PONTIFFS

POPES WHO SHAPED HISTORY

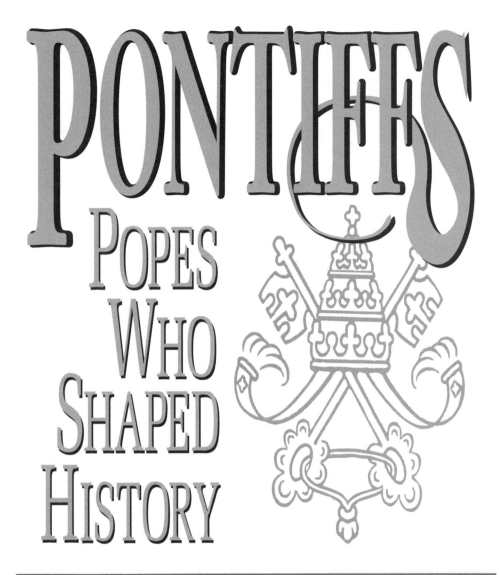

JOHN JAY HUGHES

Our Sunday Visitor Publishing Division
Our Sunday Visitor, Inc.
Huntington, Indiana 46750

International Standard Book Number: 0-87973-479-5
Library of Congress Catalog Card Number: 94-66025

Cover design by Monica Watts

PRINTED IN THE UNITED STATES OF AMERICA

479

For Joseph

a wise counselor

a faithful friend

Table of Contents

Introduction... 11

Chapter One: Simon the Rock 13

    His origins.. 14

    His call 15

    "Rock"... 17

    Simon's position among Jesus' disciples........................... 17

    Leader at Jerusalem 19

    Missionary activity 20

    Martyrdom at Rome 23

Chapter Two: Leo the Great (440-461) 27

    Leo as deacon 28

    Peter's heir.. 30

    Patriarch of the West 32

    Contention in Constantinople.. 36

    A "Synod of Robbers".. 38

    Chalcedon 41

    A new Rome? 43

    Defender of Rome 45

Chapter Three: Gregory the Great (590-604).................................. 47

    Family background and education 49

    Early career... 50

    Character and outlook.. 54

    Administration.. 58

    Evangelism 60

    Gregory's legacy... 63

Chapter Four: Gregory VII (1073-1085).. 67

    Background and early career... 68

    Church reform.. 69

    Apprenticeship... 71

Papal independence 73
Taking command 74
Lay investiture 77
The conflict escalates 78
Canossa...82
Decline and fall..83
Retrospect 85
Chapter Five: Innocent III (1198-1216) 89
Background...90
"Vicar of Christ"...91
"Less than God, but greater than man" 91
God and Caesar...93
"Where is your God?" 95
Defending the faith 98
The friars...100
Lateran IV 102
Death..104
Chapter Six: Boniface VIII (1294-1303)...................... 107
Taking charge 109
Trouble over money 110
Philip the Fair 112
The Colonna cardinals 113
A jubilee year...115
Propaganda war 116
Unam sanctam 117
A tragic denouement..118
Evaluation...120
Chapter Seven: Leo X (1513-1521)............................. 121
The Renaissance Popes...122
The need for reform 123
A Medici Pope 125
"Blameless personal morals"?....................................127
"This monster of avarice"...129
Martin Luther...130
The Ninety-five Theses 131
Justification...133
Countermeasures 134
An imperial election 136

An ambiguous condemnation 137
Evaluation 139
Chapter Eight: Pius V (1566-1572) 141
A zealot for truth and holiness 144
Religious persecution? 146
Church renewal 148
Excommunicating Elizabeth 150
Repelling the Turk 153
Chapter Nine: Pius VII (1800-1823) 157
The French Revolution 159
Conclave in Venice 163
A new century, a new Pope 164
Return to Rome 166
Concordat with Napoleon 167
The Pope in Paris 171
The Pope in captivity 175
Tightening the screws 177
Denouement 179
Restoration 181
"This beautiful figure" 184
Chapter Ten: Leo XIII (1878-1903) 187
Pio Nono 190
Youthful ambition 194
Growth in exile 197
A Vatican prisoner still 198
Recognizing civil autonomy 201
Success in Germany 203
Failure in France 206
Rerum novarum 209
Thomism and history 211
Ecumenism 215
"Americanism" 218
"Let's not set limits . . ." 221
Chapter Eleven: John XXIII (1958-1963) 225
Village boy 226
A larger world 230
Exile in Bulgaria 234
"Ant's work, bee's work" 240

"This murderous war" 242

Nuncio in France 245

A barbed wire seminary...247

Breaking out of the ghetto 248

Pastor et Pater..252

Preferring the gospel to politics.......................................255

An open conclave 257

"Vocabor Joannes"...260

Opening windows...262

A sudden inspiration? 266

The bed of thorns...269

The Roman synod...272

"On the slopes of the sacred mountain".................................274

The prophets of doom..276

Surprising Saint Joseph 279

Roses — and more thorns 282

Pacem in terris...286

"The church is no one's enemy" 288

"This bed is an altar" 291

"A death in the family"...294

Sources 297

Index... 305

Introduction

The English word "pontiff," originally used for pagan priests at Rome, is a contraction of "pontifex," itself derived from two Latin words (*pons* = bridge + *facere* = make) meaning, literally, "a bridge builder." Used as the principal title of this book, the term calls attention to an important aspect of Petrine ministry: building bridges between heaven and earth, and between people within Christ's Church as well as those without.

Writing this book has deepened my appreciation of the heavy burden laid on all those who inherit the Lord's command to Peter, to "feed my sheep" (Jn 21:17) and "strengthen your brethren" (Lk 22:32). I have tried also to be mindful of the injunction of Melchior Cano, the great Dominican theologian, at the Council of Trent:

> Peter has no need of our lies or flattery. Those who blindly and indiscriminately defend every decision of the supreme Pontiff are the very ones who do most to undermine the authority of the Holy See — they destroy instead of strengthening its foundations.

The book is not an account of "the most important popes." It seeks rather to portray representative and significant Popes from twenty centuries of Christian history who, for good or ill, "made a difference." If historical importance had been the criterion for selection, the book would have been far longer than it is. All the modern Popes from Pius IX on have been figures of major significance.

The later chapters are longer than the earlier ones not because the recent Popes are more important, but simply because we know more about them. Since this is a work for general readers and not for specialists, I have dispensed with footnotes in favor of a full listing of sources at the end.

Almost all of the research for the book was done at the Divinity Library of St. Louis University. Like all users of that fine collection, I am deeply indebted to Father W. Charles Heiser, S.J., an exemplar of the librarian's craft and of the religious order to which he belongs. *Si sic omnes!*

Father Timothy M. Dolan of the archdiocese of St. Louis kindly read one of the early chapters and offered suggestions. Professor Hermann Josef Pottmeyer of the Ruhr University of Bochum supplied valuable guidance on theological issues. Professors Gerald P. Fogarty, S.J., of the University of Virginia and Thomas Wangler of Boston College helped with the section on "Americanism" in chapter X. I owe the greatest debt to Professor Marvin R. O'Connell of the University of Notre Dame, who read the entire manuscript with meticulous care, saved me from many errors and infelicities, and offered innumerable suggestions for improvements. The defects that remain are all my own.

The best justification of this book, and of all study of Church history, is found in the words of the French Dominican Yves-Marie Congar, one of the intellectual and spiritual giants of the contemporary Church, whose ninetieth birthday (in April 1994) occurred while this work was in the press. Reflecting over three decades later on Pius XII's harsh condemnation of the French "new theology" and worker priests (briefly discussed in chapter XI of this book), Congar wrote:

> Acquiring a knowledge of history is the surest way of acquiring confidence in the church. History teaches that nothing is new and that the church has survived sadder and more difficult situations. History is a school of wisdom and of limitless patience.

To which Congar adds the historian's first law, as formulated by Cicero: "Say nothing which is false, hide nothing which is true."

Feast of Saint Charles Borromeo, 1993   JOHN JAY HUGHES

CHAPTER ONE

Simon the Rock

*"P*eter felt hurt because he said to him the third time, 'Do you
love me?' And he said to him, 'Lord, you know everything; you know
that I love you.' Jesus said to him, 'Feed my sheep' " (Jn 21:17).

If you leave Rome by St. Sebastian's Gate in the south side of the ancient
city wall, you will find on your left hand, a half mile along the Appian Way, a
small church dedicated to "Santa Maria delle Piante" ("St. Mary of the Plants").
Its more common name is the Chapel of *Domine Quo Vadis* ("Lord, where are
you going?"). An undistinguished round building, it was built in 1536 by the
English humanist, Cardinal Reginald Pole, a cousin of King Henry VIII, on the
site of an earlier church.

The church with its Latin name commemorates the supposed site of a
legend beloved of preachers ever since Saint Ambrose, who used it in one of
his sermons as Archbishop of Milan towards the end of the fourth century. The
story originated in the spurious *Acts of Peter*, a work probably composed in
Asia Minor some time before A.D. 190. It is the centerpiece of the novel *Quo
Vadis*, published by the Polish writer Henryk Sienkiewicz in 1895.

The story says that during the persecution of Christians in Rome by the
Emperor Nero, who blamed them for the great fire that devastated the capital
in July 64, Peter was persuaded to flee the capital — for his own welfare and
that of the Christian community. As he hurried along the Appian Way under
the cover of darkness, Peter encountered a familiar figure walking in the
opposite direction.

"Where are you going?" Peter asked.

"I am going to Rome," the traveler replied, "to be crucified afresh."

Peter recognized the voice at once. It was Jesus, returning to suffer death
again, this time in Rome, because his followers who were called by his name

were suffering there. Conscience stricken, Peter turned back towards the city. His companion vanished.

When Nero's officials came to arrest him the next day, Peter insisted that they crucify him upside down. He wanted to die as his Master had done, but felt unworthy to do so in just the same way.

The popularity of this legend is not difficult to understand. It goes straight to the heart: to the weakness that is in each of us, but also to our longing for one last chance to live up to the highest and best within us.

His origins

The man whose weakness and loyalty the story illustrates was born about the beginning of our era, or shortly thereafter, in the town of Bethsaida, on the east bank of the Jordan River just above its entrance into the north end of the Sea of Galilee. Bethsaida was the capital of a Roman district, rebuilt in 2 B.C. by the Tetrarch Herod Philip, who had been educated in Rome and who renamed the town "Julias" in honor of Julia, the daughter of the Emperor Augustus. The original inhabitants of the town were Jewish fishermen. Bethsaida means "House of the fisher" in Aramaic. In Peter's youth, however, the town became a center of trade. The presence of Greek-speaking merchants and government officials meant that the Jewish inhabitants of Bethsaida were bilingual.

Peter's father, Jonah, (John in English) was a fisherman. He named his boy for the second son of the Hebrew patriarch Jacob and his wife Leah: Simeon. In Greek this became Simon, the form more familiar to us. Later, however, the leader of the Christian community at Jerusalem, James, "the Lord's brother" and a stickler for the old Jewish ways, would insist on using the Hebrew name, Simeon (see Acts 15:14).

Simon's brother, apparently younger, had the Greek name Andreas, in English Andrew. Their father would not have been able to give his boys any education beyond that offered by the local synagogue school. Years later Simon and his fellow disciple John would be dismissed by the Jewish authorities in Jerusalem as "unlettered" (Acts 4:13), the same patronizing term they used for Jesus himself (Jn 7:15). As Jews living in close contact with Gentiles, however, Simon and his family would have known and practiced their faith better than many who lived in a wholly Jewish milieu — rather like Bible Belt Catholics in the United States today, whose Catholicism often has an intense quality not found in strongly Catholic areas, where it is easy to take the faith for granted.

Simon and Andrew would have helped their father, John, with the fishing from an early age. Before being called as Jesus' disciple, Simon married. It was probably at this time that he moved to Capernaum to live with his in-laws and work in their fishing business. Capernaum was a Jewish town two and a half miles west of the Jordan on the northwest shore of the lake. Modern excavations give a good idea of the houses there in Simon's day. Fishhooks have been found in the remains of one of the dwellings. Simon was a partner of the brothers James and John (Lk 5:10). Was Simon's wife their sister and their father, Zebedee, his father-in-law? We cannot say.

Mark reports that Jesus healed Simon's mother-in-law (1:30-31). Origen and other Church Fathers say that Simon and his wife had children. This may also be implied by Jesus' remark to Simon about leaving "house or brothers or sisters or mother or father or children or fields, for my sake and for the sake of the good news" (Mk 10:29). Since the gospels speak of Jesus and the other disciples staying with Simon in Capernaum, we can assume that the family fishing business enabled them to maintain one of the larger houses. This would also explain how Simon could leave home for an extended period to follow Jesus. This separation was not permanent, however. Paul says that Simon took his wife with him on his later missionary journeys (1 Cor 9:5).

His call

Through his brother Andrew, a disciple of John the Baptist, Simon came under the influence of the Baptist's preaching and was probably baptized by him. Simon was thus one of those who were expecting the coming of God's long-awaited Messiah. The fourth gospel records a meeting between Jesus and the two brothers "at Bethany beyond Jordan, where John was baptizing" (Jn 1:28 and 40-42). This was over a hundred miles south of Capernaum, near the place where the Jordan, which flows out of the Sea of Galilee at its southern end, finally empties into the Dead Sea.

Matthew and Mark both say, however, that Simon's call to be Jesus' disciple took place up north near Simon's home. Jesus encountered Simon and Andrew "casting a net into the sea" (Mk 1:16). This was a circular net thrown into the water by a person standing in shallow water or on a rock near the shore.

Jesus, who already knew the two brothers from their meeting at Bethany, said to them: "Come after me, and I will make you fishers of men" (NAB). Mark and Matthew both say that "they left their nets and followed him" (Mk 1:18; Mt 4:20).

Luke has a different story. He places Simon not on the shore with a casting-net, but in one of two boats with larger nets that required several men to handle. After a night of fruitless toil, with the nets coming back empty each time until Simon and his companions in the boat were bone weary, Jesus told them to put "out into the deep water and let down your nets for a catch." Simon knew it was useless. Once the sun was up the fish went deep, far beyond the reach of their nets. But something about Jesus made it impossible to refuse him.

"Master, we have worked all night long but have caught nothing," Simon replied. "Yet if you say so, I will let down the nets." They did so and made a big haul of fish — so big, Luke says, that "their nets were beginning to break. So they signaled to their partners in the other boat to come and help them."

Once both boats were loaded to the gunwales with fish till they were almost sinking, Simon threw himself down at Jesus' knees, with the fish flopping all round him, and said: "Go away from me, Lord, for I am a sinful man!" Jesus' words follow: "from now on you will be catching men," (NAB). Luke concludes the story by saying that Simon and his companions "left everything and followed him" (Lk 5:1-11).

This story seems to duplicate a similar one about a miraculous catch of fish in the final chapter of John's gospel, after the resurrection. The gospel writers did not have our modern interest in "exactly how it happened." They wrote not scientific history but faith-stories: inspired by faith, and designed to support faith. The writers composed their accounts freely from the many stories and sayings of Jesus that had been passed on orally in the Christian communities to which they belonged.

Many Scripture scholars believe, therefore, that Luke's account of the miraculous catch of fish was originally one of Jesus' resurrection appearances. Used, however, as the setting for Simon's call, it is highly effective. It shows that before he could be the Lord's disciple, Simon had to experience his own impotence without Jesus' help. Nowhere in the gospels do the disciples catch a single fish without Jesus' help. Left to themselves, they were failures even at the one task they thought they excelled in; a sign to gospel readers that without God, we can do nothing.

"Rock"

With his call to discipleship, Simon also received from Jesus a descriptive title: the Aramaic word *kepha*. This is not a proper name like Paul or Philip, but an ordinary noun meaning "rock." Jesus gave another title to Simon's fishing partners, Zebedee's sons James and John, whom he called *boanerges*, or "sons of thunder."

When Simon's title occurs in the Greek New Testament (for instance in the letters of Paul), it is either *transcribed* with a Greek ending "s", becoming *kephas*; or it is *translated* by the Greek word *petros*, which means "rock." The fact that the ordinary Aramaic word *kepha* was translated into Greek is significant, for proper names are not usually translated. In our English Bibles, the Greek word *petros* (rock) *is* translated, however, and written with a capital letter, becoming the proper name Peter. We come closest to the original meaning, therefore, by calling him "Simon the Rock." This is the name we have given him in the title of this chapter.

When did Jesus add this description to Simon's name? We do not know. Mark says that Jesus conferred the title when he called his twelve apostles (3:17). John, on the other hand, says that Jesus had already said to Simon, "You shall be called Cephas," on the occasion of his first meeting with Simon and Andrew at "Bethany across the Jordan where John was baptizing" (1:28 and 42). Since this is in the future tense, however ("you are to be called"), it can be understood as simply a prediction, and not the actual conferral of the title.

The same is true (though this is often overlooked) of the famous saying of Jesus reported by Matthew: "You are Peter, and on this rock [Greek *Petros*] I will build my church. . ." (16:18). That passage too is not necessarily the conferral of a new name. It could be merely the recognition that Simon already is the Rock. That is certainly the sense of Simon's words to Jesus immediately before: "You are the Messiah, the Son of the living God." Simon was not conferring something new on Jesus. He was recognizing who Jesus already was. We think of "Christ" as a proper name. It is actually a title, like Simon's title of Rock. Whether used alone ("Christ") or in combination ("Jesus Christ," "Christ Jesus") it means "Messiah," the Hebrew word for "the anointed one."

Simon's position among Jesus' disciples

"According to the united witness of the gospel tradition," writes the Protestant biblical scholar Oscar Cullmann, "Peter occupies a peculiarly representative position among the disciples of Jesus." In the so-called Synoptic gospels (Matthew, Mark, and Luke) his position is unique. In John's gospel, which gives special prominence to the unnamed "disciple whom Jesus loved" (traditionally the apostle John, though this is nowhere stated in the gospel), Simon's position is somewhat different. Yet even in the fourth gospel, Simon remains, to quote Cullmann again, "the spokesman and representative of his fellow-disciples, in good as in bad action."

Simon plays the chief role in the miraculous catch of fish (Lk 5:1-11; Jn 21:1-13), and at the transfiguration (when his two companions, James and John, say nothing: Mk 9:5). He is regularly the spokesman for the Twelve. He puts questions for them: "Lord, if another member of the church sins against me, how often should I forgive?" (Mt 18:21); "Lord, are you telling this parable for us or for everyone?" (Lk 12:41); "Look, we have left everything and followed you" (an implied question: Mk 10:28). Simon alone answers Jesus' question, "Who do you say that I am?" by confessing: "You are the Messiah" (Mk 8:29; Mt 16:16 reports the additional words, "the Son of the living God").

In the lists of Jesus' disciples, Simon's name is always given first, though the lists vary thereafter. Matthew stresses Simon's precedence by writing: "first Simon, also known as Peter" (10:2). The disciples are sometimes referred to as "Peter and those with him" (Mk 1:36; Lk 9:32). And the angel at Jesus' empty tomb commands the women: "But go, tell his disciples and Peter that he is going ahead of you to Galilee" (Mk 16:7).

When the disciples refuse to accept the necessity of Jesus' death, he first looks at all the disciples but then addresses his rebuke to Peter alone: "Get behind me, Satan! . ." (Mk 8:33). Luke reports a similar saying: "Simon, Simon, take heed: Satan has been given leave to sift all of you [plural] like wheat; but for you [singular] I have prayed that your faith may not fail; and when you have come to yourself, you must lend strength to your brothers" (22:31f: NEB).

At Jesus' arrest, according to Mark, the disciples all "deserted him and fled" (14:50). Only Simon, however, expressly denied the Master, despite his previous rash protestation of loyalty and Jesus' warning. John reports the thrice repeated question of the risen Lord at the lakeside, "Simon son of John, do you love me?" After three times exacting the affirmation that expunged the threefold denial, Jesus gave each time the command: "Feed my sheep" (21:15ff).

To these examples we could add others. So central in all four gospels is the role of the disciple whom Jesus called Rock, that it is impossible to tell the story of Jesus without relating as well the story of the fisherman Simon, son of John. This was true from the start. Even Paul's Gentile converts in distant Galatia in the mid-50s knew who the apostle meant when, without explanation, he mentioned his trip to Jerusalem "to get to know Cephas" (Gal 1:18).

Leader at Jerusalem

Simon was accorded an appearance of the risen Lord, most likely the first. Paul, writing probably in A.D. 57, states this as one of the facts he "had received" (1 Cor 15:3) — part, in other words, of the oral tradition of the Church at that time. Luke confirms this tradition by reporting that when the two disciples who had recognized the risen Jesus at Emmaus in "the breaking of the bread" returned to Jerusalem with their momentous news, the Eleven told them: "The Lord has risen indeed, and he has appeared to Simon" (Lk 24:34).

Peter, as Simon is most often called by Luke in the Acts of the Apostles, was the most important of the Twelve in the original Christian community at Jerusalem and the surrounding towns (Acts 5:16). His name heads the list of the Eleven who, following Jesus' ascension, "were constantly devoting themselves to prayer, together with certain women, including Mary the mother of Jesus, as well as his brothers" (Acts 1:14). Peter took the lead in choosing Matthias to replace Judas Iscariot (Acts 1:15-26). He was the spokesman for Jesus' followers, and the witness of their resurrection faith, at Pentecost (Acts 2), at the healing of the lame man at the beautiful Gate of the Temple (Acts 3), and before the Jewish authorities (Acts 4:8-12; 5:29). Peter exercised disciplinary authority against Ananias and his wife Saphira for lying about the price they had received from their sale of property and voluntarily donated to the Church (Acts 5:1-11). He rebuked Simon the Magician for attempting to purchase the gift of the Spirit (Acts 8:20-23).

As already noted, the purpose of Paul's first visit to Jerusalem after his conversion was to get to know Cephas. Paul stayed with him two weeks (Gal 1:18). Scholars believe this was about A.D. 35-36. Paul adds that he saw none of the other apostles "except James the Lord's brother." He was not one of the Twelve. We do not know the exact relationship between this James and Jesus. According to the ancient and unanimous tradition that Jesus was Mary's only child, however, James cannot have been her son.

In early 41 King Herod Agrippa I beheaded the apostle James, the brother of John and son of Zebedee, and arrested Peter, "intending to bring him out to the people after the Passover" (Acts 12:4). Peter's miraculous deliverance from prison frustrated the King's plan, however. Peter then "went to another place" (12:17).

In the year 41 Passover occurred on April 5th. Twelve years had passed since the presumed date of Jesus' death on April 7, in the year 30, the date of Passover that year. Several second-century works, including the apocryphal *Acts of Peter* that contain the *Quo Vadis* story (recounted at the beginning of this chapter), report that Peter led the Jerusalem Church for twelve years after the resurrection. Thereafter the local leadership passed to the Lord's brother James, to whom Peter sent news of his departure following his miraculous deliverance from prison (Acts 12:17).

Missionary activity

Where did Peter go? We do not know. Our only information about his whereabouts and activities throughout the rest of the 40s and until we can place him in Rome sometime after 55, comes from references in the Acts of the Apostles, in Paul's letter to the Galatians, and in his first letter to the Corinthians. This evidence is fragmentary, in part contradictory, and impossible to harmonize completely.

Luke is thought to have written Acts only after A.D. 80. He sometimes rearranged the order of events for dramatic or theological effect. Paul wrote closer to the events he mentions, which may make him more reliable. But when Paul is defending his standpoint against that of his opponents, we must read his statements with the caution that is always necessary in evaluating the account of one party to a dispute.

The references to Peter by Paul and in Acts place him at Lydda in northern Judea, in the nearby coastal town of Joppa, farther north at the Samarian port of Caesarea (Acts 9 and 10), at Antioch in northwestern Syria (Gal 2:11), and back at Jerusalem (Gal 2:6-10, Acts 15). We do not know, however, when or in what order Peter was in these various places.

Paul says that when he visited Jerusalem for the second time, he again met Peter. On this occasion the leaders of the Jerusalem Church recognized Paul's responsibility for the mission to the Gentiles, and Peter's for the Jews (Gal

2:6-10). This was part, it seems, of the "Jerusalem Council" described in Acts 15. This assembly waived circumcision for Gentile Christians, but imposed on them the dietary and sexual rules laid down in Leviticus 17-18 for "God-fearing" Gentiles who lived with Jews. The account in Acts shows Peter playing a mediating role between the Judaizers, led by James, and Paul, who pleaded for total freedom from Jewish rules for Gentile Christians.

This meeting must have taken place after the death of King Herod Agrippa I on March 10 in the year 44. It is most unlikely that Peter returned to Jerusalem during the lifetime of the ruler from whose clutches he had miraculously escaped at Passover in the year 41. Other evidence suggests that this second encounter between Peter and Paul at the Jerusalem Council took place in late 45 or early 46.

In the passage from Galatians in which he describes this second Jerusalem visit, Paul goes on to mention his quarrel with Peter during the latter's subsequent stay at Antioch. The dispute concerned table fellowship between Gentile and Jewish Christians. This was forbidden by Jewish law, since Gentiles did not observe the Jewish dietary rules. Paul says, however, that when Peter first came to Antioch he took a liberal view of this matter and ate with Gentile Christians. This is especially plausible if Peter's experiences at Joppa and Caesarea reported in Acts had preceded this visit to Antioch. In Joppa Peter stayed "for some time with a certain Simon, a tanner" (Acts 9:43). This was an "unclean" profession since it involved handling the carcasses of dead animals. An observant Jew could not have stayed with such a person (see Lev 11:39f).

Even more significant was Peter's experience at Caesarea, where he was asked to baptize the Roman military officer Cornelius. Peter wanted to refuse the request since it involved a forbidden visit to a Gentile house. Only a direct command from God enabled Peter to overcome his Jewish scruples and enter Cornelius' house. (See Acts 10.)

Paul says that after first sharing his meals with Gentile Christians at Antioch, Peter "drew back and kept himself separate" when "certain people came from James." The leader of the Jerusalem Church had evidently sent a delegation to investigate reports that the Antioch Christians were not following the rules formulated at the Jerusalem Council. Reminded by these emissaries of his duty to enforce the compromise he had helped produce in Jerusalem, Peter abandoned his liberal ways. Paul was furious. Writing about it some years later, he ascribed Peter's change of heart to timidity: "because he was afraid of the advocates of circumcision" (Gal 2:12).

Circumcision was a red herring. It had already been waived for Gentile Christians. The issue at Antioch was something different: the Jewish dietary laws. Like many people recounting their side of a controversy, Paul seems to have distorted the position of his opponents, to make them appear more unreasonable than they were.

There was a public meeting of the Antioch Church at which, Paul writes, "I said to Cephas, before them all, 'If you, though a Jew, live like a Gentile [i.e. by eating with those who do not observe the dietary laws], and not like a Jew [who would refuse to eat with such people], how can you compel the Gentiles to live like Jews?'" (Gal 2:14).

This reference to Peter insisting that Gentiles must live like Jews is revealing. Evidently Peter, concerned with preserving the unity of the Antioch Church, had asked its Gentile members to start observing the minimum dietary rules laid down by the Jerusalem Council to which he had agreed and of which the emissaries sent from Jerusalem by James had reminded him.

It is especially significant that Paul does not say who won the argument. The "argument from silence," normally a weak one in history, is weighty in this case however. If Paul had won, especially in a dispute over a question about which he felt so strongly, is it likely he would have remained silent about it? The Gentile Christians at Antioch appear to have accepted Peter's plea that they should observe the Jewish dietary laws, for the sake of Church unity. Paul had lost.

Paul's bitterness over this stinging defeat bleeds through his description of the incident. "Even Barnabas was led away," Paul complains. His companion on that second Jerusalem visit, when Paul had obtained recognition as "apostle to the Gentiles" (Gal 2:8), had deserted him by accepting Peter's plea for compromise. Paul was indignant for two reasons. First because Peter, the "apostle to the Jews" (Galatians 2:8), had exceeded his jurisdiction by laying down rules for Gentile Christians. More serious in Paul's eyes, however, was the question of principle: the conduct of Peter and those who sided with him "did not square with the truth of the gospel" (Gal 2:14; NEB).

We must beware of reading back into the first century, issues that belong to later history. There was no question at Antioch of "appealing to Peter as the supreme authority." Such an appeal would be possible only after centuries of historical development, including (Catholics believe) the Church's Spirit-guided reflection on this development. Then, however, a pattern visible in this early dispute at Antioch would be repeated. Not infrequently a holder of Peter's office has rejected the impassioned plea of a prophetically gifted defender of the faith who was right in principle, but whose position, if adopted at that time and place, would have injured the Church's unity.

After his defeat Paul separated from his former companion Barnabas and "went through Syria and Cilicia, strengthening the churches" (Acts 15:41). This was probably in early 48. By 49 his missionary travels would take him for the first time to Greece. There, in the early 50s, the paths of the two great apostles would cross again — at least indirectly — in the teeming port city of Corinth.

In his first letter to the Corinthians, probably written from Ephesus in the spring of 57, Paul refers to Cephas' missionary travels (9:5). And twice Paul mentions the existence at Corinth of a "Cephas party" (1:12; 3:22). Had Peter been to Corinth? Possibly. Even if he had not, these references show Peter's influence. Some of the Corinthian Christians were appealing to Peter's authority as superior to Paul's. It is noteworthy, however, especially in view of the previous difficulties at Antioch, that Paul blames these divisions not on Peter but on the immaturity of certain members of the Corinthian Church. This has compelled him, Paul writes reproachfully, to deal with them "as infants in Christ" (3:1).

Martyrdom at Rome

From the Middle Ages until our own century, people have raised doubts about whether Peter was ever at Rome. The first to deny his presence there were the Waldensians, a sect in southern France in the late twelfth century. We shall meet them later, in the chapter on Pope Innocent III. For the Waldensians the lack of any New Testament reference to Peter's presence at Rome was decisive.

Martin Luther noted doubts about Peter's Roman residence, but declined to resolve them. Surprisingly, in view of his violent attacks on the papacy of his day, Luther said that the question of whether Peter ever reached Rome made no difference. Protestant writers have disputed the matter ever since, some denying Peter's presence at Rome, others affirming it. Today, however, no serious scholar doubts that Peter suffered a martyr's death at Rome under the Emperor Nero, who reigned from 54 to 68. The evidence is fragmentary and circumstantial. Taken as a whole, however, the evidence for Peter's Roman martyrdom is so strong that Oscar Cullmann, whom we have quoted already, can write: "Were we to demand for all facts of ancient history a greater degree of probability, we should have to strike from our history books a large proportion of their contents."

When did Peter first reach Rome? Probably not before the year 55. In 49 the Emperor Claudius, concerned about bitter disputes in the large Jewish community at Rome over the claim that Jesus of Nazareth was the Jewish Messiah, issued an edict expelling Jews from the capital. This decree, which affected Jewish Christians as well, remained in effect until the Emperor's death in October 54. Thereafter the Roman Church began to revive, meeting no longer in synagogues but in the private homes of Gentile Christians.

In the final chapter of his letter to the Romans, Paul sends greetings to three of these house-churches, and to twenty-nine named individuals. Neither there nor elsewhere in the letter, however, does he mention Peter. This suggests that at the time Paul wrote this letter, no earlier than 54, Peter was not at Rome. This is consistent with the later tradition that Peter reached Rome and was martyred there during the reign of Nero.

The one hint in the New Testament of Peter's presence at Rome is in 1 Peter 5:13, which sends greetings from Babylon, almost certainly a reference to the imperial capital. If Peter wrote this letter himself, the reference to "Babylon" (which is the code name for Rome in the Book of Revelation as well) points to his presence at Rome. If the book is the work of a later writer who attributed it to a revered personage from the past (a common literary practice in antiquity), the reference to Babylon testifies to an early tradition concerning Peter's presence in Rome.

The earliest literary evidence for Peter's death at Rome is from the first letter of Clement. This was written about 96 by the Roman Bishop to the Church of Corinth. Clement warns the Corinthians, as Paul had done in his first letter to them, of the evil results of jealousy and factionalism. In a list of those who have suffered death "as a result of jealousy," beginning with Old Testament martyrs and coming down to his own time, Clement mentions the martyrdoms of Peter and Paul. The reference to Peter is vague. The context indicates, however, that Clement was reminding the Corinthians of something they already knew: that Peter, like Paul and many others, suffered martyrdom at Rome during the persecution of the Emperor Nero.

Further evidence for this tradition comes from the letter of Ignatius, Bishop of Antioch, to the Church of Rome. He wrote on his way to the capital, anticipating the martyr's death he suffered there in A.D. 117, to ask them not to try to save him. The crucial sentence reads: "I do not order you as did Peter and Paul." By itself that says very little. Read, however, in the context of the whole letter, and especially of his own anticipated martyrdom, it is clear that Ignatius was telling the Christians at Rome that he hoped soon to die there for Christ, as Peter and Paul had done half a century before.

References to Peter's martyrdom at Rome increase in Christian literature thereafter. Especially significant is the fact that the tradition was accepted everywhere, even in places such as Antioch that also claimed a connection with Peter. No other place but Rome ever claimed to be the place of Peter's death. Nor can we attribute this tradition to the desire of later Roman Bishops to bolster their claim to primacy in the Church. Universal acceptance of Peter's death at Rome came long before controversy over the prerogatives of his successors.

When did Peter die? Certainly not before Nero's mass execution of Roman Christians on October 13, 64. As we saw at the beginning of this chapter, this was the Emperor's revenge for the great fire in the capital the previous July. The Roman historian Tacitus reports suspicions that Nero had set the fire himself. Though Tacitus held Christians responsible for spreading a "deadly superstition," he regarded Nero's treatment of them as unjust. Tacitus recounts dreadful atrocities: Christians sown in animal skins to be torn to pieces by dogs; others crucified; still others daubed with pitch and set on fire at night to illuminate Nero's garden. The Emperor himself drove through these revolting scenes disguised as a charioteer.

If Peter was among the victims of this pogrom, it is unlikely that his body could have been identified and given Christian burial. Literary and archaeological evidence indicates, however, that Roman Christians knew the site of Peter's tomb on the Vatican Hill before the middle of the second century. This supports the view that he was executed alone, under conditions that permitted reverent burial. In that case we must date the martyrdom between 65 and Nero's death in 68.

Excavations under the high altar of St. Peter's Basilica carried out in the years 1940-1949 and again from 1953 to 1957 are said to have located Peter's tomb. What was actually found was a burial site at which Peter was venerated by Roman Christians seventy to eighty years after his death. The likelihood that this was the apostle's actual grave is high. But this cannot be proved with certainty.

On June 26, 1968 Pope Paul VI announced that bones found in the excavations had been convincingly identified as those of Peter. This was a statement of the Pope's personal opinion about the reliability of conclusions presented to him by the experts who carried out the excavations. Others equally competent, including a number of Catholics, believe that positive identification of the bones is impossible.

The question of whether Peter's bones have been found has no relevance for faith. Here, if ever, we should heed the question of the angel at the empty tomb: "Why do you look for the living among the dead?" (Lk 24:5). Simon the Rock, whom we know as Peter, lives on in his successors. Less than four hundred years after Simon laid down his life for the Lord he had once denied, one of those successors brought this idea of succession to Peter's office to explicit development. It is to him that we now turn.

CHAPTER TWO

Leo the Great

(440-461)

"*I*n the midst of discordant opinions and carnal jealousies I have striven for moderation" (Letter to the Empress Pulcheria: July 20, 451).

History has awarded the title "Great" to only two bishops of Rome. The first, known to us only as Leo ("lion" in Latin) was born about A.D. 400 or shortly thereafter, probably in the Etruscan town of Velathri. This is the modern Volterra in Tuscany, fifty-one miles southeast of Pisa. We know nothing of his background apart from the name of his father: Quintianus.

Leo would later refer to Rome as his *patria* or homeland. If we take this literally, it could mean that his family had joined the great migration southwards, seeking security in the capital against the danger that threatened the whole Mediterranean world in Leo's day: barbarian invasion from beyond the Alps.

Though the Romans called the Germanic tribes that lived north of the Rhine and Danube barbarians, they were by no means primitive savages. They practiced settled agriculture and had well-developed structures of social organization. These were based, however, not on a code of written law, as in the Roman system, but on tribal tradition and custom. The military prowess of these Germanic tribes gained them employment as Roman mercenaries. Even before Leo's day, most of the Empire's soldiers and many of its generals were of German origin. This led to interpenetration of two worlds: The barbarians were influenced by what remained of ancient Roman civilization, while the Empire became more and more barbarized.

The establishment of the imperial capital at Constantinople in 330 started Rome and the Western part of the old Roman Empire on a long decline. By Leo's day the Greek-speaking East had supplanted the Latin West as the center of power and wealth. It was also the source of new ideas, in theology as in other areas. Though Italy continued to be the seat of a Western Emperor, he preferred to reside closer to the threatened borders he had to defend. Diocletian moved the capital from Rome to Milan in 285. Honorius moved it again in 402, to Ravenna. This new site had important strategic advantages. A port on the Adriatic, it had access by sea to the East and was protected from overland invaders by swamps. By the fifth century, therefore, the Roman Bishop had long ceased to preside over the Church in the acknowledged capital of the world. A further sign that the old order was breaking up was the sack of Rome by the barbarian General Alaric in 410. This sent shock waves throughout the tottering Empire and occasioned the writing of one of the classics of world literature, Augustine's *City of God*, in which the great saint answers those who believed the fall of Rome in 410 was due to the debilitating effect of Christianity.

Leo as deacon

Augustine has also given us what may be the first literary reference to the future Pope. In two of his letters, the Bishop of Hippo mentions an acolyte named Leo as the bearer of letters from Pope Zozimus and his presbyter Sixtus (Pope himself from 432 to 440) to bishops in North Africa. Zozimus was Bishop of Rome from March 417 to December 418. If the acolyte mentioned by Augustine is the future Pope, Leo was not yet out of his teens. His employment at such an early age in a mission of trust indicates the high estimate his elders had formed of his character.

Leo begins to emerge from the shadows as a deacon during the pontificate of Celestine I (422-432). In the early centuries, deacons often enjoyed greater prestige than presbyters (normally called priests today, though canon law continues to give them their older designation). This was because the deacons assisted the bishop in important administrative and financial positions, whereas presbyters exercised more spiritual functions.

This situation survives today in the organization of the College of Cardinals, who are in theory the leading clergy of the local Church of Rome — which is why they elect the Roman Bishop. Since 1962 all cardinals are required to be bishops. Within the college, however, they are of unequal rank. First come the six cardinal bishops, nominally in charge of the "suburbican dioceses" surrounding the city of Rome. Cardinal presbyters, by far the most numerous group, are now almost always bishops or archbishops throughout the world. As cardinals, however, they are nominally the pastors of parish churches in the diocese of Rome. Finally there are fourteen cardinal deacons, successors of the powerful administrative officials in the ancient Roman Church. Today a cardinal deacon who is a high official in the Roman curia may exercise far greater influence than many cardinal presbyters, especially those who are archbishops of poor Third World dioceses. A further relic of the prestige once enjoyed by the Roman deacons is the privilege still enjoyed by the senior cardinal deacon of investing the newly elected Pope with the insignia of his office: formerly the tiara, now the pallium of an archbishop.

Leo's office as deacon under Pope Celestine I shows that while still in his twenties, he was a person of importance in the Roman Church. During this period the Eastern Church was convulsed by the doctrinal and jurisdictional battles that were to dominate Leo's pontificate. When the Egyptian Patriarch Cyril of Alexandria, a leading contender in these struggles, wanted support from Rome, he solicited it from the deacon Leo. For guidance in understanding the subtle theological arguments that were causing such trouble in the East, Leo enlisted the help of the foremost Western monk of the day, John Cassian.

Cassian was well-suited to this task. He had spent his early monastic years in the East and had been ordained deacon by the Patriarch of Constantinople, John Chrysostom. Following his return to the West in 404, Cassian went to southern Gaul (the ancient name for France), where he founded twin monasteries for men and women near Marseilles. In 430, on the eve of the Council of Ephesus, Cassian published his treatise *On the Incarnation*. In the introduction he wrote that he had set aside his decision to abandon literary pursuits only at the urging of "you, Leo, my honored friend, ornament of the Roman Church and of the sacred ministry." Historians believe that Leo may have gleaned most of his knowledge of the christological issues of the day from this work, written at his behest ten years before he became Bishop of Rome.

Leo's influence continued under Celestine's successor, Sixtus III (432-440), whom we have already encountered as a Roman presbyter under Pope Zozimus. In 418 Zozimus had deposed a certain Julian, Bishop of Eclanum in southern Italy, for teaching the heresy of Pelagianism: that human nature, unaided by divine grace, can take the initial steps towards salvation. A gifted controversialist, Julian was the foremost theological opponent of Pelagianism's great foe, Augustine, until the latter's death in 430. Following his banishment from his diocese, Julian traveled throughout the East soliciting support for his views. After the death of Pope Celestine I on July 27, 432, Julian returned to Italy in the hope of regaining his diocese. He was frustrated by the powerful deacon Leo who persuaded the new Pope Sixtus III not to restore Julian to his See as long as he continued to teach false doctrine.

Peter's heir

Leo's prestige also extended to the imperial court at Ravenna. In 440 the Western Emperor Valentinian III sent him to Gaul to reconcile two feuding military authorities, Aetius and Albinus. Leo was away from Rome on this delicate mission when Sixtus III died on June 24, 440, after a pontificate of eight years. A delegation of Roman clergy and laity set off for Gaul at once to fetch Leo home. Upon his arrival he was elected Pope without opposition and ordained a bishop on September 29, 440.

Leo advanced directly from the diaconate to the episcopate, without being ordained a presbyter. This was the normal practice in the early centuries, when Popes were most often selected from among the Roman deacons. Bishops were not eligible for election since a bishop was considered "married" to his diocese. Translation to another diocese had been forbidden by canon 15 of the Council of Nicaea in 325 on the ground that this would make the bishop a "bigamist." Not until 882 was a man who was already a bishop elsewhere elected Pope: Marinus I, formerly Bishop of Cere in the central Italian province of Etruria.

At his episcopal ordination, Leo preached the first of the sermons which he delivered annually on September 29th in celebration of what he liked to call his "birthday." The five anniversary sermons that have been preserved (summarized in the two paragraphs which follow) show how Leo regarded his office.

Among the bishops, to whom Jesus, the eternal high priest and supreme bishop, entrusted the care of his sheep, one outranked all others. This was Peter, who alone confessed Christ as Messiah and Son of God at Caesarea Philippi. In return Jesus gave Peter the keys of the kingdom of heaven and the legal power of binding and loosing (Mt 16:16-18), commanding him also to "strengthen your brothers" (Lk 22:32) and to "feed my sheep" (Jn 21:16f).

The Roman Bishop, Leo emphasized, is "Peter's heir." This term is crucial. In Roman law the deceased lived on in the heir. The latter replaced the former and stepped into his shoes. At death the rights and duties of the deceased passed undiminished to his heir. Peter's heir does not inherit the apostle's personal merits. Hence Leo speaks of himself as Peter's "unworthy heir." However, the one elected to Peter's office does inherit Peter's authority — conferred on him by Jesus himself in response to Peter's declaration of faith at Caesarea Philippi.

Leo was the first Pope to develop such a clear connection between Peter and his successors. Previous Bishops of Rome had spoken of their succession to Peter's "chair"; of the preeminence of Rome as the imperial capital; and of Peter's residence, martyrdom, and burial at Rome. None of these ideas provided a firm foundation for papal power, however. Since, as we saw in the last chapter, Peter was at Antioch before he went to Rome, succession to Peter's chair was also claimed by the bishops of Antioch. Rome's preeminence declined with the establishment of the imperial capital at Constantinople and the removal of the Western seat of government first to Milan and then to Ravenna. And while no one disputed Rome's claim to have been the scene of Peter's final years, martyrdom, and burial, this hardly provided a secure basis for the powers claimed by his successors.

In his extensive writings, Leo made little use of these earlier arguments for papal authority, therefore, but stressed repeatedly the theme of legal inheritance. This simple idea, firmly anchored in Roman law, had a great future. It enabled Leo to challenge the imperial government at Constantinople on its own ground — the law. Moreover Leo's argument has stood the test of time. Thousands of papal documents from his day to our own contain the ideas, and often the very expressions, that we find in Leo's anniversary sermons. The following excerpts illustrate his teaching.

> Just as Peter's faith in Christ remains valid for all times, so Christ's commission to Peter remains valid for all times. . . . Blessed Peter, who possesses for all time the strength given him as 'rock', has not deserted the church's helm. . . . Now he performs the duties entrusted to him with wider scope and greater power, and executes all parts of his obligations and responsibilities in and with that person [i.e. Leo himself] through whom he has been honored. Hence if a right action is done by us or a right decision made, if anything is obtained from God in his mercy by daily prayers, it is a consequence of his good works and merits, whose power still survives and whose authority redounds in his see.

> You will celebrate today's festival rightly, beloved, if you recognize and honor in my humble self the one with whom the care of all the shepherds remains, together with the guardianship of the sheep committed to him, and whose privilege persists even in his unworthy heir. . . . When, therefore, we utter our exhortations in your ears, holy brethren, believe that he is actually speaking, whose office we represent (*Sermon* iii, 3-4).

Though the other apostles received from Jesus an authority like Peter's, Leo says, Jesus' command to Peter to strengthen their faith (Lk 22:32) shows that they remained in some way dependent on their chief. Peter continues to obey the Lord's threefold command to "feed my sheep" (Jn 21:17) when he "strengthens us [i.e., Leo himself] by his exhortations and unceasingly prays that we may not be overcome by temptation" (*Sermon* iv, 4).

In his fifth-anniversary sermon, Leo says that he shares with his fellow bishops the care "of all the churches" of which Paul spoke (2 Cor 11:28). Nonetheless, "people come from all over the world to the see of Peter, expecting from our high priestly office the same love of the whole church that the Lord laid upon Peter" (in his threefold question, "Do you love me?"; Jn 21:15-17). Through his heir

> the most blessed Peter does not cease to preside over his see and has abiding fellowship with the eternal High Priest. For the stability which "the Rock" himself received from that rock which is Christ, he conveys also to his heirs; and wherever we see any steadfastness, this is due beyond doubt to the strength of the chief shepherd.

Previous Popes had laid the foundations for this high doctrine of the papal office. Leo, however, was the first to formulate clearly the claim that Peter lives on in his successors, who thus inherit the pastoral care of all the churches laid upon Peter by Jesus, together with Peter's plenary authority to exercise this care. Hence Leo has sometimes been called "the first Pope." The French Church historian Pierre Batiffol came closer to the truth when he wrote: "Leo is not the first Pope, but he is Pope in the full sense of the word."

Patriarch of the West

Leo's doctrine of the papal office did not remain a matter of words only. He practiced what he preached in these anniversary sermons: in the West with little opposition, in the East despite opposition that often forced him to practical concessions but never to alteration of his principles.

Leo's first concern was for the preservation of the true faith, starting in his own Church of Rome. A special problem at the beginning of his pontificate was the influx of refugees from North Africa, following the fall of Carthage to the Vandals in 439. Many of these newcomers were Manicheans, members of the heretical sect that had fascinated the young Augustine and kept him from seeking baptism until he was past thirty.

In one of his Advent sermons, Leo disclosed "as far as modesty allows" the results of an investigation of the sect's activities that he had carried out in the presence of his fellow bishops, presbyters, and prominent laity. A Manichean "bishop" at Rome had ordered ceremonial intercourse between a youth and a girl "at most ten years old." The facts had been confirmed by the testimony of the young man concerned, "two women who had raised the girl for such immoral ends", and the heretical prelate responsible for the scandal (*Sermon* xvi).

In a letter to the bishops of Italy, dated January 30, 444, and urging them to be vigilant against the spread of Manicheanism in their dioceses, Leo reported that the court he had assembled had discriminated according to the culpability of the defendants. Those who abjured their false beliefs were let off with the imposition of a penance. The obdurate were delivered to the civil authorities for punishment (another practice with a great future, in this instance a dark one). The banishment subsequently imposed on them in accordance with the existing laws against heresy explains Leo's warning to his fellow bishops. There was reason to expect that those who had refused to abjure what Leo called their "infamous heresy" would continue their immoral practices elsewhere (*Letter* 7).

Early in his pontificate, probably in 442, Leo wrote to the Bishop of Aquileia, then an important See between Venice and Trieste, expressing concern about reports that clergy who had embraced Pelagianism had been readmitted to Catholic communion without abjuring their heresy. The bishop was to call a meeting of the clergy in his province and require them to repudiate all false teaching on pain of excommunication. Leo also warned the bishop to beware of equivocal statements. "They hold that the grace of God is given only according to the merits of the recipients. But, of course, if it is not a free gift, it is not grace at all, but rather a reward and a merited compensation." He quoted Ephesians 2:8-10 to show that justification and grace are a free gift. "But those heretics say that grace comes as a result of our natural efforts" (*Letter* 1). The letter illustrates Leo's concern for pure doctrine; his consciousness of universal pastoral responsibility; and his ability to go to the heart of complex doctrinal questions in language that is simple, clear, and brief.

Leo responded similarly to the request of Bishop Turibius of Asturica in what is today northern Portugal for help in dealing with heresy there. The Pope regretted that disordered conditions in the Iberian peninsula caused by the barbarian invasions made enforcement of the strict laws of the Christian

Emperors against heresy impossible. He described his proceedings against the Manicheans at Rome and urged a general synod of all bishops in the Iberian peninsula, or failing that, a local synod. This would provide an opportunity to require the bishops, some of whom Turibius accused of favoring heresy, of confessing the true faith (*Letter* 15, dated variously between 445 and 447).

The most celebrated exercise of Leo's universal pastoral office in the West, however, concerned the diocese of Arles in southern Gaul. In 417 when Leo was only a young acolyte, Pope Zozimus had granted the Bishop of Arles considerable authority over the other dioceses in the province of Vienne, the only part of Gaul not subject to barbarian rule. When other bishops in southern Gaul protested, the successors of Pope Zozimus revoked the special privileges of Arles, but in a manner that left the limits of ecclesiastical jurisdiction in the province still open to dispute.

In 429 the Church of Arles chose as its bishop a monk named Hilary from the famous monastery of Lerins, an offshore island west of Nice. An ascetical reformer and a man of personal sanctity (he is a canonized saint, but should not be confused with his more famous namesake, Bishop of Poitiers a century earlier), Hilary possessed more zeal than tact. In the interests of Church renewal throughout southern Gaul, he acted as if the special privileges of his See were still in force. Hilary also made use of every opportunity that arose to promote to vacant Sees bishops who supported the rigorist ideas he had learned in the monastery.

Resentment over these high-handed ways boiled over in 444 when Hilary responded to complaints about a certain Bishop Celidonius of Besançon by declaring him removed from office and excommunicated. Celidonius immediately traveled to Rome to appeal his case to the Pope. Hilary followed him there, braving a winter journey over the alps on foot in order to present his side of the controversy to a Roman synod in the winter of 444-445. In doing so, however, Hilary alienated the synod by intemperate protests against papal "interference" in the affairs of a church province where, he contended, he alone possessed legitimate authority. Finding little sympathy for his position at Rome, Hilary left in a huff without awaiting a decision.

The synod found Hilary's charges groundless and reinstated Celidonius. Hilary was further humiliated when, shortly thereafter, Leo reversed the action of the impetuous bishop in another case: that of Bishop Projectus. Though his diocese was not even in the same province as Arles, Hilary had taken advantage of Projectus' grave illness to consecrate his successor, confident that Projectus was not long for this world. To everyone's surprise but his own, Projectus recovered and appealed his case to Rome. He was reinstated by the same synod that had just reversed Hilary's removal of Bishop Celidonius.

In a celebrated letter dated July 1, 445, Leo gave an account of these actions to all the bishops of the province of Vienne. He began by saying that the Lord had laid upon all the apostles responsibility for preaching the gospel, but especially on Peter, so that "anyone who dares to separate himself from the solidity of Peter . . . no longer shares in the divine mystery." Leo reminded his fellow bishops in Gaul how often they, and their predecessors, had appealed to "the apostolic see." He had acted now, he told them, not to introduce novel ties but to restore ancient discipline.

Celidonius had been restored, Leo wrote, because the charges against him were false. Leo was especially severe regarding Hilary's precipitate action in consecrating a successor for Projectus during the latter's illness. Hilary had arrived unexpectedly, Leo wrote, and departed without warning, "making many trips with great speed, rushing through distant provinces in such haste that he seems to have aimed at a reputation for giddy speed rather than for the moderation of a bishop."

For the future, Leo ordered, Hilary was to confine his activities to his own diocese of Arles. Bishops were to be chosen in accordance with the canons: by popular election of the clergy and leading laity, ratified by the common people. In this connection Leo stated a principle which, if observed today, would revolutionize church life. "He who is in charge of all should be chosen by all" (*Letter* 10).

Four days after this letter, the Western Emperor Valentinian III wrote Aetius, his military commander in Gaul, ordering him to enforce the Pope's orders. Leo was aware of the close relations between Hilary and Aetius, whom Leo knew from his mission to Gaul which had been interrupted by his summons to Rome to assume the papacy five years previously. Leo requested Valentinian's letter to his commander, therefore, to prevent Hilary from enlisting the general's support in an attempt to defy papal authority.

The Pope cannot have been happy, however, about one of the reasons Valentinian gave for the Pope's authority: "because of the importance of the city of Rome." The city's importance had already declined, and might well diminish farther in the future. Hence Leo, like his predecessors, always rejected this political argument for papal primacy. In the West, where the Emperor was weak and the Pope's authority virtually unchallenged, Valentinian's use of this argument could be ignored. This was not true in the East, however, where leaders in both Church and state did not hesitate to base Church order, and even doctrine, on the shifting sands of political power. The resulting controversies produced Leo's greatest vexations, the severest test of his pastoral leadership, but also his most important legacy to posterity.

Contention in Constantinople

Leo can hardly have imagined the sea of troubles upon which he was about to embark when, in early February 449, he received from the archimandrite (abbot) of a monastery in Constantinople named Eutyches a letter of bitter complaint about his ill-usage at the hands of the local Patriarch (archbishop) Flavian. With it came a supporting letter from the Eastern Emperor Theodosius II.

Leo would have recalled the archimandrite from their correspondence the previous spring, when Eutyches had written the Pope about efforts to revive the heresy of Nestorius: that there were two separate persons, divine and human, in the incarnate Christ. In 431 the Council of Ephesus had affirmed the orthodox belief that Christ's two natures were united in a single person. On June 1, 448, Leo wrote Eutyches commending him for his zeal in defending the true faith (*Letter* 20). The Pope would soon discover that he had been too hasty in his appreciation.

Thomas Bokenkotter has called Eutyches "a dabbler rather than a real theologian" — a judgment that must be considered charitable. Like many self-appointed defenders of the faith today, Eutyches knew little theology and was quickly out of his depth. Scholars continue to debate whether Nestorius really taught the two-person doctrine condemned at Ephesus. There can be no doubt, however, about Eutyches' teaching. Christ, he said repeatedly, had two natures before the Incarnation, but afterwards only one nature. Leo would later say of this statement:

> I am amazed that so absurd and so perverse a profession was not corrected. . . . It was as impious to say that the only-begotten Son of God had two natures before the incarnation as it was blasphemous to assert that he had a single nature after the Word was made flesh (*Letter* 28).

That was Leo's judgment in June 449. In February, however, when he received Eutyches' complaint, things were not so clear. The archimandrite portrayed himself as the victim of grave injustice. "Without any real evidence," Eutyches wrote the Pope, he had been summoned by Patriarch Flavian to answer charges of heresy before a local synod in Constantinople. He had appeared (on November 22, 448) despite "serious illness and old age," only to find that he had been judged in advance. His written profession of faith, his appeal to the Councils of Nicaea and Ephesus, and even to the Pope himself, had all been disregarded. Flavian and his allies had then issued a sentence of excommunication against him "which they had prepared before holding the trial."

Afterwards his enemies had incited people against him to such a degree, he told Leo, "that my safety would even have been endangered had not a group of soldiers snatched me from the trap through God's assistance and your prayers." After condemning all heretics back to Simon the Magician (whose attempt to purchase miraculous powers from Peter and John is recorded in Acts 8), and again professing his loyalty to "the same faith which the Council of the 318 bishops set forth at Nicaea and which the holy Council of Ephesus confirmed," Eutyches appealed to Leo as "guardian of mercy and religion" not to "allow me to be shipwrecked by rivals now that I am at the very end of my life" (No. 21 in Leo's *Letters*).

This heart-rending appeal was disingenuous in the extreme. Leo may well have suspected as much, for he did not reply to Eutyches. Instead he wrote on February 18, 449, to the Emperor Theodosius and the Patriarch Flavian asking the exact charges against Eutyches and why he had been excommunicated before his appeal to "the apostolic see" had been heard.

Flavian had already sent a report of the case to Leo in January. Lacking the archimandrite's court connections, the patriarch was unable to use the swift imperial post. It was not until April, therefore, that Leo received Flavian's original report. The patriarch's second communication, answering the Pope's request of February 18th, did not reach Rome until mid-June. The original documentation sent by Flavian in January, however, was quite sufficient to show Leo that Eutyches' claim to have been the victim of injustice was a tissue of misrepresentations from start to finish.

At no time had Eutyches responded directly to the charge of heresy (his statement that Christ had two natures before the Incarnation, but only one afterwards). Instead he tried to discredit his accusers by charging that they had departed from the statements of the last two councils: Ephesus (431) and Nicaea (325). This argument, which was to be constantly repeated in the long and involved controversy that followed, was similar to the claim of today's self-constituted "defenders of the faith" that anyone who goes beyond the verbal formulations of Trent and Vatican I is guilty of "modernism," and thus of what Pope Pius X called in 1907 "the synthesis of all heresies."

Eutyches had never told the synod, as he claimed, that he wished to be judged not at Constantinople but in Rome. He first mentioned such an appeal only after sentence had been pronounced against him, and then only in an undertone to a bishop sitting next to him. Nor was this the unique appeal to the highest authority that Eutyches made it appear in his letter to Leo. In fact, the archimandrite had solicited support wherever he thought it might be forthcoming: not only in Rome but also in Alexandria (Constantinople's longtime rival), Jerusalem, Thessalonica, and even the Western imperial capital of Ravenna — whose bishop, Peter Chrysologus, replied that the Church's faith about Christ's two natures was clearly defined; and that if Eutyches was confused on the matter, the Pope would be happy to set him straight.

It was clear that Eutyches hadn't a theological leg to stand on. What he had instead were friends. A godson, the eunuch Chrysaphios, was a powerful court chamberlain in Constantinople. A notorious intriguer, he had provided his godfather with an imposing retinue of imperial officials to supplement the crowd of monks who accompanied the archimandrite to the local synod in November. The soldiers who rescued Eutyches from his enemies following his condemnation had actually been brought to the proceedings for just such an eventuality. The archimandrite had mentioned this detail in his letter to the Pope to demonstrate the kind of support he enjoyed, in case Leo overlooked the significance of the accompanying letter from the Emperor.

A "Synod of Robbers"

By mid-April 449 Leo had concluded that Flavian's condemnation of Eutyches had been fully justified. He could also see, however, that the irresolute patriarch was no match for the contentious and well-connected archimandrite. To strengthen Flavian's resolve, therefore, and to clarify the doctrinal issues, Leo embarked on his celebrated "Dogmatic Letter to Flavian," known to history as Leo's *Tome* (*Letter* 28). While supporting the patriarch and his local synod,

Leo criticized them (as the passage already cited shows) for not clearly refuting Eutyches' heresy.

Leo then set forth what has become a classical statement of orthodox belief about Christ's two natures. At stake, in Leo's view, was the central affirmation of Christian faith. If, as Eutyches maintained, Christ's human nature had been absorbed by his divinity, he was not truly human. In that case human nature had not been redeemed. "We could not overcome the author of sin and death had not Christ taken our nature and made it his." Leo urged that Eutyches be given an opportunity of rectifying his error at a resumed session of the local synod, augmented by the presence of papal legates. "If he makes the fullest satisfaction by a condemnation read aloud and signed by him personally against all his heretical opinions, then no fault will be found with any show of mercy toward him who has repented." This sentence combined Leo's characteristic moderation with a realistic assessment of Eutyches' capacities as a trouble-maker.

On May 16, however, before this letter could be dispatched, Leo received further disquieting news from the East. On March 30 the Emperor Theodosius had summoned a general council to meet on August 1 at Ephesus to settle "new doubts about the faith." There is reason to believe that this idea may have been promoted by Eutyches himself through his protégé Chrysaphios. Be that as it may, Leo would have recognized at once that the forthcoming council would give the mischievous archimandrite ample opportunity to solicit support for his heretical views. What had been merely a local squabble at Constantinople now threatened to disturb the unity in faith of all the Eastern Churches. With as good grace as possible, Leo accepted the new situation and concentrated on limiting its potential for damage.

On June 13, 449 Leo sent a packet of seven letters to various people in the East outlining the issues in dispute and urging them to do their duty. They should insist on a clear retraction from Eutyches, but treat him mercifully once he had given it. Leo wrote in this sense to Flavian (the *Tome*), to the Emperor Theodosius, to his powerful sister Pulcheria (from Leo's point of view far more reliable than her brother: she received two letters), to Eutyches' fellow ar-chimandrites, to the bishops who would assemble at Ephesus, and to Leo's principal legate at the forthcoming council, Bishop Julian of Kos (an island off the Turkish coast). Julian was a native Italian who had been educated in Rome. As his second representative at the council, Leo appointed the Roman deacon Hilary, who would himself become Bishop of Rome on Leo's death in 461.

Preparations for the council were in the hands of Eutyches' supporters. The Emperor appointed a determined foe of Flavian, the Patriarch Dioscorus of Alexandria, to preside at the gathering, which opened on August 8, 449 amid scenes of wild excitement. Present in support of Eutyches were a large contingent of imperial troops, a horde of monks from Constantinople and Syria, and a company of muscular "hospitalers" brought from Alexandria by their Patriarch Dioscorus to lend weight to his arguments.

Dioscorus opened the council by reading a letter from the Emperor stating that the council's purpose was "to restore the faith of Nicaea" and ordering the arrest of any bishop who went beyond the dogmatic statements of that council. The Emperor ordered further that Flavian and those who had condemned Eutyches at Constantinople in November 448 were to take part only as defendants.

At the first opportunity, the papal legates requested the reading of Leo's letter to Flavian (the *Tome*). This would have blocked the planned rehabilitation of Eutyches, for Leo clearly branded him as heretical. Dioscorus temporized, therefore, by promising that the Pope's letter would be read later. This pledge was never kept. Instead Eutyches appeared before the council as Flavian's accuser, repeating the misleading account of the proceedings against him at Constantinople in November 448 that he had already sent to Leo, as well as his heretical statement about Christ's "two natures before the incarnation, one nature afterwards."

Tumultuous scenes accompanied the reading of the minutes of the synod that had condemned Eutyches. The papal legates struggled, with the help of Greek interpreters, to follow the confused proceedings. Hearing Eutyches' supporters affirm his fidelity to Nicaea, the legates unwittingly damaged their own cause by saying that the Apostolic See also supported Nicaea. In these circumstances this sounded like support for the archimandrite — which the legates of course never intended.

In the end Dioscorus declared Eutyches rehabilitated and Flavian and his principal supporters deposed for adding to the sacrosanct definition of Nicaea's statements about Christ's "two natures." When Flavian and the legate Hilary protested, Dioscorus had the doors of the church opened to admit the crowd of soldiers, monks, and ordinary laypeople who had been demonstrating outside in favor of Eutyches. The now thoroughly frightened bishops, many of whom (as modern research has shown) wanted to follow the Pope's lead and had waited in vain for the promised reading of his letter to Flavian, lined up to sign the sentence that Dioscorus had pronounced.

Hilary returned immediately to Rome. Upon hearing his report, Leo summoned a Roman synod in early October 449. This found ample grounds to declare the proceedings at Ephesus invalid. Leo's letter to Flavian had not been read. Flavian and his supporters were never heard. The bishops had been intimidated by threats from the Emperor. In reality only a minority had agreed with Dioscorus. Hence, the synod declared, Flavian remained in office and in communion with the Apostolic See. Already, however, the hapless patriarch had passed to a higher tribunal, the victim of strife among Christ's followers that has marred Church life ever since the guests at the Last Supper fought over "who should be greatest" (Lk 22:24).

Leo's celebrated description of the gathering at Ephesus in August 449 as a "Synod of Robbers," sounds harsher than it was. Leo was referring not to the bishops generally but only to their manipulation by the synod president, Dioscorus. And he had acted under pressure from the Emperor. Even under provocation, Leo remained moderate in judgment.

Chalcedon

Leo now devoted his attention to securing a new council (preferably in Italy so that Western bishops could attend) to repair the damage done at Ephesus. On October 13, 449 he fired off another salvo of letters to the Emperor Theodosius and others in the East requesting such an assembly in the name of his just concluded Roman synod, of "all the churches in our area, and all the bishops" (*Letter* 44). Subsequent letters repeated this request, which was also supported by the Western Emperor Valentinian, Theodosius' son-in-law and cousin, and Theodosius' other relatives at the court in Ravenna. As could have been predicted, these entreaties went unheeded. Theodosius saw no reason to alter a settlement of Church affairs of which he was a principal architect, and with which he was well pleased.

The resulting impasse was broken in an unexpected way when Theodosius fell from his horse in July 450 and died of his injuries shortly thereafter. He was succeeded by his energetic sister Pulcheria, a supporter of Leo. She moved swiftly to consolidate her power by marrying the powerful general Marcian and proclaiming him Emperor and joint ruler with herself. Pulcheria had the eunuch

Chrysaphios, the grey eminence behind her brother's religious policy, tried and executed. She ordered Eutyches confined to a monastery near Constantinople and recalled to their Sees the Eastern bishops who had been hounded from office because of their opposition to the troublesome archimandrite. Her husband, Marcian, in his first letter to Leo as Emperor, accepted the Pope's request for a new general council.

This met at Chalcedon, on the eastern shore of the Bosporus opposite Constantinople, on October 8, 451. With some 350 bishops in attendance, it was the largest council the Church had yet seen. The Pope was represented by five legates — three bishops and two presbyters — who were given places of honor. The actual direction of the council was in the hands of six imperial commissioners.

At the demand of the legates, Dioscorus was permitted to take part only to defend his leadership of the "Robber Synod" two years previously. Asked why he had not kept his promise to have Leo's *Tome* read on that occasion, Dioscorus claimed this had been frustrated by others. Though the issue was never resolved, the discussion served to emphasize the importance of Leo's dogmatic letter to Flavian. When it was finally read at the second session of October 10, the minutes record seventeen affirmative acclamations. The most significant from the Pope's point of view was the cry: "Peter has spoken this through Leo" — an exact echo of Leo's doctrine of the Pope as Peter's living voice that we saw at the beginning of this chapter.

Despite this positive reception of the *Tome*, however, many of the bishops were still worried that Leo's statements were an illegitimate addition to the doctrine of Nicaea. Those who took this position cited the prohibition of new credal statements by the (legitimate) Council of Ephesus twenty years before. A committee addressed this problem in an address to the Emperor called the Allocution. This said that the prohibition of new professions of faith at Ephesus in 431 applied only to heretics. The Church's pastors, however, must always be free to restate the faith in the face of error. This was what Leo had done in the *Tome*, the Allocution declared. He had not proposed a new confession of faith. Rather, as Peter's successor, he had authentically interpreted in the face of current errors the confession of faith made by Peter at Caesarea Philippi. Making use of the same right to reformulate the Church's faith that it had just vindicated for the Pope, the committee then developed its own explanation of Christ's two natures. This was based on the *Tome* and must be read together with it. But it further developed Leo's statements.

When many council fathers still could not overcome scruples about "a new profession," the imperial commissioners forced a decision by putting the following question: "Dioscorus says he accepts 'out of two natures' but rejects 'two natures.' The most holy Archbishop Leo says that in Christ there are two natures united without change, without division, and without confusion. Which do the bishops choose: Leo or Dioscorus?" The overwhelming majority voted for Leo. A small minority remained silent. They would be heard from later.

It was a watershed in doctrinal development. Stephan Otto Horn explains the significance of Chalcedon in a characteristically pregnant German sentence: "The Council's definition, together with the Allocution, became the Magna Carta for a dynamic concept of tradition which excludes an antiquarian understanding" (*Petrou Kathedra*, p. 215). We have already pointed out the relevance of Chalcedon's decision today. Once again would-be defenders of the faith are contending that dogmatic statements developed in a past historical situation may not be reinterpreted or added to in the light of changed circumstances. This argument was rejected by Pope Leo the Great and the fourth ecumenical council in the fifth century. It is as destructive of Catholic unity now as it was then.

A new Rome?

Leo's great victory was marred, however, by a dispute over the claim of Constantinople to be the second See of Christendom, after Rome. This was contained in Chalcedon's celebrated Canon 28, passed by the Eastern bishops in the absence of the papal legates on October 31st. This ascribed the primacy of "old Rome" to its status as "the imperial city." It gave "equal privileges to the most holy throne of New Rome [Constantinople]," because "the city which is honored with the Sovereignty and the Senate, and enjoys equal privileges with the old imperial Rome, should in ecclesiastical matters be magnified as she is, and rank next after her." The legates protested vigorously at the council's final session on November 1st.

In December 451 a delegation from the East visited Rome to seek Leo's consent to the disputed canon — tacit recognition that it could not take effect without papal assent. This was not forthcoming. Leo gave two reasons for his refusal. First, Rome's primacy was based not on its political status, but on the principle of apostolicity (its foundation by Peter). Constantinople could not obtain second rank by invoking its political importance. "For secular things have one basis, religious ones another." Second, Leo said that the order of precedence established by Nicaea (which had granted second and third rank to Alexandria and Antioch respectively) "cannot be changed by any innovation" (*Letter* 104).

This was a reversion to the rigid view of tradition that Leo had just rejected in matters of doctrine. If the Church was free to reformulate tradition in matters of divine faith, why not in matters of Church order, most of which derived from human law only, and hence were alterable? Leo was on firmer ground with his first reason for rejecting Constantinople's claim. He was not only insisting that Church order be built on the solid foundation of apostolicity rather than on the shifting sands of politics. He was also rejecting the claim of Constantinople (advanced when its spokesmen recognized the weakness of the political argument) to share in Peter's authority. In Leo's view this could not be divided. The rock on which Christ had founded his Church must support the whole building. The Roman See had a unique authority and a unique task, given to Peter by Christ. Diminishing the authority of his successor meant diminishing the whole Church. This claim continues to be advanced by Peter's successors today.

The East, reflecting on Leo's inflexibility over the order of precedence established at Nicaea, felt aggrieved and ill used. The dispute over canon 28 of Chalcedon sowed the seed for the division of East and West some six centuries later. Meanwhile, in the East itself, Chalcedon failed to achieve doctrinal unity. Those who had sat on their hands while the definition of Christ's "two natures, without confusion, without change, without division, without separation" was being acclaimed by the council majority, formed themselves into "monophysite" churches that exist to this day. A center of this monophysite ("one nature") teaching was Alexandria, which bitterly resented the humiliating defeat of its Patriarch Dioscorus at Chalcedon. For the rest of his pontificate, Leo labored, with small success, to heal the wounds inflicted on Christendom's second See, thought to have been founded by the evangelist Saint Mark.

The East also developed a kind of "political monophysitism." Even those who accepted the Chalcedonian definition of Christ's two natures held a "unitary" view of church-state relations which regarded the Emperor as the Church's divinely anointed ruler. The East has thus avoided the struggles between Church and state that have plagued the West. It has done so, however, at the price of "Caesaropapism": the system whereby an absolute monarch governs the Church even in matters, such as doctrine, normally reserved to ecclesiastical authority. The results were visible in the Soviet Union, where the

Russian Orthodox Church accepted (possibly reluctantly, but perhaps willingly) a measure of state control that Western Christians would find intolerable.

The West, on the other hand, developed the doctrine of "two powers," civil and religious, which parallels Leo and Chalcedon's doctrine of Christ's two natures. Often this has led to conflict between Church and state, as subsequent chapters will show. Ideally, however, the possessors of these two powers exercise them in partnership, according to this Western view: without confusion, but also without division or separation. This idea — that Church and state should cooperate to build a just society — explains the Roman suspicion (expressed in some speeches at the Second Vatican Council) of the separation of Church and state guaranteed by the United States Constitution. This suspicion is not based, as Americans often suppose, upon the desire for a theocracy, in which the church controls the state. Rather, it expresses the fear that church-state separation means hostile rivalry. The last two centuries of European history provide ample basis for this fear. Americans are convinced, on the basis of their quite different history, that separation of the two powers can be friendly. The New World experience that supports this conviction is now better understood at Rome, even though vestiges of the old suspicion recur from time to time.

Defender of Rome

The final decade of Leo's life was dominated, in addition to continuing doctrinal and political strife in the East, by barbarian invasions in Italy. The weak Western Emperor Valentinian III was unable to defend northeastern Italy against invasion by the Huns in 451. The following year Leo, at the head of an embassy from the Roman Senate, met the Hun General Attila in the neighborhood of Mantua, near the southern shore of Lake Garda and persuaded him to withdraw. Rome was saved. Leo's reputation soared.

This confrontation between the Roman Bishop and the barbarian invader was soon embellished by legend. A painting of the scene by Raphael hangs in the Stanza d'Eliodoro in the Vatican. It shows Attila struck with terror on beholding the Saints Peter and Paul descending armed from heaven. Leo, in the likeness of his feckless namesake at the time the painting was executed and whom we shall meet later, Leo X, advances on horseback followed by two cardinals. In the background is a distant view of Rome.

Leo was not so fortunate in defending Rome against the Vandal King Geiseric, who crossed by sea from North Africa to Ostia in June 455. Leo met him as he was advancing on the city. Though he was not able to prevent extensive plundering, Leo prevailed on Geiseric not to burn the city to the ground, and to spare the populace.

Leo died on November 10, 461 (some authorities say a day or two later) and was buried at the entrance to the Basilica of St. Peter of that day. His remains were moved inside the church in 688 and transferred in the sixteenth century to the present basilica. There his bones rest beneath the altar of the "Chapel of the Column" to the southwest of the papal altar under the great dome. Above the tomb is a low marble relief from the seventeenth century depicting Leo's meeting with Attila the Hun at Mantua.

Leo's contemporaries remembered him as the savior of Rome and Italy. For us his services to the papacy, and to the development of doctrine, are more important. He is the great champion, in the ancient Church, of a dynamic as opposed to a static concept of tradition. And he left a papacy fully conscious of its prerogatives as the center and foundation of Church unity. As the remnants of Rome's Empire collapsed and Europe sank into what historians call the Dark Ages, it was the papacy alone which possessed the moral prestige and intellectual power to preserve the noble elements of ancient civilization and to exercise in the new world that was struggling to be born the Lord's command to the fisherman Peter: "Feed my sheep" (Jn 21:17).

CHAPTER THREE

Gregory the Great

(590-604)

"I *have the impression that your Beatitude has not really grasped the point I was trying to make. For I said that you should not write such expressions to me or to anyone. And behold, there in the salutation of your letter I find the selfsame pompous title "Universal Pope" which I forbade you to use. I beseech your most sweet Holiness not to repeat this. For in paying unreasonable tribute to another you detract from yourself. I want to be eminent not in words, but in example. Nor can I consider something an honor which I know diminishes the honor of my brothers. My honor is the honor of the universal church. My honor is firm solidarity with my brothers. I am truly honored when no one else is deprived of the honor due to him" (Letter of 595 to the Patriarch Eulogius of Alexandria; cited by the First Vatican Council in 1870 to illustrate the rights of bishops).*

The second of the two Bishops of Rome to bear the title "Great" was born at Rome about 540 of a wealthy aristocratic family that had already given the Church two Popes. The first, Felix III, has been called "the first demonstrably aristocratic pope." His election as Bishop of Rome in 483 indicates the extent to which highly born Romans were seeking careers in the Church rather than in civil government.

Knowing the reason for this development will help us to understand Gregory's world. In 476 the last Western Roman Emperor Romulus Augustulus had been sent into comfortable retirement by the barbarian mercenary general Odoacer, who ruled Italy as self-constituted King. Odoacer, like the ruler who supplanted him, the Istrogoth Theoderic, was an Arian Christian. Both men admired the ancient Roman traditions and respected Church rights. However, the old senatorial families at Rome looked on these new rulers as parvenus and *arrivistes*. Excluded from the public offices that had been open to them in the past, the sons of these old aristocrats either left Rome to seek their fortunes at the imperial court in Constantinople, or entered the service of the Roman Church.

In 535 the relatively tranquil reign of the Arian Ostrogoths in Italy was shattered by a war of reconquest launched by the Eastern Emperor Justinian who dreamed of reviving his Western Empire. In 554 Justinian was able to issue a decree called the *Pragmatic Sanction* officially restoring Roman rule. It was a hollow victory, however. Almost two decades of war had left the Italian peninsula impoverished and depopulated.

The senatorial aristocracy at Rome, to which Gregory's family belonged, shared in this decline. Undermined by massacre, bankruptcy, and migration to the East, they were further humiliated to see many of their old government posts given to Greek civil servants imported from the East and commanded by a new imperial official at Ravenna called the Exarch.

Restoration of imperial government in Italy also had important consequences for the Church. The Arian Church was suppressed and its property handed over to the Catholic Church. In return, the Church was expected to toe the imperial line, even in matters of doctrine. The Emperor Justinian, for instance, carried off the ambitious but vacillating Pope Vigilius to Constantinople in 547 and browbeat him into signing a doctrinal statement (condemning something called the "Three Chapters") which many Western bishops believed undermined the Chalcedonian settlement under Leo. This unleashed a storm of protest in the West and caused the Churches of northern Italy to withdraw formally from communion with the Pope. The resulting Three Chapters, or Istrian Schism, lasting almost a 150 years, was one of the many problems confronting Gregory during his pontificate. Another was the pretensions of the archbishops of Ravenna, who felt that the establishment of the Exarchate there entitled them to greater importance in the hierarchy than Gregory was willing to concede.

In 568 the Italian peninsula suffered its worst disaster yet: invasion by the fierce warrior race of Lombards, who swept into northern Italy bent on plunder and conquest. Within a few years, they gained effective control of fully half of Italy. Thereafter the Eastern Emperors, preoccupied with their own problems in the Balkans and Asia Minor, could do little to defend their Western territories. In this increasingly precarious situation, the papacy inherited by default many of the functions previously exercised by the imperial government: maintenance of law and order, relief of the poor, and even military defense.

Family background and education

Gregory twice refers to Pope Felix III (483-492) as his *atavus*. Though this can mean simply "ancestor," it can also have a more precise significance. Historians are now satisfied that Felix was Gregory's great-great-grandfather. To understand how this could be, we must set aside modern ideas of clerical celibacy. Though the clergy of this early period were forbidden to contract matrimony, married men could be ordained, and many were. Celibate Popes like Leo and Gregory tried to insist on celibacy for bishops, not always with success. Even less successful were the constantly repeated papal exhortations to married clergy to live with their wives as brother and sister.

Against this background it is no surprise to learn that Gregory's ancestor Felix was the son of a priest, and himself a married man with children, when he became a deacon in the Roman Church. He was a widower when he became its bishop. Another married Pope from this period was Hormisdas, who was Bishop of Rome from 514 to 523.

Gregory's other papal ancestor is Agapitus, Pope in 535-536. He too was the son of a priest, with a wife and children when he was ordained deacon in 502. It is probable though not provable that Agapitus was Felix III's nephew. Gregory inherited his library. Agapitus had wanted to use it for a Christian University of Rome. This never materialized and the collection passed on his death to Gregory's father, Gordianus, and from him to Gregory, who incorporated it into the monastery that he founded on the family estate in Rome.

Gregory's father, Gordianus, was a *defensor*, a papal official charged with defending the rights of the Roman Church and protecting the oppressed. Technically a cleric, he had received minor orders, for which marriage and family life were of course no obstacle. His wife, Silvia (Gregory's mother), was a devout woman who retired into religious seclusion on her husband's death. The couple was wealthy, with a palatial house on Rome's Caelian Hill, farms outside the city, and extensive estates in Sicily, from ancient times the breadbasket of Rome.

The family's wealth did not save Gregory's maternal aunt Pateria, however, from falling on hard times. She received a pension from her nephew after he became Pope. Gregory's paternal aunts, Tarsilla, Aemiliana, and Gordiana, lived a strict religious life as nuns in their own house. Their nephew recounted how the first two died after seeing a vision of their papal ancestor, Felix III. Gordiana, who evidently had never cared for the cloistered life, then scandalized her relatives by throwing off the veil and marrying the steward of her estates. "Many are called but few are chosen," was Gregory's sad comment (*Dialogues* iv, 16; *Homilies on the Gospels* 38).

Gregory received the formal classical education customary for a youth of his station — one of the last to do so, since the ancient Roman schools broke up shortly after Justinian's campaign of reconquest. His later career shows that he had also studied Roman law. Although he knew the classical Latin authors and the Fathers, such as Augustine and Jerome, who had written in Latin, Gregory never learned Greek. This is especially noteworthy since, as we shall see, he was for seven years the Pope's representative in Constantinople. Gregory regarded Greek as an inferior language, and the people who spoke it as shifty and prone to heresy.

Rome, the city of the Caesars and Saint Peter, was always first in Gregory's affections, even in its decline. He could never comprehend why so many members of his social class abandoned the decaying city on the Tiber to seek their fortunes in the glittering new capital on the Bosporus. To one of them, the patrician Rusticiana, Gregory wrote: "How anyone can be so entranced by Constantinople and so forgetful of Rome I cannot understand" (*Letters* viii, 22). One suspects that Gregory would have sympathized with the stage Englishman who complains that "abroad is beastly and all foreigners are bloody."

Early career

It is likely that as a young man, Gregory gained experience in the administration of his family's extensive estates. The first secure date we know in his career, however, is 573, when he held a high position in Rome's civil government, very likely the highest. Though he performed his duties well, he remained unsatisfied. Years later he wrote about this turning point in his life in the preface to his *Morals on Job*:

> For late and long I declined the grace of conversion, and after I had been inspired with a heavenly affection, I thought it better to be still shrouded in secular habits. For although it had now been disclosed to me that I should seek the love of things eternal, yet . . . I could not change my outward habit; and my purpose still compelled me to engage in the service of this world, as it were in semblance only, but what is more serious, in my own mind. At length being anxious to avoid all those inconveniences I sought the haven of the monastery.

Gregory probably took this decision in 574-575. It appears that the step was precipitated by his father's death, his mother's religious retirement, and Gregory's inheritance of the family estates. Never one to do things by halves, Gregory used his inheritance to found six monasteries on his estates in Sicily, and a seventh in the family home at Rome, which he turned into the monastery of St. Andrew. There, with a group of companions, he formed a monastic community under an abbot.

Gregory always looked back on this period of his life as the happiest. As Pope he contrasted his recollected life as a monk with the constant distractions of the papal office.

> When I was in the monastery I could curb my idle talk and usually be absorbed in my prayers. Since taking on the burden of pastoral care, I have been unable to keep steadily recollected because my mind is distracted by many responsibilities. ... I am often compelled by the nature of my position to associate with men of the world and . . . I must frequently listen patiently to their aimless chatter. Because I too am weak . . . I soon find myself enjoying the gossip to which at first I lent an unwilling ear — and so I end by wallowing where I had first dreaded to fall (*Homilies on Ezekiel* i, 11, 4-6: Breviary reading for Gregory's feast, September 3).

The severity against himself that is reflected in this passage caused Gregory to undertake in the monastery a regimen of fasting that owed more to the ultra-ascetic practices of the early monks of the Egyptian desert than to the monastic rules of Gregory's own day. The resulting damage to his health remained with him for the rest of his life.

Gregory's monastic retirement did not last long, however. In the summer of 579, with the Lombards at the gates of Rome, the newly elected Pope Pelagius II summoned Gregory from his monastery and over his protests ordained him deacon, thus making him one of the top administrative officials of the Roman Church. To his further dismay, Gregory was then sent to Constantinople as papal envoy to the Emperor. His primary mission was to lobby for help in repelling the Lombard invaders.

It is not difficult to see why Pelagius selected Gregory for this difficult mission. His many friends among the emigré Roman aristocrats in Constantinople would be able to open doors for him at the imperial court. And as a former top administrator he was at home in the corridors of power. In the face of such compelling considerations, it is hardly surprising that Gregory's pleas to remain in the monastery went unheeded.

Gregory took some of his fellow monks with him to Constantinople, however, and installed them in the Placidia palace, the official residence of the papal representative. In addition, he soon had a circle of clerical friends in the capital, the closest being the Spanish Bishop Leander of Seville, an elder brother of the more famous Isidore, who is often called "the last Western Father." Gregory and Leander both came from pious aristocratic families, were both monks, and shared the same outlook. It was partly at Leander's instigation that Gregory began to deliver to his monastic companions in Constantinople the conferences on the book of Job that he completed as Pope and published in thirty-five books dedicated to Leander. Gregory never saw his Spanish friend after leaving Constantinople. A letter he wrote to him as Pope in 591, however, contains a touching sentence, probably unique in the whole corpus of papal writings, which shows Gregory at his most human and winning: "The image of your face is impressed forever on my innermost heart" (*Letters* i, 41).

Despite urgent reminders from Pope Pelagius, Gregory was unable to obtain much help in repelling the Lombards. Neither the Emperor Tiberius, nor his prudent and conscientious son-in-law Maurice who succeeded him in 582, could spare troops for military adventures in the West. The best Maurice could do was to send his general Smaragdus to Ravenna as exarch to organize the scanty defenses in the peninsula. Maurice also paid large bribes to the Franks to induce them to attack the Lombards from the rear, in the hope that this would relieve some of the pressure on those parts of Italy that were still under imperial control. This policy, which was to be often repeated during the two decades of Maurice's reign, achieved only limited success.

Although he failed in the principal object of his mission, Gregory formed many friendships at the imperial court that were to stand him in good stead later. In 584 he was godfather at the baptism of Maurice's eldest son, Theodosius. His seven-year residence at court deepened his loyalty to the sovereign to whom Gregory felt a double bond. As son of an ancient Roman family, Gregory saw in the Emperor, even in Byzantine exile, the heir of the men who had ruled the Empire in the days of Rome's glory. And as a Christian, Gregory revered him as the heir also of the great Emperor Constantine who, less than three centuries before, had brought the Church out of the darkness of persecution into the sunshine of public favor.

Pope Pelagius II recalled Gregory to Rome in 586. But there was no question of his resuming the monastic seclusion for which he longed. The times were too grave. Though he lived with his monastic brethren at St. Andrew's, Gregory was fully occupied with administrative duties as deacon at the Lateran palace. The Pope gave him the difficult task of healing the Istrian schism. Though Gregory did his best, it was not good enough. The northern bishops remained obdurate, and the schism continued.

The year 589 added natural catastrophes to the existing political and military difficulties. Disastrous floods devastated northern Italy and reached Rome in the fall. The Tiber overflowed, destroying several ancient churches and the papal granaries from which much of the city's population was fed. The receding waters were followed by the plague, which had ravaged Italy periodically from the mid-560s and contributed to the success of the Lombard invasion. Among the first victims was Pope Pelagius II, who succumbed on February 8, 590.

There was only one candidate for his successor. Although still the junior deacon in years of service, Gregory had a reputation for personal holiness, based upon his monastic life and rigorous fasting. This, combined with his practical experience in civic administration and as papal envoy in Constantinople, predestined him for the Church's highest office. Realizing that acceptance of the papacy would put an end to his residence at St. Andrew's, Gregory did everything in his power to ward off the inevitable. He wrote to the Emperor imploring him to refuse his consent. However, Gregory's own brother Palatinus, who was now city prefect (in all probability the office Gregory himself had held before becoming a monk), intercepted the letter and substituted one of his own telling Maurice that Gregory had been elected Pope unanimously.

The Emperor's consent did not reach Rome for six months. When it arrived at the end of August, Gregory tried to flee secretly. His plan was discovered, however, and on September 3, 570 he was brought to St. Peter's Basilica and ordained as the sixty-third successor of the fisherman over whose tomb the church had been built by the Emperor Constantine.

Gregory's letters from the months immediately following his episcopal ordination are filled with laments at having to leave the monastery. "I am tossed to and fro with the waves of business," he wrote the Princess Theoctista. "I am overwhelmed with its storms. . . . When my business is done, I try to return to my inner thoughts but cannot, for I am driven away by vain tumultuous thoughts. I loved the beauty of the contemplative life . . . but by some judgment, I know not what, I have been wedded . . . to the active life" (*Letters* i, 5).

By January 591, however, his mood had begun to change and he could write to Archbishop Natalis of Salona in Dalmatia (the Adriatic coast opposite Italy): "I undertook the burden of this dignity with a sick heart. But seeing that I could not resist the divine decrees, I have recovered a more cheerful frame of mind" (*Letters* i, 20).

Character and outlook

We know far more about Gregory than about most early Popes. Our sources are, first, his own letters: 854 have been preserved, most of them in the collection sent to Charlemagne by Pope Adrian I (772-795). There are Gregory's extensive writings. Finally there are three *Lives*: by an unknown monk of Whitby, England, in the early eighth century; by Paul the Deacon, a monk at Monte Cassino at the end of the eighth century; and by the Roman Deacon John, whose work was commissioned by Pope John VIII (872-882) when he discovered that there was no Roman *Life* of his great predecessor.

The Deacon John describes the portrait painted for the monks of St. Andrew's after Gregory's death and still in existence at the time John wrote. This showed the Pope with "a tawny beard of moderate length, rather bald [but with] two small neat curls in the middle of his forehead, darkish hair nicely curled and hanging down as far as the middle of his ear" (*Life* iv, 84). Those familiar with clerical gatherings today will recognize from this description that the wheel of tonsorial fashion has come full circle.

Prominent among Gregory's personal qualities was his fortitude in the face of physical pain, the result of excessive fasting and in his later years of gout. He was almost continuously ill as Pope, and his sufferings increased with age. "Many a long year . . . I have been afflicted by frequent pains in the bowels," he wrote one correspondent. "The powers of my stomach having broken down, I am continually weak; and I gasp under the weight of successive slow fevers" (*Letters* v, 53a). In 591 he was too ill to deliver his homilies on the gospels. They were read for him by papal notaries. Summer fevers drove him to bed in July of that year and again in August 593. "The summer which is not at all good for my body, has for a long time prevented me from speaking to you about the Gospel," he explained when he was able to resume his discourses (*Homilies on the Gospels* ii, 34, i).

From 598 until his death six years later, Gregory was almost continually bed-ridden. To his beloved Leander of Seville, a fellow sufferer from gout, he wrote in August 599: "I am myself exceedingly worn down by perpetual pain" (*Letters* ix, 227). His letters from these years are filled with harrowing details of his ailments. In August 599 he wrote that he daily expected death (*Letters* ix, 232). And in June of the following year, he told Patriarch Eulogius of Alexandria:

> It is almost two full years that I have been confined to my bed, afflicted by such severe pains of gout that I have been hardly able to rise on feast days for as much as three hours to celebrate Mass. And I am soon compelled to lie down, that I may be able to bear my torment with intervening groans. The pain I suffer is sometimes modest, and sometimes excessive: but neither so modest as to depart nor so excessive as to kill me (*Letters* x, 14).

However, Gregory's chronic illness did not lead, as so often, to self-absorption. There are many examples of his sending help to his fellow sufferers: the advice of Roman doctors for Archbishop Marinianus of Ravenna who was vomiting blood; a miracle-working charm for Patriarch Eulogius of Alexandria who was going blind; a warm cloak for Bishop Ecclesius of Clusium who was ill and suffering from the cold (this when Gregory was himself on his deathbed). His first biographer even has a story about Gregory winning the favor of a Lombard ruler who was threatening Rome by sending him a milk diet for his ailing stomach (*Whitby Life* 23). Gregory's writings show a keen interest in medical problems, perhaps nourished by conversations with the Alexandrian physician who attended him as Pope. And Gregory devoted an entire chapter of his *Pastoral Rule* to an allegorical discussion of sickness (i, 11).

Despite his frequent bouts of illness, Gregory was a tireless worker. "He never rested" Paul the Deacon wrote, "but was always engaged in providing for the interests of the people or writing down some composition worthy of the church or in searching out the secrets of heaven by the grace of contemplation" (*Life of Gregory* 15). Only the last-mentioned activity saved him from being a workaholic.

Gregory has been called "one of the great Western mystics." He believed fervently in the value of waiting upon God in silence. Nor was this something for "advanced souls" only, as the spirituality of a later age would claim. "It is not true," Gregory said in his ninth homily on the Gospels, "that the grace of contemplation is given to the highest and not to the lowest. There is no state of life of the faithful from which it is excluded. Anyone who keeps his heart within may be illuminated by the light of contemplation." And in an obvious reflection of his own experience, he added: "We see daily in holy church that very many manage external duties yet are led to mystical understandings and are gifted greatly with inward wisdom."

This inward "keeping of the heart" on which Gregory insisted so strongly consisted above all in humility. All the witnesses agree that Gregory himself manifested in outstanding measure this trait which he called "the mother and guardian of virtues" and "the root of goodness" (*Letters* ii, 52; *Homilies on the Gospels* i, 7, 4).

Gregory's concern for humility is reflected in the quotation at the head of this chapter. It was part of his protest against the use of the title "Ecumenical Patriarch" by a man named John the Faster, who was Patriarch of Constantinople. During his term as papal envoy in Constantinople, Gregory had been impressed by John's asceticism. He objected to John's adding the word "Ecumenical" to his title, however, on the ground that this impinged on papal primacy and violated humility. By hindsight it appears that Gregory's concern on the first point was based on a misunderstanding. The title "Ecumenical" had been granted in the sixth century to Popes *and* patriarchs. When used by the latter, it meant supreme within his own patriarchate, not over other patriarchs.

Gregory saw the matter differently, however. Working himself up almost to a frenzy, he denounced the title as "an act of pride in which all the bowels of the universal church are disturbed" (*Letters* v, 41). And in what Gregory called with unperceived irony "a sweet and reasonable letter," he exhorted the offending patriarch to "love humility and do not try to raise yourself by abasing your brethren. Abandon this rash name, this word of pride and folly which is disturbing the peace of the whole world." Failure to do so, Gregory warned, would make John a precursor of the Antichrist and an imitator of the fallen angel Lucifer (*Letters* v, 44).

The controversy was still unresolved at Gregory's death. In time his successors gave up the fight and adopted the title themselves. Despite this, the citation of Gregory's letter by the First Vatican Council in 1870 shows that the memory of his support for episcopal collegiality was not extinct more than thirteen centuries later. It is especially noteworthy that the council which, more than all others, exalted the prerogatives of the head of the episcopal college, also affirmed that the rights of its other members were inalienable, because divinely ordained.

For all his humility, Gregory was a strong upholder of the hierarchical order in Church and state that was so prominent a feature of his world. In Gregory's view differences of station and authority were established by God. Disturbing them could only lead to confusion and chaos. "Nature begets all men equal," he wrote in his *Morals on Job*, "but by reason of their varying merits, a mysterious dispensation sets some beneath others. This diversity in condition, which is due to sin, is rightly ordained by the judgment of God; that whereas every man does not walk through life in like manner, one should be governed by another" (xxi, 22).

Consistent with this view was Gregory's acceptance of slavery. He was glad to see slaves set free, especially if they wished to embrace a religious vocation. This required the consent of their owners, however. Otherwise relations between slaves and masters should be characterized on both sides by humility and Christian charity.

The same was true of lay rulers, government officials, aristocrats, and military commanders. They were to treat their subordinates justly. Even when they failed to do so, however, superiors were to be obeyed. "For when we offend against those who are set over us," he explained in his *Pastoral Rule*, "we offend against the ordinance of Him who set them over us" (iii, 4). And in his *Morals on Job* he wrote: "Even if the conduct of rulers is justly blamed, yet it is the duty of subjects to pay them respect" (xxv, 37). Gregory frequently reminded papal officials to cultivate good relations with the authorities, even authorizing small financial gifts to keep them well-disposed. Gregory's lofty ideals of justice were tempered by a keen sense of *realpolitik.*

Dominating all Gregory's thought and action was the conviction that the end of the world was imminent. He saw the signs of this everywhere: in the Lombard invasions, the plague and other natural disasters, and in the decay of his beloved Rome, "once mistress of the world," which he compared to an old eagle that had lost its feathers and could no longer use its claws (*Homilies on Ezekiel* i, 7, 22, 23; ii, 6, 22). His writings abound in exhortations to repentance while there was still time. A letter to the clergy of Milan is typical.

> Behold all the things of this world, which we used to hear from the
> Bible were doomed to perish, we see now destroyed. Cities are
> overthrown, fortresses are razed, churches are destroyed; and

no tiller of the ground inhabits our land any more. Among the few of us who are left the sword of man rages unceasingly along with the calamities which smite us from above. . . . View therefore with anxious heart the approaching day of the eternal judge, and by repenting anticipate its terrors. Wash away with tears the stains of all your transgressions. Allay by temporal lamentations the wrath that hangs over you eternally. For our loving creator when he shall come to judgment will comfort us with all the greater favor as He sees now that we are punishing ourselves for our own transgressions (*Letters* iii, 29).

Far from inducing fatalistic resignation, however, this conviction about the approaching end drove Gregory, as it had once driven the apostle Paul, to restless activity.

Administration

In Gregory's day the papacy was the largest landowner in Italy, with estates also in southern Gaul, North Africa, Sardinia, Corsica, and the Balkans. The papal holdings were especially rich and extensive in Sicily. The properties, called collectively the Patrimony of Saint Peter, had come to the Church by gift, inheritance, and the fortunes of politics and war. We have already noted one example: the Emperor Justinian's gift of Arian church property following his reconquest of Italy at mid-century.

Each of the patrimonies was administered by a rector, who was appointed by the Pope and held office at his pleasure. The rector had an extensive staff to oversee the operation of the individual farms — amounting in Sicily to many hundreds. The income was used for the support of the clergy, the building and upkeep of churches and monasteries, and the relief of the poor.

When Gregory became Pope, he found the patrimonial income seriously impaired: the result of plundering by the Lombards, bad administration by incompetent rectors, and looting by imperial officials, rectors, and subordinate officials. Gregory undertook a thorough renovation of the whole ramshackle system. Where necessary he replaced rectors and made all of them take an oath on the tomb of Saint Peter in Rome to administer their offices honestly and to treat everyone with strict justice.

He instituted a system of regular audits and corresponded tirelessly on matters of detail: ordering, for instance, that herds of over-age cattle be thinned out, demanding and revising lists, commanding restitution of unlawfully acquired property — including slaves — and enjoining the rectors to be constantly mindful of the needs of the poor.

The result was a marked increase in revenues. They were sorely needed. In addition to the provision of grain for much of Rome's populace (formerly the responsibility of the Emperor, but now of the Pope), the city swarmed with refugees from the Lombards, among them 3,000 nuns who looked to the Pope as their sole support.

Even the wages of the scanty imperial garrison that was supposed to defend Rome often had to be paid from the papal purse when, for months on end, no funds arrived from the Emperor. Gregory also paid huge sums to the Lombards to induce them to lift their siege of Rome — only to have the agreements repudiated by the exarch in Ravenna and the Emperor Maurice on the grounds that the Pope had exceeded his authority and was guilty of naiveté in negotiating with a treacherous foe who did not really want peace and would keep his promises only as long as it was convenient.

Gregory's correspondence makes it possible to trace his activities in considerable detail. Through them Gregory was laying the foundations for papal power in the Middle Ages. This was the result, however, not of deliberate policy, but of circumstances. Rome, once the imperial capital, first became papal Rome not by design, but simply because there was no one but the Pope to respond to the urgent needs of the hour. In Gregory Rome had a bishop who was one of the ablest administrators ever to hold the papal office. Once people had experienced his remarkable achievements, in the face of seemingly insurmountable difficulties, the demand that his successors should emulate him was inevitable. The enormously powerful medieval papacy that we shall see in the chapters following was the result.

Responsibilities similar to those thrust upon the Pope also fell on the shoulders of the bishops. Justinian's *Pragmatic Sanction* of A.D. 554 had given the bishops sweeping responsibility for overseeing local government. Deteriorating conditions in the decades following gave people further reason to expect bishops, like the Pope, to care for refugees, organize the food supply for beleaguered cities, and defend them from the barbarians. The times demanded bishops, therefore, who were not only men of God, but able administrators as well. Securing the election of such men was one of Gregory's chief concerns.

Bishops were supposed to be chosen by a vote of clergy, nobles, and people. In practice the leading clergy and nobles often arranged matters between them. The Pope was able to exert influence in various ways, however. Before the election he could suggest a particular candidate. Gregory often did this by writing to the rector of the patrimony in which the vacant See was located, urging him to line up support for a suitable candidate. The Pope could also veto an election for cause. The canons said that a man could not become a bishop if he had a criminal record, was illiterate, held government office, was a layman, had been married more than once or had married a divorcee, or was under thirty. This list of impediments tells us much about the quality of available candidates.

If the local electors were deadlocked, the Pope could choose the bishop himself. In deference to local sensitivities, however, Gregory always summoned representative electors to Rome in such cases, and negotiated the selection with them.

As in the case of patrimonial administration, Gregory's correspondence allows us to follow in some detail his efforts to upgrade the episcopate. His interventions were most frequent in the first five years of his episcopate. Thereafter, with bishops of his choice in a number of the more important dioceses, there was less need for this activity. The record shows that Gregory was a master of personnel management.

Evangelism

Though Christianity had been the official religion of the Empire for close to three centuries, paganism was by no means dead. It had once been the religion of the ruling classes. They were now the most thoroughly Christianized. It was most often peasants, especially in distant places like Sardinia, Corsica, Sicily, Gaul, and Britain, who clung to the old ways, "living like wild beasts and entirely ignorant of the worship of God," as Gregory put it with a *frisson* of upper-class aversion (*Letters* iv, 39). Gregory grieved to think that so many souls would not attain salvation. His conviction that the end of the world was imminent lent urgency to his efforts to bring as many as possible to the true faith while there was still time.

Gregory wrote numerous letters to bishops in the affected areas urging them to greater zeal in preaching the gospel. He recommended using fear of the plague or of the barbarian invaders as a motive for conversion. Although he preferred persuasion, Gregory did not hesitate to recommend coercive measures, especially for slaves and peasants, "so that those who scorn to listen to words of salvation which reclaim them from the peril of death, may at any rate by bodily torments be brought back to the desired sanity of mind" (*Letters* ix, 204).

Another concern was the extirpation of heresy, "the hot wind from the south" as Gregory called it, and the result, in his view, of pride (*Morals* iii, 43). The Arian heresy was widespread among the Lombards, though some were still pagan. In a letter to an old friend in Constantinople shortly after becoming Pope, Gregory revealed what he thought of these despoilers of his native land. "For my sins I have been made bishop not of the Romans but of the Lombards whose compacts are swords and whose favor is a punishment" (*Letters* i, 30). Such views made it difficult for Gregory to reconcile the Lombards with the Church. Realizing this, he worked through the Bavarian Catholic princess Theodelina, successively wife to the Lombard King Autharis and after his death to his successor and kinsman Agilulf. He rejoiced to hear of the Catholic baptism of their son in 603. Though Gregory could not know it, the Catholicization of the Lombards was underway. In the century following his death, Arianism would finally become extinct in the West.

Gregory's most celebrated evangelistic initiative, however, was the mission to England in 596. The Christianity that had come to Britain with the Romans had produced a Celtic Church isolated from the mainstream of Catholic Christianity. By the sixth century, it was confined to the western parts of England, Wales, and Ireland. The Angles and Saxons who had invaded the island a century before and settled in the east and north were pagan worshipers of Woden and Thor, warrior gods whose cult encouraged aggression and conquest. As these Anglo-Saxon invaders entered the period of consolidation, they sought new forms of religion more suitable to a settled society. On the continent this development had led barbarian tribes in Gaul and Spain to adopt first Arianism and finally Catholicism, the religion of the Empire and thus of civilization and respectability. The process was assisted in England by the marriage of Aethelbert, King of Kent, to the Frankish princess Bertha, who was a Christian. In July 596 Gregory wrote the Catholic Queen of the Franks, Brunhild, that he had heard of the Angles' desire for Christianity and was sending Augustine, the prior of his old monastery of St. Andrew at Rome, to bring them the gospel (*Letters* vi, 57).

It was spring 597 by the time Augustine (who had meanwhile been ordained a bishop at Lyons) reached England with his companions. They received a friendly welcome from King Aethelbert, who on Christmas Day 597 was baptized with 10,000 of his subjects. In the following year, Augustine sent two of his assistants back to Rome with a report of this initial success and a list of questions about how to organize Church life in the island.

Due apparently to illness, Gregory did not respond until 601. Then he sent a fresh company of missionary monks, sacred vessels and ornaments, relics, holy books, and a packet of letters. The one addressed to Augustine granted him the pallium of an archbishop and prescribed the organization of the Church in two provinces, based on London and York, with twelve diocesan bishops in each. These arrangements reflected ignorance of the actual conditions in England, and Augustine was able to implement them only minimally. Before his death in about 605, however, Augustine established himself at Canterbury and ordained his companion Laurentius to succeed him.

To Aethelbert and Bertha, Gregory sent congratulations on their baptism and that of their subjects and encouraged them to foster progress in the faith and prevent lapses into paganism. This raised the question of how far pagan temples and customs could be adapted for Christian purposes. Gregory's instructions on this point are worth quoting for the light they throw on what is today called "inculturation": how to establish Christianity in cultures to which it is alien without compromising doctrinal substance on the one hand or violating treasured local traditions on the other.

Gregory instructed Augustine not to insist rigidly on the customs of the Roman Church in which he had been brought up.

> If you have found any customs . . . which may be more pleasing to Almighty God, you should make careful selection of them and sedulously teach the church of the English, which is still new in the faith, what you have been able to gather from other churches. For things are not to be loved for the sake of a place, but places for the sake of their good things. Therefore choose from every individual church whatever things are devout, religious and right (Bede, *Ecclesiastical History* i, 27, ii).

> The idol temples should by no means be destroyed, but only the idols in them. Take holy water and sprinkle it on these shrines, build altars and place relics in them. For if the shrines are well built, it is essential that they should be changed from the worship of devils to the service of the true God. When this people see that their shrines are not destroyed they will be able to banish error from their hearts and be more ready to come to the places they

are familiar with, but now recognizing and worshipping the true
God (*Letters* xi, 56).

Despite two meetings with the fiercely independent Welsh bishops in 602 or 603, Augustine was unable to reach agreement with them over their non-Latin customs. However he launched the church in England on a course from which it never turned back. In the Middle Ages there was no Church in Europe more loyal to Rome than the one that revered Gregory and Augustine as its founders. It was no accident that the first *Life* of Gregory was written in England.

A century later England also produced the great missionary Boniface, summoned to Rome by Pope Gregory II in 722 and subsequently sent to Germany to do for the people of that land what Augustine of Canterbury had done for Boniface's ancestors. Gregory the Great had started the process by which the Church that was originally confined to the Mediterranean basin became the Church of all Europe. There is no evidence that this development was due to a grand design in Gregory's mind, as is sometimes claimed. Gregory does not need this inflated praise. He was simply responding to a pastoral duty, fulfilling the command of the risen Lord to Peter and his companions to "Go into all the world and proclaim the good news to the whole creation" (Mk 16:15).

Gregory's legacy

Gregory's world was much like our own. Then as now, revolutionary change and violence were the birth pangs of a new age whose contours no one could foresee. Deeply conservative, Gregory belonged completely to the old world that he saw disintegrating before his eyes. That he never despaired is one measure of his greatness. At the same time his certainty that the end of all things was at hand shows his limitation. He could not even imagine the new medieval world that was struggling to be born.

Gregory would have been astonished to know how far he shaped that world. We have already described his first contribution: the missionary activity that would capture all of Europe for the Church, bringing her new vigor, as well as new problems. It remains to look briefly at his two further contributions: his literary legacy and the impetus he gave to monasticism.

No author was more widely read in the Middle Ages than Gregory. In addition to his lectures on a number of Old Testament books, only some of which survive, we have his forty *Homilies on the Gospels*, delivered in 591-592 and published the following year, and his twenty-two *Homilies on Ezekiel*, delivered in the shadow of Rome's anguish in 592-593 but not published until 601-602. These homilies were the product of Gregory's belief that a bishop's principal duty was to preach the gospel.

This idea, rediscovered in our day by the Second Vatican Council, was prominent in one of Gregory's most influential works, the *Regula Pastoralis* or *Pastoral Rule*. This sketched his portrait of the ideal bishop, a man of personal holiness dedicated to preaching and the care of souls. The work was immensely popular, being translated into Greek during Gregory's lifetime and at the end of the ninth century into Anglo-Saxon by King Alfred the Great. Had Gregory's exhortations been as widely observed as they were read in the Middle Ages, the course of Western religious history would have been changed.

Even more popular were Gregory's *Dialogues*, subtitled "The Lives and Miracles of the Italian Fathers." Cast in the form of a conversation with his disciple Peter the Deacon, who had been Gregory's patrimonial rector in Sicily, it is a collection of edifying stories addressed to uneducated people in terms they could understand. Crowded with angels, saints, devils, and miracles, it strikes us as thoroughly medieval.

Gregory's third major work was the *Magna Moralia* or *Morals on Job*, designed not for ordinary folk but for the clergy. Richly allegorical, it presents Job as a type of Christ and the Church, suffering the assaults of heretics and unbelievers. The fruit of a mentality we have difficulty entering into today, this work profoundly influenced scriptural exegesis and moral theology throughout the Middle Ages. Gregory defended its enormous length and discursiveness with the disarming plea that it was directly inspired by the Holy Spirit — a claim which also tells us much about the quality of his faith, so unmodern in its childlike simplicity.

Gregory was not an original thinker. We have already noted his aversion to the Greeks and to what he regarded as their over-subtle theologizing, always prone to heresy. He was a theological popularizer, transmitting to posterity in easily digestible form the accepted orthodox thought of his day, especially that of Augustine.

Gregory was the first monk to become pope. So far as possible he continued a monastic lifestyle as pope, preferring his monk's habit to the pontifical robes. The monastic community that he gathered round him in the Lateran palace caused his biographer John the Deacon to write: "The Roman church in Gregory's time resembled the church as it was under the rule of the apostles or the church of Alexandria during the episcopate of St. Mark" (*Life* ii, 12).

Believing that monasticism was the ideal form of the Christian life, Gregory favored monks over clerics for appointment to Church offices. (It was unusual in this early period for a monk to be ordained, an exception, however, which Gregory strongly encouraged.) He also started the custom of granting monasteries exemption from episcopal jurisdiction. This policy, begun with the laudable intention of protecting the monks from episcopal interference, was to produce problems that perdure to the present day: the temptation to elitism on the part of religious orders, with resulting resentment by bishops and their clergy.

This ill feeling began in Gregory's lifetime. The Roman clergy resented the intrusion of his monastic friends on what they regarded as their own preserve. After the Pope's death, they moved swiftly to reclaim their old ascendancy. We have already noted the surprise of Pope John VIII at discovering, in the late ninth century, that there was no Roman *Life* of Gregory. We know why. It was the revenge of the clerical establishment at Rome for the injustices (as they saw them) received at the hands of the first monastic Pope.

Gregory is often been credited with major liturgical reforms. The best opinion today, however, is that both the so-called *Gregorian Sacramentary* and Gregorian chant (plainsong) are more properly ascribed to Gregory II, Pope from 713 to 731. Gregory the Great did compose 82 of the 927 prayers in the *Sacramentary*, however, and also established a choir school at Rome when he found that the deacons were neglecting their administrative duties in favor of singing.

Gregory's pain-wracked body finally gave out on March 12, 604. The problems he had labored to resolve survived him. The Lombards were still threatening Rome, bringing famine on the populace. Gregory was buried in the portico of St. Peter's Basilica. When Gregory IV moved his remains inside the church two centuries later, the metrical Latin inscription placed on the tomb hailed him as "God's consul." The French historian Pierre Batiffol has written: "Rome, which had no more consuls, found one again in St. Gregory, and saluted in his tomb the *Consul of God*." Equally noteworthy is the judgment of the German Protestant Erich Caspar, who called Gregory "the most Christian of all the popes."

No account of Gregory would be complete without mentioning a detail intentionally omitted in the account already given of the "Ecumenical Patriarch" controversy. Rejecting the designation for himself, Gregory proposed in its place the noblest of all the papal titles, designating for all time the essence of Petrine ministry: "Servant of the servants of God."

CHAPTER FOUR

Gregory VII

(1073-1085)

"I *have loved righteousness and hated iniquity; therefore I die in exile" (Gregory VII's dying words).*

On April 22, 1073, the Basilica of St. John Lateran, then as now the Pope's official seat and Rome's cathedral, was witness to a dramatic scene unique in papal history. It happened at the funeral of Pope Alexander II, who had died the day previously after a pontificate of not quite twelve years. A native of Milan, where he helped found the populist movement for Church reform called by its powerful enemies the *Pataria* ("Rag Pickers"), Alexander (or Anselm, his baptismal name) had been papal legate in Germany and Bishop of Lucca, northeast of Pisa. In accordance with the custom of the day, he retained that See after his election on September 30, 1061.

Presiding at Alexander's funeral was the man chiefly responsible for his becoming Pope: Cardinal Hildebrand, Archdeacon of the Roman Church, leader of the forces working for Church reform, and for more than a decade the most powerful individual in the Church's central administration. During the funeral someone shouted, "Hildebrand for Pope!" Hildebrand recounted the sequel in an anguished letter written four days later to Archbishop Wibert of Ravenna.

> While our late master the Pope was being borne to his burial . . . a great tumult and shouting of the people arose and they rushed upon me like madmen, leaving me neither time nor opportunity to speak or to take counsel, and dragged me by force to the place of apostolic rule, to which I am far from being equal. So that I may say with the prophet: "I am come into deep waters where the floods overwhelm me. I am weary with my crying; my throat is dried." And again: "Fearfulness and trembling are come upon me, and horror has overcome me" (*Register* i, 3; the citations are from Psalms 69 and 55 respectively).

Background and early career

The author of these lines was born sometime between 1015 and 1025 in the Tuscan town of Soano. His father was, according to some sources, a goatherd, a carpenter to others. While still a boy, Hildebrand was brought to Rome and enrolled in the monastery school of St. Mary on the Aventine Hill. Though Hildebrand does not seem to have taken monastic vows at this time, he was educated in personal contact with leaders in the movement for Church reform that was to play the central role in his life.

Foremost among these reformers was John Gratian, archpriest of the Lateran Basilica. John Gratian's brother Leo married Hildebrand's maternal aunt. This family connection helps explain Hildebrand's lifelong devotion to the man who, for a year and seven months (May 1045 to December 1046), ruled the Church as Pope Gregory VI. Gratian's brief pontificate tells much about the forces which formed Hildebrand and eventually raised him to the Church's highest office.

During the early decades of the eleventh century, two powerful Roman clans, the Crescentii and the Counts of Tusculum, vied to control the papacy. The latter supplied three Popes from 1012 to mid-century: the brothers Benedict VIII (1012-24) and John XIX (1024-32), and their nephew Benedict IX (1032-44). A youth of eighteen when he became Pope, Benedict's election has been called by Nicholas Cheetham, a modern papal historian, "a cynical affront to all enlightened opinion in the church outside Rome."

Whether Benedict IX was the profligate libertine portrayed in the writings of Church reformers, or merely a high-spirited youth sowing some wild oats, he had no spiritual qualifications for his office. In September 1044 the Crescentii forced Benedict to leave Rome, replacing him in January 1045 with their own candidate, Silvester III — who was himself forced to flee Rome after only a few weeks.

In this confused situation, with two rival claimants to the papacy, Benedict IX was induced to resign on May 1, 1045, in favor of his godfather, John Gratian, the reform-minded archpriest of the Lateran Basilica. He took the name of Gregory VI and promised to pay Benedict the annual receipts from England of the collection known as Peter's Pence. This constituted the canonical crime of simony or purchase of a Church office — so-called from the attempt of Simon Magus, reported in Acts 8:18-24, to purchase spiritual power from the apostles Peter and John.

It is a symptom of the desperation in reforming circles that its leading members hailed Gregory's accession as the dawn of a new day for the Church, even though he became Pope through one of the principal evils against which they fought. It was a classic case of claiming that the end justified the means.

At first all went well. Gregory VI undertook an ambitious reform program that seemed to justify his supporters' hopes. In the autumn of 1046, however, the German King Henry III came to Italy to receive from the Pope the imperial crown and the title of Roman Patrician first conferred on the Emperor Charlemagne by Pope Leo III on Christmas Day 800. According to medieval legal theory, the bearer of these honors inherited the right possessed by the old Roman Emperors (as we saw in connection with the two "Great" Popes, Leo and Gregory): giving consent to the papal election.

Henry faced a problem, however. To which of the three claimants to the papacy should he apply? Gregory VI's title was disputed both by Silvester III and by Benedict IX who swiftly withdrew his resignation. Henry III was an enlightened ruler, sincerely interested in Church reform. He met first with Gregory, who received him with all honors at Piacenza, in northern Italy. For reasons that are unclear, Henry subsequently decided that he must have a Pope of his own choosing. On December 20, 1046, therefore, the King presided over a large synod of bishops at Sutri, northwest of Rome, which declared all three Popes deposed. Henry convoked another synod at Rome three days later which confirmed this verdict. On Christmas Eve he had one of his own bishops, Suitger of Bamberg, elected Pope. On Christmas Day Suitger was enthroned in St. Peter's Basilica as Clement II. He then placed the crown of Roman Emperor on Henry III and conferred on him the right to nominate future Popes.

Hildebrand, then a young subdeacon, experienced these dramatic events as chaplain (secretary) to Gregory VI. When Henry returned to Germany in May 1047, taking the deposed Gregory with him, Hildebrand accompanied his master into exile. Hildebrand remained loyal all his life to his first papal mentor, never swerving from the belief that Gregory had been unjustly treated. Over three decades later at a crucial point in his own papacy, he would write: "I accompanied the lord Pope Gregory [VI] unwillingly beyond the mountains. . ." (*Register* vii, 14a).

Church reform

Hildebrand remained in Germany only a year and a half, living in a monastery near Cologne and being received by Henry III (as Hildebrand would write later) "with special honor among all the Italians at his court" (*Register* i, 19). It was probably during this period that Hildebrand took monastic vows. For the last time in his life, Hildebrand had leisure to study. He used it to gain the knowledge (never more than rudimentary) of canon law evident in his papal acts and letters. Hildebrand also got to know the ideas of Church reformers north of the Alps and observed first hand the evils they sought to banish. Because of the central role this struggle played in Hildebrand's life, it is important to understand the issues involved.

We have already taken note of the corruption at Rome. For two centuries many of the Popes had been personally unworthy. Entangled in local Roman feuds, and often subject to interference from the German King (the heir of the old Roman Emperor), these Pontiffs could not possibly lead the movement for Church renewal that the times required.

It is customary to describe these evils under two headings: simony and what was then called "nicolaism," a term coined by a synod at Tours in 567 (from an obscure reference in Revelation 2:6) to designate the sexual intercourse of married clergy with their wives. In reality simony and nicolaism were both symptoms of the same malady: submersion of the clergy in a lay society animated by values which contradicted the reformers' understanding of the gospel the clergy were supposed to live and preach.

It was not only the Bishop of Rome who was entangled with lay factions and magnates. Bishops everywhere were chosen by feudal rulers, enriched by royal and other benefices, and burdened with administrative duties by their temporal lords. Frequently they had bought their offices for a price. The lower clergy generally served a local landowner to whom they gave feudal allegiance in return for a subsistence income. In the German lands especially, churches were the property of the feudal lords who built and maintained them. This "proprietary church" system, though regarded by Church reformers as evil, had the paradoxical effect of gaining the support of many lay lords for the reformers' second goal: enforcement of clerical celibacy. Though this rule had been enacted for the Western Church at the Spanish synod of Elvira in 306, it was widely disregarded. Married clergy had a natural interest in providing for their children by gift or will of Church property. Moreover, under the feudal laws then prevailing, priests' children were often considered "free born." Lay rulers felt cheated both of the service they could claim from the offspring of their serfs, and of any Church property priests in their domains managed to convey to their children.

Church reformers, most of them monks or at least influenced by monastic spirituality, were convinced that only a disciplined priesthood unfettered by family ties and not dependent on secular lords could raise the moral level of society. The Church would never have such a priesthood, the reformers contended, until its bishops were freely elected in accordance with canon law, and not subject to interference by princes from whom they had purchased their offices or to whom they were otherwise bound by feudal ties. To direct this program the reformers wanted an independent and powerful papacy, spiritually upright and capable of enforcing Church law everywhere.

These were the ideas that Hildebrand had absorbed during his early formation in Rome. His experiences north of the Alps convinced him that the reformers' diagnosis of the Church's ills was sound, and their prescribed remedy correct. He would spend the rest of his life putting these convictions to the test.

Apprenticeship

Gregory VI survived only six months in exile, dying in November 1047, probably at Cologne. Clement II, who had displaced him, preceded him in death, dying on October 9, 1047, amid rumors that enemies of reform had poisoned him. He was buried in his former cathedral at Bamberg, the only papal grave in Germany. When the tomb was opened in 1942 the bones it contained were found to have a heavy concentration of lead, lending color to the contemporary reports of poison.

Clement was the first of a series of German reforming Popes. His immediate successor, Damasus II, a Bavarian aristocrat and bishop of Brixen in South Tirol, died of fever after a pontificate of only a few weeks. The irrepressible Benedict IX then judged the time ripe for another comeback attempt and managed to maintain himself as Pope for eight months.

In December 1048, however, the Emperor Henry III had his Alsatian cousin Bishop Bruno of Toul (fourteen miles west of Nancy) nominated as Pope by an imperial Diet (meeting of princes) at Worms. A strong supporter of Church reform, Bruno agreed to accept the papacy only if he was freely elected by the Roman clergy and people. When this condition was fulfilled, Bruno was crowned in the Lateran Basilica as Pope Leo IX on February 12, 1049.

Leo took Hildebrand back to Rome, ordained him subdeacon, and made him rector of the monastery of St. Paul's Outside the Walls (where nine centuries later, on January 25, 1959, Pope John XXIII would astonish the world with his announcement of the Second Vatican Council). It was hardly a prestigious appointment, but Hildebrand was still young, possibly not yet out of his twenties. Within a few years he had reinstated regular discipline in the rundown community, recruited new monks, and restored the monastery church and finances.

Leo meanwhile was assembling a team of like-minded churchmen to work for Church reform. A gifted preacher who won wide popular support for his reform measures, he traveled widely and held synods in Italy, Germany, and France which condemned simony and clerical marriage. In late 1053 or early 1054 the Pope gave Hildebrand his first foreign assignment, sending him as legate to a synod at Tours to deal with a brilliant but difficult theologian named Berengar whose spiritualizing doctrine of Christ's real presence in the Eucharist had given rise to a controversy that would continue into Hildebrand's pontificate. Though no match for Berengar as a theologian, Hildebrand walked warily through a theological minefield, fulfilling his instructions faithfully and winning from the mercurial Frenchman the statement that the young legate had treated him with exemplary fairness. While still at Tours Hildebrand learned of Leo IX's death at Rome on April 19, 1054.

On his return to the eternal city, Hildebrand was sent to Germany at the head of a delegation to ask the Emperor to nominate a new Pope. Henry chose another German bishop, Gebhard of Eichstätt. As Pope Victor II he continued the reforming program of his predecessors, though in closer political alliance with the Emperor. It was during this pontificate that Hildebrand became a cardinal. Victor attended Henry III at his death in Germany on October 5, 1056, and crowned his six-year-old son Henry IV at Aachen the following month.

Selection of the Pope by the German Emperor was difficult to reconcile with the demand for a free and independent papacy. While Henry III lived, his own commitment to Church reform made it possible to overlook this anomaly. When Pope Victor II followed Henry in death on July 28, 1057, however, the reform party at Rome quickly elected the recently professed monk and Abbot of Monte Cassino, Frederick of Lorraine, without reference to the German court. A few weeks after his consecration as Stephen IX, the new Pope sent Hildebrand to Germany to obtain imperial assent to his election from the young Henry IV's widowed mother, Agnes, who was acting as Regent during her son's minority. Stephen's pontificate lasted only eight months. He died at Florence on March 29, 1058, after exacting from the clergy and people of Rome an oath that they would not elect his successor until Hildebrand, then absent on another mission to Germany, had returned to Rome.

The Pope was no sooner dead, however, than leaders of the aristocratic party at Rome, sensing an opportunity to regain their old ascendancy, elected an Italian bishop, John of Velletri, as Benedict X. The reformers repudiated the election. Assembling at Siena, and working closely with Hildebrand, who obtained imperial support in Germany, the cardinals elected the candidate of his choice, Bishop Gerard of Florence. On January 24, 1059, after holding a synod at Sutri declaring Benedict's election invalid, he was enthroned as Pope Nicholas II.

Papal independence

In April 1059 Nicholas II held a synod at Rome attended by 113 bishops (a large number for those days) which significantly altered the method of choosing the Pope. Henceforth he was to be elected by the cardinal bishops in consultation with the other cardinals, meeting outside Rome if necessary (as they had just done in electing Nicholas himself). The Roman clergy and people were to give subsequent assent to the cardinals' choice. Diplomatic language (behind which we can recognize the hand of the man who signed the decree, with exaggerated modesty, "Hildebrand, subdeacon-monk") reaffirmed "the honor and reverence due to our beloved son Henry, who at present is acknowledged King and, it is hoped, will be Emperor, by God's grace." It was the papacy's first cautious bid for independence from imperial control, and the opening salvo in a battle between clerical and lay power that would continue into the next century and beyond.

This important synod also forbade clergy to accept any Church office at lay hands ("lay investiture") even without the payment of money. And it imposed a new sanction in the struggle for clerical celibacy by ordering the laity to boycott the Masses of married priests. Clergy who refused to put away their wives were suspended from office. Finally, at Hildebrand's insistence and as a support for celibacy, the synod ordered clergy serving the same Church to live a common life. Hildebrand's crucial role in the Church's central government was underlined when he was given the prestigious office of Archdeacon of the Roman Church following this synod.

The new provisions for the papal election were put to their first test when Nicholas II died in July 1061. Disregarding the 1059 provisions, delegations from the Roman nobility and the Lombard bishops (the area around Milan) journeyed to the German court to request the nomination of a new Pontiff. On September 30, however, before a decision was forthcoming from Germany, the cardinals, under Hildebrand's leadership, elected the reforming Bishop Anselm of Lucca as Pope Alexander II. He was no stranger north of the Alps, having served, as we noted at the beginning of this chapter, as papal legate to Henry III, from whom he received the See of Lucca.

Any hope that the deceased Emperor's heirs would accept Anselm's election was disappointed four weeks later. On October 28 a synod was convoked at Basel in the name of the eleven-year-old Henry IV which elected another northern Italian bishop, Cadalus of Parma, as Pope Honorius II. The wheel had come full circle. The German court, which under Henry III had supported Church reform, was now in league with its opponents.

Though Cadalus was never able to make good his claim to the papal throne, his supporters fought bloody battles in Rome with those of Alexander II. Finally at Pentecost 1064, a German-dominated synod at Mantua confirmed Alexander as the legitimate Pope, but only after requiring him to swear that simony had played no role in his election — a breach of the papacy's longstanding claim that a Pope could be judged by God alone.

Assisted by his Cardinal-Archdeacon Hildebrand, Alexander advanced the cause of reform throughout Europe. His support for his old friends in the *Pataria* movement in Milan brought him from 1070 onwards into conflict with Henry IV over the appointment of the city's archbishop. At the Roman Lenten synod of 1073 Alexander excommunicated Henry IV's counselors for persuading the King to name an Archbishop of Milan in opposition to the Pope's candidate — an attempt to curb Henry's activity without attacking him directly. The controversy remained unsettled when Alexander died on April 21, 1073.

Taking command

Hildebrand's election by acclamation at the funeral of his predecessor clearly violated the papal election decree of 1059, in the drafting of which Hildebrand had taken a leading part. Immediately after the funeral, therefore, the cardinals assembled in the church of St. Peter in Chains to regularize the election. The document recording their action and the assent of the Roman clergy and people is the first entry in the *Register* of Gregory's papal correspondence.

The day after the election, Gregory wrote the first of several letters giving the news to various correspondents. Addressed to Abbot Desiderius of Monte Cassino (who in 1086 would be Gregory's unwilling successor as Victor III for a troubled pontificate of sixteen months), it shows even greater distress than the letter written three days later to Wibert of Ravenna, from which we quoted at the beginning of this chapter. "As I am confined to my bed completely tired out and cannot properly choose my words," Gregory wrote, "I will not tell the story of my anxieties" (*Register* i, 1). Gregory mentions these anxieties in all his letters from these first days of his pontificate. What were they?

The election itself can hardly have been the cause, for it was no surprise. Hildebrand's name had been repeatedly mentioned as a candidate for the papacy ever since the election of Victor II in 1055. The controversy with the German court over the appointment of an archbishop for Milan, though a worry, can hardly have sent Gregory to bed unable (as he wrote) to choose his words. The most likely explanation, and the story that he would not tell Desiderius, was an oath Henry III had made Hildebrand take eighteen years previously following the death of Pope Leo IX on April 19, 1054. To succeed Leo the Emperor nominated Bishop Gebhard of Eichstätt at a Diet in Mainz in November 1054. Gebhard gave his acceptance at a subsequent Diet in Regensburg the following March and was enthroned as Pope Victor II on April 13, 1055. There is evidence that at one of these two meetings Hildebrand swore not to accept the papacy himself without the Emperor's consent or that of his heir Henry IV, then a four-year-old child.

In January 1076 a group of twenty-six mostly German bishops meeting at Worms would reproach Gregory for oath-breaking, reminding him that "there are today many bishops who witnessed that oath, who saw it with their eyes and heard it with their ears." This is probably what Gregory was referring to in another early letter in which he says that he had tried to resist his election as Pope; but that since a man's life was not in his own hands but in those of him who directs our steps, it had not been possible for him to keep the vows he had made (*Register* i, 39).

Like so many of his predecessors, Gregory was only a deacon when he was elected Bishop of Rome. He was the first one, so far as we know, who was ordained a priest after his election: on May 22, 1073. He postponed his bishop's ordination until Saturday, June 29, the Feast of the Apostles Peter and Paul. Until then he signed himself "Gregory, Roman pontiff elect." Thereafter it was "Gregory, bishop, servant of the servants of God" — the title originated, as we have seen, by Gregory the Great.

From the start, however, Gregory exercised the full powers of his office. Eight days after his election he approved a French plan for an expedition to drive the Moors out of Spain. This letter is noteworthy for its claim that "the kingdom of Spain was from ancient times subject to St. Peter in full sovereignty." Territory conquered from the Moors would therefore be held "in the name of St. Peter" (*Register* i, 7). Although Gregory advanced this claim as something well-known, it went considerably beyond anything claimed by previous Popes.

In other letters from the early weeks of his pontificate, the Pope declared his desire to come to an understanding with Henry IV "upon the matters which we think important for the welfare of the Church and the honor of his kingly office" — an obvious reference to the conflict over the appointment of an archbishop for Milan. Gregory wrote of his intention "to send pious men . . . to bring him back to loyalty to his mother, the Holy Church of Rome, and give him detailed instructions as to the proper form of assuming the empire." If Henry accepted this advice, "we shall rejoice for his sake as well as for our own. . . . But if — which God forbid! — he shall repay our love with hate and show contempt toward almighty God for the high office conferred upon him, then may the judgment which declares, 'Cursed be he that keepeth back his sword from blood!' not fall upon us in the providence of God." This text from the prophet Jeremiah (48:10) was a favorite of Gregory's. He applied it to anyone who failed to join him in rebuking the evil bishops and princes he saw everywhere who refused "to maintain justice in accordance with our advice and warnings" (*Register* i, 9, 11).

A prime concern during the first year of Gregory's pontificate was the appeal of the Eastern Emperor Michael VII for assistance against the Turks. The Pope saw this as a golden opportunity to strike a blow for righteousness (*justitia*, one of his favorite words), and heal the breach between the Eastern and Western Churches that had been opened by the mutual excommunications of 1054. On March 1, 1074 Gregory issued a general appeal "to all who are willing to defend the Christian faith" to come to the assistance of their hard-pressed brethren in the East. On December 7 of the same year, he wrote Henry IV chiding him for not having settled the quarrel over the Milan archbishopric "in accordance with your repeated letters and promises"; but announcing his intention of personally leading an army of 50,000 men to rescue the Church of Constantinople. Soliciting the German ruler's advice and help in this enterprise, Gregory said he intended to "leave the Roman Church, under

God, in your hands to guard her as a holy mother and to defend her for his honor" (*Register* i, 30, 31).

This grandiose scheme never got off the ground. The reunion negotiations failed to confirm Gregory's claim that "almost all the Easterners are waiting to see how the faith of the Apostle Peter will decide among their divergent views." His assertion that 50,000 men were preparing "to take up arms against the enemies of God and push forward even to the sepulcher of the Lord if they can have me for their leader and prelate" proved wildly optimistic. And worsening relations with the German ruler killed all thoughts of foreign adventures.

Lay investiture

Gregory's repeated expressions of goodwill for the German King in the first year of his pontificate brought friendly responses from north of the Alps. Burdened with preparations for a military campaign in Poland, and with a rebellion in Saxony, Henry could not afford a breach with the Pope. In the autumn of 1073, therefore, he wrote an almost abject letter to Gregory admitting his responsibility for simonaical appointments to Church office, misappropriation of Church property, and unlawful conduct in the affair of the Milan archbishopric. The King promised amendment and asked the Pope's advice.

Gregory responded at Easter 1074 by sending Henry a delegation consisting of two cardinal bishops and the King's widowed mother, Queen Agnes. To them Henry repeated his contrite expressions of the previous autumn, promised to support the Pope's campaign against simony and clerical marriage, and to restore unlawfully acquired Church property. Henry also sought pardon for associating with his counselors who had been excommunicated by the previous Pope Alexander II for nominating an anti-papal archbishop of Milan. The cardinals then lifted the excommunication that Henry himself had incurred through this association. On June 15, 1074 Gregory wrote Queen Agnes thanking her warmly for her help in restoring her son "to the communion of the church and delivering his kingdom from the general peril" (*Register* i, 85).

The rest of this year was taken up with efforts to hold a synod in Germany presided over by papal legates that would give effect to the measures against simony and clerical marriage passed by Gregory's first Roman synod in March. This proved impossible, partly due to German opposition to the reform program itself, partly because German bishops who supported reform insisted that the Archbishop of Mainz and not legates from Rome preside at the synod.

Undaunted by this opposition, Gregory had the Roman synod of Lent 1075 repeat the reforming decrees of the previous year, adding to them the prohibition of lay investiture first passed (as we have seen) at the Roman synod of 1059. This was an open attack on the long-standing practice by which lay rulers nominated bishops and abbots in their territories and invested them with the symbols of their office: ring and pastoral staff.

Church reformers were determined to abolish this practice. Experience had shown that it was inextricably bound up with simony. Because of the income attached to them, the Church offices in question were valuable property rights. There was no way to prevent those who awarded them from receiving payments for their patronage. Moreover lay rulers were often more interested in the personal loyalty of candidates for Church office than in their spiritual qualifications. Freedom for the Church to select its own pastors without lay interference was thus a centerpiece of the reforming program to which Gregory had dedicated his life.

Lay rulers viewed things differently. Even those who supported the campaign against simony and clerical marriage were alarmed at the demand that they yield a right which had been exercised without question for as long as anyone could remember. In the medieval feudal system, bishops and abbots were not merely spiritual leaders. They also governed the territory in which their subjects lived. Lay rulers considered it intolerable that they should have no voice in the selection of the men with whom they shared power.

The prohibition of lay investiture at the Pope's Lenten synod of 1075 thus set the stage for one of history's great confrontations — in which (as today in Israel/Palestine and Northern Ireland) the contest was not between right and wrong, but between well-founded rights on both sides.

The conflict escalates

At first Gregory remained hopeful that he could reach an understanding with Henry. On July 20, 1075 he wrote the King congratulating him for his "efforts at self-improvement," in particular for his support of the campaign against simony and clerical marriage. He asked Henry's cooperation in selecting a suitable bishop for Bamberg to replace the prelate Gregory had just deposed for simony and other misconduct (*Register* iii, 3). The Pope also told the German King that if he found anything "too burdensome or unfair" in the prohibition of lay investiture, he should "send us prudent and pious legates" to discuss the matter. If they could show "in any reasonable way how we can moderate the decision . . . we will condescend to hear their counsel" (*Register* iii, 10).

It was not to be. In June 1075 Henry put down the rebellion in Saxony. Feeling no further need to placate the Pope, he unilaterally appointed a number of bishops and abbots both in the German lands and in his sphere of influence in Italy. Gregory responded on December 8 with a long letter bitterly reproaching the King for failing to fulfill his promises of amendment or to accept the offer of negotiations.

When Henry received this letter on New Year's Day 1076, he summoned a Diet that met at Worms on January 24. Attended by few lay rulers but by the majority of Henry's bishops, it drew up a bitter indictment of Gregory for accepting the papacy in violation of his oath to Henry III (the passage already quoted) and in violation of the papal election decree of 1059; for trampling the rights of bishops by claiming the right to depose them at will; and for "filling the whole church with the stench of grave scandal by living more intimately than is necessary with a woman not of your kin." This unfounded charge, a reference to the Pope's friendship with the Countess Matilda of Tuscany, must have been a particularly bitter blow to Gregory. It reflected slanderous statements by his erstwhile supporter, Cardinal Hugh the White, who had played a leading role in Gregory's election as Pope, but who for unknown reasons had turned against him. Hugh was present at Worms, where his presumed knowledge of conditions in Rome naturally carried great weight.

For propaganda purposes Henry issued an even fiercer version of this document in which he personally denounced the Pope as "Hildebrand, no longer Pope but false monk" and challenged him to "descend and relinquish the apostolic chair which you have usurped. . . . Descend, descend, to be damned throughout the ages." Henry sent two of his bishops with these documents to a synod at Piacenza, where the Lombard bishops endorsed them and joined their German colleagues in forswearing allegiance to Gregory.

This open challenge to the papacy produced a larger than usual attendance at the Lenten synod in Rome, from February 14 to 20, 1076. When Henry's representative read the decrees of Worms and Piacenza and demanded Gregory's resignation, he was greeted with such a storm of indignation that only the Pope's personal intervention saved him from bodily attack. The next day, in the presence of Henry's mother, Agnes, Gregory excommunicated and deposed the bishops who had attacked him, and gave those who had signed under duress until June 29 to make satisfaction.

The Pope clothed his judgment against King Henry in the form of a solemn prayer to Saint Peter who, he said, had protected him from infancy against all who hated him "for my loyalty to thee." Gregory called on the apostles Peter and Paul, "and also my Lady, the Mother of God," to witness that "thy Holy Roman Church forced me against my will to be its ruler." Relying on the Petrine commission to bind and loose in heaven and on earth, Gregory declared:

> I deprive King Henry . . . who has rebelled against thy church with unheard of audacity, of the government over the whole kingdom of Germany and Italy, and I release all Christian men from the allegiance which they have sworn or may swear to him, and I forbid anyone to serve him as king. . . . And since he has refused to obey as a Christian should or to return to the God whom he has abandoned by taking part with excommunicated persons, has spurned my warnings which I gave him for his soul's welfare, as thou knowest, and has separated himself from thy church and tried to rend it asunder, I bind him in the bonds of anathema in thy stead . . . that the nations may know and be convinced that thou art Peter and that upon thy rock the son of the living God has built his church and the gates of hell shall not prevail against it (*Register* iii, 10a).

This document is like a window on Gregory's soul, revealing his almost mystical sense of personal identification with Saint Peter, and the unshakable conviction, equal to that of any Old Testament prophet, that God would infallibly ratify the judgments of his spokesman.

In subsequent letters the Pope indicated that his deposition of Henry was provisional only. "With the king of Germany . . . we desire to be at peace if only he would strive to make his peace with God and according to our repeated warnings would set right what he has done wrong to the peril of holy church and fulfillment of his own perdition" (*Register* iii, 15).

Provisional or not, the Pope's unprecedented action was a severe shock to contemporaries. No Pope had ever formally excommunicated a King or deprived him of his throne. Moreover, it was only thirty years since Henry's father had deposed three Popes and substituted one of his own. Gregory felt compelled to justify his action in several long letters to Germany. These gave details of Henry's immoral personal life, set forth the long record of his unfulfilled promises to the Pope, and argued that in view of Christ's unlimited grant of power to Saint Peter to bind and loose in heaven and on earth, his successor had authority to judge not only spiritual but worldly matters as well.

Henry's response showed that he had badly overestimated his strength. Attending Easter Mass at Utrecht in full royal regalia with a large number of bishops, the King again declared "the monk Hildebrand" deposed. When previous popes had been deposed, it was not by a mere decree issued in northern Europe, but by the King at the head of his army in Rome. During the summer Henry's support dwindled as the recently defeated Saxons made common cause with some rebellious south German princes. Meanwhile papal legates traveled through Germany to convince waverers of the correctness of Gregory's measures. In September Henry's newly united opponents met at Ulm and issued a call for an imperial Diet to meet October 15 to chose a new ruler.

Gregory wrote his German supporters on September 3 admonishing them to deal kindly with "Henry, the so-called king" and outlining the conditions for his restoration: removal of "those evil counselors who, excommunicated for the heresy of simony, have not scrupled to infect their master with their own disease"; and an acknowledgement by Henry that the Church was "his superior and mistress [not] his subject or handmaid." Only if Henry remained obdurate ("which God forbid") were they to elect a new King, informing the Pope "at the earliest possible moment in order that we may confirm your choice" (*Register* iv, 3).

Henry's foes met at Tribur, on the right bank of the Rhine, in mid-October 1076. Present were two papal legates and a number of bishops who had signed the indictment of Gregory at Worms the previous January but who now requested and received from the legates forgiveness and restoration to office. Henry waited meanwhile with his army only a few miles away at Oppenheim on the opposite side of the Rhine. After lengthy negotiations, the King finally agreed to seek absolution from the Pope. In return his opponents dropped the plan to choose a new King, but reserved the right to meet again for this purpose if Henry had not regularized his position by mid-February 1077, the anniversary of his excommunication. Finally, they invited Gregory to an imperial Diet at Augsburg on February 2, 1077, to decide who was the Empire's lawful ruler.

Both Henry and his opponents sent messengers to Rome with news of these agreements. When Gregory read the King's letter, he saw that it contained something not mentioned by the princes: a demand that the Pope clear himself of the charge of immorality contained in the indictment issued at Worms the previous January. Confronted with this fresh indication of bad faith, Gregory refused to receive Henry in Rome (where the King said he would come to seek absolution). Against the urgent recommendation of his advisers, the Pope decided to journey to Germany himself immediately after the New Year 1077.

Canossa

This was alarming news for Henry. If the Pope were to meet with the King's opponents, Henry's position could become grave indeed. To prevent this, Henry determined to seek out the Pope in Italy wherever he could find him. This proved difficult. Access to all but one of the Alpine passes was blocked by the King's opponents. With his wife and infant son, Conrad, and a few retainers, Henry set out on the arduous winter journey by the only route open to him: through Burgundy and over the Mount Cenis pass west of Turin. Gregory, on his own journey to Germany, received word of Henry's approach at Mantua in mid-January 1077. Uncertain of the King's intentions, the Pope sought refuge forty miles south at Canossa, the impregnable mountain castle of his faithful supporter, the Countess Matilda.

There Henry appeared on January 25, 1077, barefoot despite the winter weather, in the garb of a penitent. For three days he waited at the castle gate in the snow seeking absolution from the sentence of excommunication, while inside his case was pleaded by Matilda, Henry's mother-in-law, Countess Adelheid of Turin, and his godfather, Abbot Hugh of Cluny.

Gregory faced a dilemma. If he lifted the excommunication, the King might again break his promises of amendment as he had done so often before, and the Pope's German supporters would be alienated. Refusal to lift the excommunication, on the other hand, would appear like the action of a tyrant rather than a priest. Henry's supporters in the castle pressed this argument, and on January 27, Gregory yielded. Henry promised to submit to the Pope's judgment regarding his dispute with the German princes, and to grant him safe conduct to Germany or wherever else he chose to go. Gregory thereupon restored the King to communion.

Henry's humiliation was less severe than it appears today. Performing penance for sins (in Henry's case associating with his excommunicated counselors, violating the prohibition of lay investiture, and instigating the indictment of the Pope at Worms) was a familiar feature of medieval life. Moreover Henry received special treatment. The Pope permitted two bishops to swear in the King's name to the conditions for absolution. Henry gained far more than he lost at Canossa. He drove a wedge between the Pope and the German princes, who regarded Gregory's action as a betrayal. And he compelled the Pope to deal with him as a penitent sinner rather than as a political enemy.

Gregory was keenly aware of his weakened position. In letters to the German princes he stressed Henry's penitence and pleaded that, as a priest, he had had no alternative to lifting the excommunication. Restoration to the throne, however, was another matter. That was "held in suspense," the Pope wrote. He had "made no further agreements" with Henry and still hoped to judge his claim to the throne at a German Diet (*Register* iv, 12; *Epistolae collectae*, 20). Unwilling to risk further papal concessions, the German princes elected a new King on March 15: Duke Rudolf of Swabia, Henry IV's brother-in-law. During the next three years, Germany was ravaged by civil war. Gregory tried to treat the two claimants to the throne even-handedly in the increasingly vain hope that he could judge their rival claims at a German Diet, either in person or through legates.

By March 1080, however, Gregory's patience was exhausted. At the usual Lenten synod in Rome he again excommunicated Henry, this time declaring Rudolf King in his place. Once more, as at the Lenten synod of 1076, he clothed his judgment in the form of a solemn prayer to the apostles Peter and Paul whom he asked to "send forth your judgment so swiftly that all men may know that the aforesaid Henry falls and is over-whelmed, not by chance but by your power — and would that it were to repentance, that his soul be saved in the day of the Lord" (*Register* vii, 14a). Preaching at Mass on Easter Monday (April 13), Gregory predicted that if Henry did not repent, he would be dead or overthrown by the feast of Saint Peter.

Decline and fall

This rash prophecy proved to be a turning point in Gregory's pontificate. Thereafter he lost the initiative and never regained it. At Pentecost (May 13, 1080) Henry assembled nineteen German bishops at Mainz to discuss Gregory's deposition. A larger synod of some thirty bishops from Germany, Italy, and one from Burgundy, met with Henry for this purpose at Brixen in

South Tyrol on June 25. Present also was the excommunicated Cardinal Hugh the White, claiming to represent the other cardinals and adding to the charges he had brought against the Pope at Worms in January 1076, others even more outrageous: the poisoning of his four predecessors, sorcery, and heresy. The synod formally deposed Gregory and designated another former friend to replace him, Archbishop Wibert of Ravenna.

There was worse to come. In October 1080 Henry's rival, Ruprecht, died of wounds received in a successful battle against Henry's troops. Contemporaries noted that the man who had broken his oath to Henry had succumbed to the loss of his right hand (the one used for swearing). Simultaneously the Pope's attempt, with troops supplied by the ever faithful Countess Matilda, to drive his rival Wibert from Ravenna ended in disastrous defeat. In conjunction, these two events seemed like a judgment from heaven in the opposite sense to that predicted by Gregory on Easter Monday.

With his German rival dead, Henry felt able to march on Rome to place Wibert on the papal throne and receive the imperial crown at his hands. Two attempts, in May 1081 and again in early 1082, were frustrated by the continuing loyalty of Rome's populace to their legitimate bishop. On the second occasion, however, there were ominous signs that Gregory's support was crumbling. In Lent 1082 he was unable, for the first time, to hold the customary Lenten synod. When the Pope tried to pawn the Church plate to meet the expenses of defense, he was blocked by an assembly of Roman clergy, including a number of cardinals, who objected that Church property could not be used for military purposes, only for the poor, the ransom of prisoners, and for the liturgy. Gregory was forced to fall back, once again, on the assistance of the Countess Matilda who melted down her own Church plate at Canossa and gave the proceeds to the Pope.

In the spring of 1083 Henry's third attempt to enter Rome was successful. By June he controlled all of the city apart from the area around the Castel Sant' Angelo, where Gregory sought refuge. The rest of the year was taken up with futile negotiations for peace. The Pope responded to the request of the war-weary Romans that he give Henry the imperial crown by demanding that the King first do penance. The King had no appetite for repeating his experience at Canossa, however. In February 1084 he left Rome for southern Italy in pursuit of the Pope's former enemy and new-found ally, the Norman Robert Guiscard.

During this campaign the German monarch was surprised by a message from the Roman populace inviting him to return. The mood at Rome had changed completely and Gregory had lost most of his supporters, including thirteen cardinals. On March 21, 1084 Henry entered the eternal city with Wibert of Ravenna. The King immediately called a council of Roman clergy and people and invited Gregory to preside under an assurance of safe conduct. After waiting three days for the Pope to appear, this assembly met without him on Palm Sunday, deposed Gregory as a traitor to the King, and formally elected as his successor the already designated Wibert, who took the name Clement III. On Easter Day Henry and his Queen finally received from the Pontiff of his choice the imperial crowns he had sought in vain for over a decade.

Two months later Robert Guiscard moved on Rome with superior forces. Henry withdrew without a fight. After liberating Gregory from Sant' Angelo, the Norman troops proceeded to loot and plunder at will. Rome's populace blamed these disasters on their fallen Bishop, who left the city with his Norman rescuers in June 1084 amid general opprobrium. He had less than a year to live. When Gregory died in Salerno on May 25, 1085, broken in body but not in spirit, the great world in which he had played a leading role for so long took little notice.

Retrospect

In his lifetime Gregory provoked bitter enmity and devoted support. The verdict of historians about his pontificate remains divided today. It is not easy, therefore, to render a judgment that is both balanced and fair. His letters disclose a deeply religious soul, tormented by the worldliness he saw all round him. He did not have an original mind nor was he widely read. His rhetorical stock-in-trade consisted of a few quotations from the Old Testament and Gregory the Great, often repeated. Gregory had the dazzling clarity of vision of the Old Testament prophets, the same utter self-assurance, and the same limitations. Like them, he felt himself driven by superior force. In his second deposition of King Henry in 1080, Gregory called on Saint Peter to witness

> that I entered holy orders not of my own pleasure, and that I accompanied the Lord Pope Gregory [VI] unwillingly beyond the mountains, but still more unwillingly returned with my master Pope Leo [IX] to your special church, where I have served you as best I could; and then most unwillingly and unworthy as I was, to

> my great grief and with groans and lamentations I was set upon
> your throne (*Register* vii, 14a).

Gregory's frequently repeated expressions of personal unworthiness were clearly sincere. Equally clear was his exalted conception of his office. This is best seen in the twenty-seven sentences inserted in his *Register* in 1075 under the title *Dictatus Papae*. Scholars today believe they were an index to a lost or planned collection of canons on papal primacy. These sentences state in the starkest language imaginable the universal jurisdiction of the Pope in both worldly and spiritual matters.

In Gregory's view, the apostle Peter continued to live on in his successor, who inherited Christ's command to bind and loose in heaven and on earth. This single text from Matthew 16:19 was almost the sole basis for Gregory's unprecedented claim of authority to depose Kings and release their subjects from allegiance. The canonical arguments and alleged precedents with which Gregory attempted to bolster this claim were hastily assembled and weak. Later defenders of papal absolutism repeated few of these arguments, preferring to state their case afresh.

Gregory's choice of a papal name was a tribute to the first Pope he served, Gregory VI. He felt an even closer bond, however, to Gregory the Great. In reality it would be difficult to find two men more different. The first Gregory was a born aristocrat who moved easily among the great and powerful. A courtly Roman bred in the traditions of the city's imperial glory, he treated Kings and bishops as his equals, at least in courtesy. Gregory VII treated them like servants, sometimes like naughty children. His opponents constantly stressed his humble birth and unimpressive physical appearance. He was a "populist" pope, who incited people against the aristocratic establishment that had ruled the Church for as long as anyone could remember.

Like his first papal namesake, Gregory was a monk. He had none of the contemplative spirit, however, which we saw in the first Gregory. Gregory the Great was torn by the conflicting demands of monastic solitude and Church administration. Gregory VII, an activist to the core, felt no such tension.

When opponents attacked him as a "false monk" (Henry's charge at Worms in 1076), or as "monk in dress but not in life" (according to the synod of Brixen in June 1080), Gregory did not deign to reply. Though he always wore the monk's habit under his papal robes, he never emphasized his monasticism. It influenced him nonetheless. Combined with his humble birth, his monastic status freed him from the establishment ties to the existing order that fettered so many medieval bishops and Popes from aristocratic backgrounds.

Despite his lengthy apprenticeship as a papal diplomat, Gregory lacked even the rudiments of tact. Those who did not support his efforts for "righteousness" (*iustitia*, a word that appears more than 200 times in the letters) were, in Gregory's view, in the grip of the devil. This harsh rigorism alienated even close friends: Wibert of Ravenna, Abbot Hugh of Cluny, Abbot Desiderius of Monte Cassino — and at the end thirteen cardinals including three of his own creation. Not all of these defectors can be written off as opportunists or turncoats (like Cardinal Hugh the White). Many were sincere supporters of reform. The loss of so many allies suggests a fatal flaw in Gregory's character. This helps explain a remark of the gentle saint, Peter Damian, who was dragged from his hermitage in 1057 to become Cardinal Bishop of Ostia and help with Church reform. Damian (who died the year before Hildebrand became Pope) called him "a holy Satan."

The dying Pope's well attested words, "I have loved righteousness and hated iniquity; therefore I die in exile," sound to us like a cry of disillusionment. For Gregory and his contemporaries, they were something quite different. The words are a variation of a psalm verse used in the Middle Ages at the consecration of bishops and the coronation of Kings: "I have loved righteousness and hated iniquity; therefore you have anointed me with the oil of gladness before my fellows" (Ps 45:8). A tradition that goes back to the Church Fathers applies the verse to Christ. Numerous references in his letters show that Gregory saw himself as an *alter Christus*, reproducing in his struggle for the Church's freedom aspects of Christ's passion. By citing the verse as death approached, the Pope was reiterating the guiding principle of his life: the imitation of Christ.

Moreover, to the medieval mind, the variation in the second half of the verse was not the bitter sarcasm claimed by so many modern writers. The words refer to Gregory's sufferings for righteousness' sake — for which he would surely receive his promised reward: "the kingdom of heaven" (Mt 5:10) or (in the psalmist's words) "the oil of gladness before [his] fellows." Far from being a cry of despair, the Pope's dying words were a final affirmation of the unshakable faith that never left him, even in his darkest hours. It was this faith that led to his canonization by Pope Paul V in 1606.

Gregory's personal isolation at the end is deceptive. The great cause for which he spent his life triumphed. Many of Europe's leading bishops and cardinals were convinced Gregorians. Gregory VII had laid the foundations for the free and independent papacy of the high Middle Ages that, at the end of the next century, would reach a pinnacle of combined ecclesial and worldly power never equaled before or since.

CHAPTER FIVE

Innocent III

(1198-1216)

*"*W*e are the successor of the prince of the apostles, but we are not the vicar of any man or apostle, but the Vicar of Jesus Christ himself"* (PL 214, 292A).

"In truth the Pope may not flatter himself with his power and praise his magnificence and honor to excess, for the less he is judged by men the more he will be judged by God" (Sermon IV on his consecration; PL 217, 670B).

One of history's curiosities is the appearance — in times when the average life span was, by modern standards, pathetically brief — of individuals whose longevity astonishes us even today. An example is Pope Celestine III (Giacinto Bobone), who became Bishop of Rome in April 1191, at the age of eighty-five. An important Pope despite his years, he survived into his ninety-third year.

The ancient adage, "No one is as dead as a dead pontiff," was abundantly verified at Celestine's death on January 8, 1198. Most of the attending cardinals, fearing the disorders that frequently accompanied papal elections, immediately left the Lateran palace, where the Popes lived from the time of Constantine until their departure for Avignon in 1309, for the fortified Septizonium of the Emperor Septimius Severus on the southern slope of the Palatine Hill.

One of the few who remained for Celestine's funeral, which was held the same day, was the youngest cardinal, the 37-year-old deacon, Lothar of Segni. By nightfall he had received a majority of votes among four candidates in the first ballot of the papal election. Following some discussion of his youthfulness, the cardinals unanimously elected him Pope on the second ballot. He took the name Innocent III.

Background

Lothar was born in 1160 of aristocratic parents. His father, Trasimund, was Count of Segni, southeast of Rome. His mother, Claricia, belonged to the Roman patrician family of the Scotti. Lothar received his early schooling in Rome in contact with highly placed clergy such as Paul Scolari, the future Pope Clement III (1187-1191), who were friends or relatives of his family.

Lothar studied philosophy and theology at the University of Paris, then the leading center of learning in Europe. As Pope, he would make a number of his teachers bishops and cardinals. Toward the end of his student days in Paris, probably at the beginning of 1187, Lothar made a pilgrimage to the shrine of Archbishop Thomas à Becket at Canterbury, murdered in his cathedral by agents of the English King Henry II in 1170 and canonized two years later. This visit to the tomb of a recent martyr for Church liberty appears to have made a deep impression on Lothar. As Pope he would make the vindication of Church authority against encroachment by state power a central element in his policy.

From Paris Lothar went to study law at the University of Bologna under the famed canonist Huguccio of Pisa. It was probably there, in late November 1187, that Lothar was ordained sub-deacon by Pope Gregory VIII during the latter's seven-week pontificate. Lothar's legal studies were brief. His reputation as a great lawyer-Pope is based on his administrative ability and practical wisdom. In this respect he resembles certain justices of the United States Supreme Court, who, though not legal scholars, have shaped constitutional history with their judicial decisions.

Lothar's patron, Paul Scolari, who succeeded Gregory VIII as Clement III in December 1187, made the twenty-eight-year-old Lothar a cardinal-deacon just two years later. The sun of pontifical favor shone on the young cardinal only fifteen months, however. With the accession of the aged Celestine III in April 1191, enmity between the new Pope's family and that of Lothar's mother, and even more the age difference of more than half a century between Celestine and his junior cardinal-deacon, combined to exclude Lothar from all but routine curial business. To these years belong Lothar's treatises *On the misery of the human condition*, *On the 'fourfold species' of marriage*, and *On the mysteries of the Mass*. Works of no particular originality which would probably have been forgotten had their author not become Pope, they reflect Lothar's frustration at being passed over when his connections and ability qualified him for a position of influence.

At his election to the papacy on January 8, 1198, Lothar was little known outside the curia. A German chronicler reported a contemporary lament: "Oh, the Pope is so young! Lord, help your church." Still a deacon, like so many of his predecessors, Innocent was not ordained a priest until February 21. The day following, a Sunday and the feast of Peter's Chair, he became sacramentally what he already was juridically: Bishop of Rome.

"Vicar of Christ"

For centuries Popes had expressed an almost mystical identification with Saint Peter. We have seen this in a particularly striking form in the case of Gregory VII, who clothed his excommunication of the German King Henry IV in the form of a personal prayer to Saint Peter. The conviction that the first Bishop of Rome lived on in his successors, and guaranteed their acts, led Popes to call themselves "Vicar of Saint Peter." In an age in which Rome was no longer a political center, but a city of shrines and relics, this title expressed the Pope's link with Rome's first bishop.

Until the mid-twelfth century, the title "Vicar of Christ" was used by Kings and priests, but never by Popes. They considered it too vague. However, the papacy's struggle to vindicate Church sovereignty against encroachments by lay rulers, which reached an initial climax in Gregory VII's contest with Henry IV, made Popes desire a title that supported their claim to universal sovereignty.

From the mid-twelfth century onwards, therefore, the title "Vicar of Christ" increasingly displaced the Pope's older designation as "Vicar of Saint Peter." That had looked backwards, emphasizing the Pope's function as Peter's trustee, charged with preserving his legacy. The new title made a more sweeping claim, emphasized in the first quotation at the beginning of this chapter. He was Peter's successor, Innocent insisted, "but we are not the vicar of any man or apostle, but the vicar of Jesus Christ himself."

"Less than God, but greater than man"

Preaching at his episcopal ordination (or possibly on its anniversary), Innocent went farther, calling the Pope "the mediator between God and man, placed below God but above men, less than God, but greater than man" (*PL* 217, 658A). The language shocks us — until we know the context. Innocent was commenting on the text: "Who, then, is the faithful and wise slave whom his master has put in charge of his household, to give the other slaves their allowance of food at the proper time?" (Mt 24:45) He identified himself as this servant: set over his fellow servants, but with them subordinate to their common Master. In language that today sounds unpardonably exaggerated, Innocent was contrasting the inferiority of his person with the dignity of his office. He would use the method often. Innocent liked to state clearly at the outset the most extreme position which he was prepared to defend — only to back off from it and say that in this case there was no need to go so far.

Many of Innocent's pronouncements sound like radical assertions of unlimited papal power not only in spiritual but in worldly affairs. In fact, he was deeply conservative, a venerator of tradition and respectful of the limits it imposed on the exercise of his office. In important respects Innocent's view of papal power was more limited than that of some of his predecessors.

In all his difficulties with Kings and Emperors, for instance, Innocent never claimed, like Gregory VII, the right to depose rulers. Nor did he accept the extreme "two sword theory" expounded a half-century before by Saint Bernard of Clairvaux. Based upon a typically medieval allegorical interpretation of Scripture, this said that the "two swords" offered to Jesus following the Last Supper (Lk 22:38) represented spiritual and worldly power respectively. The Pope, as successor of Peter, possessed both swords. He bestowed the worldly sword on the Emperor, to be used on behalf of the Church. When the Emperor failed to do so, however, the Pope could take it back and depose him. This theory, already impiicit in Gregory VII, would be revived by Innocent's successors, most explicitly by Boniface VIII a century later.

Innocent, who was familiar with Bernard's views and often followed him in other matters, held that worldly rulers received their sword directly from God. The spiritual power was far higher, in Innocent's eyes, than the temporal power. He likened the two to the sun and moon. Yet Innocent maintained that worldly rulers were autonomous in their domain, as the Church was in spiritual things.

Even the Pope's spiritual power, upon which Innocent insisted so strongly, was not unlimited. The Pope's duty to show charity and justice to all forbade any arbitrary use of his power. And he must yield both to divine law, and to the voice of conscience. An example of the former limitation was Innocent's refusal of the insistent demand of King Philip II of France for dissolution of his marriage. This would contravene the Lord's words: "What God has joined together, let no one separate" (Mt 19:6). Were he to grant the petition, Innocent told the King, he could be charged with heresy, thereby forfeiting his office (*PL* 215, 1494-98; 216, 617f).

Conscience, Innocent held, was to be obeyed, even when contrary to decisions of the Church, indeed of the Pope himself. This was because the tribunals of God and the Church did not always agree. God's tribunal was based on the truth, which neither deceived nor could be deceived. The Church's decisions, on the other hand, reflected human opinion, which often deceived and was deceived. Yet the person claiming to follow conscience against the Church must accept the consequences. A spouse, for example, with positive knowledge of a marriage impediment, but unable to prove it before the Church, must not continue the marriage in obedience to a Church tribunal, even if such refusal resulted in excommunication (*PL* 215, 1585C).

An interesting case illustrating Innocent's insistence on the superiority of divine to human law concerned a man who had been ordained subdeacon after separating from his wife. The Pope compelled the man to continue his marriage, even though this entailed forfeiture of the right to exercise the order to which he had been ordained. Innocent's reasoning was that the wife's right to her husband was based on divine law, whereas the law imposing continence on clerics was human (*PL* 215, 1518D-1519A).

In one case, however, Innocent held that the Roman Bishop could dispense even from divine law: the resignation of a bishop from his See, or his translation to another. We have already noted the belief of the ancient Church that a bishop was "married" to his diocese (see p. 30 above). This spiritual union, symbolized by the bishop's ring, was by God's law as indissoluble as the corporal union of marriage. Innocent held that God had empowered his earthly vicar to dissolve the bishop's bond, however, by a special privilege. In support Innocent cited canonical decrees and existing custom, the best interpreter of law (*PL* 214, 291C-293A; 306C-308A). Innocent was the first Pope to insist that he alone could permit a bishop to resign or be translated from one See to another. By reserving such *causae majores* to himself, Innocent greatly enhanced papal power.

God and Caesar

"Then repay to Caesar what belong to Caesar," Jesus had said, "and to God what belongs to God" (Mt 22:21; NAB). The often conflicting claims of worldly and spiritual rulers were high on the papacy's agenda throughout the Middle Ages. Like Gregory VII, Innocent insisted tenaciously on the Church's rights and freedom. Innocent was more careful than his embattled predecessor, however, to respect the rights of Caesar. Only when each power was free in its own domain, Innocent believed, could Christendom enjoy true peace.

This was a crucial factor in the Pope's annulment of the Magna Carta in 1215. Innocent, who probably never saw the text, could not foresee that it would be transformed, after he and the English King John were dead, into an acceptable constitutional document. Innocent did know, however, that the document had been extorted from the King "by force and fear," as he protested to the English barons. It was thus a violation of the King's sovereign rights and hence not binding.

England, however, was far away. Far more important to Innocent was his relationship with the Holy Roman Emperor. Innocent came to the papal throne at a time of unique opportunity for the papacy. Like previous popes, Innocent wanted imperial protection but not hegemony. Territorial claims were at the heart of the problem.

For as long as anyone could remember, the Popes had controlled extensive Italian territories thought to have been given to them in the fourth century by the Emperor Constantine in thanksgiving for his baptism and recovery from leprosy. The "Donation of Constantine" on which the papacy's territorial claims were based, was actually an eighth-century forgery. This was not known, however, until the fifteenth century. In Innocent's day the Pope's position as a feudal lord was seldom challenged.

As such, he was inevitably caught up in the struggle for territory and power that engaged all medieval rulers. The papacy's chief rival was the Emperor, Roman in name and crowned by the Pope, but in fact a German chosen by the great feudal lords ("Electors"), some of them bishops, in the German lands. When Innocent became Pope in January 1198, the imperial throne was vacant, its previous occupant Henry VI having died in Sicily on September 29, 1197. Innocent moved at once to take advantage of this power vacuum, consolidating his position in Rome and throughout central Italy, where he instituted a policy of "recuperations" to reclaim for the papacy territories wrested from it by the deceased Emperor.

Innocent was especially concerned about Sicily. An Emperor in control both of northern Italy and the island kingdom to the south could subject the

Pope to his will. Shortly after Innocent's accession, Henry VI's widow Constance, who ruled Sicily during the minority of her son, Frederick II, born in 1194, ceded the kingdom to the Pope as a feudal fief. In November 1198 Constance died, having appointed Innocent regent of Sicily and Frederick's guardian, an office the Pope discharged with increasing difficulty until 1208, when Frederick reached his majority at age fourteen.

Meanwhile a protracted struggle over the imperial succession enhanced Innocent's power, though at the cost of problems that were to vex him for over a decade. By June 1198 there were two claimants to the Empire, the Staufen candidate Philip of Swabia, brother of Henry VI, and the Guelph Otto of Brunswick. Each had been chosen by a different set of electors.

Unlike Gregory VII, Innocent was reluctant to make a political decision between the two rivals. However he claimed the right, as possessor of the fullness of spiritual power, to judge the moral qualities of the man he was being asked to crown as "Emperor of the Romans" and the Church's protector. Crucial for Innocent's decision was the willingness of the rival claimants to respect papal territorial claims in Italy and the independence of Sicily.

A power struggle of Byzantine complexity continued for a decade, ending only with Philip's murder at Bamberg on June 21, 1208. On October 4, 1209 Innocent finally crowned Otto at Rome, having received his promise to respect papal interests in Italy and Sicily. When Otto immediately broke this promise, the Pope excommunicated him as an oath-breaker and threw his support to his former ward, Frederick II, whom the German electors hostile to Otto chose as King in 1212.

The contest had lasted fourteen years. Throughout Innocent showed himself a master of timing. Neither indecisive nor impulsive, he had the steady patience to await the right moment for his next move. And despite his exalted notion of the superiority of spiritual to worldly power (exemplified in the metaphor of papal sun and imperial moon), Innocent on the whole respected the boundary dividing spiritual leadership from theocracy. His successors would be less circumspect, with disastrous consequences for Church and state alike.

"Where is your God?"

In an address from the first year of his pontificate, summoning Christendom to a crusade to liberate the Holy Land from Mohammedan rule, Innocent portrayed the infidels taunting Christians with the words:

> Where is your God to rescue you from our hands? We have
> desecrated your holy places. . . . We have broken the lances of
> the French, brushed aside the assaults of the English, cut to
> pieces the forces of the Germans, and tamed the Spaniards. . . .
> Where is your God? May he rise up, help you and protect himself
> and you! (*PL* 214, 509 A-B)

Few aspects of medieval religion are so foreign to us today as the idea of a holy war. We have great difficulty seeing the crusades for what they originally were: an outpouring of religious fervor on a mass scale.

Following the capture of Jerusalem and most of Asia Minor by Turkish troops in 1071, the Eastern Emperor appealed for help to Gregory VII. The Pope planned to lead an expedition which would culminate in a pilgrimage to Jerusalem. Nothing came of it. In 1095, however, Pope Urban II appealed to Western knights to cease fighting among themselves and help their Eastern brethren liberate Jerusalem from the infidel. The response exceeded all expectation. On July 15, 1099 the armies of the First Crusade captured Jerusalem. The Latin Kingdom of Jerusalem which the crusaders established proved so fragile, however, that two further crusades were mounted, in 1147-1149 and 1188-1192 respectively, to keep it precariously alive.

Twentieth-century historians, influenced by Marxist ideas of economic determinism and unwilling to believe that religious motives could launch movements as vast as the crusades, have assumed that the prospect of material gain was an important stimulus to crusading recruitment. The medieval reality was quite different.

Even without twentieth-century weapons of mass destruction and bureaucratically planned genocide, medieval society was extremely violent. Though everyone in Europe nominally accepted the Christian faith (apart from a small minority of Jews), there was a great gulf between faith and life. Almost the only places where a serious attempt was made to live by gospel standards were the reformed monasteries.

The crusades offered the ordinary layman an opportunity to respond to the gospel as wholeheartedly as the monk. By sacrificing property, health, and often life itself, to assist his suffering brethren in danger and to liberate from infidel rule the places hallowed by Christ's life and death, knights could assure for themselves, and for their families who shared their sacrifices, a place in heaven. Despite the profiteering that accompanies all military enterprises, far more crusaders impoverished themselves by "taking the cross" (as the crusader's vow was known) than became rich — to say nothing of the huge number who died, Kings and princes along with ordinary knights. Monastic writers were deeply impressed with the way these ordinary layfolk faced death for the sake of their faith. They saw this as evidence that the reform movements of the eleventh century had been successful. The laity had taken up the Christian ideals which were formerly the virtual monopoly of the monks.

Innocent III shared this view. In making the crusade a central concern of his pontificate, he believed he was expanding the serious practice of Christian faith from a small elite in the monasteries to ordinary laypeople living in the world. In a society dominated by warriors (the knights), surely it was better that they should fight infidels rather than other Christians.

As so often in human affairs, however, reality fell short of the high ideals it was supposed to embody. The crusade for which Innocent appealed in 1198 did not get underway until 1202. It was decided to go by sea from Venice. Too many ships were ordered, and when the crusaders came to embark, they could not meet the charter fees. To discharge the debt, the Venetians demanded, over the Pope's protests, that the knights first help them take the Adriatic port of Zara.

There was worse to come. From the Adriatic the expedition sailed not to Egypt (the base originally planned) but to Constantinople, where further support had been promised. When this was not forthcoming after a year's wait, the frustrated crusaders stormed the city, which fell in April 1204 amid a three-day orgy of pillage that permanently crippled the Byzantine Empire and inflicted on Eastern Christians a wound which continues to fester today. In May the Venetians established a Latin Emperor and patriarchate, with a Venetian as first patriarch. Innocent, delighted at what he mistakenly supposed was the reunion of the Eastern and Western Churches, acquiesced in these arrangements, while continuing to press the crusaders to proceed to Jerusalem. They never got there. It was the most bitter disappointment of Innocent's pontificate.

Still the Pope refused to abandon the dream. In 1213 he tried again, seeking this time to avoid the pitfalls that had ruined the previous undertaking. Funding was increased through a tax on the clergy, the cardinals, and the Pope himself. Approved at the Fourth Lateran Council of 1215, this was greater than the tax levied for the Fourth Crusade. Transport of the crusaders was not to be a business transaction, nor were they to be dependent on a single power (Venice) over which the Pope had no control. Innocent even set a date for the embarkation. On June 1, 1217 the Lord's warriors were to gather at Brindisi, Messina, and the neighboring harbors. The Pope promised to be present himself to oversee the embarkation and give his blessing.

It was not to be. On July 16, 1216, during a journey to reconcile hostile factions in Italy so that they could join in the crusade, Innocent died in Perugia.

Defending the faith

Innocent took the spiritual duties of his office very seriously. His concern for the unity of the flock entrusted to him and the purity of its Christian faith produced the most serious blemish on his pontificate, as well as its greatest achievement.

From the start Church unity had been marred by divisions between Christians. Paul identified the two principal forms of disunity in his first letter to the Corinthians. "I hear that there are divisions [*schismata*] among you; and to some extent I believe it. Indeed, there have to be factions [*haireseis*] among you, for only so will it become clear who among you are genuine" (11:18-19). Innocent shared Paul's concern. We have noted his joy over the establishment of the Latin patriarchate of Constantinople. Though misplaced, it showed his deep desire to heal schisms in the Christian community.

Innocent was equally zealous to root out false doctrine. Medieval heresy was a complex phenomenon. At its simplest it represented revolt against the establishment. The medieval Church was rich and powerful. Its clergy enjoyed privileged status. Its laws were complex, its sacraments and other devotional practices imposing but, for many, unnecessarily complicated. Spiritually sensitive souls sought a simpler, more direct approach to God. They were disturbed by the glaring contrast between the hierarchical Church all round them and the simple life of the poor Carpenter of Nazareth whom it claimed to represent.

At a deeper level, there were dualistic theories of good and evil, spirit and matter, reminiscent of the Manichaeism that had fascinated the young Augustine. Some heretical teachers held that an evil agent and not God had created the material world. Salvation, for them, meant escape from the body into the pure spiritual realm of God — a radical denial of the sacramental system and of the incarnational principle on which it is based. The Church, in this view, was the corrupt descendant of an originally pure body. Its doctrines were false, its sacraments impositions of an unspiritual clergy on the credulity of simple believers.

In its most highly developed forms, medieval heresy was a form of Gnosticism: a sophisticated doctrinal system known only to the gifted initiates capable of understanding it, which nourished their sense of spiritual and intellectual superiority. Characteristic of medieval heresy in all its forms was voluntary poverty and lay preaching — protests against the wealth of the Church and its hierarchically commissioned preachers and theologians.

Using the method of allegorical interpretation so popular in the Middle Ages, biblical commentators and preachers identified heretics with the "little foxes, that ruin the vineyards" (Song 2:15). Samson, they held, had shown how to deal with these "ravenous wolves" in "sheep's clothing" (Mt 7:15) when he tied 300 foxes in pairs, set their tails alight, and sent them into the grain fields of the Philistines (Judg 15:4-6).

Innocent's attitude was more enlightened. He recognized that many of those who attacked powerful prelates and wealthy monasteries sincerely wanted to imitate the Christ they encountered in the gospels. From the time he became Pope, therefore, Innocent urged his fellow bishops to treat cases of suspected heresy with great care, lest they uproot the grain along with the weeds (Mt 13:29-30), thus injuring the Church more than the heretics. Preachers of poverty and other suspect doctrines were to be treated with kindness, in the hope of reconciling them with the Church. Stronger measures were justified only against the incorrigibly contumacious.

This policy was partially successful. In northern Italy Innocent was able to reconcile with the Church two groups previously condemned as heretical: the Italian Waldensians (followers of Peter Waldo, a pious layman from Lyons) and the lay brotherhoods known from their voluntary poverty and simplicity of life as "Humiliati."

Heretics in southern France proved less tractable. Here they were called Cathari ("the pure") or Albigensians (after Albi, one of four towns which were seats of Albigensian bishops). In its extreme form, the sect taught the dualism described above and condemned all religious practices involving material things, including baptism, matrimony, and other sacraments.

Innocent sent Cistercian monks including the abbot of Cîteaux into the region of Toulouse, the principal Albigensian stronghold, to preach against the heresy. They accomplished little. People contrasted the luxurious way of life of the Pope's spokesmen with the austerity of "the pure," and drew their own conclusions. When the papal legate, Peter of Castelnau, was assassinated in January 1208 by an officer of Count Raymond of Toulouse, Innocent was shocked. He appealed to King Philip II of France to launch a crusade against the heretics. While the King hesitated, the French nobles took up the challenge. Disregarding Raymond's protestations of orthodox belief and his repeated offers to do penance, they plundered his lands in a savage campaign that culminated in the massacre of some 20,000 people at Bézieres on July 21, 1209.

Modern historians agree that Innocent was badly informed, and ill-served by representatives who spurned the conciliatory policy he repeatedly urged in favor of punitive revenge. While these considerations mitigate his personal responsibility, the bloody "Albigensian Crusade" remains the most serious blot on Innocent's eighteen-year pontificate.

The friars

With spiritual insight all too rare in medieval prelates, Innocent recognized that heresy's appeal could be countered only by genuine Church renewal. Where others saw in the popular movements for poverty and preaching only threats to the established order, Innocent viewed them as movements of the Spirit. They were also symptoms of spiritual illness in a Church grown rich and lax. And since depravity had started from the clergy, Innocent told the Fourth Lateran Council in 1215, purification must begin in the sanctuary (*PL* 217, 675f).

Church renewal seldom proceeds from the top down, however. It comes from the grass roots through prophetic, charismatically gifted individuals who are most often perceived by contemporary Church authority as trouble-makers and worse. Most prophets and reformers encounter hostility and persecution. Yet it is one of the ironies of history that their efforts become truly fruitful only when taken up by the hierarchy.

Innocent encountered two such Spirit-gifted individuals. The first was Dominic, an Augustinian Canon from Spain who crossed the Pyrenees with his bishop in 1203 intending to preach the gospel in faraway Denmark. He never got beyond Provence, where he gathered companions, founded a convent of nuns in 1206, and preached against the Albigensians. In 1215 he visited Rome to seek the Pope's approval for a new "Order of Preachers" — an innovation with potentially disturbing implications for a Church in which preaching was normally restricted to bishops. Innocent recognized the needs of the day, however, and blessed Dominic's project.

Since the Lateran Council had just forbidden the establishment of new orders, the Pope told Dominic to choose an existing rule for his proposed foundation. Dominic naturally chose the rule of Saint Augustine, with which he was already familiar. From it he fashioned an elaborate constitution that replaced the patriarchal system of government of the monastic orders with a limited form of democracy in which religious superiors were elected by their subjects for limited terms only. (Abbots, like bishops, held office for life.)

Even more original than Dominic was Francis, born in 1181 or 1182 at Assisi as the son of a wealthy cloth merchant. Converted from a prodigal and comfortable youth, he put aside his dreams of knightly glory, gave away his inheritance despite the protests of his outraged father, and embraced the life of a homeless worker and simple preacher. Others joined him to form a primitive brotherhood living by a few gospel texts in radical poverty, preaching conversion of life, and united by brotherly love. As such they were indistinguishable from innumerable heretical groups. Innocent discerned the purity of Francis' intention, however, and in 1210 gave verbal approval to his foundation.

Dominicans and Franciscans are today so integrated into Church structure that we have difficulty perceiving just how revolutionary they were for a Church in which monks and nuns were the only vowed religious. The older monastic orders met the needs of the individual searching for God. The friars (as the new recruits were soon called) existed to meet the needs of the Church and world for teachers, preachers, and missionaries.

Unlike the monks, who vowed stability to a particular monastery, the friars were organized in provinces. Their superiors could send them throughout the province, or even to another. This made them dynamic, in contrast to the monks, who were static. Closely allied with the papacy from the start, the friars provided the Church with a militia that Popes could use as they had never been able to do with the monks and secular clergy.

The friars also revived a dimension of Church life essential for its spiritual health in all ages: the missionary outreach. Dominic discovered his vocation, as we have seen, while on his way to preach to the heathen of Scandinavia.

Francis journeyed to the Orient to conquer the Saracens not with arms, like the crusaders, but with the force of love. After two frustrated attempts, Francis reached Egypt on a crusader ship. Closing his ears to all pleas for prudence, he walked unarmed into the Sultan's camp, obtained an audience, and talked to him about the love of God. For the first time in his life, the Sultan said afterwards, he had encountered a Christian who was a friend and not an enemy. We can only guess what the world might look like today had Francis' example been more widely followed.

By 1228 provinces of both Dominicans and Franciscans had been established in the Holy Land, and members of both orders were encouraged to learn Arabic in order to preach to Muslims.

Innocent opened the door to Francis and Dominic, men whom more conventional Popes would have considered dangerous innovators. To that extent we are justified in saying that the record of the friars, one of the great success stories of the medieval Church, must be counted among Innocent's greatest achievements.

Lateran IV

"I have eagerly desired to eat this Passover with you before I suffer" (Lk 22:15). With these words of Jesus at the Last Supper, Innocent opened the Fourth Lateran Council on November 11, 1215. Attended by 412 bishops, some 800 abbots, the 21-year-old Holy Roman Emperor Frederick II, the Kings of France, England, Aragon, and Hungary, and many other representatives of Church and state, it was the largest Church council until Vatican II.

Innocent told the assembly he had summoned them for two purposes: to support the forthcoming crusade, and to reform the Church by restoring the virtuous life of former times. The council approved the plans for the crusade described above. In matters of Church reform, Innocent got most of what he wanted, but not all.

A fundamental problem of the medieval Church was the large number of clergy who sought ordination not for the sake of pastoral service, but to enjoy the emoluments of a Church benefice, and the exemption from civil law granted to clerics, including those in minor orders only.

The evil began with the bishops. They were elected by their cathedral chapters, most of them dominated by the younger sons of the local nobility.

Many of these clergy led worldly lives in which religion played, at best, a purely formal role. The system tended to produce bishops who were no better than their electors. They in turn were responsible, through the ordination of candidates also motivated by worldly motives, for the creation of a large, mostly quite uneducated, clerical proletariat far in excess of any conceivable pastoral needs. This situation, which continued throughout the Middle Ages despite repeated attempts at reform, would be a major cause of the sixteenth-century Reformation.

Innocent was fully aware of the problem. A genuine solution would have entailed abolishing the system that permitted the nobility to regard Church benefices as their private preserve. An aristocrat himself, Innocent was unwilling to attempt so radical a cure. Instead he tried palliative measures: supporting zealous, pastorally minded bishops (who were never lacking even when their numbers were insufficient), and encouraging others to do better.

At the Pope's instigation, the council passed a number of measures reminding bishops of their pastoral duties. Since many bishops could not themselves preach the gospel throughout their large dioceses, because of other duties, "not to say for lack of knowledge" (as Innocent delicately put it to the council), the bishop was to appoint competent vernacular preachers and confessors in his cathedral and other major churches. Bishops were also to provide for the adequate education of future clergy, and to ordain only properly qualified candidates.

"Pluralism" (the holding of more than one benefice at the same time, for the sake of the income), another great evil of the medieval Church, was forbidden. Absentee pastors, who enjoyed the fruits of a benefice without providing pastoral care, were required to appoint a permanent vicar and to pay him an adequate stipend. Annual provincial synods, and for the religious orders general chapters, were to oversee the implementation of the council's reforms.

The council also legislated for the laity. It reduced the number of impediments to marriage and forbade clandestine marriages. To curb abuses in popular devotion it forbade the public veneration of newly discovered relics without papal permission. Pulpit appeals for alms required episcopal permission; and preachers were to limit themselves to the terms of their authorization.

A provision of major importance, which remains in force today, was the requirement that all Catholics receive the sacraments of penance (if conscious of unforgiven grave sin) and communion annually during the Easter season.

However minimalistic this law seems today, it was a major advance in an age when people could remain away from the sacraments for years and still consider themselves good Catholics. A notorious case, by no means unique, was that of King Richard I ("The Lionheart") of England (1157-99), who put off receiving communion for years because he was unwilling to be reconciled with his enemy, King Philip II of France.

Innocent's reform proposals for support of the Roman curia failed. The rapid growth in curial business, due to the flood of legal appeals from people all over Europe convinced that they could vindicate their rights only before the Pope's court in Rome, required more officials, and more money. Innocent proposed that the financial support of the curia be placed on a secure basis through an annual tax on cathedral chapters and other collegiate bodies. All cases brought to Rome could then be litigated free, and the system of fees and gifts (often indistinguishable from bribes) abolished. Despite support in high quarters, the proposal provoked strong opposition and the Pope dropped it. In the ensuing three centuries, the escalating fiscal demands of the curia would become another major cause of Church revolution in the sixteenth century.

The council's legislation against Jews, accompanied by harsh language about their having foully murdered Christ, shocks us today. Even here, however, pastoral motives were at work. The curfew imposed on Jews during Holy Week was designed to prevent the popular outbreaks of anti-Semitism endemic throughout the Middle Ages. The requirement that Jews wear distinctive clothing (which applied also to Mohammedans living in Christian countries) was to prevent Christians becoming intimate with non-Christians through ignorance. It would be many centuries before Catholics began to discern the un-Christian basis of such laws. And even today we are still struggling to put into practice the principles of religious liberty enunciated at the Second Vatican Council.

Death

The man who, as a young cardinal deacon of thirty-seven, had arranged single-handedly for the proper burial of the aged Celestine III, was less fortunate when, at age fifty-five, he fell victim to the fever that had more than once brought him close to death. A quarter century before, in his work *On the misery of the human condition*, the young cardinal had reflected on the passing nature of human glory:

> He who so recently had been sitting in great glory on the throne, now lies unnoticed in his grave. He who so recently had been shining in brilliant array in the great hall now decays naked in his coffin (*PL* 217, 737).

The words became literally true at the death of their author in Perugia on July 16, 1216. The same night burglars plundered Innocent's corpse, which was found stripped and decomposing in the summer heat the next morning. He was buried in the church of St. Lawrence at Perugia. Later his remains were thrown together with those of two successors, Urban IV (died 1264) and Martin IV (died 1285), in a box which was stored in a cupboard in the new cathedral at Perugia. When the box was opened in 1605 it was found to contain only a few broken bones.

In 1892 Pope Leo XIII ordered the remains of his great predecessor to be given worthy burial in the Church of the Lateran, to this day the Bishop of Rome's cathedral. A priest brought the bones to Rome on a train, packed in a suitcase.

CHAPTER SIX

Boniface VIII

(1294-1303)

*"**A**ntiquity shows us that the laity has always been exceeding hostile to the clergy"* (Bull *Clericis laicos,* February 25, 1296).

"There is only one, holy, catholic, and apostolic church . . . and there is no salvation or remission of sins outside of her . . . Consequently we declare, state, define and pronounce that it is altogether necessary for salvation for every human creature to be subject to the Roman Pontiff" (*Unam sanctam,* November 18, 1302).

In Boniface VIII we encounter a Pope whose pontificate was so closely linked to that of his immediate predecessor that we must tell his story first. He was Celestine V, the only Pope in history to resign. The origin of his five-month reign was as bizarre as its conclusion. Celestine's predecessor, Nicholas IV, the first Franciscan among Peter's successors, died at Rome on April 4, 1292. For twenty-seven months the twelve cardinals (soon reduced by death to eleven) were unable to muster the eight votes necessary to elect a successor. Though not quite a record (Gregory X had been elected Pope in 1271 after a thirty-three month conclave, the longest in papal history), the protracted deadlock caused mounting concern.

Among those who protested was an eighty-five-year-old monk celebrated throughout Italy for his sanctity, the hermit Peter of Morrone. In April 1294 Peter wrote to a patron of his congregation, the Dominican Latino Malabranca, dean of the cardinals (who had been meeting at Perugia since the previous October), relating a vision he had received of divine punishment for the Church if there were no Pope by All Saints' Day. On July 5, at a crucial point in the discussions, Malabranca told his colleagues about the letter and suggested that its celebrated writer was the Pope the times demanded. This broke the impasse. In short order eight cardinals, and finally all eleven, gave Peter of Morrone their votes.

Vigorous arm twisting overcame the old man's reluctance to accept the election. Declining urgent invitations from the cardinals to join them on papal territory at Perugia (since disorders at Rome made his coronation there impossible), the new Pontiff went instead in company with King Charles II of Naples to L'Aquila, which he entered at the end of July riding on an ass amid scenes of wild excitement. There, in a Church of his order, he was ordained a bishop on August 29, 1294, and crowned as Pope Celestine V. The Neapolitan King stage-managed the entire ceremony, down to ordering the wine for the banquet afterwards.

Things went swiftly downhill from there. Within days Charles was giving orders for the journey of the Pope and his curia to Naples. On October 6 Pope and King started south. Traveling by slow stages, they reached Naples a month later. During his visit to Monte Cassino, which lay on the travelers' route, Celestine tried unsuccessfully to incorporate the famed Benedictine abbey into his own order. The granting of privileges to his monastic brethren (two of whom he made cardinals) and to their churches was a prominent feature of Celestine's brief reign.

Place seekers quickly swarmed round the papal court to take advantage of a situation ready made for exploitation. Charles II controlled Celestine politically. Others discovered in his chaotic administration a rich source of patronage. The Pope was probably not as naive as he has sometimes been portrayed. He had organized into a flourishing monastic order the numerous disciples attracted by his reputation for sanctity. But at eighty-five he was too old to master the intricacies of curial politics.

In late November Celestine announced his intention of retiring for his customary Advent fast to a cell to be erected in his palace, leaving Church affairs in the hands of three cardinals. When the cardinals refused to acquiesce in what amounted to temporary resignation, Celestine hinted that he might lay down his office permanently. This occasioned panic in those who saw their own fortunes sinking with the beleaguered Pontiff. On December 6 the King and Celestine's monastic supporters organized a mass demonstration among the people, who considered the Pope a saint, and elicited his promise to stay on "unless circumstances intervene to compel his conscience."

The escape clause hinted at the Pope's personal crisis. Realizing that he was out of his depth, and tormented by fear that the Church was suffering in consequence, Celestine had already sought private counsel about resignation from Cardinal Benedict Caetani, an expert canonist and a forceful personality. After initial attempts to dissuade the harassed Pontiff, Benedict advised that there was no legal barrier to resignation. Other canonists, cardinals among them, concurred in this opinion. Following a final attempt by the cardinals on December 8 to persuade the Pope to remain in office, Celestine formally presented his resignation to the cardinals on December 13, 1294. Stripping himself of the pontifical vestments and insignia, he withdrew to his room and returned in the coarse grey habit of his order to sit on the lowest step of the papal throne, where he implored the cardinals (now shedding tears of pity for the poor man, as they had wept for joy at his election in July) to elect a successor as soon as possible. A pontificate of five months had demonstrated that personal sanctity alone does not qualify a man to exercise the office of chief pastor in the Church.

The debacle left the cardinals emitting mating calls for a crisp leader. Following the prescribed ten-day waiting period, the conclave assembled in Naples on December 23. On Christmas Eve 1294 (apparently on the second ballot) they elected Cardinal Benedict Caetani. He took the name of Boniface VIII. Among those who voted for him were two cardinals who would soon become his arch-enemies: James Colonna and his nephew Peter.

Taking charge

Born at Anagni about 1235, Benedict had been a cardinal since 1287. A tall handsome man (as we know from the description of his almost incorrupt body at the opening of his tomb in 1605), he possessed keen intelligence, a sharp tongue, and an impetuous temper. Through extensive land purchases he had raised the Caetani family to a position of power and influence in the papal states. As Pope he continued the aggrandizement of the family fortunes on a larger scale. During the first year of his pontificate, he awarded cardinals' hats to three of his nephews, one of them a married man. The nephew's enforced separation from his wife, and her banishment to a convent, earned Boniface the enmity of her family. Never a man to suffer fools gladly, Boniface made enemies with a lack of concern that was to prove his undoing.

Immediately after his election, Boniface started cleaning up the mess he had inherited — something Celestine himself had requested when he asked Boniface to rectify any errors in the previous pontificate. On December 27, the new Pope issued a wholesale revocation of Celestine's appointments and grants of privilege (many signed in blank or in ignorance of their contents). Only creations of cardinals and appointments to bishoprics were exempt — and Boniface subsequently cancelled many of the latter individually. Boniface also declared his independence from Charles II at the beginning of January by leaving Naples for Rome. There, on January 23, 1295, Boniface was crowned Pope in a ceremony of great splendor.

Since no Pope had ever resigned, it was unclear how Celestine should be treated. On leaving office he had announced his intention of returning to monastic solitude. He asked permission to do so from the new Pontiff immediately after his election. Boniface temporized, fearful that his unpredictable predecessor could become a pawn in the hands of those who bitterly resented his replacement by a Pontiff who (whatever else might be said of him) was all business. It was even conceivable that Celestine might be prevailed on to revoke his resignation, reclaim power, and lead a schism. These fears were not groundless. Within a year of his election, Boniface's enemies were accusing him of having engineered Celestine's resignation and his own election.

Boniface tried, therefore, to keep Celestine under surveillance. He was unsuccessful. Aided by his monastic brethren, the old man managed to slip away to his former hermitage at Morrone. When Boniface sent agents to bring him to Rome, Celestine eluded them until May 10, 1295, when he was finally apprehended at Vieste, on the spur of the Italian boot, as he was attempting to reach Greece by ship. Brought back under honorable conditions to papal territory at Anagni, he was housed next to the papal palace where, eight years later, Boniface would suffer the greatest humiliation of his life. In August Boniface had Celestine moved to the nearby Castle of Fumone, where he lived under honorable but strict house arrest until his death on Trinity Sunday 1296.

Trouble over money

The medieval Church was enormously wealthy. Centuries of donations and legacies, undiminished by inheritance (since a celibate clergy had no legal heirs), had given abbots, bishops, cathedral chapters, and religious orders enormous holdings in land and buildings. The income greatly exceeded pastoral needs. It was only natural that secular rulers increasingly cast covetous eyes on this wealth as a source of revenue for their rising national states.

The Church resisted taxation. In 1179, for instance, the Third Lateran Council forbade levies on the goods of the clergy without episcopal consent.

Complaining that this had sometimes been granted too freely, Innocent III sharpened the prohibition in 1215 by decreeing that the Pope must be consulted before the clergy could confer any grant on lay princes.

Another attempt at fiscal defense was the distinction between the Church's temporal and spiritual goods. The latter category embraced all property connected, however remotely, with the care of souls. These were held to be "in God's possession" and hence exempt from taxation. Temporal goods were those acquired by saving, or not attached to a particular church. The distinction, never very clear, proved difficult to maintain in practice.

Medieval Popes were themselves great tax collectors. Papal levies on Church wealth to support the crusades were diverted in time to other uses: the support of anti-heresy campaigns and other European conflicts (designated crusades for recruiting and tax purposes), and of the papal bureaucracy itself, rapidly increasing in size not so much from a desire for aggrandizement as from the increasing number of legal appeals to Rome by people unsatisfied with the justice available to them closer to home.

The efficiency and success of the Popes in collecting taxes from their subjects led secular rulers to emulate them. Responding to complaints of English and French prelates about the fiscal demands of their respective Kings to support their war with each other, Boniface forged a new defensive weapon. This was the bull *Clericis laicos*, issued with the consent of the cardinals (but not immediately promulgated) on February 25, 1296. This began by repeating earlier papal statements about the perennial rivalry between laity and clergy, but in a needlessly provocative form: "Antiquity shows us that the laity has always been exceeding hostile to the clergy."

The statement was not really true. Had it been true, it might well have been the occasion for inquiry into the reasons for the alleged hostility — the results of which could hardly have fallen out to the sole discredit of the laity. The medieval papacy was incapable of such self-examination. Moreover, it would have required better historical evidence than the age afforded. (Boniface himself, doubtless in good faith, had responded to Celestine's request for advice about papal resignation by citing several supposed precedents now known to have been purely legendary.)

Clericis laicos went beyond invective to forbid, under pain of automatic excommunication, the imposition of any tax on Church goods by the laity — as well as the payment of such a tax — without the permission of the Holy See.

This was sharper than Innocent III's requirement that the Pope be consulted; or the prohibition by Alexander IV in 1256 of clerical taxation, but not of free grants to secular rulers.

The bull touched the vital interests of both Church and state. In an age of rising national states, secular rulers could hardly accept without protest the exemption from taxation of their wealthiest subjects. On the other hand the papacy's interests went beyond questions of law and prestige. The more taxes the Church had to pay to secular rulers, the less would be left for the steadily increasing expenses of Pope and curia. *Clericis laicos* thus set the stage for a power struggle of epic proportions.

Philip the Fair

Well-favored physically but indolent, with a show of piety (he would die rejecting a cup of chicken broth because it was a fast day), Philip IV of France had surrounded himself with a group of able civil lawyers contemptuous of the traditional rights of church and castle, and wholly devoted to the service of the King upon whom their fortunes depended. In the summer of 1296, Philip responded to the Pope's bull by prohibiting the export of money and valuables from his realm and ordering the expulsion of all foreigners. This was a double blow to Boniface. It stopped both the flow to Rome of papal taxes on Church wealth and the activities of the Roman legates who collected them.

Beset by enemies at home (as we shall see shortly), Boniface compromised. On September 25, 1296 the bull *Ineffabilis* condemned Philip's infringement of Church rights, but declared that the Pope would order the French clergy to pay taxes to their sovereign in case of real need. This new bull also explained that *Clericis laicos* did not restrict the payment of levies arising out of age-old feudal obligations.

These concessions did not satisfy Philip. His counselors carried on a vigorous pamphlet war against *Clericis laicos*. Through strong-arm methods they secured the support of most of the French clergy, who were too dependent on the King to resist him. In 1297, therefore, Boniface retreated farther. In February he wrote the French bishops giving permission for "voluntary" payments to the King. And in July he authorized Philip and his successors to tax the clergy without consulting the Pope in cases of genuine necessity — the definition of which he left to the King. With *Clericis laicos* tacitly withdrawn,

Philip revoked his prohibition of payments to Rome and the expulsion of foreigners from his realm. On August 11, 1297 Boniface showed his gratitude by canonizing Philip's grandfather, Louis IX.

The Colonna cardinals

The initial contest between Boniface and Philip had ended with the French King's victory. A Pope as domineering as Boniface would never have made such sweeping concessions had his position not been undermined by enemies at home. Leading them were two cardinals whose votes had helped Boniface to the papacy: James Colonna and his nephew Peter.

The Colonna family, long one of the wealthiest and most powerful in the papal states, had often been at odds with the reigning Pope. Within a year of Boniface's election, uncle and nephew were leading figures among those who objected to the new Pontiff's high-handed, despotic manner. Allied with them were influential Franciscan "Spirituals," so called because they insisted on a strict interpretation of their vow of poverty. They bitterly resented the resignation of the Pope who had bestowed rich privileges on their order. The two Colonna cardinals enlisted their aid to spread rumors about Boniface's alleged immoral personal life and heretical views. They also sent a secret appeal to the University of Paris, the leading intellectual center of the day, for an expert opinion about the legality of Celestine's abdication and his successor's election. King Philip was able to use his knowledge of these intrigues to increase pressure on the Pope. Aware of his opponents' activities, Boniface had several times clashed with the two in meetings of the cardinals.

On Friday, May 3, 1297, a considerable treasure belonging to the Caetani family was plundered at the gate of Rome by Stephen Colonna, younger brother of Cardinal Peter. Such escapades, common enough among the Roman aristocracy, were normally resolved by negotiation. Instead Boniface saw an opportunity to settle with his opponents once and for all. He ordered the Colonna cardinals to appear before him in consistory on May 7, "to hear what it pleased him to say, and to answer what he wished to know, whether he was Pope or not."

When they appeared, Boniface demanded restoration of the stolen treasure, the surrender of Stephen Colonna, and of the family's castles at Palestrina, Zagarolo, and Colonna, which lay south of Rome on the route to the papal residence at Anagni. The two cardinals agreed to restore the money, but refused to surrender their brother and castles, which would have put them at the Pope's mercy.

On May 10 the Colonna cardinals, who had fled to yet another family castle at Longhezza, issued the first of three manifestoes, co-signed by important Franciscan Spirituals, charging that Celestine's abdication and hence Boniface's election had been illegal, calling for a general council, and appealing to the faithful to withdraw allegiance from the illegitimate occupant of the papal throne. The manifesto also charged Boniface with heresy, simony, and personal immorality, and with murdering his predecessor — charges which, though never proved, were to follow the Pontiff into his grave and beyond.

On the same day, but before he had knowledge of this attack, Boniface castigated the two cardinals in an impassioned speech before their peers, vowing to punish their "accursed family with its tainted blood, full of pride and contempt, ever ready to rise in rebellion." The Pope followed this intemperate attack with the bull *In excelso throno*, which deprived the two cardinals of their offices and incomes, and excommunicated them and other members of their family.

The Colonnas protested in a second manifesto, which added new attacks on the Pope and renewed the appeal to a general council. Boniface responded with yet another bull, *Lapsis abscissus*, which extended the previous penalties to the whole Colonna family, confiscated their property, and declared them incapable of holding any office in Church or state.

Confident of support from the French King, the two cardinals issued a third manifesto with even graver charges against the Pope, which they sent to Philip, the University of Paris, and numerous Church dignitaries. The anticipated support from Philip never came. Satisfied with the sweeping papal concessions with regard to the taxation of Church property, the French King saw no reason to assist the two rebellious cardinals. Recognizing their hopeless position, the Colonnas surrendered and appealed to the Pope's mercy.

Boniface responded by ordering a ruthless campaign against the Colonna family which culminated in the capture of their principal stronghold at Palestrina. Churches as well as buildings that went back to Roman times were leveled to the ground. The Pope ordered their replacement by a new city, to be called *Civitas Papalis* (Papal City). This act of unbridled vengeance inflicted a grave blow on the moral authority of the papacy.

Deposed from their offices and the clerical order, and publicly branded as heretics and schismatics, the two cardinals fled to Philip, whose failure to support them had precipitated their ruin. At the French court the Colonnas continued their intrigues against Boniface. Meanwhile the Pope divided the rich spoils of the Colonna family between his relatives, the rival Orsini family, and a younger branch of the Colonnas, who had taken his side in the conflict.

A jubilee year

As the century drew to a close in 1299, rumors multiplied that the Pope would open the new century with a Jubilee Year. After consultation with the cardinals, he did so on February 22, 1300, the Feast of Peter's Chair, granting a plenary indulgence for visits to the Roman basilicas of Peter and Paul — the first grant of such an indulgence in history for visits to specified churches.

Since indulgences will play a prominent role in the following chapter, we need to understand what they are. Experiencing a slow and gradual growth, indulgences came to their full flowering only in the late Middle Ages. An indulgence has to do not with the forgiveness of *guilt* for sin, but with sin's *consequences* — the weakening of character that remains after the guilt of sin has been taken away through confession and absolution. Guilt for the sin of laziness (to take a simple example) is forgiven totally and immediately upon sincere confession. The *consequences* of laziness remain, however, even after its guilt has been forgiven. Removal of these consequences requires a prolonged effort at self-discipline.

It was to remove the consequences of serious sin (not sin's guilt) that the Church of the early centuries instituted lengthy works of penance. In time these penitential works were replaced by works of piety: pilgrimages, prayers, almsgiving. The reckoning of indulgences in days and years refers to an equivalent time of penitential discipline in the early Church.

An indulgence is an assurance of the Church's prayer — which is certain to be effective because of the Church's holiness — for the overcoming of sin's consequences. Available only for sins whose guilt has been forgiven through confession and absolution, an indulgence is said to be partial if it removes some of the consequences of sin, plenary if it removes all consequences.

Distinctions as subtle as these have never been easy to grasp or to maintain. The misunderstanding of indulgences as a short-cut to forgiveness of sin's guilt has always been as common as it is understandable. In theory Boniface excluded this misconception by making his plenary indulgence for visits to the Roman basilicas available only to those who had received forgiveness for the guilt of their sins through a sincere confession.

The jubilee indulgence of 1300 made a tremendous impact nonetheless. How much was due to misunderstanding, how much to sincere repentance and the desire for spiritual renewal, we cannot say. In any case a flood of humanity descended on Rome, eager to win the Pope's *gran perdono*. Contemporaries overestimated the financial advantages to the papacy. The offerings of the pilgrims were gathered in day and night in the Roman basilicas by clerics with rakes. But they benefitted mostly the churches that received them.

For Boniface the principal result was psychological. The success of the jubilee led the Pope to underestimate his loss of prestige and moral authority arising from the bitter struggle with the Colonnas and the attacks by them and others on his person and the legitimacy of his pontificate. Surrounded by masses of pilgrims, Boniface imagined himself impregnable, wielding the "two swords" of spiritual and worldly power against all challengers. It is reliably reported that the Pope appeared several times during the jubilee year in imperial attire, proclaiming: "I am Caesar, I am the Emperor."

Propaganda war

The truce between Philip and Boniface had not resolved their underlying conflict. The Pope continued to hold an extreme version of the "two swords" theory which he expressed in the most provocative form. The French King, on the other hand, embodied the new spirit of nationalism that would undermine the feudal system and with it the medieval alliance of throne and altar which, despite tensions, had been for centuries the basis for public order in Europe.

Conflict broke out afresh in December 1301. Incensed by Philip's harassment of a contentious bishop, Bernard of Saisset, in the south of France, Boniface revoked his previous concessions on the ground that the King had failed to respect Church rights. At the same time the Pope summoned the French hierarchy as well as Philip, to meet in Rome on November 1, 1302 to consider further measures to preserve Church liberty in France. Citing one of his favorite texts from the prophet Jeremiah, "I appoint you over nations and over kingdoms" (1:10), Boniface told the King in the bull *Ausculta fili*: "Let no one persuade you that you have no superior or that you are not subject to the ecclesiastical hierarchy, for he is a fool who so thinks." Anyone who persisted in such folly, the bull added, was an unbeliever who did not belong to the Church of the Good Shepherd.

Scorning self-justification, Philip decided on all-out war. His ministers suppressed the bull and published in its place a crude forgery which overstated the Pope's arguments to the point of absurdity. With it they issued a reply *Sciat maxima fatuitas* ("Be it known to your high and mighty fatuousness") stating that the King could not be judged by anyone in worldly affairs. Philip's ministers used these documents at a National Assembly in Paris in April 1302 to discredit the Pope and drum up support for the King, who again forbade the export of gold and valuables from his realm and the attendance of French clergy at the Roman synod on All Saints' Day.

Thirty-nine French prelates traveled to Rome despite this prohibition, suffering the confiscation of their property in consequence. There is no record of the proceedings. They are assumed, however, to have included discussion of the most celebrated and controversial of Boniface's bulls, issued on November 18, 1302 —

Unam sanctam

Beginning with the statement, "that there is only one holy, catholic and apostolic church . . . and that there is no salvation or remission of sins outside of her," the bull used formal logic, buttressed by appeals to scriptural proof texts cited by theologians and Popes for centuries, to develop this fundamental tenet of Catholic faith into the ringing conclusion quoted at the beginning of this chapter: "that it is altogether necessary for salvation for every human creature to be subject to the Roman Pontiff."

Along the way, the Pope reaffirmed the "two swords" theory propounded by Saint Bernard a century and a half before (see p. 92 above). Both the spiritual and temporal swords were in the power of the Church. The spiritual sword was wielded "by the church . . . by the priest." The temporal sword was wielded "for the church . . . by kings and knights, but at the will and sufferance of the priest. . . . For the spiritual power has to establish the earthly power, and to judge it, if it be not good." A lesser spiritual power might be judged by a competent higher one. But the supreme spiritual power, vested in the Pope, could be judged by God alone.

These arguments were not novel. Even the bull's celebrated conclusion was a direct citation from the tractate *Contra errores Graecorum* of Saint Thomas Aquinas. A claim that offends modern ideas of religious liberty seemed perfectly logical to the medieval mind. The only people then known to have rejected the Pope's authority were Jews, Moslems, and Eastern Christians ("Greeks"). They were assumed to have made a deliberate choice for which they must accept the consequences.

Commonplace though the bull's arguments were, their reaffirmation by a Pope whose position had been gravely weakened in a bitter struggle with the most powerful monarch of the day was bound to provoke opposition. *Unam sanctam* represented a serious miscalculation in terms of *realpolitik.*

A tragic denouement

An indication of this miscalculation was Boniface's continuing belief that he could reach an accommodation with Philip even after the harsh provocation of *Unam sanctam.* A week after the bull was issued, Boniface appointed Cardinal John the Monk, whom the Pope knew was agreeable to the French court, as nuncio to negotiate a settlement with Philip.

When John presented the Pope's terms at Paris in February 1303 Philip prevaricated. Behind the scenes his new chief minister, William of Nogaret, was preparing a fresh attack on the Pope. Launched at a meeting of the King's ministers in March, and expanded at a meeting of leading French clergy and nobles in June, this embodied the accusations of the Colonna cardinals, who finally received the support they had hitherto sought in vain.

Philip charged Boniface with being a heretic and simonist, and with grave offenses against faith and morals: He denied the immortality of the soul, had compelled priests to violate the seal of the confessional, regularly consulted a private devil, was a sodomite, and his predecessor's murderer. The King declared that since he had been anointed to administer justice, he was appealing to a general council, before which he would prove these charges. The motive behind this attack was clear. If Boniface was not the legitimate Pope, his threats of excommunication were without effect. The stage was now set for the final showdown.

News of this fresh attack reached the Pope at his summer residence in Anagni. There on August 15 Boniface held a consistory at which he indignantly denied the charges against him, excommunicated Philip and his advisers, and threatened further sanctions. These were contained in the bull *Super Petri solio*, which released Philip's subjects from their allegiance to him. Promulgation of the bull was planned for Sunday, September 8, 1303. One day before that, events took a dramatic new turn.

Some months previously William of Nogaret, at Philip's behest, had slipped into Italy to organize a direct attack on the Pope. The lack of concern with which the hot tempered Pontiff had made enemies now came home to haunt him. A conspiracy was organized among his numerous foes, beginning with the Colonnas, and reaching even leading citizens of Anagni and at least two of the cardinals.

Learning of the planned promulgation of the Pope's bull on September 8, William entered Anagni the previous morning at the head of an armed band carrying the papal and French flags and crying, "Long live the King of France and the Colonnas!" After storming the residences of several cardinals, the conspirators, joined by many of the townsmen, attacked the papal palace. When Boniface requested a truce, his attackers offered to spare his life if he would restore the Colonnas' offices and confiscated wealth, deliver the Church's treasury to the senior cardinals, resign the papacy, and surrender. When the Pope refused these terms, the attack on him was renewed.

Towards evening of Saturday, September 7, the attackers confronted the Pope, arrayed now in his pontifical robes, and again demanded that he accept their terms. Boniface declared his willingness to die rather than yield. This courageous response saved his life. The conspirators had failed to agree beforehand on the purpose of their attack. An extreme faction, led by Sciarra Colonna, was bent on assassination. William of Nogaret, on the other hand, wanted to take Boniface back to France to be tried before the general council to which Philip had appealed. The Pope remained a prisoner while his captors argued all day Sunday over what to do with him.

Early Monday morning the citizens of Anagni, remorseful over the shameful treatment of their patron and most distinguished fellow citizen, freed the Pope and drove his attackers from the town. That evening Boniface appeared on the balcony of his palace to bless the crowd and to forgive those who had aided his attackers.

Following these traumatic events, it was understandable that Boniface no longer cared to remain at Anagni. He set out for Rome, which he reached on September 25. He survived the ceremonies that greeted his return by less than three weeks. Broken in health, Boniface received the last sacraments and died in the Vatican Palace on October 12, 1303. His enemies rejoiced and spread the false report that he had gone out of his mind and died in a fit of delirium through self-inflicted wounds. He was buried in the elaborate tomb he had prepared for himself in St. Peter's Basilica.

Evaluation

Boniface's conflict with the French King Philip was not the whole story of his pontificate. An accomplished lawyer, he made a major contribution to the development of canon law through the promulgation in 1298 of what would became the third volume of the *Corpus Iuris Canonici*. He intervened in the often bitter rivalry between the parish clergy and the friars by limiting the rights of the latter to exercise pastoral ministry, especially in the confessional. He was a major benefactor of the Vatican library and archives.

Despite these achievements, posterity has judged his pontificate harshly. The distinguished medieval historian, Brian Tierney, writes that the tragedy of Boniface's reign lies in "the disproportion between the ends he set himself and the resources of his own personality. All his diplomacy aimed at establishing peace and concord in a Christendom guided and led by the Pope. But his inability to comprehend the new forces of nationalism that were stirring into life, his excessive preoccupation with the advance of the Caetani family, his impatient and irascible disposition, all made the attainment of such an end impossible."

Aiming to strengthen the papacy, Boniface left it weaker. He thus helped prepare the day when Christians would dispense with Peter's successor entirely, confident that in so doing they were returning to an older Church and a purer gospel.

CHAPTER SEVEN

Leo X

(1513-1521)

"G*od has given us the papacy. Let us enjoy it."*

The two centuries following the death of Boniface VIII were not happy ones for the papacy. This was the period of the Avignon Captivity, the Great Western Schism, and Conciliarism.

From 1305 to 1378 seven Popes, all Frenchmen, ruled the Church from Avignon, where they were largely dependent on the goodwill of the French King. Several of them worked strenuously for Church renewal, only to be defeated by forces beyond their control. The Hundred Years War in France (1337-1453), and the Black Death, which first broke out in 1348, devastated Europe's population, including that of the monasteries, and led to the widespread breakdown of law and order.

Escalating costs were a further problem. In an age of increasing nationalism, most of the Avignon Popes tried to bolster their claims to supreme spiritual power by maintaining the most splendid court in Europe. This entailed further development of the powerful engine of papal taxation which had been at the heart of the conflict between Boniface VIII and the French King. Harsh spiritual sanctions were imposed to collect a vast array of taxes and fees. In a single papal audience on July 5, 1328, for example, John XXII imposed excommunication for non-payment of taxes on one patriarch, five archbishops, thirty bishops, and forty-six abbots. Long smoldering resentment at the insatiable fiscal demands of the papacy would help fuel the outbreak of the Reformation less than two centuries later.

The seventy-year absence of the Popes at Avignon ended with the return to Rome of Pope Gregory XI in January 1377 — to be followed a year later by the Great Schism, when first two and then three Popes contended for the tiara.

This fresh disaster for the papacy had its origin in the election of a non-cardinal, Archbishop Bartolomeo Prignano of Bari, as Pope Urban VI on April 8, 1378. Although the cardinals acted under extreme pressure from the Roman populace, they accepted the new Pontiff and tried for a few weeks to work with him. From the start, however, Urban subjected them to violent abuse and terrible tirades. On the plea that his unexpected elevation had unhinged his mind, a group of cardinals declared in August that Urban's election the previous April was invalid, since it had been made under fear of mob violence. When Urban declined the invitation to resign, the cardinals opposing him declared him deposed and elected another Pope, Clement VII. The resulting Great Schism lasted almost four decades, until 1417.

Uncertainty over who was legitimate Pope led to the development of the legal theory called Conciliarism, which claimed that a general council of the Church was superior to the Pope, and thus could judge between rival claimants to the papal throne — and elect a new Pontiff if necessary. When the Council of Pisa proceeded to do just that in 1409, the Church found itself with three Popes.

People later canonized as saints supported rival Popes. Cynics concluded that the controversy was unimportant: Everything continued much as before even though no one knew who the real Pope was. In 1454 the learned humanist Enea Silvio Piccolomini, later Pope Pius II, reported following a trip through Germany as papal legate: "Christianity has no head whom all will obey. Neither the Pope nor the Emperor is accorded his rights. There is no reverence and no obedience; we look on Pope and Emperor as figureheads and empty titles." The time was not far distant when religious reformers, fired with the vision of a radically different New Testament Church, would claim that the papacy itself was an illegitimate development and the enemy of gospel truth.

The Renaissance Popes

The closing decades of the fifteenth century saw a series of Popes for whom the routine business of the Holy See took second place to the aggrandizement of the papal state, the enrichment of their relatives, and an opulent building program in the city of Rome. The most notorious of these Renaissance Popes was the Spaniard Alexander VI, who reigned from 1492 to 1503. A lavish patron of the arts and the father of several illegitimate children as cardinal and Vice Chancellor of the Holy See, Pope Alexander arranged one magnificent marriage after another for his favorite daughter, Lucrezia, whom he even left in charge of official business during his absences from Rome. His death in August 1503 is believed to have been due to poisoned food mistakenly given to him and his son Cesare instead of to the cardinal who was their host. Cesare, whose survival may have been due to his youth (he was twenty-eight) and stronger constitution, had been made a cardinal at eighteen but resigned the dignity five years later.

Following the twenty-three-day pontificate of the reform-minded but sickly Pius III, a one-day conclave on All Saints' Day 1503 unanimously elected Cardinal Giuliano della Rovere, who took the name Julius II. An enemy of Alexander VI for political reasons, he achieved the Church's highest office through massive bribery of his fellow cardinals.

Eschewing the nepotism of his predecessors, Julius threw his tremendous energy into restoring the finances and territory of the papal state, frequently leading his troops into battle in full armor. Ruthless, violent, and sensual (as cardinal he had fathered three daughters), he was nicknamed *Il terribile* by contemporaries. The Florentine historian Guicciardini wrote that there was nothing of the priest about him but the dress and the name.

At his death of fever in February 1513, Julius was hailed as the liberator of Italy from foreign domination. Art historians honor him as the patron of Michelangelo, the youthful Raphael, and Bramante, whom Julius commissioned to design the present Basilica of St. Peter. He presided at the laying of the foundation stone on April 18, 1506, after arranging for the costs to be defrayed through the sale of indulgences.

The need for reform

Discussions of the causes of the Reformation often focus on resentment over the excessive fiscal demands of the medieval papacy. While this was important, other factors were no less crucial. A major irritant was the enormous number of clergy, far in excess of pastoral needs. It has been estimated that in many countries, priests numbered one percent or more of the total population. (In the contemporary United States, that would be two and a half million priests.) Mostly ill-educated (seminaries did not come into existence until the Council of Trent, which concluded in 1563), many had no obligation beyond daily Mass and the recitation of the Breviary.

Worst of all was the tremendous growth of *religiosity* in the late Middle Ages: pilgrimages, relics, indulgences, endowed Masses (the stipends for which supported the huge clerical proletariat), the cult of the saints with legends of fantastic miracles. Designed to guarantee personal salvation, this jungle growth of religiosity obscured the truth, writ large in the New Testament and in the teachings of great theologians like Augustine and Aquinas, that God "saved us, not because of any righteous deeds that we had done, but because of his mercy" (Titus 3:5; NAB). For growing numbers of increasingly individualistic and spiritually sensitive souls in Western Europe, all this religion hindered direct access to God.

This helps explain the succession of attempts at religious simplification in the late Middle Ages, starting with the Franciscan movement of the thirteenth century. One of the best known was the *Devotio moderna* movement which originated in Holland in the late fourteenth century. Its celebrated classic, *The Imitation of Christ,* is strikingly individualistic. The Church, while never denied, is mostly absent from a work that teaches a spirituality, by turns stern and fervent, of the soul alone with God.

This religious ferment, as well as the pent-up, unsatisfied need for reform, is evident in the account of a tour of Germany in early summer 1517, only months before the outbreak of the Reformation, by the Italian Cardinal Luigi d'Aragona, the widowed husband of a granddaughter of Pope Innocent VIII (1484-1492).

> The palace of the Fuggers [at Augsburg] is the most beautiful building in Germany.... The Fuggers ... have continually 300,000 Ducats at their disposal besides other resources which are not small. They acquired these riches by lending money to those who had to pay tribute to Rome at their installation as bishops, abbots and holders of other great benefices. Jacob Fugger said that in his lifetime, although he was not over seventy, he had helped at the installation of every bishop in his diocese in Germany and sometimes two or three times. . . .

> [In Germany] there is no talking about business in the churches as in Italy. The whole attention is centered on the Mass . . . and all kneel when praying. . . . They pay much attention to the Mass and other services in the churches, and many new churches are built. . . .

> [At Aachen are] the following relics: a garment of the Blessed Virgin, the loin cloth of our Lord on the cross, stockings of St.

Joseph, the bloody cloth in which the head of St. John the Baptist was wrapped after beheading, and many other relics. . . . A plenary or jubilee indulgence, as they say, can be gained. There is no papal authorization for it, but since the veneration was such an old one, Pope Alexander could not stop it, and it is kept up. . . .

"For over a century," writes the great historian of the Popes, Ludwig von Pastor, "a cry for reform of both the head and members of the church had resounded from all parts of Europe. . . . With the dawn of the new century [1500] the cry for reform sounded louder and louder from both sides of the Alps. . . . To many the church seemed to be as rotten as the Holy Roman-Teutonic Empire."

At this fateful eleventh hour, with "the signs of the times [becoming] more and more threatening," the cardinals, following the death of Julius II in February 1513, turned to "a man who was not equal to the serious duties of his high office, who, in fact, knew scarcely anything about them" (*Pastor*).

A Medici Pope

His name was Giovanni de' Medici. Born at Florence on December 11, 1475, he was the second son of Lorenzo the Magnificent and his wife, Clarissa Orsini. Tonsured as a cleric at the age of seven, he was made a cardinal at thirteen. He received an excellent classical education from leading humanist tutors, and studied theology and canon law at Paris from 1489 to 1491.

Following family reversals at Florence in 1494, he traveled to France, Germany, and Holland, where he met the celebrated humanist Erasmus. From 1500 he resided at Rome, becoming a great patron of the arts, literature, music, and the theater and gaining widespread favor as one of the most gentle and affable members of the Sacred College.

In April 1512, while serving as papal legate to Bologna and the Romagna, he was taken prisoner at Ravenna by French troops fighting against the Spanish-papal army of Julius II and carried off to Milan. He managed to escape, however, and made his way to Florence, where he devoted himself to the restoration of his family fortunes. News of the death of Julius II on February 20, 1513 called the thirty-eight-year-old cardinal to the conclave at Rome.

This began on March 4, with twenty-five cardinals in attendance. Cardinal de' Medici had to be carried in on a sedan chair, suffering from a fistula which would require surgery even as the conclave was meeting. Five days were taken up with preliminary business including the drawing up of the customary election "capitulation." This was the program for the coming pontificate. Though sworn to by all the cardinals, it was actually little more than a wish list, since there was no way of forcing a Pope, once elected, to adhere to it.

The capitulation included a provision binding the future Pope to implement plans drawn up by Julius II for reform of the curia in head and members, and to conclude the Fifth Lateran Council convoked by the late Pontiff in 1512 to deal with Church reform and the war against the Turks — long the great enemies of Western Christendom. Significantly the cardinals exempted themselves, however, from taxes to support this struggle. Finally the conclave listened to a bull of Julius II forbidding in the fiercest terms any repetition of the simony which had brought him to the papal throne — a prohibition which, contemporary witnesses agree, was for once strictly observed.

Balloting began on March 10, with Cardinal de' Medici receiving only one vote. By nightfall, however, his election appeared imminent. As senior cardinal deacon, it fell to him to read out the names on the ballots. When he did so early on March 11 (calmly and modestly, according to a contemporary witness), it was clear that he had received the necessary two-thirds majority. He took the name of Leo and his motto from the opening verse of Psalm 119: "In my distress I called to the LORD,/ and he answered me" (NAB).

The new Pope owed his election to the support of the younger cardinals, who were attracted by his gentleness, kindness, and love of peace, and by his blameless personal morals. Those who considered him too young were swayed by the argument that a cardinal who had undergone surgery during the conclave was unlikely to enjoy a long pontificate.

The new Pope (like almost all his early predecessors) was only a deacon. He was ordained a priest on March 15 and bishop two days later. On Saturday March 19, the eve of Palm Sunday, he received the triple crown in a ceremony of great splendor. Even this was surpassed, however, on April 11, when Leo took possession of the Lateran Basilica, to this day the cathedral or official seat of the Bishop of Rome. Pastor calls the procession "the most magnificent spectacle which Rome had witnessed since the days of the Emperors." It included a tabernacle containing the Blessed Sacrament, born on the backs of white horses. The Pope, wearing a richly jeweled tiara, rode the same Turkish horse that had carried him at Ravenna twelve months before, when he was taken prisoner.

Wealthy Romans vied with each other to contribute to the splendor of the occasion. Among the many triumphal arches along the traditional "Via Papale," the most splendid was that erected by the banker Agostini Chigi. Adorned with pagan figures, it bore an inscription referring to the pontificates of Alexander VI and Julius II: "First Venus ruled, then Mars; now Pallas Athena [goddess of wisdom and learning] holds sway." Rome would not have been Rome without a riposte: a statue of Venus erected by the celebrated goldsmith Antonio de San Marino with the inscription: "Mars has reigned; Pallas followed; but the reign of Venus will never end."

"Blameless personal morals"?

Leo was in his element. Blameless only with regard to sexual morality, he was in all other respects an insatiable lover of pleasure. The Venetian ambassador described him in 1517 thus: "A very good-tempered and generous man, who shrinks from severe exertion and desires peace. . . . He loves the sciences and is well versed in literature and canon law; but above all else he is an excellent musician." Another observer added: "He fulfills his religious duties conscientiously, but he will live and enjoy life. He takes special pleasure in the chase." At the request of the King of Portugal, Leo forbade the clergy of that country to hunt, only to spend weeks on end in this pursuit himself, surrounded by hundreds of attendants.

The words attributed to him at the beginning of the chapter, "God has given us the papacy, let us enjoy it," rest on weak authority. It is beyond question, however, that they aptly characterize Leo's attitude to his high office. As news of the new Pontiff's tastes spread, European rulers vied with each other to satisfy them.

In March 1514 a delegation from the King of Portugal, seventy strong, brought Leo the following gifts: Persian horses, Indian poultry, parrots, a young panther, two leopards — and a white elephant which bowed the knee three times to his Holiness and delighted the Roman crowd by spraying them with perfumed rosewater from its trunk. Ridden by a richly dressed Moor, the elephant carried on its back, under an ornamental canopy, a chest surmounted with a silver many-towered fortress containing further presents: vestments embroidered in gold and precious stones, monstrances and chalices of pure gold, a beautiful altar-cloth, and costly books.

Unable to satisfy his appetite for pleasure and display through the generosity of others, Leo spent vast sums himself. In two years he squandered the considerable surplus left him by Julius II. Thereafter he never dreamed of economizing and was perpetually strapped for cash. He shrank from no method of making money and even the highest Church offices were sold. In his pontificate no less than 2,200 curial positions, cardinals' hats included, were available for purchase. The huge sums that flowed in melted away, however, and the Pope had to borrow continually, sometimes at up to forty-percent interest. The Romans who were the principal beneficiaries of this largesse (along with the hordes of Florentines who swarmed into the Eternal City to get in on a good thing), said that Leo had eaten up three pontificates: the treasury of Julius II, his own revenues, and those of his successor.

Personally abstemious, Leo ate only one meal a day, but then heartily. He was temperate at parties and fasted three days a week. A passionate lover of music, he liked to have music played during meals and afterwards. He entertained lavishly, taking the greatest pleasure in the low jokes of the many professional buffoons, jesters, and clowns with whom he surrounded himself. His successor would be amazed at the enormous kitchen bills, in which peacocks' tongues occupied a prominent place.

A late riser, Leo heard Mass daily but celebrated infrequently himself, always going to confession, however, before he did so. A man of consummate tact, he hated to refuse requests and knew how to soften a rejection with hints of favors to come.

In political affairs Leo was a master of the double-dealing in which so many of his countrymen, before and since, have excelled. A contemporary said that he never sailed with one wind, a modern historian that he habitually steered by two compasses. He knew how to keep his thoughts, plans, and intentions concealed even from intimates, speaking little and often replying only with a smile. He thought nothing of making secret treaties simultaneously with rivals (such as the French King Francis I and Charles V, King of Spain and Holy Roman Emperor), the objects of which were irreconcilable with the intentions of their respective signatories.

Under such a Pontiff, it is no wonder that the official world of Rome lulled itself into a sense of false security. In 1516, for instance, the self-important but well-informed papal emissary to Germany, Hieronymus Aleander, told Leo that thousands north of the Alps were just awaiting the right opportunity to rise in open revolt against the Holy See. But German protests had become so frequent that no one in Rome took such warnings seriously.

"This monster of avarice"

Typical of the bitter feeling against Rome is a pamphlet that circulated in Germany in 1518 protesting against the latest attempt of the Pope to collect tithes for the war against the Turks. The anonymous author declared that the real Turk lived in Italy, a "hound of hell" who could be appeased only with streams of gold.

> From his own dominions streams of wealth flow in to the Pope as to no other Christian prince; yet we have to pay for palliums, and send asses laden with gold to Rome, and exchange gold for corn, and rest content with blood-lettings — pardon me, I mean with indulgences! Woe to this monster of avarice which is never satisfied! The craftiness of the Florentine discovers a thousand devices, each one more execrable than the last. Let German freedom be mindful not to become tributary, and not to pay tithes.

The Fifth Lateran Council, summoned by Julius II in 1512 and continued by his successor, was supposed to deal with these and like matters. Shortly after his election in 1513, Leo X had received a lengthy report from two Venetian Camaldolese monks, Giustiani and Quirini, outlining the reforms needed to achieve the long-postponed reform of the Church in head and members. Their proposals went beyond negative criticism to recommend positive measures: revision of canon law, simplification of the religious orders and the liturgy, reunion negotiations with the Eastern Orthodox, and even missions to the New World.

This program would become the basis of Church renewal at the end of the century, following the Council of Trent. Under Leo X, however, the will to reform was too weak for effective action. Lateran V adopted some reforms but left the worst abuses untouched. When the council ended in March 1517 no effective measures had been taken, for instance, to curb pluralism (the holding of several benefices by one person, for the sake of the income each provided), or its closely allied evil, non-residence (many Church office holders never set foot in the territories they were supposed to shepherd).

Nothing throws into sharper relief the paralysis of reform efforts than the correspondence of the Roman curia with a youthful German princeling,

Albrecht, in May 1514. This twenty-four-year-old playboy, already Archbishop of Magdeburg and Administrator of Halberstadt, had just been elected Archbishop and Prince Elector of Mainz by the cathedral chapter there. To enjoy the fruits of this office, however, Albrecht had to pay enormous fees to the curia: for the dispensation necessary to hold these benefices in plurality, and for the documents appointing him to his new office. To meet these expenses, Albrecht took out a loan with the Fuggers.

Along with a copy of the latest reform decrees passed by the council at its just concluded ninth session, the curia sent Albrecht a proposal for repaying his huge debt. He should permit the preaching in his territories for eight years of the indulgence for the building of St. Peter's. Half the proceeds would go to Rome, the other half (less a percentage demanded by the Emperor) to Albrecht for payment of the Fuggers loan.

Albrecht accepted these arrangements and they were confirmed by Leo X in the bull *Sacrosanctis salvatoris et redemptoris* on March 31, 1515. Preaching of the indulgence in the province of Magdeburg was entrusted to the Dominican Johannes Tetzel, who received generous compensation for his efforts. Representatives of the Fuggers accompanied him to ensure that they got their share of the receipts. Modern Catholic historians have called the affair "an open scandal" which "degraded the indulgence to a bargaining chip in a big business deal."

Martin Luther

Especially scandalized was the thirty-four-year-old Augustinian friar Martin Luther, who had already made a name for himself as a preacher and Scripture professor at Wittenberg in the eastern German province of Saxony. Tetzel was forbidden to preach in Saxony by the local Prince Frederick the Wise, who did not want his subjects' money to benefit his rival Albrecht, and who feared competition with the enormous collection of over 17,000 relics in his Castle Church of All Saints in Wittenberg. Frederick had secured from the Pope an indulgence of 1,902,202 years and 270 days plus 1,915,983 "quarantines" (equivalent to performance of a Lenten penance of 40 days) for each visit to this bizarre collection.

In April 1517 Tetzel preached the indulgence in nearby Jüterbog. Crowds flocked there from Wittenberg "like men possessed," Luther wrote. In the confessional he learned the ideas they brought back with them. Tetzel improved on the popular verse, "As soon as the coin in the coffer rings, the soul from purgatory springs," by telling the people that delivery was instantaneous, whereas the coin required time to fall. Confession of sins and contrition were not necessary to obtain a plenary indulgence for the dead. A cash contribution was sufficient, Tetzel assured his hearers, even if the donor was in mortal sin.

Tetzel was also authorized to sell "confession letters" for future use. These enabled the purchaser to obtain from any priest absolution for sins reserved to the Pope. Luther would later claim that this entailed a promise of absolution from sins not yet committed. While this was not strictly true, the letters were sure to mislead people not schooled in theological hair-splitting.

Luther was outraged. A preacher officially commissioned by the Church was putting ideas into people's heads, Luther contended, which crassly violated the gospel call to contrition and repentance. His protest would have consequences that no one foresaw, and which Luther himself never intended.

The Ninety-five Theses

On October 31, 1517 Luther wrote Bishop Schulz of Brandenburg and Archbishop Albrecht of Magdeburg and Mainz (the two prelates in whose dioceses the indulgence was being preached), complaining that the preachers were "lulling people into a feeling of security and fearlessness through lying fairy-tales and promises of indulgences." He asked that the preachers be given new instructions. He enclosed some theses to show how uncertain Church teaching on indulgences was.

These were Luther's famous Ninety-five Theses. The story, celebrated in floods of Protestant pulpit oratory on Reformation Sunday, that Luther nailed the theses to the door of All Saints Church in Wittenberg on October 31 is almost certainly apocryphal. Luther wanted to end a grave pastoral abuse, not to make a public protest. For the rest of his life, he claimed that he did not make the theses known to others until the bishops responsible had failed to act. The picture of Luther bringing down the rotten fabric of the medieval Church with his hammer blows on the church door at Wittenberg derives from an account written after Luther's death by his disciple Melanchthon, who errs in other details as well.

The theses were a mixture of stirring calls to repentance, challenging questions about matters which were then freely debated by theologians, and demagoguery. Luther emphasized that he merely wished to provoke discussion and would change his views if they were refuted. Inevitably it was the polemical theses which attracted the most notice.

> Previously rich people were caught with the net of the gospel; now they fish with the net of indulgences for the people's riches (*Th.* 65-66).

> Christians should be taught that, if the Pope were acquainted with the exactions of the indulgence preachers, he would prefer that St. Peter's be burnt to ashes rather than that it be built with the skin, flesh, and bones of his sheep (*Th.* 50).

> Why does not the Pope empty purgatory for the sake of most holy charity and the supreme necessity of souls — this being the most just of all reasons — if he redeems an infinite number of souls for the sake of that most fatal thing, money, to be spent on building a basilica — this being a very slight reason (*Th.* 82).

> Why does not the Pope, whose riches are greater than the wealthiest of the wealthy, build the Basilica of St. Peter with his own money rather than with that of poor believers? (*Th.* 86)

This was explosive rhetoric. Once printed, the theses spread like wildfire. Their effect was electric, kindling into flame the long smoldering resentments against Rome. Theologians who would later become Luther's opponents greeted the theses. Bishop Adolf of Merseburg said they should be posted everywhere "to warn the poor people against Tetzel's swindle." The Franciscan Prior Johannes Fleck spoke for many when he told his brethren after reading the theses: "There is the man who will do it." Luther himself regarded the reception of his theses as proof that he had given utterance to grievances which no one had previously dared express "for fear of the Jews."

In May 1518 Luther published a theological defense of his views to justify himself to his superiors and the Pope. In an accompanying letter he assured Leo that he desired "to say and claim nothing but what is contained above all in Holy Scripture, but also in the Fathers who are recognized by the Roman Church, in canon law and in the papal decrees." The theses were intended only to provoke discussion among scholars. Luther said he was surprised at their rapid spread, and chagrined at "this conflagration which enkindles the whole world." They were "theses to be discussed, not doctrines. Had I known what would happen, I would have made them more understandable." Luther concluded: "Therefore, most Holy Father, I throw myself at the feet of your

Holiness and submit myself with all that I am and have. . . . I acknowledge your voice as the voice of Christ, who reigns and speaks through you."

That no one in a position of leadership was able to build on these protestations of loyalty and obedience to harness Luther's great gifts as a theologian and preacher for the Church was tragic. In this failure of pastoral responsibility, more than in all the practical abuses recounted above, lies the Catholic guilt for the separation of entire nations from Catholic unity that followed.

Justification

Luther's indulgence theses were the outgrowth of an intense inner struggle that he had waged for years over the question of his own personal salvation. How could he, a miserable sinner, be accepted ("justified," in the language of theology) by the all-holy God? A man of passionate intensity with an innate tendency toward introspection and brooding, Luther belonged to a people who, if they are to have a religion at all, must take it with deadly seriousness. Preaching on baptism in 1534 Luther would say: "I was a monk for fifteen years. But I was never glad of my baptism. For I asked myself constantly: Oh, when will you finally become devout and do satisfaction for your sins, that you may find a merciful God?"

This question of satisfaction was crucial. Both the language of the Church's public prayer and the great theologians like Saint Thomas Aquinas clearly taught that justification was God's free gift. The religious atmosphere in which Luther lived, however, had buried this fundamental Catholic truth beneath what the Catholic historian Joseph Lortz has called "externalism run riot." Luther assumed that to be accepted by God, he must first make atonement for his sins. He labored mightily to do so, often receiving the sacrament of penance daily, fasting and praying until he was exhausted.

"I was a pious monk," Luther would write later, "and kept the rule so strictly that I can say: if ever there was a monk who got into heaven through monkery, then I wanted to get there by that route too. All my fellow monks, who knew me in the monastery, will testify to this. For if I had held out any longer I would have done myself to death with watching, praying, reading and other works."

Luther says that at his first celebration of Mass he was so overcome by the thought of his sinfulness that he wanted to run away from the altar at the opening words of the Canon, *Te igitur clementissime Pater* — and this despite the fact that the prayer addresses God as "most merciful Father."

Some time before the indulgence controversy (the exact date is disputed) Luther had an insight which supplied the solution to his problem. This is the famous "Tower Experience," so-called because it happened in the tower-room Luther used as his study. He says he had long "hated" Paul's words in Romans 1:17, "the justice of God" (NAB). Construing this as the justice by which God rightly punishes sinners, Luther says this and similar texts drove him to despair — until he realized one day that the justice referred to in those passages was that which God gives us as a free gift, and which we lay hold of by faith.

> I felt as one new born and as if I had gone in through the open doors of paradise. The whole of holy scripture appeared to me in a new light. I went through scripture then, as I had it in my memory, and found a corresponding meaning in many passages: thus "God's work" is the work he does in us, "God's strength" is the strength with which he makes us strong, and "God's wisdom" is that with which he make us wise."

Luther worked out the consequences of this insight between 1512 and 1517 in his university lectures on *Psalms*, *Romans*, *Galatians*, and *Hebrews*. An expositor of texts rather than a systematic thinker, Luther emphasized the gratuitous work of Christ in the life of the believer, which heals concupiscence (the innate inclination to sin and the root of all actual sin), and imparts a justice unattainable by even the greatest human effort.

There was nothing in this that departed from Catholic teaching. Luther's tone, however — highly personal and charged with deeply felt emotion — contrasted sharply with the cold and dry scholastic theology of the day. Moreover the more radical corollaries which Luther drew from his teaching *were* departures from traditional views: his denial of free will, and his contention that the faith by which the sinner accepted justification was personal certitude that one's sins had been forgiven. The controversies to which these views gave rise remained confined, however, to academic circles. Only when Luther attacked indulgences — something which touched the lives of just about everyone — did the world at large take note of the startling views of the young Wittenberg professor.

Countermeasures

Archbishop Albrecht was financially damaged by Luther's criticisms of the indulgence campaign Albrecht had commissioned in order to repay his debt to the Fuggers. In December 1517, therefore, Albrecht sent Luther's indulgence theses to Rome with the request that the troublesome friar be silenced. When no action was taken, Albrecht lapsed into inactivity, not wishing to be bothered with the affair further.

Not so the Dominicans, who rallied to support their colleague, Tetzel. Defending Tetzel's statement that souls were released from purgatory *before* the coin reached the bottom of the box, since the coin took time to fall, the Pope's official theologian, Sylvester Prierias, said that his fellow Dominican was no more blameworthy than a cook who added spices to food to stimulate a jaded appetite.

In March 1518 the Dominicans initiated a formal process at Rome against Luther for heresy. Leo X was too busy with the activities recounted earlier in this chapter to devote time to what he regarded as "a monk's squabble" in distant Germany. The Augustinian General was ordered "to quiet down" his obstreperous German subject. Luther received a friendly admonition from his superior, Staupitz, and nothing more. Instead the Augustinians closed ranks behind Luther, as the Dominicans had behind Tetzel.

In July 1518 Luther was summoned to Rome to answer the charges of heresy. Frederick the Wise, wishing to support his newly famous professor, got the Pope to transfer the case to Germany. Leo ordered his Legate Cardinal Cajetan, who was at the Diet of the German princes at Augsburg to obtain their help for the war against the Turks, to hear Luther's case in that city. There Luther met on October 12 with Cajetan, who according to Luther's own account received him "most graciously, with almost excessive reverence." Things went swiftly downhill from there, however.

Cajetan had prepared carefully, taking the trouble to read Luther's writings on indulgences, and to formulate his own moderate views on the disputed points. The legate tried to avoid a disputation by demanding that Luther retract his erroneous statements and promise to keep peace in the future. Luther saw in Cajetan not the Pope's legate but an enemy: a Dominican and worse, an exponent of the Thomist scholasticism which Luther hated as the bloodless, logic-chopping adversary of gospel truth. Luther wrote his friend Karlstadt from Augsburg, that Cajetan was "as fit to judge this matter as an ass is to play the harp."

For his part Cajetan, a cultivated Italian and one of the most learned theologians of the day, was offended at the presumption of this hot-headed German with his wild ideas who claimed that he was not understood or taken seriously. A bitter dispute ensued, in which there was never any real meeting of minds.

With characteristic acumen Cajetan identified a crucial error in Luther's teaching: the claim that, to be forgiven, one must first be certain that one *was* forgiven. Pointing out that this gave an entirely novel meaning to the faith which the Church had always said was necessary for fruitful reception of the sacraments, Cajetan told Luther he was constructing "a whole new church." This Luther could not concede. Subjective certainty of justification was a key element in the theology forged in the fires of his own inner struggle.

The three-day meeting ended on October 14 when Cajetan dismissed Luther and told him not to return until he had changed his mind. Three days later Luther, at the urging of Augustinian colleagues, wrote Cajetan apologizing for his hot-headedness and lack of respect, and promising to write no more against indulgences if others would observe silence also.

Simultaneously, however, Luther issued a formal appeal "from the poorly informed Pope to the better informed most Holy Father and Lord, Pope Leo X" asking him to clarify the disputed points of Church teaching regarding indulgences. The Pope obliged on November 9 with the Constitution *Cum postquam*, which was drafted by Cajetan. At the same time, the legate demanded that Frederick hand over Luther for trial as a notorious heretic. On November 29, 1518 Luther responded with a public appeal to a future general council which, he contended, was superior to the Pope in matters of faith. Three weeks later Luther wrote his friend Wenceslaus Link that he was beginning to think "that the true Anti-Christ rules the Roman curia," and that Rome was "worse than the Turk."

An imperial election

A new factor altered this rapidly deteriorating situation with the death, on January 13, 1519, of the Holy Roman Emperor Maximilian. For reasons of papal and family politics, Pope Leo was determined at all costs to prevent the election of the Spanish King Charles V. To achieve this he needed the vote of Luther's protector Frederick, one of the imperial "Electors."

On March 29, in a fatherly letter full of disingenuous optimism, Leo invited Luther to come to Rome to make before Christ's Vicar the retraction of his errors which, the Pope pretended, the German theologian was now prepared to give. This had been prevented hitherto, Leo stated, only by Cajetan's hostility and favoritism for his fellow Dominican Tetzel.

The Pope's courtship of Frederick (and Cajetan's humiliation) reached its breathtaking climax in June, a week before the Electors met to choose Maximilian's successor. Leo asked Frederick to do everything in his power to secure the election of King Francis I of France. If that proved impossible, he was to accept the imperial crown himself. In return the Pope would do all he could for Frederick — and make "his friend" a cardinal.

Though surrounded with enough ambiguity to permit disavowal later, the most obvious interpretation of this astonishing offer was that Leo was prepared, in return for Frederick's help in the imperial election, to make Luther a cardinal. By a supreme irony, the Pope himself furnished the best possible evidence to support a central charge of his now thoroughly aroused critics: that the Church of Jesus Christ had become a mere political organization more interested in power politics than in the gospel.

An ambiguous condemnation

The election of Charles V as Emperor on June 28, 1519 made further papal concessions to Luther's patron, Frederick the Wise unnecessary. Leo continued, however, to be preoccupied with political concerns and the unending quest for pleasure and money. Nothing further happened with regard to the pending case against Luther until well into 1520.

Meanwhile, in contravention of pledges he had given not to stir up new controversy, Luther was disseminating views that clearly contradicted Church teaching. In formal disputations, and in a series of brilliant polemical works that made him overnight the hero of everyone with a grievance against Rome, Luther jettisoned four of the traditional seven sacraments, retaining only baptism, the Eucharist, and penance. He denied the priestly power of forgiveness, saying that any Christian could absolve, provided that the penitent was certain of forgiveness. He attacked transubstantiation (though retaining belief in the Real Presence) and the sacrifice of the Mass, said that the Church was a purely spiritual fellowship of believers with no earthly head, and that the Pope was anti-Christ.

Finally in June 1520, more than two years after the original charges of heresy, the Pope acted. In the bull *Exurge Domine*, Leo condemned forty-one sentences extracted from Luther's works as "heretical, or scandalous, or false, or offensive to pious ears, or seductive of simple minds, or repugnant to Catholic truth." No attempt was made to say into which of these categories each of the condemned doctrines fell. The boundary between dogma, disputable theological opinion, and heresy remained unclear — thus robbing the bull from the start of its intended effect. Amazingly this ambiguous condemnation remained the only pronouncement of Church authority on Luther's teaching until the Council of Trent over a quarter century later.

Luther was given sixty days from the promulgation of the bull in Saxony to retract. The language in which Luther framed his rejection of this ultimatum helps explain his enormous popular success.

> The Roman See is finished. God's wrath has come over it without ceasing, it is the enemy of the general councils, will listen to no instruction nor be reformed, and is incapable of restraining its flagrant, un-Christian temper. . . . This is the cause, O pious Leo, why I have regretted from the beginning that you, who are worthy of being Pope in better times, should be Pope in this age. The Roman See is not worthy of you nor the likes of you. The Evil One himself should be Pope. . . . O most unhappy Leo, verily I speak the truth, for I wish you naught but good. . . . But that I should retract my teaching, nay, that will come to naught.

Luther also scored points by pretending (contrary to his real conviction, as revealed in his private correspondence) that he doubted the bull's true authorship.

> I summon you, Leo X, and you cardinals, and all others of any importance in the Curia and say to your faces: if this Bull has really gone forth over your names and with your knowledge, then I exhort you in virtue of the power which I, like all Christians, received at baptism — repent and cease such satanic blasphemies against God, and that right speedily. Otherwise you must know that, with all worshippers of Christ, I shall regard the see of Rome as possessed by Satan and as the throne of Anti-Christ. If you persevere in this madness I condemn you and deliver you with this Bull and your decretals to Satan for the destruction of the flesh that your spirit may be saved with us on the day of the Lord. In the name of him whom you persecute, Jesus Christ our Lord.

What Leo made of these fulminations, or indeed if he ever read them, history does not record. On December 1, 1521, six weeks after conferring on Henry VIII, for his *Defense of the Seven Sacraments* against Luther, the title

"Defender of the Faith" (which the English King had long coveted and which his successor bears today), Leo X died suddenly of malaria. He left Italy in political turmoil, Europe north of the Alps in religious revolt, and the papal treasury deeply in debt.

Evaluation

Leo never really grasped the grave situation that faced him. Though aware of the need for practical reform, he lacked the will to carry it out. Pastor writes:

> While the tempest was ready to break in which a third part of Europe was to be torn from the chair of St. Peter, Leo gave himself up with a light and joyous mind and without anxiety to the enjoyments and preoccupations of the world. In all respects a true child of the Renaissance, Leo, surrounded by his artists, poets, musicians, actors, buffoons and other parasites of a court, flung himself with a terrible nonchalance into the vortex of secularity without troubling himself to ask whether such pursuits were in accordance or not with his position as a spiritual ruler.... Under Alexander VI there was certainly a greater depravity of morals, but it is hard to say whether the subtle worldliness of Leo X was not an evil more difficult to counter and of greater danger to the Church.

Worst of all was Leo's failure to understand that Luther's primary concern was *theological* and *pastoral*: reaffirming the gratuitous nature of justification in the face of religious practices that suggested that it must be earned; and correcting widespread errors in the minds and hearts of believers about their relationship with God based on these practices — and on the explanations of them given in medieval pulpits and theological schools.

A religious protest originally aimed at renewal of the existing Church, rather than at founding a new one, was first ignored, then met with juridical half-measures. Failing "to catch the foxes while they were small" (in the words of a contemporary Catholic opponent of Luther), Leo allowed a volatile situation to get beyond the power of anyone to control. The resulting religious divisions continue today, impoverishing all the followers of Christ, and seriously weakening their witness to the world.

CHAPTER EIGHT

Pius V

(1566-1572)

*"G*od has called me to be what I am, in order that I may serve the church, and not that the church might serve me."*

We take it for granted today that the Pope is a religious man, acting from spiritual motives to serve the best interests of the Church and humanity as he sees them. Though most Popes have fulfilled this expectation, many have not. The first Pontiff in modern times to fit our stereotype was Pius V, with his namesake Pius X (1903-1914) one of only two post-Reformation Popes to be enrolled in the Church's official list of saints.

Even after Luther's challenge became too clear to ignore, it was decades before the Church found the bold spiritual leader the times demanded. Leo X's successor was a Dutchman, Adrian VI, the last non-Italian Bishop of Rome until the election of John Paul II in 1978. Sincerely interested in Church reform, Adrian had his legate Chieregati tell the Reichstag at Nürnberg in January 1523:

> We know full well that for years the Holy See itself has been guilty of grave abuses in spiritual things, violations of the commandments, and all kinds of evil. . . . All of us, prelates and priests, have left the right way. "There is not one that does good, no not one" (*Ps.* 14:3).

This call to repentance fell on deaf ears. The prelates of Renaissance Rome closed ranks against the simple-minded barbarian from the north and defeated all reform efforts. Discouraged by the insurmountable obstacles in his path, Adrian died on September 14, 1523 after a pontificate of just thirteen months. The inscription on his tomb in the German church of the Anima at Rome reflects his heart-breaking experience: "Oh, how much depends on the times in which the work even of the best man falls."

The Renaissance returned to power with Clement VII, like his cousin Leo X, a Medici, though of illegitimate birth. The Catholic historian Philip Hughes describes both Popes as "blown all over the sky by the contrary winds of [German] and [French] policies . . . their habitual duplicity in politics matched only by the incompetence of their practical judgment. Time and again they changed sides — just as the side they deserted was about to win." Clement failed to support the movements of renewal and reform which were already at work in the Church. His eleven-year reign witnessed a series of disasters: the sack of Rome in 1527 by the troops of the Catholic Emperor Charles V, and the loss to the Church of England, Scandinavia, much of Germany and Switzerland, and parts of Austria.

The next two Popes, Paul III (1534-49) and Julius III (1550-55), continued the traditions of the Renaissance. Pleasure-loving, generous to relatives, artists, writers, and scholars, they recognized the need for reform, but lacked the will to carry it through with the necessary vigor. To Paul III belongs the credit, however, of convoking the council for which all Europe had been clamoring since Luther's first protest in 1517. It met in the northern Italian city of Trent in 1545, after many delays due to political factors. Julius III, a typical Renaissance Pontiff who caused scandal by his infatuation with a fifteen-year-old youth whom he picked up in the streets of Parma and named a cardinal, reassembled it in 1551 after a three-year suspension.

The frustrated friends of Church reform rejoiced at the election of Marcellus II in April 1555. Upright, zealous, and learned, he was one of the presidents of the Council of Trent, once again suspended. Retaining his baptismal name, he cut his coronation expenses to a minimum, using the money saved to repay his predecessors' debts and relieve the poor, and forbade his relatives to come to Rome. When he succumbed to a stroke after a pontificate of only twenty-two days, a contemporary applied to him some words of Virgil about another Marcellus: *Ostensus est nobis non datus* — "He was shown to us, not given." The German Cardinal Joseph Ratzinger would recall the words following the death of Pope John Paul I on September 28, 1978, after a six-week reign.

Marcellus' successor, Paul IV, was seventy-nine at his election in May 1555. Personally ascetic, autocratic, and a man of incandescent hatreds, he was an aggressive leader of the reform party. Violently anti-Protestant, he refused to recall the suspended Council of Trent, convinced that he could carry through the necessary reforms more swiftly himself by strengthening the Roman Inquisition (at the head of which he placed the Dominican Michele Ghislieri, the future Pius V) and instituting the Index of Forbidden Books.

Paul IV's ferocity against heresy carried over the political sphere, involving him in warfare with Catholic Spain and intransigent policies toward England and Germany which had the effect of favoring the cause of Protestantism in both countries. At his death on August 18, 1559 the citizens of Rome expressed their hatred of Paul's harsh reign by storming the palace of the Inquisition and liberating its prisoners, among them Cardinal Morone, himself an upright champion of reform unjustly accused of heresy.

Reaction came with Pius IV, elected on Christmas Day 1559 after a four-month conclave. The father of three illegitimate children in his earlier years and not known as a champion of reform, he nonetheless reconvened the Council of Trent, suspended since 1552, and carried it through to a successful conclusion, despite grave obstacles and crises, in December 1563. President of the council during its final sessions was Cardinal Morone, imprisoned for heresy by Paul IV and rehabilitated by Pius IV.

Despite this signal achievement, the Church's situation at Pius IV's death on December 9, 1565 was bleak. Only the Italian and Iberian peninsulas were religiously secure. In France militant Calvinism threatened to repeat the victory it had already won in Scotland. Though the first Elizabeth had sat on the throne of England for seven years, hopes were still entertained at Rome that the schism over which she was presiding with shrewdness and increasing success might yet prove to be temporary.

No such prospect was thinkable in Scandinavia, which was already lost to the ancient Church. In Poland the Catholic monarchy, and with it the faith, were at risk. In the German lands the Peace of Augsburg (1555), which permitted local rulers to determine the faith of their subjects ("a victory for territorialism, not toleration"), consolidated Lutheran gains. Most of north Germany had gone over to the Reformation. Elsewhere the Catholic cause was dependent on dynastic fortunes and political considerations. The religious issue was in doubt in Austria, Bohemia, and Hungary. The Swiss Confederation had already split into the confessional kaleidoscope still manifest in that country today.

That the Church was able to recover from this crisis and move forward into a new century with fresh spiritual élan was due to forceful leadership from the top. At long last the papacy, which for half a century had lagged behind the forces of renewal already at work in the Church, seized the initiative by insisting that Trent's doctrinal clarifications and practical reforms be incorporated into the Church's daily life.

In so doing it fashioned the Church that perdured, with variations in different countries and periods, until the Second Vatican Council in 1962: a clerically-dominated organization that mistrusted to the point of persecution the theological and liturgical pluralism which had flourished in the ancient and medieval Church; exalted obedience as the supreme virtue; and regarded all forms of Protestantism as scarcely worthy of the name of Christian.

A zealot for truth and holiness

The funeral rites for Pius IV, celebrated with a magnificence not seen in Rome since the death of Paul III in 1549, concluded on December 19, 1565. The conclave to choose his successor began the same evening. Contemporaries estimated that it would last six months to a year. There was general surprise, therefore, when, on January 7, 1566, the cardinals unanimously chose the Dominican Cardinal Michele Ghislieri. In deference to the late Pontiff's nephew, Cardinal Charles Borromeo of Milan, who was chiefly responsible for the conclave's decision, the new Pope took the name of Pius, rather than that of his mentor and patron, Paul IV.

He had been born in 1504 in northwest Italy to poor parents who named him Antonio. As a boy he worked as a shepherd before entering the Dominican order at fourteen — a normal age for entry into religious houses in Italy until past the middle of our century. Professed in 1521 under the name of Michele, he was ordained a priest in 1528, and spent many years as a teacher of philosophy and theology in the Dominican convent at Pavia and commissary (agent) of the Inquisition there. His asceticism, zeal, and piety led to leadership positions within his order, which he accepted unwillingly.

In 1550 Ghislieri was named Inquisitor at Como, where his relentless pursuit of Protestants from nearby Switzerland brought him to the attention of that arch hammer of heretics, Cardinal Carafa. In 1551 Carafa persuaded Pope Julius III to call Ghislieri to Rome as Commissary General of the Inquisition. When Carafa became Pope Paul IV in 1555, he overruled the Dominican's objections to further advancement by making him Bishop of Sutri and Nepi in 1556, cardinal in 1557, and Grand Inquisitor the year following.

The new Pope owed his rise solely to his zeal in the service of the Church. Though only sixty-two at his election, years of ascetical living had given him the appearance of a much older man. Emaciated, bald, with a long white beard and aquiline nose, he impressed all who saw him as a man of unshakable firmness, his inner vision fixed entirely on spiritual things. "People were captivated," writes the German Protestant historian Ludwig von Ranke, "when they saw him walking barefoot and without head covering in procession, with an expression of deep devotion on his face. It was said that Protestants had been converted by the mere sight of him."

Like his predecessor Gregory the Great, Pius said he had known true peace of soul only in the quiet of the cloister. He was so imbued with the responsibility of his high office that he looked on it as an obstacle to his salvation, fearing that he would fall under the heavy burden.

Pius viewed everything from a supernatural point of view, refusing to take any account of political considerations or worldly wisdom. He told the cardinals at the start of his pontificate that Rome needed no fortifications: its best defense was prayer, fasting, tears, and the devout reading of Holy Scripture. However edifying, this other-worldliness proved problematical in a day when the rising national states of Europe were increasingly subordinating religious considerations to secular concerns.

Though Pius said that he realized he had been called to rule men and not angels, his actions belied his words. Wishing to raise the moral tone of daily life in Rome, he insisted on receiving lists of everyone who left the Vatican after nightfall. He even tried to enlist physicians in the campaign for holiness by ordering them to refuse treatment to patients who would not receive the sacrament of penance. Not surprisingly, such measures did more to raise the level of hypocrisy than of virtue.

No one could fault the Pope's own example, however. He continued to wear a rough tunic under his white Dominican habit — the origin of the white papal cassock familiar to us today. He celebrated Mass daily (then a novelty), slept only five hours a night, ate very abstemiously and alone. Solitude at table continued to be the rule for papal meals until finally abolished by that most human of all modern Pontiffs, John XXIII.

The Pope was also strict in appointments to his household. He insisted that priests in his service celebrate Mass thrice weekly, and that others communicate at least fortnightly. All were to attend regular lectures on philosophy and theology. The need for such requirements shows clearly the lax standards prevailing at the papal court. Pius was equally careful about the selection of cardinals, refusing the customary advice of princes on the ground that this was based on political considerations, and choosing candidates solely on the basis of spiritual and intellectual merit.

As part of his insistence on vigorous enforcement of the decrees of Trent, he campaigned especially against the evils of non-residence and pluralism. In general the least flexible of men, he waived Trent's requirements, however, to keep Cardinal Charles Borromeo with him at Rome, saying he was the only person who told him the truth. And in time he also permitted some German prelates to hold more than one Church office in order to exclude Protestants from benefices, especially in north Germany.

Religious persecution?

Zeal in the defense of the true faith, which in the sixteenth century included ferreting out and punishing heretics, first brought the friar Michele Ghislieri to the attention of the Church's highest authorities. It would remain a central concern throughout his pontificate. Such an attitude is difficult to view sympathetically today, in an age which values religious freedom and toleration.

We might be less quick to condemn past heresy hunters if we reflected that our own century has witnessed the persecution of *political* heresy on a scale undreamed of by the inquisitors of four centuries ago: anti-Communist crusades in the West, and the bureaucratically organized slaughter of millions for alleged ideological deviance in the Soviet Union and China.

Today's high level of religious toleration, at least in Western countries, is a fruit of two ideas: the Enlightenment belief that religion is a purely private affair (like stamp collecting or chess); and its liberal corollary, that there is no such thing as absolute truth, only a variety of equally legitimate opinions. Even in countries which today pride themselves on religious toleration, however, it remains fragile. This is evident from the hostile reactions of political conservatives to Church statements about social justice; and of their liberal opponents to condemnation of legal abortion by Church leaders.

To Pius V and his contemporaries — Protestant as well as Catholic — the idea that religious belief had no consequences in the public sphere, or that there were no religious or philosophical absolutes, would have seemed as absurd as belief in a flat earth is to us today. In the sixteenth century, people viewed the eradication of false religious doctrines, and of those who spread them, in much the same light as many Americans regard the campaign against illegal drugs today. A generation which is witnessing widespread demands for the execution of illegal drug dealers is hardly well-positioned to condemn people who used the ultimate penalty against the purveyors of ideas considered, in their day, to be equally dangerous to society.

Pius V recognized that the low morals of the Catholic clergy gravely weakened the ancient faith in its contest with Protestantism. In the Pope's eyes, this justified zeal in the campaign for Church renewal, but not the setting up of altar against altar. If Protestants still refused to submit to the one true Church of Jesus Christ after its claims, and the falsity of the reformers' teaching, had been amply demonstrated, this could only be due, Pius V reasoned, to obstinacy and pride.

This view, which some Catholics did not abandon until the Second Vatican Council, overlooked the *theological* appeal of Protestantism: its insistence on justification by grace over against a Church which (to state the matter charitably) seemed to tolerate, if not actually to encourage, the idea that salvation could and must be earned; and Protestantism's appeal to the power of God's word over against a Church which all too often treated Scripture simply as a quarry of loose stones to hurl at opponents, and a source of proof texts to demonstrate the power of the hierarchy and the sacraments.

None of this came within Pius V's range of vision — nor could it have done so in the conditions then prevailing. In Italy Protestantism did not appear openly (as in Germany), but surreptitiously. Books containing the new gospel were circulated secretly. Protestant preachers went about in disguise. Worst of all (in the Pope's eyes) were preachers who, still dressed as Catholic priests, imperiled the eternal salvation of their unsuspecting hearers by proclaiming from the pulpit the pernicious errors of Luther and Calvin.

Added to these considerations was the Pope's personal experience. The heretics he had encountered seldom exhibited courage. When apprehended, few persisted in their opinions until death. Pius was keenly aware, moreover, of the horrors visited on France by the Huguenot wars of religion — the result, he was convinced, of the French crown's leniency towards heretics. In season and out, he contended that the only remedy for heresy was sternness. To this end he founded a new Roman Congregation to administer the Index of Forbidden Books (abolished only in 1966), issued harsh laws against Jews, and ordered in 1569 that a person convicted of heresy, or who had confessed to it, be forced to fuller confession by torture. We find such measures shocking. By using them, however, Pius V, who knew all too well the capacity of his compatriots for violence, spared Italy the rivers of blood that would have flowed in a religious war, as well as the destruction of art which such a conflict would have entailed.

Moreover, Pius V's severity toward heretics had abundant parallels on the Protestant side. In 1569, for instance, forty Spanish and Portuguese Jesuits, voyaging to Brazil as missionaries, fell into the hands of the Huguenot Vice-Admiral Jean Sore in the Canary Islands. After maltreating them in various ways, he threw them all into the sea, alive or dead, as heralds of papist superstitions.

Finally, it is only just to record a protest by Pius V against excessive persecutorial zeal. He resisted strong pressure by King Philip II of Spain to confirm the condemnation of Archbishop Bartolomé Carranza of Toledo by the Spanish Inquisition, which had imprisoned him for seven years while the King enjoyed the revenues of the See. Insisting that the statements of the archbishop be read in context, Pius V said that the methods used against him would have made a heretic out of Saint Augustine. In 1566 he had Carranza brought to Rome, where the case dragged on and was still unsettled at the Pope's death in 1572.

Church renewal

Pius was not satisfied with combatting enemies without. Four centuries before the Second Vatican Council told Catholics that their "primary duty" in the work of Christian reunion was "to make a careful and honest appraisal of whatever needs to be renewed and done in the Catholic household itself" (*Decree on Ecumenism*, 4), Pius V labored untiringly to implement the reforming decrees of the Council of Trent.

Impressed with the enormous success of Luther's *Little Catechism* (1529), the Council of Trent resolved at its opening session in 1546 to issue a Catholic catechism. Nothing was done, however, until 1563, when the council entrusted the work to the Pope. Within a year four theologians had prepared a complete text, probably in Italian. This was translated into classical Latin by two leading humanists. Pius V was able to publish it in 1566. Popularly known as the *Catechismus Romanus*, its title page stated that its publication had been "decreed by the Council of Trent for pastors." Even today catechetical experts praise the work's Christocentric and non-polemical presentation of Catholic doctrine. Especially noteworthy, in view of the sixteenth-century controversy over justification, is the catechism's teaching that obedience to the commandments and prayer are the believer's grateful response to God's gift of salvation, rather than good works performed to earn God's favor.

Following initial publication of the catechism in Latin and Italian, Pius V ordered translations into German, French, and Polish. A Spanish translation remained unpublished because of the nervousness of authorities in that country about theological works in the vernacular.

In 1568 the Pope authorized a revised Breviary. This eliminated numerous duplications and many readings in bad Latin containing spurious legends of the saints. The Psalter and Holy Scripture were restored to their proper significance, and complexities arising from accretions over the ages (a recurring feature of liturgical development in all periods) were reduced or expunged. For the first time the Latin Church honored the four great Eastern "Doctors" (official Church teachers): Athanasius, Basil, Gregory Nazianzen, and John Chrysostom. Pius V also added Saint Thomas Aquinas to the four Western Doctors: Ambrose, Jerome, Augustine, and Gregory the Great.

Reform of the eucharistic liturgy followed two years later with the publication in 1570 of the *Missale Romanum*. This was made obligatory for all local churches of the West which had not possessed a liturgy of their own for at least two hundred years. Like the *Breviarium Romanum*, the Missal would bear on its title page for almost four centuries the name of the Pope who issued it. Alterations in both books were reserved to the Holy See, a change in the toleration previously extended to local rites and an important instrument in the increasing centralization of Church governance in Rome which would continue down to the present, when modern means of communication have made possible closer supervision of local churches than ever before.

Pius V insisted that bishops reside in their Sees and threatened absentees with loss of jurisdiction and (more to the point) of revenues. As a religious himself, he gave special attention to the reform of religious orders. In many places monasteries and convents, richly endowed by the piety of previous generations, had become dumping grounds for the unmarried sons and daughters of the nobility. Elsewhere numbers and finances were so reduced that regular observance was impossible.

Pius V insisted that the religious of both sexes live a strict, disciplined life in accord with the spirit of their founders. To this end, he did not hesitate to suppress religious houses, and even whole orders — or decree their merger with others in better condition — when laxity, or the decline of numbers or material resources, made such measures necessary.

Even the reforming zeal of Pius V was powerless, however, to alter a centuries old custom which was responsible for some of the worst abuses in religious life. This was the practice of awarding the income of a monastery *in commendam* to a titular abbot who neither resided in the house which supported him, nor lived a religious life. France alone had in Pius V's day over a thousand such commendatory abbots. The Pope grieved over this abuse, but was unable to abolish the system which supported it.

Previous Popes had undermined efforts for Church reform by a policy of liberal dispensations. Pius V was the first Pontiff who really took reform seriously. Pastor writes:

> By his unflagging zeal the dead letter of [Trent] gradually became a living force and changed the whole appearance of the church. It is with deep emotion that one may see today in the church of S. Maria Maggiore, among the relics of the great Pope, the printed copy of the Tridentine decrees which he used. This little book became in his hands the lever by means of which he uprooted from its bed a whole world of disorders.

Excommunicating Elizabeth

Secular historians know Pius V chiefly for his ventures into politics. As we might expect, however, from a man who judged everything by spiritual criteria and scorned *realpolitik*, Pius V's record as a statesman was mixed at best.

The worst political miscalculation of the pontificate was the bull *Regnans in excelsis* (February 25, 1570), which excommunicated and deposed "the servant of vice, Elizabeth, pretended Queen of England," and released her subjects from allegiance to her. This was the result of wishful thinking, and misinformation about the true situation in England.

As already noted, hopes were still entertained at Rome at the start of Pius V's reign in 1566 that Queen Elizabeth might return to the original faith of her father, Henry VIII (a rather typical Catholic ruler of his day until his quarrel with Pope Clement VII over the annulment of Henry's first marriage with Catherine of Aragon), and of her predecessor and half-sister, Mary.

As these hopes faded, the Pope tried to interest continental rulers, starting with Philip II of Spain (who as Mary's widower and thus ex-King of England was considered the protector of Catholics in that country), in restoring England to the papal allegiance by political and military means. When all upon whom Pius pressed his suit declined to act, he turned to his British followers.

Prominent among them was Mary Stuart. Born in Scotland in 1542, she had been educated in France and was a staunch adherent of the old faith. Queen since infancy of the separate kingdom of Scotland, Mary was a great-granddaughter of Henry VIII's father, Henry VII. As such she was thought by many to have a stronger claim to the English throne than her cousin Elizabeth. Catholics considered Elizabeth illegitimate, since the marriage of her parents, Henry VIII and Anne Boleyn, had never been recognized by the Pope.

In 1568 reversals in Scotland forced Mary to flee to England, where she remained for the rest of her life the prisoner of her rival, Elizabeth. From this time onward, Mary was the focus of special interest on the part of English Catholics troubled on the one hand by Elizabeth's anti-Catholic policy, and on the other by scruples about the legitimacy of opposing a sovereign who had not been excommunicated by the Pope.

In the spring of 1569, the Pope sent Nicholas Morton, a former prebendary of York who had become penitentiary of St. Peter's in Rome, to England to find out how a possible excommunication of Elizabeth would be received in that country. His inquiries gave English Catholics their first direct news of Pius V's hostility to their Queen. Without action against her in Rome, however (which Morton was unable to report), scruples about an armed revolt remained. The report which Morton carried back to Rome encouraged the Pope to remove these scruples by excommunicating Elizabeth.

Revolt came in November 1569, led by the northern Earls of Northumberland and Westmoreland. Declaring their loyalty to Elizabeth, they protested that "evil counsellors" had introduced a false religion and were plotting the destruction of the ancient nobility. Despite initial success (a Catholic Mass was celebrated in Durham Cathedral on November 14), the revolt failed to achieve its chief aim: the liberation of Mary Stuart. Within weeks it had been put down with great severity.

News of the rising did not reach Rome until mid-January 1570. Unaware that it had already failed, the Pope ordered prayers for its success. On February 5, encouraged by the report of his envoy Nicholas Morton, by letters from

England stating that English Catholics had refrained from taking up arms against Elizabeth only because she had not yet been declared a heretic and deposed by the Apostolic See, and by advice from English exiles in Rome (who, however, had been out of touch with their country for years), Pius V opened a formal process against the English Queen. Witnesses testified that Elizabeth had made herself head of the English Church, had deposed and imprisoned Catholic bishops and replaced them with laymen and schismatics, had permitted the preaching of heresy, and lived as a heretic herself.

The process concluded on February 12. The bull *Regnans in excelsis* followed on February 25. In it the Pope declared that by embracing heresy Elizabeth had incurred excommunication and forfeited her "pretended right" to the English throne. Her subjects were thus released from their oath of loyalty and, under pain of excommunication themselves, could no longer yield her obedience.

The bull's strong language was in marked contrast to the use made of it. It was never published in the usual form. Kept virtually secret in Rome, copies were sent to the Low Countries and France for the information of Catholic exiles from England. An Italian banker in London received copies for distribution there. On May 25 a copy was found affixed to the door of the Bishop of London's palace — an act which cost the perpetrator, John Felton of Southwark, his life.

Pius V always insisted that he had issued the bull only in response to the pleas of his English subjects for relief of their conscientious scruples. In the event, however, most English Catholics ignored it, pleading loyalty to their Queen and allegiance to the Pope only in spiritual matters.

Not so the English government, which used the bull to intensify persecution of Catholics in England, on the ground that their loyalty to the Pope made them enemies of the state. In 1582 Bishop Jewel of Salisbury, in his day the leading apologist for the Church of England, mocked the Pope for an action that would have occasioned little surprise in the days of Innocent III and Boniface VIII: "O vain Man! As though the coasts and ends of the world were in his hands, or as if no prince in the world might rule without his sufferance."

The bull was the last papal sentence of deposition against a monarch. Seventy years later, when the Spanish government demanded that Pope Urban VIII excommunicate and depose Louis XIII of France, the plea was rejected on the ground that such measures had proved useless in the case of Henry VIII and Elizabeth.

Issued, as we have seen, primarily to relieve the scruples of English Catholics, the bull greatly increased them. For centuries it was a heaven-sent weapon in the armory of Protestant polemic. Bishop Jewel's argument influenced Englishmen's view of Catholics for centuries. It lives on today in Northern Ireland in the extremist rhetoric of Ian Paisley. Few papal actions in the modern era have proved so disastrous for the Catholic cause as the bull *Regnans in excelsis* of Pius V.

Repelling the Turk

If the excommunication of Elizabeth was Pius V's gravest miscalculation, negotiating an alliance with the proud and mutually suspicious papal rivals, Spain and Venice, was his greatest political success. The purpose of this Catholic League was to repel the Turks. Masters of the Holy Sepulchre in Jerusalem (for the liberation of which crusaders, at papal urging, had for centuries expended so much blood and treasure), the Turks constituted for Pius V and his contemporaries a threat as menacing as the Soviet Union was for the West at the height of the Cold War.

Eliminating this danger was a central concern of the pontificate from the start. As always, Pius turned first to spiritual weapons. On July 28, 1566 he was observed praying fervently, with tears in his eyes, as he walked in the first of three Roman processions to avert the Turkish peril. In a brief on the reform of clerical morals from the same year, the Pope stated: "I am taking up arms against the Turks, but the only thing that can help me in that is the prayers of priests of pure life."

Building a coalition against the Turks proved as difficult, however, as convening a Middle Eastern peace conference today — and for similar reasons. None of the parties trusted each other. Each feared that concessions would be exploited by rivals for their own advantage. France even had a treaty of friendship with the Turks.

In the summer of 1570 several years of wearisome negotiations produced a combined Spanish-Venetian-Papal naval expedition to lift the Turkish siege of Nicosia, the capital of Cyprus in the eastern Mediterranean. This consisted of 198 galleys (137 supplied by Venice, 49 by Spain, and 12 by the Pope) with 1,300 cannons and 16,000 soldiers — a formidable force for those days. The effort failed at the eleventh hour when the Spanish admiral, piqued by the appointment of a papal commander-in-chief and fearful of losses to his own ships, snatched defeat from the jaws of victory by refusing to commit his forces. On September 9, 1570 the hard-pressed defenders of Nicosia surrendered. The Turks broke the terms of capitulation and put 20,000 men to the sword. When the news reached Pius V, his grief and anger were beyond words.

Sixteenth-century warfare was suspended in the winter. While the soldiers repaired their losses and rested, therefore, the politicians returned to the bargaining table. By May of 1571 an agreement for the renewal of the triple alliance was imminent. The ancient Roman saying, still current, that in the Eternal City "everything is a mystery and nothing is secret," was verified once again. Though the negotiations had been conducted in the deepest secrecy, rumors swept through Rome the second week of May that an agreement would be concluded on the 19th. People even knew the names of those who were to command the papal galleys.

The new triple alliance was agreed to only a day later than predicted. On Friday, May 25, the pact was read at a consistory, approved by the cardinals, and sworn to by the Pope and the ambassadors of Spain and Venice. Two days later Pius presided at a solemn Mass in St. Peters which included a sermon explaining the terms of the treaty. The next day the Pope took part in the first of three processions to implore divine favor for the intricately constructed alliance.

It took all summer to assemble the combined fleet at the Sicilian port of Messina, opposite the toe of the Italian boot. For three months the Pope was in a fever of anxiety: impatient at the repeated delays, urging haste, and all the while praying for success in a cause he never doubted was that of God himself. On August 27 he asked the cardinals to fast weekly, and to give extraordinary alms, since penance alone could obtain the favor of God in a time of such peril.

Supreme command was entrusted this time to Don John of Austria, a natural son of the Emperor Charles V and thus a half-brother of Philip II of Spain. Only twenty-four years old, with blue eyes and fair hair, he was to prove, despite his youth, a happy choice. After spending most of the summer at Genoa, he reached Naples on August 14. Amid scenes of wild enthusiasm, the Pope's representative gave the romantic young prince his commander's baton and the sacred standard. Of blue silk damask, it displayed beneath an embroidery of the Crucified Savior the arms of Pius V flanked by those of Spain and Venice. Linking the three shields was a golden chain, from which hung Don John's personal arms. The banner may still be seen in the cathedral of Toledo in Spain.

Don John's arrival at Messina on August 24 provoked the same outbursts of popular acclaim seen shortly before in Naples. Disagreements between the commanders kept the fleet in port, however, until September 16. When it finally put to sea, the leading ships carried relics of the true cross, sent by the Pope. His nuncio, in full pontificals, stood on the breakwater blessing each vessel as it passed.

They sailed for the island of Corfu and reassembled at Gomenitsa on the Albanian coast immediately opposite. There scouts brought word that the Turkish fleet was at Lepanto at the western end of the Gulf Corinth, around the corner to the south and east.

Just as a fresh quarrel between the commanders (the bane of all international military undertakings) threatened to fracture the fragile alliance, news was received of the capitulation, on August 1, of Famagusta, the last remaining Venetian stronghold on Cyprus. Again breaking the terms of surrender, the Turks had flayed the Venetian General Bragadino alive, stuffed his skin and, clothing the mutilated body in his uniform, had dragged it through the city. The report of this atrocity concentrated all minds in a manner thoroughly gratifying to the allied commanders. On Saturday, October 6, the fleet of over 200 vessels, manned by more than 85,000 men thirsting for revenge, set sail.

The Turkish ships, slightly superior in numbers, were sighted next morning, advancing from the east against a light head wind with the sun behind them, as the allied fleet approached the narrow strait at the western end of the Gulf of Corinth. Don John gave the signal to attack by firing a cannon and hoisting the blue silk standard of the Catholic League from the masthead of his flagship *Real* (*Royal*). Crews aboard all ships knelt at their battle stations to receive general absolution from their Capuchin and Jesuit chaplains, and from thousands of throats came the cry: *"Vittoria! Vittoria! Viva Christo!"*

Battle was joined at noon, when the wind died away, leaving the ships to be maneuvered by the rowers. For three hours peasants in the mountains on both shores heard the dull sound of booming cannon fire. When the smoke cleared the Turks had been vanquished. All but 40 of their more than 280 vessels, the largest fleet ever assembled up to that time, were smashed, burning, or sunk. Only the springing up of a violent storm, and the exhaustion of the rowers, prevented Don John from pursuing the defeated enemy.

Contemporaries would soon be reporting that the same Sunday afternoon Pius V, discussing financial affairs with his treasurer in far off Rome, broke off the audience to go to an open window and look heavenward. "This is no time for business," he exclaimed, "but to give thanks to Jesus Christ, for our fleet has just conquered."

Two agonizing weeks went by, however, before the first messenger reached Rome to confirm the Pope's premonition. The cardinal who received him in the early hours of October 22 had Pius wakened at once. Breaking out in tears of joy, the Pontiff repeated the words of the aged Simeon at the sight of the infant Jesus: *"Nunc dimittis servum tuum in pace"* ("Lord, now let your servant depart in peace").

The victory had come on Sunday, October 7, the day on which the Roman rosary confraternities held their annual processions. Attributing the victory to Mary's intercession, Pius V ordered a feast of Our Lady of Victory to be kept on the first Sunday in October every year. In 1573 his successor, Gregory XIII, renamed it the feast of the Holy Rosary.

In the weeks following the Battle of Lepanto, Pius V wrote all Christian rulers, and even non-Christian rivals of the Turks in Persia and Ethiopia, inviting them to join in banishing the Turkish danger forever. It was not to be. National jealousies, and continued French friendship with Turkey, frustrated all attempts at concerted action. The articles of peace signed in 1573 contained so many concessions to the Turks that Voltaire could remark, two centuries later, that the treaty was shaped as if the Turks had won the Battle of Lepanto.

Pius V was spared this humiliation. He died the evening of May 1, 1572 at the age of 68. Immediately venerated by the people of Rome as a saint, his cause of canonization was introduced in 1588 by Pope Sixtus V. Beatified by Clement X in 1672, he was canonized by Clement XI in 1712. In a pontificate of only six and a half years, Pius V had accomplished much. He had banished the worldliness of his Renaissance predecessors. The papacy, previously ambivalent with regard to Church renewal, was now firmly committed to enforcing spiritual and doctrinal purity in all areas of Church life and teaching.

The price of these achievements was the creation of the siege mentality which regarded the Church as a beleaguered fortress, threatened on all sides by hostile foes. Understandable in its day, this mentality long survived the causes that produced it. It would dominate Catholic life and thought for almost four centuries, until it was finally dismantled in our own century by a Pope whose pontificate was even briefer than that of Pius V, John XXIII.

CHAPTER NINE

Pius VII

(1800-1823)

*"T*he Catholic Church has always confronted its great spiritual task in the times of its suppression and persecution. Its great spiritual challenge has always occurred in the time of its unquestioned popularity and support by the secular powers of the state"* (John Lukacs).

Few of the thousands of tourists who stand each year on the quay of San Marco in Venice, between the Doges' Palace and the Old Library, looking south to the island and church of San Giorgio, realize that they are viewing the site of papal election. The fourteen-week conclave which elected Pius VII took place there in the winter of 1799-1800, when the Church was at the nadir of its fortunes.

The closing decades of the eighteenth century had brought the papacy a mournful succession of humiliations and defeats. It was the age of the Enlightenment, an intellectual movement which mistrusted authority and tradition, and held that truth (including religious truth) could be discovered only through reason, observation, and experiment.

Even Catholics who continued to believe in a Church divinely commissioned to teach the truth were affected by Enlightenment ideas. Then as now, progressive Catholics contended that the papacy should jettison historical baggage, modify its claims, and seek reconciliation with a world come of age through the blessings of science and learning freed from religious tutelage.

These ideas crystallized in the demand for greater independence of local churches from Roman control. In France this was called Gallicanism, from the four Gallican Articles drawn up by the famed Bishop J. B. Bossuet and adopted by an assembly of French bishops and deputies in 1684. The Gallican Articles denied that sovereigns were subject to the Pope in temporal matters or could be deposed by him. They reaffirmed the teaching of the Council of Constance (1414-1418) that the Pope was subject to the authority of a general council, adding that his judgments were not binding until ratified by a council.

Although rejected by Pope Alexander VIII in 1690, Gallican ideas continued to be taught in French seminaries. In the eighteenth century, they found fresh nourishment from the Enlightenment and from an idea advanced by the theologian Edmond Richer (1559-1630): That as the bishops were successors of the twelve apostles, so parish priests were descendants of the seventy-two sent out by Jesus. As such they were entitled to a voice in dogmatic definitions and in serious disciplinary decisions such as excommunication.

In Germany similar ideas were advanced in 1763 by an auxiliary bishop of Trier, J. N. von Hontheim. Writing under the pen name, Febronius, Hontheim attacked medieval accretions of temporal power by the papacy and contended that bishops and civil rulers were better protectors of the Church than Popes, whose claim to supreme sovereignty undermined legitimate Catholic pluralism. Febronius also gave his ideas an ecumenical thrust by contending that reducing papal power would facilitate reunion with Protestants.

In Austria-Hungary the Holy Roman Emperor Joseph II (1765-1790) combined Febronian ideas with Enlightenment demands for religious toleration (regarded by Catholics of the day as an attack on the one Church which taught the whole truth) into a governmental program of Church reform known as "Josephinism."

Common to all these proposals for Church reform was the appeal to national rulers to protect the Church against the encroachments of papal power. In reality the power of the Popes was greatly reduced in the eighteenth century. Throughout Europe bishops were normally chosen by civil rulers. Seldom did a Pope decline to institute the candidate proposed. It was natural that such prelates, feeling primary loyalty to their civil patrons, should support Gallican and Febronian ideas.

The one group in the Church which refused to do so was the Society of Jesus, whose members took a special vow to support and obey the Pope. Jesuits were the great defenders of "ultramontanism" — the appeal to Church power "beyond the mountains" (the Alps). Jesuits were banished from Portugal by government decree in 1759, from France in 1764, and from Spain three years later. In 1773 the Franciscan Pope Clement XIV, yielding to pressure from these and other Catholic powers, suppressed the entire Society of Jesus.

Famed since the seventeenth century as "confessors to kings," the Jesuits had made friends in high places, but powerful enemies as well. Though many were motivated by resentment of the Jesuits' political influence, some of the opposition arose from higher motives. In the seventeenth century, Blaise Pascal had excoriated the Jesuits with the zeal of an Old Testament prophet as lax in their moral teaching and confessional practice. Jesuit elitism, expressed in their custom (which continues today) of referring to members of the Society as "ours," gave offense by suggesting that those so designated were the "real" Catholics.

While the Jesuits were thus not blameless in the troubles which came upon them, their suppression was a grave injustice, and for the papacy a disaster. For the Pope to dissolve, at the behest of jealous Catholic monarchs, the one religious order which, more than all others, upheld a high view of papal independence, was an act of craven weakness.

The loss to Catholic missionary works in the New World especially, and to Catholic education, was enormous. Ironically, the two countries in which the Society's suppression was never promulgated, thus permitting it to maintain a shadow existence until its restoration by Pius VII in 1814, were ruled by non-Catholic sovereigns: the Protestant King of Prussia and the Orthodox Czar of Russia. Both regarded the continued existence of Jesuit schools as a matter of national self-interest.

The modern historian of the Popes, J. N. D. Kelly, says of the Pope who suppressed the Jesuits: "His reign saw the prestige of the papacy sink to its lowest level for centuries." The road to recovery would lead through worse disasters still.

The French Revolution

A cynic, improving on Holy Scripture, has observed that it is not the love of money, but its lack, which is the root of all evil. In 1789 the coffers of King Louis XVI of France were empty. To replenish them, new taxes would have to be approved by parliament. It had not met for a hundred and fifty years. Called the Estates General, it consisted of the First Estate (bishops, abbots, and parish priests), the nobility (the Second Estate), and commoners (the Third Estate). They met at Versailles on May 4, 1789.

As the King surveyed this anachronistic body, it was not difficult to see who had the deepest pockets. The Church owned, by the best modern estimate, as much as ten percent of all the land in the kingdom. While this might seem modest, it produced an income (exempt from ordinary taxation) nearly enough to pay a living wage twice over to every priest in France. In addition there was the Church tax, or tithe, which produced half as much revenue again.

The distribution of this wealth, however, was horribly unequal. Bishops, cathedral canons, and commendatory abbots (absentees, often aristocratic playboys, who received up to half the income of the monasteries of which they were the titular heads) enjoyed lavish incomes, while many parish priests lived in penury. These injustices were magnified by the fact that the high paying benefices were reserved, in almost all cases, for those of noble birth.

Since mid-century, therefore, the parish clergy had been seeking an improvement of their lot. The ideas of Richer, described above, supplied them with theological arguments. What their representatives at Versailles observed of the character and life-style of the prelates who sat with them in the First Estate filled up the measure of the lower clergy's resentment, and strengthened their desire for reform.

Once assembled, the six hundred commoners who made up the Third Estate turned their attention not to the provision of revenue sought by their King, but to radical social reform. A society based on privileges due to birth was contrary to reason. And the Enlightenment had taught people that reason was the supreme authority.

Battle was joined over the desire of the commons to abolish the three separate Estates and form a single National Assembly. On June 13 three parish priests broke ranks by leaving the First Estate and crossing over to the commons. Others joined them in the days following, motivated chiefly by resentment at the aristocratic prelates with whom they found themselves allied in the First Estate. Within a week this trickle had become a flood. On June 22 the Archbishop of Vienne led 150 clerical deputies (out of a total of 295) to join the commons.

At stake were not merely the privileges of the Church and nobility, but the claim of the King to rule by divine right. After fighting a desperate battle to retain the system of privilege on which his power rested, Louis XVI yielded on June 27 and ordered the first two Estates to join the third. In theory the newly constituted National Assembly would share power with the King. It would soon become clear that he was actually the assembly's hostage.

Though the Church's representatives had saved the revolution by joining it, there was no way that the Church could escape the radical restructuring which now ensued. On August 4 the privileges of the *ancien régime* were formally abolished. A week later the clergy renounced their right to collect tithes. On November 2 the assembly declared that Church property was "at the disposal of the nation," which henceforth would pay the clergy and care for the poor.

The new arrangements were formalized in the Civil Constitution of the Clergy, promulgated by the assembly on July 12, 1790. This greatly reduced the number of parishes and dioceses in France, provided for election of bishops and pastors (who could choose their own curates rather than having to accept those sent to them by the bishop), and provided state salaries for all clergy. Episcopal incomes were greatly reduced, those of the parish priests on average doubled. The Pope's right to institute bishops (chosen by the King) was abolished. In the future a newly elected bishop would merely send the Pope a letter affirming unity of faith.

Left out of these arrangements were the religious orders. Since French taxpayers could not be expected to support people who (as far as anyone could see) did nothing but pray, the religious orders were abolished except for a few congregations of women engaged in educational and charitable work.

The Civil Constitution was Gallicanism carried to its logical conclusion. Its authors pleaded that they had not touched faith or morals. They were merely restoring the Church to its primitive simplicity and creating a structure acceptable to the nation which had now agreed to pay for it. There was, however, one major defect. The Church had not been consulted.

The bishops, who were the greatest losers, immediately objected to the new arrangements. Even the parish clergy were critical, despite their enhanced position. To force the issue, therefore, the assembly on November 27, 1790 imposed on all clergy an oath accepting the Civil Constitution. All but two of the bishops, and roughly half the other clergy in France, refused to swear. Those who acquiesced came to be known as the Constitutional Church. Its clergy were not motivated simply by the desire for self-preservation. Many of them, together with the new bishops elected and consecrated as the assembly had provided, pleaded that they were merely accepting arrangements they could not alter as the price of continuing the pastoral care of their flocks.

The Civil Constitution created a schism in the French Church which would continue for over a decade. Most of the clergy who refused the oath, possibly as many as 40,000, went into exile along with almost the entire episcopate of the *ancien régime*. Those who remained had to go into hiding. When found and denounced by twenty citizens, they could be put to death.

As the Revolution grew more radical, it swept away the monarchy and then turned on the Constitutional Church it had created. Starting in October 1793 measures were adopted substituting for Christianity a new Religion of Reason. Deprived of their state salaries, the lot of the Constitutional clergy was especially bitter since they lacked the support of Catholics still loyal to their faith, who for the most part regarded the constitutionals as traitors. In the Reign of Terror which followed, it is estimated that at least two thousand priests were executed, and possibly as many as five thousand. Many more were imprisoned.

A turning point came with the decree of February 21, 1795 extending toleration to all religions in France. Catholics in France, deprived of their ancient endowments, of the state support briefly extended to the Constitutional Church, and even of such external signs as the wearing of clerical dress and the ringing of church bells, rushed to refurbish and reopen their churches.

In 1796, however, the Revolution reached its long arm into Italy. The new star in the French firmament, Napoleon Bonaparte, occupied Milan and set up a number of republics in northern Italy on the French model. Napoleon demanded that the worthy but worldly Pius VI, Pope since 1775, withdraw his longstanding condemnations of the Civil Constitution and the Revolution. When the Pope refused, Napoleon invaded the papal states and imposed a huge indemnity, including valuable manuscripts and works of art, and cession of substantial territory.

When, during a riot at Rome on December 28, 1797, a corporal of the pontifical guard killed a French general, French troops were sent to occupy the Eternal City. On February 15, 1798 the Pope was deposed as head of state and a new Roman Republic proclaimed. For a time Pius was permitted to live in the Carthusian monastery at Florence, cut off from his advisers.

In the spring of 1799, however, the French authorities, fearful that the Pope would be rescued by the European powers now allied against them, carried him across the Alps to the citadel at Valence, in the Rhône valley. There the eighty-one-year-old successor of Peter died on August 29, 1799, after murmuring a prayer of forgiveness for his enemies. The prefect of the town recorded in the municipal register the death of "Citizen Braschi, exercising the profession of pontiff."

All over Europe enlightened people told each other that the papacy was finished, and with it the superstition which had supported it. The world would never see another Pope.

Conclave in Venice

The man whose body lay in a sealed coffin in the citadel at Valence (because the local clergy, who belonged to the Constitutional Church which he had condemned, would not bury him) had reigned as Pope Pius VI since his election in a 134-day conclave in 1775. The son of down-at-the-heel aristocrats, he had risen through the favor of the mighty. Benedict XIV, the best of the eighteenth-century Popes, made him his private secretary in 1758. A cardinal since 1773, he owed his election as successor to the Pope who suppressed the Jesuits to his ability to persuade their supporters in the conclave that he was pro-Jesuit, while convincing their foes that he was not. Proud of his good looks, he was a lover of ostentation and obsolete ceremonial, a lavish patron of the arts, and a notable nepotist. In January 1797, and again in November 1798, Pius VI had provided for the election of his successor under emergency circumstances. The conclave was to be summoned by the senior cardinal in any place of his choice which enjoyed the protection of a Catholic ruler.

A conclave at Rome was problematical. Though the republic established there by Napoleon had collapsed, the city was now occupied by troops of the kingdom of Naples. The situation in the Eternal City remained unstable. Moreover, since the autumn of 1798, the Holy Roman Emperor Francis II of Austria, who regarded himself as the Church's anointed defender against French atheism and lawlessness, had been encouraging the cardinals to collect at Venice, which was under the protection of Austrian troops, in preparation for the coming conclave. This was part of an ambitious plan to secure the election of a Pope friendly to Austrian interests and to bring all of northern Italy, including the papal states north of Rome, under Austrian hegemony.

By the time of Pius VI's death, therefore, a number of cardinals were already in Venice. When Francis II offered to pay the expenses of the conclave, and the reluctant Benedictines on the island of San Giorgio were prevailed upon to host it, even the cardinals who preferred Rome agreed to join their brethren in Venice. The conclave opened there on the first of December 1799, with thirty-four cardinals in attendance.

As so often before, the electors were soon deadlocked. For weeks the twice daily ballots produced majorities of eighteen to twenty-two in favor of Cardinal Bellisomi, the Bishop of Cesena, and a blocking minority between ten and thirteen for the Austrian candidate, Cardinal Mattei, the Archbishop of Ferrara. In 1797 Mattei, on behalf of Pius VI, had signed the Treaty of Tolentino which ceded large portions of the papal states to Napoleon. Francis II hoped that with his troops in command of northern Italy, Mattei as Pope would prove equally accommodating to Austrian interests.

In early March intricate negotiations between key members of the conclave and the Catholic sovereigns of Europe produced an ingenious solution to the impasse. Representatives of the minority supporting Mattei would designate a Bellisomi voter acceptable to them. The majority would then be invited to transfer their votes to the new candidate. This would reconcile the two factions and permit both to feel that they had played a role in selecting the new Pope. The choice fell on the Benedictine Bishop of Imola, Cardinal Chiaramonti. He was duly elected on March 14, 1800 by the votes of all the cardinals save his own, which went, out of respect, to the cardinal dean. In deference to his predecessor he took the name of Pius VII.

Though the Austrian Emperor had agreed to the election, he showed his displeasure by refusing to permit the new Pope's enthronement to take place in the Venetian Cathedral of St. Mark. The ceremony was held on March 21 in the much smaller monastic church of San Giorgio. Curious spectators jammed the small piazza outside, while others observed from gondolas thronging the island or peered through telescopes from the Venetian piazzetta opposite. Less than four months into the new century, after a fourteen-week conclave and a papal vacancy of six and a half months, the Church had a new Pope.

A new century, a new Pope

He was born on August 14, 1742, at Cesena in northeastern Italy to noble parents who christened him Luigi Barnaba. His comparative youth (he was fifty-seven) counted against him with his electors, who in 1800 (as so often in papal history) preferred to give the Grim Reaper timely opportunity to correct a mistaken choice.

At fourteen Luigi had joined the Benedictines, who gave him the monastic name Gregorio. Following studies at Padua and Rome, he taught theology in Parma and from 1772 to 1780 at the Benedictine college of San Anselmo in Rome.

In the fall of 1773, Dom Gregorio met Cardinal Braschi, soon to become Pope Pius VI. Both men were from Cesena and were linked by family ties. In 1781, learning that his friend was supporting the young monks at St. Paul's-Outside-the-Walls, where he resided, against arbitrary rule by their abbot, the Pope rescued Dom Gregorio from this monastic squabble by sending him back to his home monastery in Cesena as a titular abbot.

In December 1782, at the age of forty, Chiaramonti was named Bishop of the small diocese of Tivoli near Rome, a position which kept him in contact with the Pope. Two years later he became Bishop of Imola, near Cesena, and a cardinal. It was as bishop of that See that he attended the Venetian conclave which elected him Pope.

As diocesan bishop the kindly and mild-mannered Benedictine showed qualities which Church leaders sorely needed (but did not always manifest) if they were to shepherd their flocks through hostile terrain for which past experience provided no maps. From the start of his episcopate, Cardinal Chiaramonti was generous to the large number of former Jesuits (estimated at 180) who had sought refuge in Imola following the suppression of their Society by Spain in 1767 and by the Pope in 1773. He made one of them, the Spaniard Diego José Fuenzalida, his personal theologian. Following his election as Pope, he asked Fuenzalida to accompany him to Rome as pontifical theologian, a post the Spaniard declined out of concern that he might compromise the new Pope with Spain. Cardinal Chiaramonti was also resourceful in providing for the sixty French refugee priests who arrived in Imola in the 1790s.

Of greater significance was the combination of prudence, flexibility, and firmness with which the Cardinal Bishop of Imola confronted the French revolutionary regimes which replaced the papal states of northern Italy ceded to Napoleon in February 1797 by the Treaty of Tolentino. Chiaramonti accepted the title of "Citizen Cardinal," took down the canopy over his throne in the cathedral, and even used the Republican calendar in his correspondence. He had the words "Liberty" and "Equality" printed at the top of his stationery. In between, however, he placed not "Fraternity," but "And peace in our Lord Jesus Christ," to emphasize that the bond which held society together was not human affection but that which arose from being God's children.

Chiaramonti recognized that these matters did not touch the substance of faith. For the same reason he told his flock (many of whom resisted the imposition of French revolutionary rule, some for patriotic, others for religious reasons) to accept the new order. Pressed by the regime to publish a pastoral letter stating that there was no contradiction between the gospel and the revolutionary principles of liberty, equality, and fraternity — a demand flatly refused by his brother cardinals at Ferrara and Bologna — Chiaramonti preached at Christmas 1797 a sermon which the Catholic historian E. E. Y. Hales has called "one of the key documents of modern Catholic history."

In this discourse, which was immediately published and widely circulated, Chiaramonti said that the revolutionary regime was "not repugnant to the gospel; it demands, on the contrary, those virtues which are acquired only in the school of Jesus Christ." Under the *ancien régime* the subjects needed only to obey the government. In a democracy they were subjects no more, but autonomous citizens, helping by their franchise to shape society. Precisely because of this new responsibility, the guidance of the Church and the supernatural grace available through her sacraments were more necessary than ever.

This was hardly what the new regime had envisaged when they demanded that the cardinal commend revolutionary and democratic principles to his flock. It was equally disturbing to the large majority of Catholics. As late as 1837 Chiaramonti's first biographer, Artaud de Montor, was still scandalized by the sermon. He ascribed the offending passages to "timid men in the cardinal's entourage, who plucked the pen from the hands of His Eminence." There is no evidence for this claim. Hales says that the sermon expressed "a point of view entirely characteristic of Chiaramonti ever since the time when, as a young man, he had defended the novices of a monastery in Rome against the oppressive rule of their masters."

Return to Rome

In the final days of the Venetian conclave, the Austrian Emperor Francis II, realizing that he could not control the outcome, had pressed Chiaramonti to pledge the appointment of an Austrian nominee as Secretary of State. The Benedictine replied blandly that any candidate making such a commitment would incur excommunication. When the demand was renewed three days after the election, Pius VII told the Austrian representative (who had just assured his master in Vienna that the new Pontiff was "inexperienced in affairs") that since he was not yet in possession of a state, he required no Secretary of State. Instead he appointed as Secretary to the Pope the adroit secretary of the conclave, Ercole Consalvi.

A cleric in minor orders, Consalvi had accompanied Pius VI in exile. Elevated to Cardinal Secretary of State in August, following the new Pope's entry into Rome, and ordained a deacon (but never a priest) in 1801, Consalvi soon became one of the leading diplomats in Europe and the key adviser to Pius VII throughout his twenty-three-year pontificate.

Francis II then urged Pius VII to come to Vienna, promising to pay all the expenses of the journey and pleading that it was essential for the head of Christendom and his principal protector to confer on the state of affairs. Consalvi and the Pope had no difficulty discerning the Emperor's real object: to obtain cession of the papal territories in Italy wrested by Austrian troops from French rule. Pius VII replied that his first visit must be to Rome. Possibly he could come to Vienna later in the year.

Wishing to avoid a triumphal progress through territory controlled by his army, the Austrian Emperor arranged for the Pope to voyage by sea to the Adriatic port of Pesaro, and proceed overland from there to Rome. Not until June 6 was all in readiness. The ship provided was so badly run down and poorly manned that a passage which should have taken a mere twenty-four hours stretched to twelve days.

Wearied by their pelagic wanderings, the papal party staggered ashore at Pesaro on June 17 to the salute of Austrian guns. Consalvi recorded in his diary that the journey through the towns of central Italy to Rome was "a continuous triumph." Underway came news of the defeat of Austrian troops by Napoleon at the Battle of Marengo in northwest Italy on June 14.

Pius VII made his formal entry into Rome on July 3 amid scenes of popular acclaim. He went first to St. Peter's to pray at the tomb of the city's first Bishop, then to his residence in the Quirinal Palace. In the four weeks since his departure from Venice, the whole balance of power in Europe had changed. Henceforth the Pope would negotiate not with the Emperor at Vienna but with the First Consul in Paris.

Concordat with Napoleon

By November 1799, when the thirty-year-old Napoleon Bonaparte ousted the incompetent and corrupt Directors at Paris in a *coup d'état* and declared himself First Consul of the French Republic, he had left his Catholic upbringing on the island of Corsica far behind him. He could still be sentimental about his First Communion. At heart, however, he was a deist with a soldier's fatalism.

Napoleon was also an administrative genius and a pragmatist. As such he recognized the power of religion in human affairs. During his Egyptian campaign of 1798-1799 (intended by Napoleon to crush the British Empire by isolating India, and encouraged by the Paris Directors hopeful that failure would rid them of the ambitious young general), Napoleon had posed as the protector of Islam and talked of conversion to that faith. Upon learning that this would require circumcision and lifelong abstinence from wine, he settled for "a certificate of competence in Mohammedan religious knowledge."

"If I were to govern a nation of Jews," Napoleon later declared, "I would rebuild the Temple of Solomon." He considered the religious policies of his revolutionary predecessors madness. In a flight of Gallic logic out of control, Napoleon said that the Revolution's persecution of the Church was "worse than a crime: it was an error." Catholicism, after all, was the religion of the vast majority of Frenchmen, and of almost all Italians. Napoleon once estimated the Pope's power as equivalent to "a corps of 200,000 men." A force of that magnitude should be utilized, not combatted.

One of Napoleon's first acts as First Consul, therefore, was to order the magistrates at Valence to pay full honors to the body of "Citizen Braschi," still lying unburied in its sealed coffin in the citadel where he had died. On June 5, 1800, nine days before defeating the Austrians at Marengo, Napoleon told the clergy in the Milan Cathedral: "The French are of the same religion as you. Admittedly we have had our quarrels, but all will be arranged, all will be adjusted."

On his way back to France following the battle, Napoleon told Cardinal Martiniana of Vercelli (midway between Milan and Turin): "Go to Rome and tell the Holy Father that the First Consul wishes to make him a gift of thirty million Frenchmen."

Martiniana's letter containing this momentous news reached Pius VII only hours after the Pope's arrival in Rome. Napoleon had proposed, the cardinal wrote, a completely new settlement of Church affairs in France. Both the old Bourbon bishops and those of the Constitutional Church should resign. Napoleon would appoint new bishops for a reduced number of dioceses, and the Pope would invest them with their Sees. The Church would waive all claims to its expropriated property. In return the state would pay all clerical salaries. If agreement could be reached on these points, Napoleon would endeavor to see that the Pope recovered all his territories.

Pius VII lost no time in responding positively to this overture. It was early November, however, before his emissary, Monsignor Giuseppe Spina, reached Paris to open negotiations. Spina had attended Pius VI at his death in Valence. Napoleon had encountered him there in October 1799, still guarding the body of his late master, when the General was on his way to Paris to seize supreme power.

Intransigents on both sides made agreement difficult. Embittered *ancien régime* bishops in exile and their curial supporters in Rome were indignant at the suggestion of compromise with the Church's persecutors. Equally hostile were the French free-thinkers, who feared that an agreement with their principal ideological enemy would betray the liberal and egalitarian achievements of the Revolution. The apostate bishop Talleyrand, now married and Napoleon's Foreign Minister, was suspicious. So was Bishop Grégoire, consecrated by Talleyrand as head of the Constitutional Church condemned by the Holy See and now about to be repudiated by the French state as well.

Difficult negotiations continued through the end of February 1801, when a draft agreement was sent to Rome for approval. Consalvi and the other cardinals advising Pius VII felt unable to reply before Easter (April 5). In Holy Week Napoleon sent word that his patience was exhausted. If the Holy See did not accept his generous offer within five days, he would deal with the Church as Henry VIII of England had done less than three centuries before. This threat concentrated all minds in Rome, where memories have always been long. Immediately after Easter Consalvi journeyed to Paris to complete the negotiations himself. He had long conversations with both Talleyrand and Napoleon, who alternately flattered, cajoled, and threatened the Pope's emissary.

Napoleon's aim throughout was reestablishment of the Church in France under the control of the state, namely himself. Consalvi demanded recognition of Catholicism as the state religion. Napoleon would concede only that it was the religion of "the great majority of Frenchman." There were arguments over the extent to which the state could interfere in the bishops' appointment of parish priests, over the provisions for restored seminaries and cathedral chapters, and especially over the "police supervision" of the Church upon which the First Consul insisted. Consalvi was told not to worry: at stake was merely good order in outdoor ceremonies.

At the last minute, after all points had been resolved, the draft presented to Consalvi differed from that to which he had agreed the day before. Warned of the subterfuge, Consalvi balked. Following a final twelve-hour negotiating session, the definitive text was signed by both sides just before midnight on July 15.

Napoleon told Consalvi to be back in Paris with the Pope's signature on the agreement within forty days. Allowing himself only a day's rest at Florence, Consalvi reached Rome in twelve days. Summoned from their summer villas, the cardinals examined the text in the August heat with misgivings. The reference to police supervision was troubling. So was the article renouncing all claims to confiscated Church property in France.

In the end, however, Pius VII and Consalvi were convinced that the agreement contained more advantages for the Church than disadvantages. The Secretary of State was back in Paris with papal ratification three days under the deadline given him. On August 15 Pius VII showed his good faith by publicly requesting (with a heavy heart, as he explained privately) the resignation within ten days of all the exiled legitimate bishops in France, and by removing their Constitutional successors. Ratifications of the accord were exchanged privately in Paris on September 10.

Rome was mystified, however, when Napoleon, who in July had pressed for swift agreement, now declined to publish it. Despite this ominous silence in Paris, the Pope continued to keep his part of the bargain by issuing in early December a bull suppressing the 135 Sees of the *ancien régime* and paving the way for the erection of 60 new Sees. Finally, in March 1802 Napoleon sent the Pope word that he was ready to announce the restoration of Catholicism in France.

When he did so in a ceremony at Nôtre Dame in Paris on Easter (April 18), Pius VII and Consalvi were shocked. Published along with the treaty they had signed were seventy-seven "Organic Articles" affirming precisely those measures of state control over the Church which Consalvi had refused to concede during his negotiations in Paris. Papal communications with the French Church were to be subject to government control, as were seminaries, which were required to teach the Gallican Articles of 1664. Bishops were to administer their dioceses as prefects did their *departements*, under close state supervision. Police regulation of Church activities (still undefined) was reaffirmed.

Hard liners in Rome saw their previous opposition to the agreement vindicated. In France, however, people saw things differently. The opponents of the Concordat were delighted to see Napoleon take back with his left hand what he had so improvidently given with his right. Returning *ancien régime* bishops, sixteen of whom received Sees in the diminished new hierarchy, saw in the Organic Articles merely a revival of the Gallicanism which they had always accepted. Constitutional bishops, of whom twelve received new Sees, could hardly object since they had already accepted state control of the Church.

The Church had paid a high price for the right to resume in France, still glorying despite the Revolution in the title of Catholicism's "eldest daughter," its pastoral and evangelical work. That much even contemporary supporters of the agreement conceded. The judgment of history is different.

The Concordat greatly strengthened the power of the bishops over their clergy. Henceforth they alone would appoint parish pastors and their assistants. The patronage which, from time immemorial, had resided in the hands of local aristocrats and gentry, was gone forever. The lower clergy, who must now look to their bishop for promotion, lost the independence they had once enjoyed. The bishops, now nominated and salaried by the state, lost the independence of their *ancien régime* predecessors.

The great gainer in the new arrangements (though few recognized this at the time) was the papacy. For the first time in history, the Pope's power to remove a bishop from his See was recognized. Only by granting him this power could Napoleon rid himself of the competing claims of the old Bourbon bishops and their Constitutional rivals and start afresh.

Though Pius VII conceded the state's right to nominate bishops, his twentieth-century successors would see this concession lapse as the separation of Church and state (proclaimed in France in 1905) caused governments to lose interest in selecting bishops. In the meantime the lower clergy had come to see the papacy as their bulwark against arbitrary episcopal rule.

By hindsight, therefore, we can see that Pius VII's Concordat with Napoleon laid the foundations for the papal autocracy proclaimed by the First Vatican Council in 1870. The agreement's immediate result, however, was fresh humiliations for the Pope who had signed it.

The Pope in Paris

In May 1804 the papal nuncio in Paris, Cardinal Caprara, sent word to Rome that Napoleon had had himself proclaimed Emperor by the subservient

French Senate and wanted the Pope to come to Paris to crown him. The cardinals, whom Pius VII consulted before all important decisions, had serious misgivings.

How could the Pope crown the man who had insulted him by unilaterally attaching to the Concordat the offensive Organic Articles? How could he thus honor the man who continued to rule large areas in northern Italy which, from time immemorial, had belonged to the Pope?

Consalvi had carefully excluded the question of the papal states from the Concordat negotiations, to avoid any suggestion that territorial concessions could induce the Pope to yield on matters affecting the Church's pastoral role. But Napoleon had coupled his original offer of a Concordat with an assurance that he would give the Pope back his lands. Not only had Napoleon failed to do so; he had set up revolutionary governments which had introduced on papal territory civil marriage and divorce, a scandal scarcely to be endured.

Finally, what would the legitimate sovereigns of Europe, starting with the Holy Roman Emperor Francis II (whose pressing invitation to visit Vienna from Venice Pius VII had refused) think of a Pope who gave this young Corsican *arriviste* who was troubling all Europe the cachet of anointing by the head of Christendom?

Despite these troubling questions, only two of the twenty cardinals consulted recommended flat rejection of Napoleon's invitation. The others advised acceptance under conditions. Pius VII and Consalvi judged that the arguments for going to Paris were weightier than those against. A personal conversation might achieve more than months of diplomatic negotiations through emissaries. Napoleon might be induced to modify the Organic Articles. There would be an opportunity to discuss the offensive laws imposed by Napoleon's puppet rulers in the Pope's Italian territories. And the Pope could confront the former Constitutional bishops invested with new Sees who had refused to abjure their acceptance of the Revolution.

Efforts to obtain advance assurance on these points were not successful. All the new Emperor would promise was that once the Pope was in Paris all outstanding questions could be fully discussed. When Napoleon's formal invitation arrived on September 29, it was so brusque that Pius VII wanted to refuse it. He accepted nonetheless, and finally left Rome on November 2, 1804, leaving the trusted Consalvi behind in charge of normal Church business.

The journey north was another triumph: "We passed through France," he reported to Consalvi, "in the midst of a people on their knees." In a calculated breach of diplomatic protocol, Napoleon contrived to avoid the customary honors by encountering the papal party while he was hunting in the forest of Fountainbleau. To prevent manifestations of popular acclaim, the Emperor rode into Paris in the Pope's coach at night. Upon arrival Napoleon gave his guest a bedroom in the Tuileries with a view of the square where, not many years before, thousands of Frenchmen (hundreds of priests among them) had died under the guillotine. This slight, like many others which Napoleon perpetrated to show that he was master of the man he had summoned to grace his crowning, was only partially requited by the crowds which appeared beneath the Pope's apartment to seek his blessing.

Only four days remained between Pius' arrival in Paris and the coronation in Nôtre Dame Cathedral on December 2. The Pope learned that the ceremonial previously agreed to had been changed. He would anoint the Emperor and bless the crown. Napoleon would place it on his head himself. Moreover, the Emperor would not receive communion, since he was unwilling to make his confession beforehand. Napoleon later explained this refusal as due to his having too much faith to wish to commit a sacrilege. Ever the gentle pastor, Pius accepted even this rejection of the Church's greatest gift, hopeful (as he explained) that "a time would without doubt come when the Emperor's conscience would advise him differently."

On one point, however, Pius was unyielding. Upon learning that Napoleon and his consort Josephine had undergone only a civil marriage (and were thus not married at all in the eyes of the Church), the Pope insisted on a religious ceremony. This was performed the afternoon before the coronation by Napoleon's uncle, Cardinal Fesch, who as French ambassador to the Holy See had been closely involved with negotiations for the Pope's visit from the start. Since the ceremony was private and without witnesses, Napoleon was able, five years later, to obtain from a compliant French court an annulment of his marriage to Josephine, who had failed to produce the desired heir. He then married the Hapsburg princess Marie Louise, daughter of his arch rival, the Holy Roman Emperor Francis II of Austria.

In 1804, however, there was bitter hostility between Paris and Vienna. There could be no question of obtaining from the Hapsburg ruler's treasury the loan of some of the regalia from Charlemagne's coronation, which Napoleon wanted to replicate. He had to make do with modern copies.

Coronation day brought snow and fog. Napoleon kept Pius VII, who was fasting from the previous midnight so he could celebrate the Mass, waiting from ten-fifteen till almost noon in the frigid cathedral. While the Pontiff meditated and prayed, vendors did a brisk business selling sausages and rolls to the packed congregation in the nave.

The days following brought further difficulties over the gifts required by protocol. Pius VII would have preferred that they be omitted entirely. He could not help but notice, however, that the presents to the cardinals were exceedingly modest; that the two state coaches he had been promised never appeared; and that the large emerald in the tiara presented to him had been taken from the tiara of his predecessor as part of the tribute exacted by Napoleon in the treaty of Tolentino in 1797. When Consalvi heard about this, he was wild.

As Christmas came and went, and then the New Year, Napoleon found that his guest was in no hurry to leave. The Pope still hoped to obtain concessions in the Organic Articles and related matters. This proved impossible. The Emperor yielded on a few peripheral points, but gave only vague assurances regarding differences of substance.

A further reason for the Pope's delay was that, apart from the Emperor's *brusqueries* (which his guest mostly contrived not to notice), he was having a thoroughly good time. Paris proved to be quite different from the hotbed of disbelief of which he had heard so much at Rome. Everywhere he went crowds thronged to receive his blessing and kiss his ring. This popular acclaim would prove, in the long run, to be the most significant result of the Pope's trip to Paris. The faith was still alive in French hearts — and a faith focussed, for the first time, in personal devotion to a kindly, deeply spiritual pastor strikingly different from so many of his worldly predecessors and *ancien régime* prelates.

Napoleon had already left for Italy when Pius VII finally set out for Rome in early April 1805. The memory of the happy months he had spent in Paris would sustain him later when, by order of the Emperor he had anointed, the Pope had to spend years isolated from his advisers and the world at large. Frenchmen still loved him. They still believed in his role as their divinely commissioned chief pastor. Pius VII would never forget that. The moving scenes through which he had passed assured him it was true.

The Pope in captivity

Napoleon, on the other hand, drew quite different conclusions from the forbearance of his distinguished guest. Having restored religion in France and shown his regard for Christendom's head by inviting him to grace his coronation, the Emperor expected the Pope to show himself grateful: He must recognize the changed times in which they were living by accepting civil marriage and divorce in France and in Napoleon's newly constituted Italian kingdom. He must concentrate on his spiritual duties and abandon his outmoded preoccupation with his "petty duchy" in Italy. And as temporal ruler of the diminished territories which the Emperor, for reasons of expediency, graciously left to him, the Pope must make common cause against their "heretic enemies," England and Russia. "Your Holiness is Sovereign of Rome," Napoleon wrote the Pope in February 1806, "but I am the Emperor. All my enemies must be his."

The Pope's reply was unyielding. He reminded Napoleon that he was Emperor of France (and an elected one at that), but not of Rome. The successor of Peter was not free to relinquish the sacred patrimony held by his predecessors for a millennium. As a man of peace, he could not be the enemy of any nation, and certainly not of empires as vast as those of Russia and England, with their millions of Catholics who (the Pope remarked pointedly) "enjoy freedom in the practice of their religion and are protected" by their governments.

Enraged at his inability to make use of the Pope for his increasingly grandiose schemes (as he was already doing with the Pope's bishops in France), Napoleon demanded the replacement of Consalvi, whom he held responsible for Rome's insane intransigence. This was a serious miscalculation. The Secretary of State was a lonely voice for moderation. His resignation in June 1806 strengthened the position of the hard-liners in the curia who felt the Pope had already gone too far in accommodating the French Emperor.

Over the next two years, relations worsened as the Pope refused Napoleon's escalating territorial demands in Italy and the appointment of French cardinals (named by the Emperor) up to a third of the whole number. In February 1808 French troops occupied Rome, training their cannons on the Pope's apartment in the Quirinal Palace, and expelling from the Eternal City fifteen of the cardinals considered to be most hostile to French interests.

Still Pius VII refused to be intimidated. He recalled his nuncio in Paris, the compliant Cardinal Caprara, whose efforts at appeasement had included anointing Napoleon King of Italy at Milan in April 1805, approval for France of a new obligatory feast on August 16 of "Saint Napoleon" (an obscure figure of dubious authenticity), and acceptance of a French catechism inculcating "love, respect, obedience, loyalty, military service and taxes for our Emperor Napoleon I." More ominous (because the results were cumulative and long lasting) was the Pope's refusal to institute any more of Napoleon's nominees to French dioceses, as called for in the Concordat.

On May 17, 1809 Napoleon, now master of continental Europe, declared the rest of the Pope's territory annexed to France in order (he explained) to end for all time "the abusive confusion of temporal and spiritual power." On June 10 Pius and his sole remaining adviser, the uncompromising Secretary of State Cardinal Pacca, watched from the Quirinal as the French tricolor replaced the papal flag over the Castel Sant' Angelo, and listened to the proclamation of Rome as "a free Imperial City" with the Pope as its bishop in possession of his palaces and a suitable revenue, but shorn of temporal power.

At once Pius VII signed a bull (prepared long beforehand, as everybody knew, for just such an eventuality) excommunicating all "robbers of the Patrimony of Peter," but not mentioning Napoleon by name. By nightfall copies had been posted on walls throughout Rome — to the fury of the French General Radet, who had already complained to Napoleon that "the Pope rules by moving his finger far more effectively than we with our bayonets."

News of the excommunication reached Napoleon as he was preparing to crush an abortive attempt by the Austrians to overthrow French rule (the Battle of Wagram, July 6, 1809). He feigned indifference, calling the Pope "a raving madman who must be shut up," and ordering the arrest of "Cardinal Pacca and the Pope's other adherents." Emboldened by this ambiguous command, and fearing an insurrection of the Roman citizens, the nervous French authorities spirited Pacca and the Pope out of Rome in a sealed carriage in the early hours of July 6. Following an exhausting month-long journey northwards over the Alps to Grenoble and then back again (in response to Napoleon's angry protest that subordinates had exceeded his instructions), the Pope was finally lodged in the episcopal palace at Savona, on the Italian Riviera twenty-five miles west of Genoa.

There he remained, as the Emperor's guest, guarded from rescue or escape by fourteen hundred soldiers, for almost three years. The municipal prefect attended the Pontiff's daily Mass in the tiny chapel, paid him a daily courtesy visit, read all his mail, and was present whenever the Pope received visitors from the town. Cut off in this way from all advisers and the great world, Pius let it be known that he could no longer function as Pontiff. He would become, once again, "the poor monk Chiaramonti."

While bishops and heads of religious congregations died, the man who alone could invest their successors with the authority of office passed his time in prayer, reading, meditation, and simple tasks such as mending his soutane. All over the world the ordinary business of the Church ground to a halt.

Tightening the screws

Though Napoleon treated his excommunication with contempt, he did what he could to minimize its significance. French Catholics were told that the quarrel between Pope and Emperor was purely political. The Vicar General of the Lyon archdiocese informed his priests: "The French clergy have been deprived of their property, and the Pope of his. This does not affect religious matters, or the Pope's spiritual jurisdiction."

In February 1810 Napoleon ordered the curial cardinals and heads of religious orders to Paris, where they were at first given every honor. This ended abruptly, however, when Napoleon, who in January had obtained from the archdiocesan tribunal in Paris an annulment of his marriage with the still childless Josephine, married the Austrian princess Marie Louise. The French bishops, following Gallican principles, accepted the decision of the Parisian court. Not so Consalvi, who insisted that the case should have been submitted to the Holy See. Thirteen of the cardinals refused to attend the religious ceremony. Enraged at this public rebuff, Napoleon forbade the offenders to wear the insignia of their dignity, and banished them from the capital.

As reports circulated about these "black cardinals," along with copies of the bull of excommunication (eagerly distributed by Napoleon's enemies), the true nature of the quarrel could no longer be concealed. Moreover, Pius rejected the Emperor's repeated pleas (brought to Savona by emissaries thought most likely to sway the isolated Pontiff) that he come himself to Paris, or at least to Avignon. He insisted that he could make no decision regarding the government of the Church without the counsel of advisers of his choice — a demand which Napoleon steadfastly rejected.

By the summer of 1810 twenty-seven French dioceses were vacant — a consequence of the advanced age of so many of the bishops nominated by

Napoleon at the time of the Concordat. Paris had been vacant since June 1808, when Archbishop Belloy had died at the age of ninety-nine.

To break this increasingly embarrassing impasse, Napoleon resolved on a National Council to revive the "ancient custom" (conveniently discovered by a committee of obliging theologians) whereby bishops could be invested with their Sees by the metropolitan (archbishop). The council met in Paris on June 17, 1811, with 140 bishops in attendance from France, and from French-ruled territories in Italy and Germany.

Though many of them felt that the Pope was too unbending, they informed the Emperor that they could not act without papal approval. Furious at this fresh frustration of his plans, Napoleon dissolved the assembly and imprisoned three of its leaders. In the weeks following he managed to browbeat eighty-five of the bishops who remained in Paris into signing a private statement accepting investiture by the metropolitan after a six-month delay. A reconvened session of the council on August 5 approved this measure, but still with the proviso that it required papal approval. A twelve-man deputation (eight bishops and four cardinals, all of them "red," i.e., collaborators with Napoleon) departed at once for Savona to obtain the Pope's consent.

Buoyed by their expressions of loyal support, and impressed by what he was told was the considered opinion of his bishops, and by assurances that the Emperor sincerely desired a just settlement, Pius yielded. Instead of simply ratifying the action of the Council of Paris, however, the Pope on September 20, 1811 issued a new brief emanating from himself as sovereign Pontiff and excluding the bishops of the former papal states (now under French rule) from investiture by the metropolitan.

Incredibly, Napoleon rejected this capitulation. Calculating that he could now dictate terms to the Pope, the Emperor insisted on unconditional surrender. Despite continued pressure by the Emperor's emissaries, Pius VII refused to go beyond the position set forth in his brief.

In February 1812 Napoleon ordered the prefect in Savona to read Pius a harsh letter upbraiding him for damaging the welfare of Christendom, ignoring the advice of his bishops, and refusing to render to Caesar what was rightly his. Since the Pope was unable to see the distinction, clear to any seminarian, between what was dogmatic and thus essential to religion, and what was temporal and thus subject to change, why (the letter asked rhetorically) did he not resign?

Asked by the prefect two days later whether the letter had caused him to change his mind, Pius said it had not. The prefect then informed him that Napoleon regarded the Concordat as abrogated and the powers of the papacy suspended.

Denouement

On May 21, 1812 Napoleon sent orders from Dresden, where he was on his way to invade Russia, that the Pope was to be removed from Savona. Alleging a planned British naval expedition to kidnap the Pontiff, Napoleon ordered that he be transported secretly to Fountainbleau. There the Emperor intended to confront his prisoner personally later in the year, after vanquishing his enemies in the east.

Not until five-thirty in the afternoon of June 9 was Pius told of this plan. He was to depart that night, disguised in the black cassock of an ordinary priest. When no black shoes could be found to fit him, his white satin papal slippers were dyed with black ink.

At midnight the Pope and his personal physician were bundled into a sealed carriage. To avoid detection the wheels were wrapped in cloth, the horses unshod. For ten days the papal apartment was kept in full running order: meals were carried in at the regular hours, the prefect paid his daily call of courtesy.

There followed a frightful twelve-day journey during which the Pope, who suffered agonies from a urinary infection, was thought by his doctor to be dying, and the Abbot of the Benedictine hospice at Mont Cenis gave him the last sacraments. To prevent scenes of popular acclaim, the carriage passed through Lyon at night, and at a gallop. As they bounced over the cobblestones, the doctor tried to alleviate his patient's sufferings by holding his stomach and head. When they reached the country north of the city, the Pope was heard murmuring a prayer for the forgiveness of his tormentor.

Upon arrival at Fountainbleau at midday on June 20, there was a further delay while the custodian of the chateau (who, for reasons of secrecy and contrary to Napoleon's assurances, had not been informed of the visitor's arrival) sent to Paris for instructions. In the weeks following, Pius slowly recovered from his harrowing ordeal.

The Russian campaign, which Napoleon thought would be successfully concluded by autumn, proved a disaster. Half a century later John Henry

Newman would write in his *Grammar of Assent* that Napoleon had asked upon learning of his excommunication by the Pope: "Does he think the world has gone back a thousand years? Does he suppose the arms will fall from the hands of my soldiers?"

In the winter of 1812/1813 the unthinkable happened: "No miracle," Newman wrote, "but a coincidence so special, as rightly to be called a Divine judgment." It was a beaten Emperor who finally confronted Pius VII at Fountainbleau on January 19, 1813.

Napoleon did not act like a beaten man, however. For six days the Pope had to endure threats, cajolery, and violent invective. At one point Napoleon gripped him by the buttons of his cassock, and shoved him back and forth to drive home his point. Gallican bishops and "red" cardinals were brought in to urge agreement to whatever terms the Emperor might propose. They were present on January 25, when Pius VII signed a provisional agreement conceding most of Napoleon's demands. Three days later, tormented by remorse, the Pope sent Napoleon another document which declared his previous agreement "cancelled, abrogated, and annulled" — along with the brief he had issued (only to have the Emperor reject it) at Savona on September 20, 1811.

Ignoring this retraction, Napoleon announced the Pope's agreement to the "Concordat of Fountainbleau" — despite the document's clear statement that it was merely a basis for future negotiations and would not be published. Simultaneously Napoleon ordered *Te Deums* sung in all churches and amnesty for the imprisoned "black" cardinals who had opposed him. Informed of these measures, Pius VII declared: "He has betrayed me."

The Pope's last Secretary of State, Cardinal Pacca, who hastened to Fountainbleau from the fortress in the French Alps where he had languished for the last three and a half years, found Pius in mid-February "bent, pale, emaciated, with his eyes sunk deep into his head, and motionless as though he were dazed." To Pacca's words of admiration for the fortitude with which he had borne his long ordeal, Pius replied sadly: "But in the end I was defiled. Those cardinals — they dragged me to the table and made me sign."

Though the Pope still had eleven months of enforced residence at Fountainbleau, the tide of events was running strongly in his favor. Cheered by the presence of Consalvi, who resumed his former post as Secretary of State, and the other black cardinals, Pius quickly regained his health and good spirits. In March he wrote with his own hand another letter to Napoleon again repudiating the agreement he had signed on January 25. The Emperor kept this letter secret and never acknowledged its receipt.

Napoleon's military position deteriorated steadily during the summer and fall of 1813. In January 1814 he offered the Pope a treaty of peace and restoration of all his territories in Italy. It was too late. On the advice of Consalvi and Pacca, who realized that Napoleon no longer had the power to redraw Europe's boundaries, Pius rejected the offer.

On January 21 Napoleon ordered the Pope's removal to Savona, to prevent his rescue by the enemy armies which were nearing Paris from the east. The journey south was another triumphal progress. The enthusiastic crowds which greeted him everywhere showed how deeply offended Catholics had been by Napoleon's treatment of their chief shepherd.

On April 12, 1814 Napoleon abdicated. Now it was his turn to travel south. He did so in a coach with blinds drawn, passing through Lyon and other major centers by night, to avoid detection by a now hostile populace.

Meanwhile the Pope had reached Italy. He spent Holy Week and Easter (April 10) in Imola and two weeks thereafter in his home town of Cesena, where he baptized and confirmed his grand-nephews and visited the monastery of his monastic profession. On May 24 he reentered Rome after an absence of almost five years. At the Porta del Popolo, the papal coachman took the horses out of the shafts so that the sons of the Roman nobility could draw the carriage up the Corso. As on his first entry into the city fourteen years before, he went first to St. Peter's, to thank God for deliverance from his enemies.

Restoration

Pius VII was in his seventy-second year when he returned to Rome. He would live another nine years. Not surprisingly, given the chaos resulting from the French revolution, it was a time of restoration. He was the only ruler in continental Europe who had withstood Napoleon. Deprived of his territories, without arms, isolated from his advisers, and relying only on spiritual weapons and his own inner strength, the gentle monk on the papal throne bent but never yielded to Napoleon's unceasing drive to dominate the Church.

The lesson was not lost on the European powers who gathered at the Congress of Vienna in September 1814 to redraw the map of Europe. With remarkable diplomatic skill, Consalvi managed to recover for the Pope all his former territories, save the enclave around Avignon in southern France. It was not merely personal modesty, however, but the historical record which caused Consalvi to write afterwards: "Without the immense personal reputation of the Holy Father, and the view that is held about his sanctity and his character, it would have been useless to have made claims, and negotiated, and cajoled; or at least we should have gained very little."

What appeared at the time to be the papacy's gain proved in the end, however, to be a misfortune. Whatever view one takes of such matters as civil marriage and divorce (which seemed so scandalous to churchmen in the nineteenth century), the administrative reforms introduced by Napoleon in the former papal territories had been a real advance.

The restoration of the papal states meant that such matters as taxation, legislative and judicial power, postal service, the police, and even the military (for as a temporal ruler the Pope had a minister of war, a cardinal, responsible for the defense of his realm) were all returned to clerical control. As time went on, the resulting situation was increasingly felt by all save the most diehard supporters of the status quo to be at best anachronistic, at worst ludicrous and unjust.

Small wonder that, as the century progressed, bits and pieces of the papal states threw off the papal yoke until only Rome itself was left. In 1870 this too went. For almost six decades each successive Pope would style himself "the prisoner of the Vatican," while all over the world Catholics were encouraged to demonstrate their loyalty by protesting, in public addresses and mass meetings, against the godless politicians who had "robbed the Holy Father of his just possessions." Only in 1929, did another courageous Pontiff, Pius XI, resolve the impasse by the Lateran Treaties which ceded the erstwhile papal territories to Italy and left the Pope temporal ruler only of Vatican City. The papacy's gain in spiritual freedom and prestige is recognized by all today. Tragically, it took over a century for this recognition to become general.

Within the Church the policy of restoration brought more positive results — though even here it was not all gain. The most immediate result was the restoration of the Society of Jesus by Pius VII on the feast of Saint Ignatius (then celebrated on August 7) 1814. The years following saw an enormous revival of the traditional religious orders — always dependent on the papacy — and the foundation of countless new ones. Not surprisingly France, which had given the Church so many martyrs, provided the firstfruits of this spiritual harvest, demonstrating once again a truth first stated by Tertullian: "As often as we are mown down by you, the more we grow in numbers; the blood of the martyrs is the seed" (*Apology* 50:13).

While the Church benefitted greatly from this revival of religious life, it also paid a price. Too many orders were founded. The exemption of religious orders from episcopal control created administrative and pastoral problems. And the gifts lavished, on the men's orders especially, by lay Catholics impressed by a charismatic founder, or by exaggerated emphasis on the vows taken by religious (as opposed to the "mere promises" of the diocesan clergy — a distinction more important in theory than in fact) often undermined the spiritual health of the recipients.

In theology Gallicanism was finally discredited as first the Catholic people and their priests — followed, as the nineteenth century progressed, by more and more of the bishops — concluded from the experience of the French Revolution and its aftermath that papal power was a stronger guarantor of the Church's liberties than national hierarchies. Pius VII's pontificate assured the triumph of ultramontanism.

The shadow side of this development became manifest at the First Vatican Council in 1870, when the majority, with scant attention to the dogmatic and prudential objections of the minority (who made up in learning what they lacked in numbers), declared the Pope infallible. Sympathy for the popular Pius IX, beset on all sides by enemies imbued with the principles of the French revolution, played a major role in gaining support for the definition.

For almost a century the worst fears of the Vatican I minority seemed to be justified, as the policies of Popes, and those who claimed to speak and act in their names, often displayed the excesses of absolute rulers in all ages, and a kind of "creeping infallibility" was extended to every Roman utterance or document, no matter how minor.

Today we better understand the contemporary judgment of Newman, who reassured a correspondent troubled by alarmist accounts of the Vatican I declaration: "As little as possible was passed at the Council — nothing about the Pope which I have not myself always held," adding: "Perhaps the definition will *limit* the Pope's power." By attaching strict conditions to papal infallibility, the council limited the Pope's dogmatic authority rather than (as is still often assumed) enlarging it.

The historian, assessing the gains and losses from Pius VII's heroic resistance to Napoleon, and the policy of restoration which followed, sees the greatest loss in the inability of Catholics, for almost two centuries, to appropriate the positive elements in the French Revolution. How many Catholics today see anything objectionable in the demand for "liberty, equality, and fraternity"? Who is not embarrassed by the declaration of Pius IX in his 1864 Syllabus of Errors, that the Roman Pontiff can never be reconciled with "progress, liberalism, and modern civilization"? Why did Vatican II's Declaration on Religious Liberty provoke such bitter opposition — at the council itself, and afterwards by the schismatic Archbishop Lefebvre and his powerful supporters in the Roman curia?

History alone supplies the answer: because all these ideas, accepted in varying degrees by Vatican II as just, good, and even necessary, were originally promoted by the embittered enemies of Christianity and the Church. To a degree which was, in the circumstances, remarkable, Chiaramonti as Bishop of Imola and later as Pope was able to distinguish between the Revolution's admissable ideas and the inadmissable policies of its promoters and heirs. His successors were less skilled in reading the signs of the times. For almost two centuries the Church was the loser.

"This beautiful figure"

The modern historian Jacques Droz praises this Pope's "infinite goodness, his total disinterestedness, and his innate tendency to forgive enemies." Never was the last named quality better displayed than in 1817, when he pleaded for mitigation of Napoleon's internment on the island of St. Helena:

> We remember that, after God, it is to him chiefly that is due the re-establishment of religion in the great kingdom of France. The pious and courageous initiative of 1801 has made us long forget and pardon the wrongs that followed. Savona and Fountainbleau were only mistakes due to temper, or the frenzies of human ambition. The Concordat was a healing act, Christian and heroic.

In the summer of 1817 Pius VII had a bad fall and for a time his life was thought to be in danger. He recovered, but his activities thereafter were restricted. On July 6, 1823 he fell again and broke his thigh. Though the doctors pronounced him in no immediate danger, the French minister to the Holy See reported to Paris that with the Pope's fall the next conclave had begun.

For six weeks he lingered, the faithful Consalvi, still a deacon, constantly at his bedside. On the morning of August 20, in the twenty-fourth year of his pontificate and a week after his eighty-first birthday, Pius VII died. He was buried on September 1 in St. Peter's, where his monument may be found in the Clementine Chapel (east of the south transept) on the left of the altar which contains the tomb of Gregory the Great.

The French minister Étienne Pasquier wrote in his memoirs: "His reign was filled with the most terrible vicissitudes; this beautiful figure is one of the most remarkable of the great epoch through which he lived." More recently, the French historian Bertier de Sauvigny, writing at the time of the Second Vatican Council, called the long pontificate of Pius VII "one of the most decisive and significant in history."

CHAPTER TEN

Leo XIII

(1878-1903)

**"*I* **intend to carry out a grand design of statesmanship"* (Leo XIII on the day after his election).

The Holy See did not move willingly into the new world which emerged from the French Revolution and the Napoleonic wars. It was dragged along, kicking and screaming, by inexorable historical forces whose origins we have traced in earlier chapters of this book. Medieval christendom had accepted without question the idea of divine sovereignty over human affairs, mediated by the Pope for the spiritual realm, the Emperor for temporal things. Medieval feudalism was a system of checks and balances in which the different orders of society balanced each other through mutual rights and duties. Bishops, chosen by Kings from their aristocratic subjects, were instituted by the Pope. Many cared little for spiritual matters and valued their offices principally for the income they provided.

The bishops with pastoral concern, however, considered themselves to be not papal functionaries, but shepherds of the Churches entrusted to their care. This reflected the *communio* ecclesiology of the ancient Church (rediscovered in our day by Vatican II), which views the universal Church as a fellowship of local churches. In terms of *realpolitik*, however, what made this episcopal independence possible was the protection extended to bishops by their royal patrons.

The first assault on this system came with the sixteenth-century Reformation, which destroyed Europe's religious unity. The eighteenth-century Enlightenment demolished the remaining intellectual foundations of social unity by exalting reason over authority. National states replaced the old idea of christendom, presided over by Pope and Emperor. The power of the aristocracy, based on land, was replaced by the power of the middle classes, based on trade, manufacture, and industry. The *ancien régime* did not go quietly into history's night, however. It yielded only to force: the French Revolution and the Napoleonic wars.

Following Napoleon's fall representatives of the *ancien régime* attempted its restoration at the Congress of Vienna (1815). They succeeded only on paper. The intellectual legitimation of the old order was gone. Few people believed any longer in the divine right of Kings. It was replaced in the nineteenth century by the absolute sovereignty of national states, enforced by positive law, central administration, and armed force (the police and army). The Kings who remained, or were recalled from exile, were constitutional monarchs, not absolute rulers.

Epochal changes of this magnitude are never well understood at the time. It is hardly surprising, therefore, that the Popes who succeeded Pius VII did not realize that the world had changed forever. They expected that in time people would abandon their revolutionary madness and return to the eternal verities proclaimed by the divinely commissioned teacher of the truth, the Catholic Church. To prepare for that happy day, the Church must itself return to the good old ways. In Roman eyes this meant restoration of the papal states. For without territory, how could the Pope maintain his independence?

The insistence on temporal sovereignty arose not merely from the desire of the Popes to hold on to their "just possessions." Under international law the papacy needed territory to qualify as a treaty partner able to negotiate concordats with other sovereigns for the protection of Church rights. This was especially important in the nineteenth century, when national episcopates no longer had the power possessed by the aristocratic hierarchies of the *ancien régime*.

The French Revolution showed that bishops could not protect the Church's liberty. To regain the right to preach the gospel and carry on pastoral work, the Holy See agreed in the 1801 Concordat with Napoleon to remove the entire French hierarchy and start afresh. A further weakening of episcopal power came two years later, when Napoleon transferred to civil administration the extensive territories ruled by German prince bishops since the Middle Ages. With bishops throughout Europe increasingly subject to state control, only the Pope could defend Church rights. But if the Pope was no longer a territorial sovereign, what government would take him seriously as a treaty partner?

Parallel with these political developments was the rise of ultramontanism in theology: the idea that the Pope is the Church's absolute ruler, who appoints bishops all over the world to carry out his orders. Ultramontanism was bolstered by the growing conviction of Catholics that the papacy was a stronger guarantor of the Church's liberties than national hierarchies.

In the nineteenth century, few Catholics perceived the grave disadvantages of maintaining papal sovereignty over large territories in Italy. It put the Pope on the level of other national rulers. It involved him in bitter quarrels with Italian nationalists. Fearful of threats to their own rule, the successors of Pius VII told Catholics everywhere to submit to their legitimate rulers — even when (as was the case in Ireland, Belgium, and Poland) Catholics were seeking liberation from religious and political oppression. This policy made it impossible for the Popes to deepen the alliance between the papacy and Catholic peoples of Europe which had been forged during the French Revolution.

A man who urged the Pope to stride boldly into the new order was the French priest Felicité de Lamennais. A convert from Enlightenment rationalism and a writer of prophetic power, Lamennais contended throughout the 1820s that the evils of the day could be overcome only by a theocracy, with the Pope as supreme leader of Kings and peoples. Lamennais's ideas received the approbation of Leo XII, Pope from 1823 to 1829, who seems to have considered making their proponent a cardinal.

Lamennais overplayed his hand, however, when he suggested in later publications that the new revolutionary freedoms — separation of Church and state, secularization of education, freedom of the press — offered the Church a unique opportunity to exercise its spiritual mission unhindered by state interference. Gregory XVI, a Camaldolese monk who was Pope from 1831 to 1846 and an uncompromising reactionary (he banned railways from the papal states on the ground that locomotives were "engines of hell") condemned the ideas of Lamennais in the encyclical *Mirari vos* (1832). Exhorting Catholics everywhere to be loyal to their legitimate rulers, the Pope condemned

> the erroneous and absurd opinion — or rather, delirium — that freedom of conscience must be asserted and vindicated for everyone. . . . Prosperous states have perished through this one evil, the immoderate freedom of opinions, licence of speech, and love of novelties. Linked with this is that abominable and detestable freedom of the press which some dare to demand with much noise and zeal.

Lamennais's demand for a theocracy under papal leadership may have been unrealistic. He was correct, however, in saying that after the French Revolution society could be organized only on the basis of individual freedom. *Mirari vos* jettisoned any chance of using the alliance between the Catholic peoples of Europe and the papacy to reshape society. Fearing that any encouragement given to Lamennais's program would only encourage his enemies in Italy, with disastrous consequences for the papal states, the Pope remained loyal to the discredited *ancien régime* and was forced to watch in self-imposed isolation as society was reorganized by anti-Catholic liberals. This fateful policy received its fullest expression under Gregory XVI's successor, Pius IX, whose thirty-two year pontificate (1846-1878) was the longest in history.

Pio Nono

Cardinal Mastai-Ferretti came to the papal throne as a compromise candidate with the reputation of a moderate progressive. As a young priest he had read books on social justice and supported the right of workers to share in the fruits of their labors. This was exceptional in a day in which, as late as 1842, a French priest, the Abbé Luc, could write that poverty was "by no means an evil. It serves as a basis for authority, increases courage, shows up merit, works marvels, and is useful and advantageous for government."

As Bishop of Imola from 1832, Mastai-Ferretti had spoken about the compatibility of Catholicism and democracy. His sympathy with the aspirations of Italian nationalists and their criticisms of the papal states (more the result, however, of a warm heart than a clear head) incurred the displeasure of Gregory XVI. When he made Mastai-Ferretti a cardinal in 1840, the Pope expressed the hope that the red hat would make its wearer more devoted to the Holy See.

The new Pope took the name of Pius in honor of the man who, as Bishop of Imola, had tried to reconcile Catholicism and democracy in his Christmas sermon of 1797; who had been imprisoned by Napoleon; and who, on his return to Rome had befriended Mastai-Ferretti before his ordination to the priesthood in 1819.

Pius IX's election was warmly welcomed by progressives throughout Europe, including non-Catholics, as the dawn of a new age. Their optimism appeared justified when the new Pope proclaimed amnesty for more than a thousand prisoners in the papal states and introduced constitutional and administrative reforms, including the appointment of a lay Prime Minister.

These measures displeased the Austrian Prime Minister Metternich, a leader of European conservatism since the Congress of Vienna and an unbending Catholic of the old school.

Each day the Pope shows himself lacking in any practical sense [*Metternich wrote early in Pius IX's pontificate*]. Warm of heart and weak of intellect, he has allowed himself to be taken in and ensnared, since assuming the tiara, in a net from which he no longer knows how to disentangle himself; and if matters follow their natural course, he will be driven out of Rome.

Metternich's prophecy was fulfilled in 1848, the year of revolutions throughout Europe. The papal Prime Minister, Count Pellegrino Rossi, was murdered as he entered the legislative chamber at Rome on November 15. The Pope was forced to flee in disguise. He returned seventeen months later, under the protection of French troops, as the determined opponent of all democratic and liberal ideas. For the rest of his life, Pius IX was surrounded by advisers who told him that there was a direct connection between the overthrow of legitimate authority in the French Revolution and the murder of Count Rossi together with the indignities to which the Vicar of Christ had been subjected by men infected with the falsehoods that had poisoned social life ever since 1789.

Could the Pope remain silent while these dangerous ideas continued their destructive work? A man who urged that he could not was the thirty-nine-year old Archbishop of Perugia, Gioacchino Pecci (the future Pope Leo XIII). In 1849 Pecci proposed that the Pope issue a comprehensive list of modern errors. The idea bore fruit ten years later, when the Pope began a five-year process of consultation. This produced the encyclical *Quanta cura*, issued on December 8, 1864, which condemned the leading errors of the day.

Appended to the Pope's letter was a list (signed by the Secretary of State Cardinal Antonelli) of eighty false ideas, and identifying the previous papal document in which each one had been condemned. This was the famous Syllabus of Errors. It culminated in the proposition (which like the previous seventy-nine was rejected as erroneous) that "the Roman Pontiff can and ought to reconcile and harmonize himself with progress, with liberalism, and with modern civilization."

The Syllabus was a public relations disaster. The Church's enemies seized on it with glee as final proof that the Pope was completely out of touch. Catholics who had been striving for decades to build on all that was good and true in progress, liberalism, and modern civilization felt betrayed. The only people who welcomed the Syllabus were reactionary Catholics, like the French journalist Veuillot, who considered monarchy the only governmental form compatible with Catholicism, and contended that "the parliamentary system rests on an heretical principle."

As late as 1930, when it had long been clear that the propositions had to be taken in their historical context (the "liberalism" condemned by the Pope, for instance, was only the kind which had led to the murder of his Prime Minister), Abbot Cuthbert Butler called the final proposition of the Syllabus, with characteristic English understatement, "singularly unfortunate."

When the Vatican Council proclaimed papal infallibility six years later, few people outside the small circle of learned theologians realized how few papal pronouncements fell within the scope of the definition. For decades the infallibility decree was used to justify the "creeping infallibility" noted at the end of the preceding chapter.

The Vatican Council ended abruptly in July 1870 when French troops, whose presence was the Pope's sole defense against the loss of his remaining territories to Italian nationalists, were withdrawn from the Eternal City. Governmental power passed at once to nationalist hands, and the Pope went into self-imposed seclusion as the "prisoner of the Vatican." Pius IX's isolation from the contemporary world was thus complete.

In the hearts of Catholics everywhere, however, he had become, more than all the Popes before him, their beloved "Holy Father." Though Pius IX personally sought the infallibility definition, and did not hesitate to intimidate those who opposed it, prior to 1860 the escalation of papal power had come not from Rome, but from the Catholic people (laity and lower clergy) demanding that the Pope defend them against anti-Catholic forces in society. As Alexis de Tocqueville wrote in 1856: "The faithful were more influential than the Pope in making him the church's absolute ruler. Rome's attitude was more a result of this development than its cause."

The nineteenth-century papacy would never have achieved the position it did, however, without Pius IX's winning personality. The papal personality cult which we know today did not exist prior to 1846. A priest visiting Rome in 1842 noted that men did not even raise their hats to the Pope when he passed on the street. Pio Nono (to give him the name by which he is most often known) impressed people with his charm and deep if simple piety. Though irascible and easily influenced by the last person he had talked to, he had a sense of humor remiscent of John XXIII in our own day. When some visiting Anglican clergymen asked his benediction, he responded with the blessing of incense at

Mass: "May you be blessed by him in whose honor you are to be burned."

John Henry Newman, who had no great opinion of the Pope's intelligence or wisdom, expressed the view of many when he wrote:

> His personal presence was of a kind that no one could withstand. The main cause of his popularity was the magic of his presence . . . his uncompromising faith, his courage, the graceful mingling in him of the human and the divine, the humor, the wit, the playfulness with which he tempered his severity, his naturalness, and then his true eloquence.

There was even something impressive about Pio Nono's consistent rejection of the modern world. Hand in hand with this unbending counter-culturalism went tremendous growth, during his long pontificate, in popular piety and priestly spirituality (encouraged by the Pope's personal example), and in missionary outreach. In thirty-two years Pius IX established 206 new dioceses and apostolic vicariates (missionary territories entrusted to a bishop).

As the shadows of the longest pontificate in history lengthened, however, an undeniable air of stagnation surrounded the aging "prisoner of the Vatican." Visiting Rome in 1876, the redoubtable champion of papal infallibility, Cardinal Manning, noted:

> Six years have passed over the Holy See since 1870, and its organization has been dying out year after year. All this darkness, confusion, depression, with inactivity and illness, made me understand the *Tristis est anima mea usque ad mortem* ["My soul is sorrowful even unto death" — Jesus' words in the garden of Gethsemane: Mk 14:34].

The Pope himself recognized that he had played out his hand. Shortly before his death on February 7, 1878 Pius IX is reported to have said:

> I can see that everything has changed. My system and my policies have had their day, but I am too old to change my course. That will be the task of my successor.

The conclave which assembled on February 19 to select him was the shortest in history up to that time. On the third ballot the cardinals chose Cardinal Pecci, the *camerlengo* in charge of their meeting. He took the name of Leo in honor of the Pope who had befriended him as a young student at Rome a half-century before.

Admirers of Pius IX who were troubled by reports of the new Pope's greater flexibility noted with satisfaction that he was sixty-eight years of age, noticeably frail, and in delicate health. If the Sacred College had made a mistake, it could surely be corrected before too many concessions were made to a world gone mad.

Youthful ambition

The new Pontiff had been born on March 2, 1810 in the remote mountain village of Carpineto, some seventy miles south of Rome in the papal enclave of Benevento, as the eighth child and sixth son of Ludovico Pecci and Anna Prosperi Buzi. They gave him the baptismal name Gioacchino Vincenzo (Joachim Vincent). The Peccis were an old patrician family who had left their native Siena in the sixteenth century to settle in papal territory to the south. Joachim's father was proud to be called "Count" by the local peasants. The "Palazzo" which accommodated his large family was a modest two-storey building, six windows wide across the front.

From childhood on Joachim was keenly aware that his family had "come down in the world." His dearest desire, repeatedly expressed in youthful letters which were published while he was Pope, was to restore the family name and honor. The first document to bear his signature as Pope would be a letter informing his "dearest brothers" of his election to the papacy "this morning." As Pope he revived the court ceremonial (discontinued by Pius IX in 1870 as a sign of mourning for the end of the papal states) which required mounted members of the Noble Guard to accompany his daily carriage drives through the Vatican gardens.

At the age of seven, Joachim was sent to the Jesuit boarding school in Viterbo. His mother wanted him to be a priest. That meant receiving tonsure and putting on a cassock — not unusual in Italy, where until past the middle of this century one could still see little boys playing soccer in cassocks and clerical collars. Joachim balked. In 1824, however, when his mother was dying, he yielded. Before her death Anna Pecci was consoled by the sight of her fourteen-year-old son in cassock and biretta. The future Pope was not the first young man, nor would he be the last, to become a priest to fulfil a mother's wish rather than an inner call.

Once embarked on this path, however, Joachim never wavered. (The identity crisis had not yet been discovered. And lifelong commitments, undertaken even in youth, were considered as normal as their abandonment in middle life, or later, is today.) In the more than two hundred published letters written by Joachim Pecci prior to his ordination as priest, there is, however, not a single reference to vocation, to ascetical practices, to the motto of his Jesuit teachers *Ad majorem Dei gloriam* (to do all "for the greater glory of God"), to a desire to save souls. Through all the letters (affectionate ones to his brothers, more formal communications to his widowed father) runs one constant theme: to have a priestly career which would bring honor to his family, winning for the Pecci name the renown too long withheld by an ungrateful world.

To attain this goal the young Pecci was prepared to spend lavishly the only capital he possessed: his wits. While still a schoolboy at Viterbo he mastered Latin so fully that it became his first language, Italian almost a dialect. This did not prevent his learning by heart most of Dante's *Divine Comedy*. He could still recite long passages as Pope. In the closing months of his long life, he was working on Latin verse of his own composition.

From the age of fifteen, Joachim continued his education with the Jesuits at the Collegio Romana. His burning wish was to enter the Roman academy for Ecclesiastical Nobles, the elite training school for future papal diplomats and curial officials. For that he needed an acceptable pedigree and powerful patrons. From his meager financial resources he commissioned genealogical research which produced a family tree attesting a sufficient number of noble ancestors. It may still be seen in the "Palazzo Pecci" in Carpineto.

Patrons were more difficult to come by. He gradually acquired them by inviting cardinals, prelates, and professors to witness his success in the academic disputations for which he prepared through ceaseless study even during the heat of the Roman summer, when his teachers and fellow students relaxed in the cooler mountain air.

Gradually the great Roman world became aware of the brilliant young student with his polished manners and ingratiating ways. Admitted to the Noble Academy at the age of twenty-two, he began to prepare for a diplomatic career. His letters from this period read like diplomatic dispatches: reports of visiting princes, a cholera epidemic, horse races, the Roman carnival, the deaths of high prelates, cardinals, and popes (his first patron Leo XII in 1829, Pius VIII the year following), and rumors about the elections of their successors, the cowardice of papal functionaries. Never does Pecci touch on matters of deeper concern to the Church of his day: the growing movement for Italian unity, the chaotic administration of the papal states, Church-state relations, social justice.

The young seminarian's joy was unbounded when Pope Gregory XVI made him a monsignor in the autumn of 1837, prior to his ordination as a priest. Prospects of a brilliant career unfolded before him. Letters written just before his ordination on the last day of the year, however, reflect a changed mood. For the first time he realized that the priesthood was not a career but a service. "This world offers no happiness sufficient to satisfy the heart's desires," he wrote a cardinal who had befriended him. He would like to leave the world and devote himself wholly to spiritual things. On his ordination day he experienced a deep sense of his unworthiness.

This sudden accession of piety proved short lived. Learning that he was being considered as papal governor of Benevento (precisely the kind of position for which he had worked so tirelessly for years), he was momentarily depressed. When the appointment came, however, Pecci's mood changed again. He wrote home in excitement that the papal guards now saluted him "as if I were a prince."

After only three years at Benevento, he was made papal governor of Perugia, where he built roads, founded a savings bank for farmers, and won the affection of the populace. His management of the visit of Gregory XVI to Perugia so impressed the aged pontiff that he promised to remember his young protégé upon returning to Rome. The Pope was as good as his word. In January 1843, a month short of his thirty-third birthday, Pecci became a titular archbishop and nuncio to Belgium. He had his portrait painted in the robes of his new dignity and sent it to Carpineto to grace the walls of his ancestral home.

In Belgium, a bastion of "liberal Catholicism" viewed by Rome with deep mistrust, the young nuncio was quickly out of his depth. Pecci got embroiled in a controversy over the Catholic University of Louvain, newly refounded by the bishops in 1834, and had to be recalled in May 1846. The Pope consoled him by sending word of his appointment as Bishop of Perugia, hinting that a cardinal's hat was only a matter of time.

On his way back to Rome, Pecci visited England. There word reached him of the Pontiff's death on June 1. This news, coming on top of his diplomatic failure, was a bitter blow. Not many years before, Pecci had written his brother: "In Rome protection is one of the indispensable prerequisites for a career." Now he was naked to his enemies. To be, at age thirty-six, an Italian diocesan bishop among some three hundred others, was hardly the position Pecci had worked so hard to achieve. How long would his exile in Perugia last?

Growth in exile

Pecci had ample time to ponder this question. He would remain in Perugia for thirty-two years. Those years changed him, as exile and disappointment had changed the patriarch Jacob from the youthful deceiver fleeing his brother's vengeance to the man who could say in the fullness of years: "LORD . . . I am not worthy of the least of all the steadfast love and all the faithfulness that you have shown to your servant, for with only my staff I crossed this Jordan; and now I have become two companies" (Gen 32:9-10).

Pecci was a conscientious pastor and efficient administrator. He showed special concern for the education of his seminarians, who shared part of his episcopal palace. He liked to read aloud to them from Dante's works, previously banned from the seminary. Influenced by his Jesuit brother, Joseph, who taught at the seminary until 1848, he founded the Academy of St. Thomas in 1859 to promote the renewal of Thomism, still virgin territory to most Catholics. (In 1846 John Henry Newman, preparing at Rome for ordination as a Catholic priest, had been surprised to find his teachers ignorant of both Aristotle and Saint Thomas.)

In 1853 Pecci received the cardinal's hat promised him seven years before. This did not prevent Pius IX's Secretary of State, the reactionary Cardinal Antonelli (like Consalvi a deacon to the end of his life, and unlike him a nepotist with an illegitimate daughter who used his position to enrich himself and his family), from placing Pecci on his blacklist of prelates considered too open to the spirit of the age. Antonelli blocked Pecci's attempt to escape from Perugia by becoming Bishop of Albano, one of the suburbican Sees surrounding Rome still reserved for the highest of the three ranks of cardinals.

A subsequent basis for Antonelli's suspicions, however slender, might be seen in pastoral letters issued by Pecci between 1874 and 1877 advocating reconciliation between the Church and the positive elements of contemporary culture. These advocated the reform of criminal justice and praised in romantic terms the achievements of the industrial revolution such as the lightning rod, telephone, and steam engine. Only later did Pecci learn from others about the dark side of nineteenth-century industry. His only personal experience in this area (and of parliamentary government as well) came from his three years in Belgium, with brief visits to the Rhineland and England.

Pecci's relationship with Pius IX is unclear. In September 1877, following Antonelli's death the previous November, the 85-year-old Pontiff named Pecci *camerlengo* (chamberlain) of the Roman Church, thus placing in his hands the organization of the next conclave. While the appointment indicated confidence in Pecci's administrative abilities, it may also have been intended to reduce his chances of succeeding to the papacy, since there was a tradition that the conclave did not elect the *camerlengo*.

When this tradition was breached five months later, diehards opposed to the new Pope claimed that Pius IX had said towards the end of his life: "Dying is a small matter. What worries me is that I shall have as my successor Cardinal Pecci, who would ruin the church, if that were possible, by his statesmanship and his diplomacy."

The quotation rests on the authority of witnesses hostile to Leo. Solidly attested, on the other hand, is Leo's statement on the day after his election to Cardinal Franchi, whom he would soon appoint Secretary of State: "I intend to carry out a grand design of statesmanship."

A Vatican prisoner still

The grand design got off to a bad start. To show his goodwill, Leo wanted to give his first papal blessing *Urbi et Orbi* (to the city and the world) from the outside loggia of St. Peter's. Though merely symbolic, a public blessing would have been a break with the practice of Pio Nono, who since 1870 had immured himself within the Vatican to protest the takeover of Rome by Italian nationalists. Anticipating the possibility of a conciliatory gesture, the authorities had ordered the soldiers in the piazza to present arms, if the Pope should appear on the balcony above.

It was not to be. Cardinal Bartolini, the hard-line master of ceremonies at the conclave, announced that a public appearance was out of the question. To make sure that his advice was followed, Bartolini, in true Roman fashion, hid the key to the loggia door. Leo had to impart his blessing from the balcony inside St. Peter's Basilica.

(This little drama would be repeated, with different actors, at the election of Leo's successor, Pius X, on August 4, 1903. And on October 16, 1978, when the newly elected Pope John Paul II succeeded in breaking tradition by delivering a brief speech in Italian before the blessing *Urbi et Orbi*, television viewers round the world heard the voice of a prelate near the Pope saying with obvious displeasure: "*Basta* — enough." Rome is, in more senses than one, the Eternal City.)

Leo sent the customary diplomatic notifications of his election to governments outside Italy, expressing the Holy See's desire for good relations. He ignored the Italian authorities, whom he considered usurpers. His coronation on March 3, 1878 took place not in St. Peter's (since the Italian government said it could not guarantee maintenance of good order), but in the Sistine Chapel.

On April 21 Leo published his first encyclical, *Inscrutabili Dei*. This ascribed all the evils of modern society to rebellion against the truth and its divinely commissioned teacher, the Catholic Church. Sounding a theme he would repeat in many future encyclicals, the Pope said that the Church, and in particular the Holy See, had been the constant promoter of culture and progress, in Italy especially, and not their foe — as charged by the Church's enemies. Not from any desire for honor or power, but simply for reasons of conscience and to fulfill his duty to society, the Pope must continue to demand the restoration of his stolen territories and sovereignty. The moderate Italian journal *Riformi* commented: "The form is sweet, but the substance is absolute, hard, intransigent."

Relations between the papacy and the kingdom of Italy would remain tense throughout Leo's twenty-five-year pontificate. There were a number of attempts behind the scenes to achieve a rapprochement through third parties. They foundered on the opposition of embittered hard-liners on both sides. Powerful members of the Roman curia resisted the Pope's willingness to consider acceptance of sovereignty over a small territory in and around Rome and insisted on full restitution of the papal states. On the Italian side nationalists, many of them fiercely anti-Catholic freemasons, were unwilling to consider reconciliation with the age old foe on any basis.

Isolated in the Vatican, Leo became obsessed with the idea that a "masonic conspiracy" was responsible for all the Church's woes. He even gave credence to the writings of a pseudonymous "Leo Taxil" about a satanic "masonic pope." When Taxil was exposed as a forger in 1896, a papal commission of inquiry tried to cover the Pope's embarrassment by assigning responsibility to gullible lay Catholics in France and Germany — thus provoking resentment from some of the Pope's most devoted adherents.

The Vatican and the Quirinal (formerly the Pope's Roman residence, after 1870 the seat of the Italian government) carried on sporadic warfare by means of celebrations, staged with all the drama of which Italians are capable, of anniversaries significant to the two sides: the centenary of Voltaire's birth in 1878, the dedication of a Garibaldi monument (placed ostentatiously within sight of the Vatican) in 1895, and in the same year the twenty-fifth anniversary of the nationalist takeover of Rome. Counter-demonstrations by Catholics included Leo's golden anniversary of priesthood in 1887, dedication of the year 1890 to the founder of the papal state, Gregory the Great (elected Pope in 590), and the Holy Year of 1900.

The Pope appeared at these and numerous other celebrations borne aloft on the *sedia gestatoria* accompanied by all the pomp of a royal court. With considerable skill Leo used these occasions to demonstrate his popularity with Catholics throughout the world, while complaining to the crowds of pilgrims in attendance of his mistreatment by the Italian authorities. These carefully staged demonstrations deepened both government resentment and the sympathy of the faithful for their beleaguered Holy Father.

The most overt act of hostility in this protracted cold war came during the night of July 12-13, 1881 when a vast crowd of the faithful accompanied the body of Pius IX from St. Peter's to the Basilica of St. Lawrence, designated by the late Pope as his final resting place. Nationalist demonstrators attacked the procession, threw mud at the coffin, and tried to throw it into the Tiber. It took the police three hours to restore order.

Fearing that this attack on the deceased Pontiff presaged an assault on his living successor, Leo XIII opened secret negotiations in August 1881 with the Austrian Emperor Franz Josef for transfer of residence to Trent or Salzburg (both in Austrian territory). The result was a standoff. The Emperor said that he would welcome the Pope (though not his large court of prelates, monsignors, and other hangers on); but he could do nothing to jeopardize his good relations with Italy — whose King Umberto (to Leo's chagrin) was received with high honors during a state visit to Vienna in October 1881. Thanking the Austrian Emperor for his offer of hospitality, the Pope said he would never leave Rome unless forced to it by his enemies.

Throughout his pontificate Leo maintained the decree *Non expedit* ("it is not expedient") issued by Pius IX in 1871 forbidding Catholics to take part in national elections either as candidates or voters. (Participation in local elections was permitted.) Though the prohibition was widely ignored, it had the effect of excluding Italian Catholics from influence on the political life of their country. Efforts to found a Catholic party in Italy foundered on the opposition of the Roman curia, which feared dependence on laypeople not subject to hierarchical control.

As we shall see below, Leo's steadfast refusal to be reconciled with the new order in Italy was in marked contrast to his efforts for improvement of Church-state relations elsewhere. The reasons for this inconsistency must be sought in his personal background, and his situation as Pope. Leo had been born in the papal states and had served all his priestly life under Popes who rejected all compromise. Well into the present century, powerful members of the Roman curia viewed Italy as a geographical entity only and thought the papal states would be restored. As Pope, therefore, Leo had to defend himself against critics in his own entourage who charged him with excessive leniency toward an upstart kingdom which was too artificial to last.

It is unfair, therefore, to judge Leo's "grand design of statesmanship" by the impasse in Italy. Elsewhere there was genuine progress.

Recognizing civil autonomy

This began only three years into the pontificate with the encyclical *Diuturnum*, issued on June 29, 1881. It was occasioned by the assassination in March of the Russian Czar Alexander II, who had attempted to carry out a revolution from above, liberating the serfs and introducing other reforms. He was killed on the day he signed a new liberal constitution.

One could only expect such outrages, the Pope commented, as long as people disregarded the Church's teaching about the rights of rulers and the duties of subjects. The Enlightenment philosophers had said that governmental power derived from the people. The Church insisted, on the other hand, that all power came from God. In a crucial advance over previous papal teaching the Pope added, however, that the citizens of a state had the right to determine how power should be exercised, by giving themselves the kind of government they desired.

Leo further developed this position four years later in the encyclical *Immortale Dei* (November 1, 1885). People would respect constituted authority, the Pope wrote, only

> when they are convinced that their rulers hold authority from God, and feel that it is a matter of justice and duty to obey them, and to show them reverence and fealty, united to a love not unlike that which children show their parents. . . . The right to rule is not

> necessarily, however, bound up with any special form of government. . . . The Almighty has appointed the charge of the human race between two powers, the ecclesiastical and the civil, the one being set over divine, the other over human things. Each in its kind is supreme, each has its fixed limits within which it is contained. . . .

The Pope contrasted this true doctrine with the widely accepted false opinion, destructive alike of individual happiness and social welfare,

> that sovereignty resides in the multitude, and this without any reference to God . . . [and] that princes are nothing more than delegates chosen to carry out the will of the people; whence it necessarily follows that all things are as changeable as the will of the people, so that risk of public disturbance is ever hanging over our heads. . . . In a society grounded upon such maxims, all government is nothing more nor less than the will of the people, and the people, being under the power of itself alone, is alone its ruler. . . . The authority of God is passed over in silence, just as if there were no God, or as if he cared nothing for human society.

A state rightly governed, on the other hand, was one in which the civil authority, acknowledging the rule of God, the source of all authority, did all in its power to apply divine law to human society, including the obligation of worship. It was a grave error to hold that the state was not obligated to profess any religion,

> or to inquire which of the very many religious is the only true one; or to prefer one religion to all the rest . . . but on the contrary, is bound to grant equal rights to every creed, so that public order may not be disturbed. . . . And it is a part of this theory that all questions that concern religion are to be referred to private judgment; that everyone is to be free to follow whatever religion he prefers, or none at all if he disapprove of all.

The consequence of such religious freedom, the Pope wrote, was "the same thing as atheism, however it may differ from it in name."

The doctrine expounded in *Immortale Dei* would remain the official teaching of the Catholic Church on Church-state relations until 1965, when it was modified by Vatican II's Declaration on Religious Liberty. This replaced Leo XIII's teaching that it was the duty of the civil power to promote the cause of "true religion" (i.e., the Catholic Church) with the statement that "the human person has a right to religious freedom."

In nineteenth-century Europe religious freedom meant either religious indifference or outright hostility to religion ("freedom from religion"). Hence Leo's statement that religious freedom was "the same thing as atheism" caused little comment. Not so his teaching about the autonomy of the civil power. This was a clear departure from the medieval "two swords" theory, which held that the temporal power was subject to the spiritual power. (Cf. pp. 92 and 117 above.) This would provoke a protest from traditionalist Catholics, in France especially, as violent as the rejection of Vatican II by their ideological heirs today.

Success in Germany

Leo inherited a major crisis in Germany. Formerly a patchwork of loosely allied kingdoms and principalities, Germany had organized itself in 1871 under the Prussian "Iron Chancellor" Otto von Bismarck into a federally structured Reich dominated by its largest state, Prussia. German liberals (who considered religion a purely private affair) and conservative Protestants (the self-appointed guardians of the torch of authentic German culture lit by Martin Luther) viewed Catholics with suspicion. Too often, it seemed, their first loyalty was to a foreign sovereign in Rome. Suspect too was Catholics' preference for a "Greater Reich" (including Catholic Austria) as opposed to Bismarck's "Small Reich" dominated by Protestant Prussia.

The proclamation of the Pope's universal primacy and infallibility in 1870 deepened these suspicions. Bismarck contended that the Vatican I decrees had made the once proud German bishops (many of whom, until 1803, had been the civil as well as spiritual rulers of their dioceses), into mere lackeys of the Pope. At the council most of the German bishops had belonged to the minority (superior in theological learning though not in numbers) who opposed the infallibility definition — some for theological reasons, others because they considered it inopportune or unnecessary. Once it had been promulgated, however, they accepted the Church's decision.

A small group of Catholic intellectuals in Germany, Switzerland, and Austria refused to do so and formed the schismatical Old Catholic Church. The papal excommunication which inevitably followed emptied the lecture halls of Old Catholic theology professors (and the classrooms of schoolteachers who followed their lead), since Catholic students refused to attend the classes of teachers censured by the Church.

Claiming that the civil rights of German citizens had been violated, Bismarck retaliated with a series of harsh anti-Catholic laws. These expelled most religious orders and subjected all aspects of Church life to state control: the appointment of bishops and parish priests, seminaries, and Catholic schools. When the bishops refused to comply, they were ordered to pay heavy fines. Five of the eleven Catholic bishops in Prussia went to jail.

The resulting "Kulturkampf," as it was called, proved counter-productive. German Catholics rallied round their bishops and celebrated them as martyrs. In the large north German diocese of Münster, for instance (where Catholics boast, even today, "We're staying Catholic, no matter what they do in Rome"), Bishop Brinkmann refused to pay his fine. When his furniture was auctioned in the cathedral square to settle the debt, the purchasers carried it back into the bishop's house from which it had just been removed. The authorities were not amused.

Bismarck's anti-Church laws were opposed in parliament by the Center Party, founded in 1870 under a brilliant political tactician, Ludwig Windhorst, to protect Catholic interests. Even Protestants felt there was justice in the Center's plea that the constitutional rights of Catholics were being violated. Support from this quarter dwindled, however, when Pius IX wrote Kaiser Wilhelm I in August 1874 protesting his government's laws and claiming that "anyone who has been baptized belongs in some way to the Pope" — an argument hardly calculated to enlist the sympathy of the letter's Protestant recipient.

By the time of Pius IX's death in 1878 the two sides had fought to a standstill. In Prussia a number of dioceses had no resident bishop, and over a thousand parishes were without a pastor. The houses of Jesuits and of other religious orders were closed and their residents exiled. The new Pope was eager to find a way out of the impasse. To regain liberty for the Church to pursue its spiritual mission, Leo was willing to make broad concessions. He also looked forward to an agreement with Europe's leading conservative statesman, whose anti-revolutionary policies the Pope admired as the best defense against socialism. A treaty with the German Reich would show the papacy's enemies, in Italy especially, that the sovereign Pontiff remained a force to be reckoned with.

In the letter informing Kaiser Wilhelm of his election to the papacy, therefore, Leo expressed his desire to do all in his power to end the conflict.

This was a godsend to Bismarck. He too wanted peace, but not at any price: "We'll never go to Canossa," the Chancellor had said, recalling the German Emperor who had done so eight centuries before. (See p. 82 above.) With the Pope now in the role of petitioner, Bismarck proceeded to test the Church's readiness for concessions while skillfully avoiding commitments himself.

Negotiations dragged on for nine years (1878-1887). At no time did Bismarck consider the bilateral treaty envisioned by the Pope. The Chancellor would end the conflict unilaterally, by modifying German laws. Agreement on acceptable terms was rendered difficult by diverging views on both sides. Bismarck had to consider the conflicting views of his fellow politicians and the imperial court. The Pope had to contend with the German bishops, the Center Party, and the nuncios in Munich and Vienna.

Leo never grasped the role of a Catholic political party, free of Church control. When he tried to make Bismarck more amenable to Church demands by suggesting that the Center support the Chancellor's request for increased military expenditures, the Center politicians, with the support of the German bishops, said that they were not subject to ecclesiastical control in purely political matters.

A breakthrough came in 1885-1886. True to the policy adopted by Pius VII in the 1801 Concordat with Napoleon, of sacrificing individuals for the sake of principles, Leo requested the resignation of the two German archbishops most offensive to Bismarck because of their leadership in the Kulturkampf: Melchers of Cologne and Ledóchowski of Gnesen-Posen (who for a decade had administered their dioceses from exile). Both became curial cardinals and were replaced by prelates more acceptable to the government. Bismarck responded by asking Leo to mediate his dispute with Spain over ownership of the Caroline Islands in the Pacific — and was rewarded for this recognition of the Pope's sovereignty by the papal "Order of Christ."

The final settlement was negotiated secretly between emissaries of the Pope and Chancellor, with all other parties excluded. Bismarck abandoned the most objectionable restrictions on Church freedom: control of seminaries, the appointment of bishops, prohibition of religious orders. To the dismay of the German bishops and the Center party (which had borne the heat and burden of the struggle), Leo conceded state supervision of Catholic schools, state consultation in the appointment of parish pastors, obligatory civil marriage (prior to the Church ceremony), continued prohibition of political topics in the pulpit and of the ban on Jesuits (revoked only in 1917).

Resentful of their exclusion from the final negotiations, the German bishops, and even more the Center politicians, complained that the Pope had yielded too much. Bismarck's critics raised the same charge against him. The sequel showed, however, that German Catholicism possessed a vigor which in practice did much to nullify the continuing restrictions on Church freedom.

Using his favorite language, Leo called the settlement *aditus ad pacem* ("an approach to peace"), suggesting that he expected further concessions to match his own. These were never forthcoming. Disappointment on this score was a factor in turning the Pope's attention to the position of Catholics in Germany's neighbor, France.

Failure in France

There is no clearer example of the Church's capacity for renewal following disaster than nineteenth-century France. As we saw in the previous chapter, the Church of the *ancien régime* was outwardly powerful, but inwardly weak. Its aristocratic prelates were isolated from their people and clergy. It was top-heavy with religious of both sexes, far more than needed to serve the Church's pastoral needs. Their numbers peaked in 1765. Many of them led comfortable lives whose spiritual or social value was not easy to perceive. When the revolutionary storm broke over the rotten fabric of this *ancien régime* Church, much of it collapsed.

In 1878, the year of Leo XIII's election to the papacy, a survey of the French Church by the Revolution's heirs (then in firm control of the French Republic) presented an astonishing picture. Membership in religious orders (many of them new foundations) almost equaled that in 1765. There were over 30,000 male religious — three times the number of diocesan priests — including 3,350 Jesuits. The women's orders numbered almost 128,000. They maintained some 16,500 schools for girls. Under the provisions of the 1801 Concordat (still in force) most of these orders — for both men and women — were illegal.

Resentful of the Church influence reflected in these figures, successive French governments sought to reduce the Church's dominant role in education and charitable works. Civil prefects kept a vigilant eye on religious processions, sermons, sodalities, Church courts, hospitals, and even cemeteries. In 1882 the cardinals of Paris and Rouen protested that the government had proposed more than twenty laws to control the Church. In a fiery speech in the Chamber Deputies on November 5, 1883 the sole clerical member, Bishop Freppel of Angers, accused the Church's foes of promoting social division:

Separation — that is your goal. Yesterday separation of church and school; today separation of parish and town; tomorrow separation of church and state. [*Wild applause from the left.*] Always and everywhere, separation.

Though left-wing politicians pressed for abrogation of the Concordat, the government was never willing to take this ultimate step. They feared that the financial saving to French taxpayers (who continued to pay clergy salaries) would be offset by Catholic resentment of a measure that could cast the clergy in the role of martyrs. Through the reports of their prefects the government was well aware of widespread monarchist sentiment among Catholics. The authorities also knew, however, that a sizable minority of clergy accepted the ideas of Lamennais and saw the new world of liberty, equality, and fraternity as an opportunity for the Church. Most important of all, the Concordat gave the government a crucial measure of Church control: the right to negotiate with the Church about the selection of bishops. By nominating candidates of moderate views, the republic could ensure that the clergy would be governed by men more interested in collaboration than confrontation.

The "separation of church and school" referred to by Bishop Freppel began with a law passed in March 1882 secularizing all elementary schools in France. The Minister of Education moderated this administratively by introducing a "conscience clause" for Catholic teachers. The government also lost no opportunity to remind the Pope's Secretary of State of its protection for Catholic missionaries in the French overseas colonies.

The most famous among them was Charles de Lavigerie. Professor of church history at the Sorbonne at twenty-nine (in 1854), he became Bishop of Nancy in 1863, and Archbishop of Algiers in 1867. There he founded the missionary order of White Fathers. A man of unusual ability and vision, he urged missionaries to respect the positive values of native culture and pagan religion. In 1882 Leo XIII made Lavigerie a cardinal. His prestige among his countrymen made Lavigerie uniquely qualified to serve as an agent of peace in France's protracted religious strife.

In 1890 Cardinal Rampolla, the ablest of Leo XIII's advisers and Secretary of State since 1887, urged Lavigerie to make a public appeal for French Catholics to support their government. Fearful of jeopardizing support for his missions, Lavigerie hesitated. It took five separate requests from Rome before Lavigerie agreed in October 1890 to appeal to French Catholics on the Pope's behalf.

On November 12, 1890, toasting the French navy (a hotbed of monarchism) at a dinner in Algiers, Lavigerie urged Catholics to "rally" to the support of the republic, assuring them that they "would not encounter disapproval from any authorized quarter." Before the thunderstruck admirals could respond to this unwelcome toast, a White Fathers band struck up the stirring strains of the *Marseillaise.*

The response was a storm of indignation from monarchist Catholics throughout France. In a flood of vituperative articles and speeches, they accused Lavigerie of selling his ecclesial birthright for a mess of revolutionary pottage. For over a year, Rampolla and the Pope (at whose behest Lavigerie had spoken) left the beleaguered cardinal without support. Only two French bishops defended him publicly. "Rabbits in mitres," Lavigerie called the rest.

Finally, on February 17, 1892, Leo addressed French Catholics in their own language (*Au milieu des sollicitudes*). Reminding them that "the civil power is always of God," the Pope urged them to defend Church rights as participants in political life, rather than as protesting exiles.

It was asking too much. As the modern historian, John McManners, has written, the Pope wanted French monarchists to desert a hopeless cause which they loved (restoration of the Bourbons) for a hopeless cause which they detested (rallying to the republic). For a century they had lived as opponents of the regime, revering its martyrs (most recently Archbishop Darboy of Paris, executed by a firing squad with twenty-four of his priests on May 24, 1871). Modifying this stance would have been difficult. Abandoning it for its opposite exceeded human powers.

Surprising in the circumstances was the amount of support that the Pope's *ralliement* policy did receive from Catholics who had learned to read the signs of the times. Hampered, however, by the celebrated individualism which has long been both the glory and distress of French life, Catholics were unable to unite for effective political action. "We need a French Windhorst," was the comment of one frustrated Catholic politician in a reference to the successful Center Party leader in Germany.

Church-state tensions continued to the end of the century and beyond. In 1905 the French government abrogated the 1801 Concordat and carried out the total separation of Church and state prophesied by Bishop Freppel a quarter century before. The bitter divisions among French Catholics continued up to our own day, when the ideological heirs of the nineteenth-century monarchists became the core supporters of the schismatic Archbishop Lefebvre.

Not long before his death in 1903, Leo XIII commented sadly on the limits of papal power to a French priest who had supported his *ralliement* policy, the Abbé Frémont: "By their disobedience to my program of 1892 the French clergy rendered me powerless to help them."

That was the short-term view. For the long-term, Leo had established the principle that Catholics could support any form of government which preserved order, respected morals, and left the Church free to pursue its mission. This was a necessary precondition if Catholics were to respond to the challenge Leo issued in one of his most memorable encyclicals: to join the fight for social justice.

Rerum novarum

Despite Pecci's 1849 suggestion, as the young Archbishop of Perugia, that the Pope issue a list of modern errors, his attitude toward the modern world was never really negative. And over the next three decades he grew — personally, but also intellectually. Through reading and contact with visitors from outside Italy, Pecci was aware of developments elsewhere, especially of what was coming to be known as "the social question." His pastoral letters between 1874 and 1877 reflected this awareness. (See p. 197 above.)

The French and industrial revolutions drove masses of agrarian workers into cities. By mid-century Europe's factories and mines employed millions of men, women, and children in dangerous work, for long hours, at miserably low wages. For traditional Catholics, these industrial masses were "the new poor," objects of charity. For nineteenth-century socialists, on the other hand, they were a new class, the proletariat. It was to them that Karl Marx and Friedrich Engels addressed their *Communist Manifesto* in 1848.

Even before that, however, some Catholic voices were being raised on behalf of the oppressed working class. One of the first was Denis-August Affre, Archbishop of Paris from 1840 to 1848. He said that an industrial system which treated workers as "mere chattel" was unjust and should be changed. In England the convert Cardinal Manning, Archbishop of Westminster from 1865, espoused similar views.

In Germany the leading advocate of social justice (as opposed to mere charity) was Wilhelm Emmanuel von Ketteler, Bishop of Mainz from 1850 to 1877. Ketteler's Advent sermons in 1848 (before he became a bishop) criticized the prevailing economic system which produced injustice and established his reputation as "the founder of social catholicism." Decades later Pope Leo would call Ketteler "my great predecessor, the man from whom I learned."

The Pope incorporated the fruits of this learning in the encyclical *Rerum novarum*, dated May 15, 1891. Drafted for him by others (like most papal documents), it was the one on which Leo worked hardest. Starting with a clear portrayal of "the misery and wretchedness which press so heavily at this moment on the large majority of the very poor," Leo set forth a broad middle course between contemporary socialism and laissez-faire liberalism.

Rejecting socialist contentions that private property was inherently unjust and class warfare inevitable, the Pope vigorously defended private property as "a right given to man by nature." Only if this right were respected would citizens, including workers, have a stake in the social order. It was the Church's task, Leo said, to overcome class warfare by "binding class to class in friendliness and good feeling."

Against contemporary liberals, who said religion was a private affair which should not influence public policy, Leo insisted on certain postulates of social justice developed from the Thomist doctrine of natural law. Workers were entitled, for instance, to a just wage. The Pope defined this as one

> sufficient to support the worker, provided he is thrifty and well behaved. If the worker is compelled to accept harsher terms, or is induced by fear of worse hardships, and these have to be accepted because they are imposed by a master or employer, this is submission to force and therefore repugnant to justice.

Workers also had the right to organize trades unions to obtain just wages, and if necessary to strike; and the state must protect these rights. The state must also protect the family, society's basic unit, rejecting both communal ownership and excessive taxation, which in their different ways were equally destructive of family life. The state could not be indifferent to injustice and poverty (as liberals contended):

> Whenever the general interest of any particular class suffers, or is threatened with harm, which can in no other way be met or prevented, the public authority must step in to deal with it. . . . Still, when there is question of defending the rights of individuals, the poor and badly-off have a claim to special consideration.

A century later Church documents would speak of a "special option for the poor."

By today's standards *Rerum novarum* is patriarchal and conservative. A century ago it was radical. In 1891 most Catholics would have found the view of poverty expressed by the Abbé Luc in 1842 quite acceptable. (See page 190 above.) After *Rerum novarum* it was acceptable no longer. Leo XIII initiated a major development in papal and conciliar teaching on social justice which continues today.

Thomism and history

The doctrine of social justice set forth in *Rerum novarum* was drawn, as we have seen, from the Thomist philosophy of natural law. Twelve years previously, in the encyclical *Aeterni Patris* (1879), Leo had called for a revival of Thomism. This foundational document for the whole pontificate praised the teaching of Saint Thomas Aquinas as so perfect that anyone who followed it could never depart from the way of truth.

Though the encyclical insisted on the need to study Saint Thomas himself, what continued to be taught in most seminaries was not classical Thomism but neo-scholasticism. Propositions drawn from the writings of Saint Thomas (or alleged to be contained therein) were used without regard for their historical context to erect a rigid intellectual system that was then declared to be the final statement of philosophical and theological truth. Other philosophical schools were labeled unworthy of serious consideration. Those who followed them were suspect of heresy. The intellectual hubris characteristic of this mentality would weigh heavily on Catholic life right up to Vatican II.

The weakness of *Aeterni Patris* was ignorance of history. The encyclical portrayed doctrinal development as a smooth and uninterrupted continuum from the early Church Fathers through Augustine to Aquinas, whose doctrine it pronounced so perfect that it possessed timeless validity.

Though Leo was no historian, he was indignant at the falsification of history by the papacy's political opponents in Italy, who portrayed the Popes as enemies of Italian freedom and prosperity. To Leo this was a travesty. A frequent theme of his encyclicals was the blessings conferred on Italy by the papacy.

When the Roman Empire collapsed, it was the papacy which preserved Italy from the worst consequences of barbarian invasion. In the Middle Ages, Popes had defended Italy against the power of German Emperors. In the sixteenth and seventeenth centuries, Popes had defended Italy from Turkish raids, and helped Austria to defend all Europe from Turkish conquest. In Leo's own century the papacy had defended Italy from Napoleon Bonaparte. Far from being the enemy of Italian liberty, the papacy had been its principal defender, as well as the patron and protector of Italian culture, art, and literature.

It was one thing to assert these things, another to convince liberal skeptics that they were true. The nineteenth century witnessed the rise of the scientific study of history, based on archival research. Dominating the field were Germans, most of them Protestants with an innate bias against all things Catholic.

An exception was the Catholic historian Ignaz von Döllinger, professor of church history in Munich. The intellectual leader of the opponents of papal infallibility at the Vatican Council of 1870, Döllinger had been excommunicated in 1871 because of his continued opposition to the council's definition. Support for the papacy could hardly be expected from such a source.

One of Döllinger's pupils, however, Josef Hergenröther, professor of church history at Würzburg, had remained within the fold. A crashing bore in the lecture room, his writings were respected by the scholarly world. In his first consistory in May 1879, Leo made Hergenröther a cardinal, along with another scholar whose elevation was momentous for the Catholic study of history: John Henry Newman. Within weeks the monsignor in charge of the Vatican archives died. Leo immediately made Hergenröther his successor.

It was a brilliant appointment. By placing a cardinal with a European reputation as a historian in a post previously held by a mere monsignor Leo was signaling both his curia and the scholarly world that he intended the archives to be used. A mediocre teacher, Hergenröther was eminently qualified as an archivist. He was determined to make the documents now entrusted to him freely available to his fellow scholars.

This was easier said than done. The archives were in terrible disorder. Between 1810 and 1813 Napoleon had carted them all off to Paris as part of his grandiose scheme to make the French capital the world-center of learning and culture. The monumental task of organizing and cataloguing had only begun when Napoleon fell from power and Pius VII demanded his papers back.

The new French government was prepared to pay for their transport only a tenth of the sum which Napoleon had expended for their acquisition. The Pope contributed what he could, but it was not nearly enough. To reduce costs, much material was burnt. Parchments were sold by weight to a French grocer for packing purposes. Fragments could still be bought in Parisian shops at the end of the century. Some volumes found their way to the Bibliothèque Nationale in Paris, others to Trinity College, Dublin (a bastion of Protestantism until after Vatican II).

About a third of the collection never returned to Rome. Some of the material that did come back suffered water damage: during the crossing of streams for packing cases sent by land, by bilge water in the case of those sent by sea. The archives were disorganized before their kidnapping. The chaos following their return can easily be imagined.

Added to the practical difficulty of using a vast collection for which there was no catalogue was the reluctance of the curia to open to unfriendly eyes the record of past mistakes, injustices, and follies. The English Catholic historian, Lord Acton, noted privately: "What archives reveal is the wickedness of men. . . . The one constant result is to show that people are worse than their reputation." Though this severe judgment was known only to its author, curial officials acted as if it were true.

Throughout the nineteenth century a sign over the archives threatened excommunication to anyone who entered. (The archivist and his tiny staff were of course excepted.) Hergenröther's predecessor, Monsignor Rosi-Bernardini, called by Owen Chadwick (author of the best account of the opening of the archives in English) "the stuffiest head of the Vatican Archives during the entire nineteenth century," worked under the motto: "No one goes in and nothing comes out."

Exceptions were occasionally made, however, for a few selected individuals. They worked under frustrating conditions. Unable to enter the archives themselves, and with no catalogue to guide their search, they had to request specific items. Documents could be copied only by the staff, whose work had to be paid. Because of the risk of fire there was no heating. Radiators, connected to a distant boiler, were not installed until 1900.

In 1880 Leo had a room constructed for the use of researchers. Previously they had had to sit at a table in the Vatican library. On January 1, 1881 the archives were officially opened to qualified scholars. In reality, however, access continued to be restricted by curial resentments and suspicions. The Pope himself shared this reluctance to open family secrets to hostile eyes. Research by friendly scholars like Hergenröther could be useful in refuting the historical calumnies of the papacy's opponents. Caution was still needed, however, in the case of Protestants.

Ironically it was a Protestant, Theodor Sickel, Director of the Austrian Institute in Rome, who helped to remove this prejudice. From 1881 he had been working in the archives on the *Privilegium Ottonis*, a grant by the German Emperor Otto I in 962 which formed the basis for the papal states. The document was widely assailed as a forgery. In 1883 Sickel published a book defending its authenticity.

Hergenröther immediately saw an opportunity to counter curial efforts to restrict access to the archives. Since Leo did not read German, Hergenröther wrote a report on Sickel's book and gave it to the Pope. On April 10, 1883 Leo received Sickel in private audience and expressed himself delighted with the historian's findings. Sickel received the distinct impression that Leo thought his visitor had abandoned Protestantism. It speaks volumes for the Pope's mentality that he equated a non-Catholic scholar's resolution of a disputed point of history in favor of the papacy with agreement in faith.

Be that as it may, the Pope's friendly conversation with a Protestant visitor, eagerly reported by Hergenröther, was soon the talk of the small curial world. On August 18, 1883 Leo published his "Letter to the Three Cardinals": the Vice Chancellor de Luca and the Frenchman Pitra, both protectors of the Vatican library, and Hergenröther as prefect of the archives. Chadwick calls it "one of the most important utterances of a pope in modern times."

The letter deplored the corruption of history by the Church's enemies. The Church had nothing to fear from true history. This would show how much the Italian people owed to the Popes of past ages. Let scholars work at the sources: prudently, impartially, avoiding rashness in judgment. This the Church had always encouraged. "The first law of history," Leo wrote in a frequently quoted passage, "is not to dare to utter falsehood; the second, not to fear to speak the truth."

Chadwick calls Leo's opening of the papal archives "one of the most liberal acts in an illiberal century. . . . The opening of the archives brought general understanding and new confidence among instructed non-Catholics that the Catholic Church cared about truth." The Pope's action was the more creditable since he acted against the advice of his own curia, and sustained his decision in the face of continued curial resentment.

Among the many fruits of Leo's policy, which continue today, pride of place belongs to the forty-volume *History of the Popes* (from 1417 to 1799) by the German Catholic layman Ludwig von Pastor, a product of the author's lifelong research in the papal archives and a primary source for earlier chapters of the present work.

Ecumenism

Leo's French policy ended the Church's sole reliance on monarchy and made it possible for Catholics to participate in the political life of modern democracies. *Rerum novarum* showed that charity was not enough: Catholics must also be concerned with social justice. Leo may also be regarded as the founder of modern Catholic ecumenism.

A modern historian has identified thirty-two documents from Leo's pontificate which speak of reunion with Eastern Christians. The first was the encyclical *Grande munus christiani* (September 30, 1880), devoted to the Slav apostles Cyril and Methodius, whose feast Leo extended to the whole world. Two years later, responding to a request from the Greek government, Leo announced that titular bishops appointed to defunct dioceses in Greek territories would no longer be styled "*in partibus infidelium*," a designation appropriate only for non-Christian territories. Leo was also the first Pope to refer to Eastern Christians as "separated brethren" rather than as schismatics and heretics.

Where previous papal documents granted at best a grudging toleration of Eastern liturgical rites, Leo repeatedly expressed respect. The papal brief *Orientalium dignitas* (November 30, 1894) forbade the imposition of Latin rites and discipline on Eastern Rite Catholics, whose traditions the Pope called "a wonderful adornment of the universal church which confirms the divine unity of Catholic faith."

Leo knew that these were small steps. He was saddened by the continued refusal of members of his curia, and Latin Rite missionaries in Eastern countries, to show the respect he had enjoined for oriental Christians. Reunion was for the distant future, the Pope realized, and would be especially difficult with the Russian Orthodox. He could hope for no more, Leo told the Austro-Hungarian ambassador to the Holy See on New Year's Eve 1897, than to see the dawning rays of a future for which he longed with his whole soul.

Another ecumenical initiative, this one with Anglicans, ended in disaster. It began in 1890 with a chance meeting, on the island of Madeira, between Lord Halifax, a devout member of the Church of England whose spirituality reflected the catholicizing influence of the Oxford Movement of 1833, and a French Vincentian, the Abbé Fernand Portal. Like almost all Catholics of the day, Portal considered Anglicanism to be merely another Protestant sect, nourished spiritually not by liturgy and sacraments but by Bible reading and preaching. Through conversation, correspondence, and visits to England, Halifax opened the eyes of the abbé to a religious world of whose existence Portal had not even dreamed.

Together the two friends considered how this world might become better known to Catholics. Above all, how could theologians of two churches be brought into friendly conversations, in which the two sides would look first of all not for what was wrong in the other's position (the traditional polemical approach) but for areas of agreement (what we now call dialogue)?

Portal suggested discussion about the validity of Anglican ordinations. Anglicans insisted that Catholic rejection of their orders as invalid was based on misinformation and prejudice. Portal urged that since the dispute concerned historical facts, it was a good place to begin. Discussion about more difficult matters, in particular the crucial question of the Pope's universal primacy and infallibility, could follow.

This suggestion, though made in good faith, was somewhat naive. In reality the dispute about Anglican orders involved not only the preservation of an historically unbroken succession of episcopal ordinations in England (which was fairly easy to demonstrate), but dogmatic questions as well: the doctrine of eucharistic sacrifice and the nature of the Church's ordained ministry.

Portal's suggestion, reported to Rome by friends, brought him, in September 1894, an invitation to visit Leo XIII's Secretary of State Cardinal Rampolla. Following close on the French priest's visit to England, Portal was able to report that only weeks before he had witnessed liturgies remarkably like Catholic models being celebrated in Anglican churches. He had visited religious communities for men and women shaped along Catholic lines. The Archbishop of Canterbury, whom he had visited with Lord Halifax, had been somewhat nervous about the rapprochement Portal was urging. But the Archbishop of York had received the two visitors warmly, had said that he tried to follow the methods of Saint Charles Borromeo in the administration of his diocese, and expressed the hope "that we are at the beginning of something really great in the interests of the church."

Rampolla considered Portal's report so important that he had him repeat it to the Pope the very next day. Deeply moved, Leo said that no one had ever talked to him about England as Portal had done. What could he, as Pope, do? Portal suggested a friendly letter to the two English archbishops, suggesting conferences on the subject of Anglican orders as a point of contact which would give theologians on both sides an opportunity to discuss their respective positions.

Clearly no initiative could be taken without consulting the Catholic hierarchy in England. Realizing this, Halifax had kept the Archbishop of Westminster, Cardinal Vaughan, informed about his hopes and Portal's suggestion. Vaughan was horrified. By letter, and personally in Rome, Vaughan warned the Pope that he was being lured into a trap. Halifax and his coreligionists had no interest in reunion, Vaughan alleged. They merely hoped for a Roman declaration in favor of Anglican orders in order to keep individual Anglicans from submitting to Rome, and to shore up their own wavering faith in a sham church presided over by lay archbishops.

The idea that anything could be gained through a discussion of Anglican orders was absurd, Vaughan contended. The only way to reunion was for Anglicans to admit their errors and submit their proud wills to the Vicar of Christ. The question of Rome was crucial. It was the question which would have to be settled in the end. Therefore it was better to begin with it.

Vaughan went farther. Now that the question of Anglican orders had been raised, he argued, the Holy See must issue a solemn and public declaration of their invalidity. Since the Church had always treated them as invalid, any other judgment, even a decision that the orders were doubtful, would be tantamount to an admission that the Church had been wrong — which would scandalize the faithful. To strengthen their case, Vaughan and his allies promised that a solemn condemnation of Anglican orders would produce a flood of converts eager to abandon a Church which dispensed worthless sacraments for the only body which offered the genuine article.

The result was a foregone conclusion. The bilateral discussion of Anglican orders, which Halifax and Portal had proposed as a means of initiating dialogue, was replaced by a secret Roman investigation of Anglican orders, from which Anglicans were excluded. The result of this investigation became known only in 1968. Only four of the eight experts appointed to investigate the question voted for invalidity. Two found the orders valid, the remaining two said they were doubtful.

With the Pope's commission divided (though this was carefully concealed at the time), Cardinal Vaughan's arguments carried the day. On September 13, 1896, in the bull *Apostolicae curae*, Leo XIII chose polemic over dialogue. The bull's crucial sentence said, in the triumphalistic language of the day: "We pronounce and declare that ordinations carried out according to the Anglican rite have been and are absolutely null and utterly void." Halifax and Portal, though heartbroken, remained confident that the day for dialogue would ultimately come. The flood of Anglican converts which the English cardinal had predicted never materialized.

One should not be too hard on Vaughan. Like Catholic royalists in France unable to accept Leo's policy of *ralliement*, the English cardinal felt that rapprochement with the Church of England meant betrayal of the English Catholic martyrs. What was surprising, in a pre-ecumenical age, was not the negative attitude of Vaughan and his supporters, but the broad positive response which Halifax and Portal received from Catholics, including many in England, as well as from Anglicans. Polemic had triumphed for the moment. But the future would belong to dialogue.

"Americanism"

During Leo's pontificate the number of Catholics outside Europe grew rapidly. Nowhere was this growth more dramatic than in the United States. These years also witnessed an acrimonious conflict between American bishops over the best way to preserve the faith of their immigrant flocks in the predominantly Protestant culture. On the one hand were those who believed that this required preservation of Old World customs and languages. Arrayed against them were bishops who wanted to shed European ways and attitudes in order to fashion a distinctively American church in a land where "liberty, equality, and fraternity" had none of the negative connotations which this revolutionary slogan had in the continent of its origin.

The Americanists, as the latter group were called, had no thought of establishing a national church, separate from Rome. They, no less than their opponents, were constantly appealing to Rome for support. What they sought above all was an understanding of the great opportunity offered to the Church by the separation of Church and state decreed in the American Constitution. In Roman eyes separation of the two powers was the cardinal sin of the French Revolution: the rejection not only of the Church's domination of national life which had characterized the *ancien régime* (in particular, Church control of education), but also of the partnership, for the common good, advocated by Leo XIII in the encyclical *Immortale Dei.*

The Americanists insisted that in the United States, which had never experienced anything like the *ancien régime*, separation of Church and state meant not mutual hostility but liberty for the Church to pursue its mission untrammeled by the state interference which was so prominent a feature of Church life in Europe.

Though the Roman authorities neither accepted nor understood this view (any more than American Catholics comprehended Leo's doctrine of the partnership of Church and state), they were prepared to tolerate it as long as it was not exported. When American Catholics contended that separation of Church and state was the wave of the future elsewhere, and when Old World Catholics (in France especially) embraced this program, there was trouble.

It is not difficult to see why. If separation of Church and state was a positive good, rather than an evil to be endured, what reason did the Pope have to continue protesting the violation of his rights as temporal sovereign by the anti-Catholic kingdom of Italy? If Leo's *ralliement* policy in France meant not merely an appeal for Catholics to take their proper political role in a democratic state but (as the Americanists seemed to claim) endorsement of democracy as a better form of government than monarchy, could the demand for introduction of democracy into the hierarchical church be far behind?

A key figure in exporting Americanist ideas to Europe was John Ireland, Archbishop of St. Paul, Minnesota, from 1884 until his death in 1918. Brought to this country in 1848, at the age of ten, as a penniless immigrant, John Ireland grew into the flamboyant, romantic prelate who could walk in the front door of the White House and discuss affairs of state with the President. A fervent American patriot, Ireland acquired fluent French during his seminary studies in France. During a number of protracted episcopal preaching tours in that country, Ireland had ample opportunity to spread his gospel of democratic freedom on the American model, with its corollary of Church freedom from state interference.

Though this political Americanism made people in Rome nervous, it might have been tolerated but for the introduction, by Ireland and his friends on both sides of the Atlantic, of a kind of religious Americanism as well. This began in 1887 when the Americanists began publishing in Europe French translations of their reform ideas. This propaganda campaign culminated with the publication in the summer of 1897 of a French version of the biography of the American convert-priest Isaac Hecker, who had died in 1888. In contrast to American prelates of the day, whose primary concern was preserving the faith of their immigrant flocks, Hecker was interested in converting American Protestants. He was convinced that they had preserved the basic elements of Christianity. Catholicism should be presented to them positively, therefore, as the completion of the faith they already possessed. This was a radical departure from the polemical method of contemporary proselytizers, who sought first to discredit Protestantism in order to fill the resulting void with the true faith of Catholicism.

The Abbé Félix Klein, a friend and warm admirer of Archbishop Ireland, saw in Hecker's biography an ideal vehicle for presenting Americanist ideas to French Catholics. To do so he adapted the English original and added a preface of his own, to portray Hecker as the ideal Catholic priest of the future, who harmonized Catholicism with modern thought, emphasized the active virtues which produced modern "saints of the marketplace" rather than anachronistic imitations of medieval monks and nuns, and placed the interior promptings of the Holy Spirit ahead of exterior direction by the Church's hierarchy.

Publication of Klein's book provoked a violent controversy, first in France, then in Rome. This culminated on January 22, 1899 with the publication of Leo XIII's letter *Testem benevolentiae* to the only American cardinal of the day, Archbishop James Gibbons of Baltimore. The Pope addressed "certain contentions" among American Catholics — but softened his criticism by ascribing the disputed ideas to the French life of Isaac Hecker. The letter condemned "religious Americanism": watering down Catholic doctrine to attract converts, introducing democracy and individual liberty into the Church, replacing hierarchical guidance with the interior action of the Holy Spirit, exaggerated emphasis on the "active" virtues, and denigration of religious vows as relics of a past age.

Political Americanism, on the other hand, was approved as long as it designated "the characteristic qualities which reflect honor on the people of America, just as other nations have what is special to them." If used, however, to promote "a church in America different from that which is in the rest of the world," Leo expressed confidence that his bishops in America would reject political Americanism as firmly as he did himself.

From the vantage point of Rome, the condemnation of Americanism was a relatively minor incident in the long pontificate. For the young Church in the United States, however, it was a body blow. Combined, as it would be a few years later under Pius X, with the draconian measures against modernism (which, like Americanism in its pure form, never really existed in the United States), *Testem benevolentiae* crippled the efforts of American Catholics at theological scholarship for a half century.

A result of this condemnation, which was provoked by the imprudent enthusiasm of John Ireland and his friends, remains visible in the character of the American hierarchy today. In contrast to countries like Germany, Belgium, and Ireland, where professional theologians are regularly appointed to major Sees, the United States still has no tradition of scholar-bishops — and this despite the declaration of Vatican II that the "office of teaching is conspicuous among the principal duties of Bishops" (*Decree on the Pastoral Office of Bishops*, 12; a footnote refers to the almost identical statement in *Lumen gentium*, 25).

"Let's not set limits . . ."

At Leo's election in 1878 people had commented on how frail the new Pope looked — as if the first strong wind might blow him away. His electors anticipated a brief pontificate. Leo buried all of them but one: the arch-conservative Cardinal Oreglia, who in 1878 had voted against Pecci to the bitter end. As the new century dawned, one of the few cardinals who could still remember the last conclave remarked: "We thought we were electing a Holy Father, not an eternal father."

On March 2, 1900 Leo completed his ninetieth year. Told by the cardinal dean that the *porporati* (as cardinals are called in Rome) were praying that he might celebrate his hundredth birthday, Leo replied with characteristic humor: "Let's not set limits to the providence of God." His biographer Eduardo Soderini would write three decades later: "Leo loved life and considered longevity a gift from heaven."

The twenty-fifth anniversary of his election on February 20, 1903, however, would be his last. On July 3, following a carriage drive in the Vatican

Gardens, the Pope took to his bed. Two days later the doctors diagnosed pneumonia, called by the medical profession prior to the discovery of antibiotics "the old man's friend." For two weeks more the wraith-like Pontiff clung tenaciously to life, hovering between unconsciousness and times of lucidity during which he was able to discuss business with Rampolla (his faithful Secretary of State since 1887) and the other cardinals, receive the last sacraments, participate in the prayers for the dying, and take leave of those who gathered round his bed. At four o'clock in the afternoon of July 20 the stout heart in the frail body beat its last. It had kept Joachim Pecci alive for ninety-three years, four months, and nineteen days, more than twenty-five of those years as the two hundred and fifty-third successor of the fisherman Peter.

Leo wanted to be buried in St. John Lateran, the Pope's cathedral, near his great hero, Innocent III, whose remains Leo had brought there from Perugia in 1892. (See p. 105 above.) While a suitable tomb was prepared, Leo's mortal remains found a temporary resting place in St. Peter's. Fearing repetition of the ugly scenes which had accompanied the translation of Pius IX's body in 1881 (see page 200 above), the authorities postponed the transfer until 1924, when it was carried out secretly. The tomb, in the left transept opposite that of Innocent III, is surmounted by a standing, bowed figure of the Pope, his hand raised in blessing. On his right is a pilgrim clothed as a worker, commemorating Leo's pioneering plea for social justice.

Leo accomplished both less and more than the "grand design of statesmanship" of which he spoke on the day after his election. He wanted above all to bring the Church out of the cul-de-sac into which it had been led by the radical rejection of the post-revolutionary world under Gregory XVI and Pius IX. Within limits he succeeded.

Leo failed to solve "the Roman question": his successors would remain "prisoners of the Vatican" until Pius XI broke the impasse with the Lateran Treaties of 1929. Elsewhere Leo had considerable diplomatic success. The enhanced political importance of the papacy during Leo's pontificate was evident in his final months of life, when the two mightiest Protestant sovereigns of the day came on state visits: King Edward VII of England on April 29, 1903, and his cousin Kaiser Wilhelm II of Germany three days later. One of the witnesses who was impressed with the panoply surrounding these events was a twenty-three-year-old student at the Roman seminary named Angelo Roncalli. Fifty-five years later he would succeed Leo as Pope John XXIII.

Further evidence of the increased importance of the papacy on the world stage was the keen interest of European governments in the election of Leo's successor. During the 1903 conclave, the Emperor of Austria-Hungary exercised his veto against the pro-French Cardinal Rampolla. (The gesture was futile, since the voting showed that Rampolla never had enough votes for election. And the veto was immediately abolished by the new Pope, Pius X.)

Leo greatly increased the self-confidence of Catholics in the face of the modern world. By ending the Kulturkampf in Germany, he made it possible for Catholics in that country to emerge from political isolation. And although most French Catholics failed to embrace the Pope's *ralliement* policy, Leo's appeal opened the door to Catholic participation in twentieth-century political life throughout the world.

Leo XIII's enormous output of teaching documents, eighty-six encyclicals in addition to numerous apostolic letters and addresses, began the tradition of papal teaching on a host of subjects which we take for granted today. Leo's ecumenical stance fell far short of the standard set by Vatican Council II. Yet without his initiatives, modern Catholic ecumenism would be unthinkable. Equally unthinkable, but for the pioneering breakthrough of *Rerum novarum*, would be the great social encyclicals of this century's Popes, from Pius XI to John Paul II.

Like every Pope, Leo XIII was a man of his time, limited by background, education, and experience of life. No one familiar with his youthful ambition could have predicted the degree with which he transcended those limits to become, as he truly was, the first modern Pope.

CHAPTER ELEVEN

John XXIII

(1958-1963)

*"O*ne of my favorite phrases brings me great comfort: We are not on earth as museum-keepers but to cultivate a flourishing garden of life and to prepare a glorious future. The Pope is dead, long live the Pope!" (On hearing of Pius XII's death)

"Third day of the conclave. . . . Invoked with special tenderness my saintly protectors: St. Joseph, St. Mark, St. Lawrence Justinian and St. Pius X, asking them to give me calmness and courage. I thought it wiser not to eat with the cardinals. I ate in my room. At the eleventh ballot I was elected Pope. O Jesus, I too can say what Pius XII said when he was elected: 'Have mercy on me, Lord, according to thy great goodness' [Psalm 51]. One would say it is like a dream and yet, until I die, it is the most solemn reality of all my life" (Diary, October 28, 1958).

"Will things be done differently when I'm gone? That's none of my business. I feel joy in the contemplation of truth and in duty done." (Words on his sickbed in consciousness of approaching death, May 21, 1963).

"We've worked together and served the church without stopping to pick up and throw back the stones that have sometimes blocked our path" (To his secretary, Monsignor Loris Capovilla, May 31, 1963, three days before death).

Leo XIII's successors are all buried in the Vatican Grottoes under St. Peter's Basilica. Though not visited by most tourists, the tombs are accessible to the public. One tomb in particular is the goal of countless pilgrims, who come daily to pray, bringing flowers and candles. The tomb bears the simple inscription: "Joannes PP. XXIII."

Pope John XXIII's cause of canonization is pending. So is that of his immediate predecessor, Pius XII, who is buried nearby. A master diplomat whose literary output exceeded even that of Leo XIII, Pius XII gave new meaning to the ancient title "Sovereign Pontiff." At his death his legacy was considered to be so imposing that the cardinals decided not to attempt a replacement. They chose instead a "transitional Pope," the genial 77-year-old Patriarch of Venice, Angelo Roncalli, to keep the papal chair warm until a suitable successor was found for the great Eugenio Pacelli.

Few of his electors took Roncalli seriously. Some were openly contemptuous of him. On the eve of the conclave, Cardinal Lercaro of Bologna told his secretary: "Don't book the Venice express, please. I don't want to have to travel with that bore Roncalli." Back in New York Cardinal Spellman, who had built his entire career on friendship with Pacelli, remarked to aides of the man he had just helped elect: "He's no Pope. He should be selling bananas."

Yet today it is the banana vendor's tomb which is the focus of popular devotion and not that of his fellow candidate for sainthood nearby — who in his lifetime had taken the modern papal personality cult to previously undreamed of heights. Canonization is the one thing in the Catholic Church which is, by the Church's deliberate choice, democratic. In accordance with ancient tradition, a cause for sainthood must arise spontaneously from the faithful, first in the candidate's local church, and must continue for decades to elicit their prayers and other manifestations of devotion.

Kenneth L. Woodward, author of *Making Saints* (1990), the best study in English of the modern canonization process, reports being told in Rome that Pope John's cause had run into "impediments" sufficiently serious to cast doubt on his heroic virtue. As a result, Woodward learned, "the cause was stymied, but not officially stopped." In the hearts and minds of countless souls the world over, however, John has been canonized already. The pages which follow attempt to explain why.

Village boy

He was born on November 25, 1881 in the village of Sotto il Monte, ten miles from Bergamo (the seat of a bishop) in northern Italy, the fourth of thirteen children, and the eldest son, of peasant farmers. On the day of his birth, he was given the name Angelo Giuseppe in baptism.

Angelo could never remember a time when he did not want to be a priest. In the autumn of 1892 he left home to attend the junior seminary at Bergamo. Almost four decades later, he would write his parents:

> Ever since I left home, towards the age of ten, I have read many books and learned many things you could not have taught me. But what I learned from you remains the most precious and important, and it sustains and gives life to the many other things I learned later in so many years of study and teaching.

At the age of fourteen, Roncalli started to keep a diary, a practice he would continue all his life. He wanted to record graces received and spiritual insights, his good resolutions and failures to keep them. The entries for his seminary years contain many self-reproofs about his tendencies to gossip, to overeat (a lifelong problem, evident from photographs), to pride, and to ambition (in a celibate priesthood the clerical form of lust).

Read today, Roncalli's constant laments about what seem at worst petty faults appear scrupulous. When the diary was published (as *The Journal of a Soul*) after its author's death, the English Cardinal Heenan remarked that the work contained the sort of thing every seminarian since the Council of Trent had written and thrown away. The entries are significant nonetheless. They show how much Angelo Roncalli was the product of the Tridentine Church which flourished from Pius V to Vatican II. And they show too that the simple goodness which impressed the whole world in "good Pope John" was the fruit of a lifelong inner struggle against what the New Testament calls "the world," and Catholic theology terms "original sin."

In January 1901, at age nineteen, Angelo was sent to Rome to study theology. He took to his new life like a duck to water, doing well in his studies and enjoying the sights and ceremonies of papal Rome, presided over by the ninety-one-year-old Leo XIII. At year-end, however, Angelo was devastated by the call to compulsory military service. He was unprepared for the barrack-room tales of sexual exploits he had previously not even imagined. His diary speaks of "the year of Babylonian Captivity . . . a real purgatory." He did well in the army nonetheless. As Pope he would proudly recall his rise, inside a year, to the rank of sergeant.

Discharged at Christmas 1902, Roncalli returned to his Roman studies with fresh enthusiasm, being ordained sub-deacon in April 1903 and deacon in December. In between these two events he witnessed the funeral of Leo XIII in July and the proclamation of the newly elected Pope Pius X on August 14, 1903. On August 10, 1904 Roncalli was ordained priest in Rome. None of his family were present. They could not afford the train fare.

Following home visits and Masses in Sotto il Monte and Bergamo, Angelo returned to Rome in November to begin graduate study of canon law. He had barely started when his life took a wholly unexpected turn. Monsignor Giacomo Radini-Tedeschi, the newly appointed Bishop of Bergamo, chose Roncalli as his secretary and took him north in April 1905.

Responsible for this sudden reversal of fortune was a change of papal policy. Radini-Tedeschi, a Bergamo priest and a protégé of Leo XIII's Secretary of State Cardinal Rampolla, had an important curial position as director of the *Opera dei Congressi*, the great meetings through which Italian Catholics, forbidden by Leo XIII to take part in national politics, influenced public life.

When Pius X, as part of his repudiation of his predecessor's policies, abolished the Congress movement on July 28, 1904, a job had to be found for the man who had directed it with great success, while making the change appear like a promotion. The Bishop of Bergamo having conveniently died in October 1904, Radini-Tedeschi was named to the vacant See. On January 29, 1905 Pius X himself ordained him bishop in the Sistine Chapel.

There was nothing unusual in this. It was the time honored Roman principle of *promoveatur ut amoveatur* ("promote him — get him out of here"). Roncalli was well aware of the real reason for his new bishop's promotion. As he held the book of the gospels over Radini-Tedeschi's head during the latter's episcopal ordination, Roncalli was being initiated into a clerical system which often lays the heaviest burdens on those who serve it most selflessly. His own promotion to the episcopate in 1925 would come about under similar circumstances, as we shall see.

Roncalli's training in this system continued over the next decade. The village boy Roncalli admired the grace with which the highly born and cultivated Radini-Tedeschi accepted his banishment from the center of power and threw himself into a job he had never expected. Roncalli developed genuine affection for his first mentor, whose biography he would later write under the title of *My Bishop*, a work of filial piety.

Service as episcopal secretary brought him into contact with other prelates. The most prominent was the Archbishop of Milan, Cardinal Andrea Carlo Ferrari. Despite a thirty-one-year difference in age, the two became friends. Roncalli consulted Ferrari on all important decisions and met him almost monthly until Ferrari's death in 1921.

In the Church of Pius X this was a dangerous friendship for a young priest. A leader of the progressive forces in Italian Catholicism, Ferrari was a victim of the anti-modernist campaign which dominated the pontificate. Pius X ordered no less than four "apostolic visitations" of the Milan archdiocese (Ferrari called them "apostolic vexations"). No grounds for action were found, but the Pope's mistrust of his Milan cardinal was an open secret. In the last four years of his life, Pius refused even to see Ferrari. On February 10, 1963 Roncalli had the satisfaction of opening, as Pope, the beatification process for his old friend. In doing so he said that God "often permits bitter situations to arise which have nothing to do with the personal merits of the saints." In Ferrari's case, John added, "those responsible were gravely wrong."

From 1906 Roncalli combined his work as episcopal secretary with the teaching of church history at the major seminary in Bergamo. In the heyday of "the church that never changes" that too was "dangerous." In 1870 minority bishops at Vatican I who appealed to history in the debate over papal infallibility had found themselves suspect of heresy. During the anti-modernist campaign, this suspicion was directed with intensity at one of the leading church historians of the day, the French priest Louis Duchesne. In 1912 his three-volume *History of the Ancient Church* was placed on the Index of Forbidden Books.

In June 1914 Roncalli, alarmed by a letter from a curial cardinal reporting information that Roncalli was "a reader of Duchesne and other unbridled authors," protested that he had "never read more than fifteen to twenty pages" of Duchesne's first volume and had "never seen the other two volumes." Even if this were true (and there is evidence it was not), one could ask whether a seminary professor was not obliged to read the offending work, in order to refute its errors. Roncalli's letter of terrified self-defense betrays human weakness. The letter is an even graver indictment, however, of a system that did not hesitate to force an ardently loyal thirty-two-year-old priest into evasions and selective recollection in order to salvage his reputation.

Roncalli's historical studies, and his friendship with the Milan cardinal, had a happier sequel which bore lasting fruit. In 1906 Roncalli discovered in the Milan archiepiscopal library thirty-nine parchment volumes containing the records of Saint Charles Borromeo's visitation of the diocese of Bergamo after the Council of Trent. He realized that they were a precious record of religious renewal under a diocesan bishop who was also a canonized saint. Editing the material for publication became a lifelong task which produced five volumes, published between 1936 and 1957.

The first day of August 1914 saw the outbreak of World War I. On the twentieth of the month Pius X died, grief-stricken at his inability to prevent the conflict. Two days later Bishop Radini-Tedeschi, having told his secretary "I can hear our Holy Father calling me from paradise," died in Bergamo. It was the end of Roncalli's youth. He was ready to move into —

A larger world

Roncalli realized that he could not expect to have with his new bishop the close relationship he had enjoyed with Radini-Tedeschi. On retreat at the end of September 1914, Roncalli resolved "not to feel any anxiety about my future." He would concentrate on his seminary teaching, renouncing all "fantastic dreams in which my pride may indulge, thoughts of honors, positions, etc. . . . They upset one's peace of mind, sap one's energy, and take all real joy and all value and merit from anything good one may do."

When Italy entered the war on the side of the Allies in May 1915, Roncalli was recalled to military service with his old rank of sergeant. At first a hospital orderly, he became a chaplain in March 1916. Pastoral ministry to the troops, many of them from peasant families like his own, gave him insight into qualities in his fellow soldiers which he had not previously discerned. Decades later he would recall his wartime ministry thus:

> After days of intensive work, when all one's limbs were aching, I would return to my room, fall down on my knees, and tears of consolation would run down my cheeks. What tremendous reserves of moral energy are present and at work among our people.

This was far removed from his reactions to army life as a seminarian. Roncalli had spent the first decade of his priesthood at headquarters, not in the trenches. But he had developed the heart and soul of a true pastor.

The end of the war in November 1918 brought Roncalli fresh challenges as director of a hostel for forty students in Bergamo, and spiritual director of the Bergamo seminary. On retreat at the end of April 1919 he looked backward and ahead.

> In the four years of war how good the Lord has been to me! . . . I call to mind all those young souls I have come to know during these years, many of whom I accompanied to the threshold of the other life; the memory of them moves me deeply, and the thought that they will pray for me is comforting and encouraging. . . .

> I will never say or do anything, I will dismiss as a temptation any thought, which might in any way be directed to persuading my superiors to give me positions or duties of greater distinction. . . . My main task is here, the apostolate among students.

Other tasks crowded in upon him nonetheless. He was in demand as a preacher. In September 1920 he achieved great success with an address in Bergamo before a large crowd which included many bishops, at the first post-war Eucharistic Congress. Two months later Roncalli's bishop told him that he would be going to Rome as National Director of the Propagation of the Faith, responsible for organizing support for the missions throughout Italy.

Roncalli protested that he lacked organizing ability. "I am by nature lazy, I write very slowly and am easily distracted." A letter from his old friend Cardinal Ferrari, dying of throat cancer in Milan, reassured him: "Go ahead. Whenever God calls, one goes, without hesitation, abandoning oneself in everything to his divine and loving providence." Roncalli realized that he had no choice but to accept. In a letter to a friend, however, he confessed that "this sudden change in the direction of my life has left me astonished and terrified."

Ferrari died on February 2, 1921, having served as Archbishop of Milan for twenty-seven years. Roncalli's contemporary tribute to his old friend and mentor described the person he would one day become himself.

> He always preferred to affirm rather than to deny, to act rather than to criticize. Pettiness was foreign to him. He overcame every obstacle with unvanquished constancy, drawing his inspiration not from worldly criteria but from the Christian faith and piety that filled the depths of his spirit. . . . He sought the kingdom of God and Its Justice, and nothing else. He knew that he had to become holy in order to make others holy.

The following months brought Roncalli the honors customary for a cleric now in the service of the Holy See: Honorary Canon of the Bergamo Cathedral in March and Domestic Prelate in May. About the latter Roncalli wrote his family with greater piety than realism: "This dignity is a great responsibility."

On January 22, 1922 Benedict XV, the Pope who had approved Roncalli's appointment, died. His efforts to terminate his predecessor's anti-modernist campaign had achieved only limited success. His initiatives for peace during the World War gained him the title of *Franzosenpapst* ("French Pope") in Berlin and *le Pape boche* in Paris. Recognition of his efforts came, of all places, from the government of Turkey, which in 1920 erected his statue in Istanbul saluting him as "the great Pope of the world tragedy . . . the benefactor of all people, irrespective of nationality or religion." Benedict would be known also as "Pope of the missions" because of his exhortation to bishops in mission territories to recruit a native clergy and put the welfare of the people they served above the imperial interests of the countries from which (in those days) they all came.

The longest conclave of this century took fourteen ballots to elect Achille Ratti as Pope Pius XI on February 6. An expert paleographer who had worked for twenty-three years at the Ambrosian Library in Milan and from 1911 at the Vatican Library (of which he became prefect in 1914), he had served as nuncio to Poland from 1918 to 1921, when Benedict XV rescued him from the maelstrom of Polish nationalism by making him Archbishop of Milan. He had been there only five months when he was elected Pope. His first papal act was to give the blessing *Urbi et Orbi* from the outside loggia of St. Peter's — the first Pope to do so since 1870. (No one attempted to repeat with the new Pontiff, a choleric man with a notably short fuse, the "lost key" scam which had prevented his predecessors from imparting this public benediction.)

The new Pope continued his predecessor's support for the missions by issuing on May 3, only three months after his election, the Motu proprio *Romanorum Pontificum*. This transferred to Rome the office for promoting missionary work which had been founded in Lyon a century before, and elevated it to the Pontifical Society for the Propagation of the Faith, under the direction of the cardinal prefect of the identically named congregation. Roncalli had a major role in the preparation of this decree, initiated by Benedict XV. He learned in this way how papal documents are produced.

Roncalli's work took him to every part of Italy, including Sicily. He was careful to recognize previous efforts for the missions, thus retaining the goodwill of people who could easily have resented the intrusion of a newly important curialist. Roncalli more than doubled the annual collection for the missions in Italy and founded a magazine in which he appealed not only for funds but also for prayers on behalf of the missions.

In November 1921 Roncalli was appointed professor of patristics at the Pontifical Lateran Athenaeum (his old seminary, upgraded; today the Lateran University). This was a part-time position, normal for a curial official at that time. He was an immediate hit with the students, who are reported to have applauded his lectures.

Roncalli was shocked, therefore, to be summoned on February 17, 1925 to Cardinal Secretary of State Gasparri, who told him that he would shortly leave Rome to become Apostolic Visitor to Bulgaria (an Orthodox country with few Catholics). It was a temporary appointment only, the cardinal assured him. After a brief stay in this Balkan "purgatory" (as Gasparri termed it), Roncalli would formally enter the Vatican diplomatic corps with a posting to Argentina.

What had happened? One story is that someone had denounced Roncalli's Lateran lectures as "modernist." Meriol Trevor, his first serious English-language biographer, reports on the authority of an anonymous eye-witness that shortly after he became Pope in 1958, Roncalli found in his Vatican personnel file a notation from this period: "Suspected of modernism." He immediately seized a pen and wrote: "I, John XXIII Pope, declare I was *never* a modernist!" (How many others, one wonders, had their careers and lives ruined and never received a chance to vindicate themselves?)

Another hypothesis is that Roncalli was removed for political reasons. From late 1922 Italy was governed by the Fascist party of Benito Mussolini. He was opposed by a Catholic party, the *Partito Popolare Italiano* (PPI), led since its foundation in 1914 by the Sicilian priest Don Luigi Sturzo. To consolidate his power, Mussolini knew he had to achieve a rapprochement with the Church. Secret negotiations with Cardinal Gasparri began in January 1923. They would terminate in the Lateran Treaties of 1929, in which the Italian state pledged to respect Church rights and to pay a huge indemnity for the confiscation of the papal states in 1870. In return the clergy were to withdraw from party politics.

To demonstrate the Church's goodwill, Don Sturzo was ordered by Cardinal Gasparri to resign as Secretary of the PPI in July 1923. He went into exile, first in London, later in the United States. Pius XI and Gasparri had decided to abandon the PPI in favor of "Catholic Action," which organized the Catholic laity for social action under the direction of the hierarchy.

Since this decision was not made public, however, many Italian Catholics continued to support the PPI as the best bulwark against Fascism. Roncalli was one. Another was the young priest Giovanni Battista Montini, son of a Brescia newspaper editor and PPI parliament member — and Roncalli's successor as Pope Paul VI. The two men first met in the autumn of 1924, when Montini had just received a junior appointment to the Vatican Secretariat of State. They became lifelong friends.

Roncalli expressed support for the PPI in a sermon preached in the Bergamo Cathedral on September 1, 1924 at a tenth anniversary Mass for Radini-Tedeschi. Fascist dignitaries were present in the congregation. Though Roncalli was never a political activist, his name may have appeared on a list of "unreliable" priests submitted to Gasparri by Mussolini's representatives as part of the ongoing negotiations.

For whatever reason — whether as a suspected "modernist" in theology or because someone considered him politically "mistaken" — Roncalli was marked for removal from Rome. The time-honored way to accomplish this was through promotion. When Pius XI received Roncalli on February 21, four days after Cardinal Gasparri had dropped his bombshell, the Pope told him he would be made an archbishop. He did not want anyone in Bulgaria pulling rank on his envoy — as the Polish hierarchy had done on him, Achille Ratti, when he was representing Pope Benedict in that country. On March 3, 1925 *Osservatore Romano* announced that the forty-three-year-old Monsignor Roncalli had been appointed titular Archbishop of Areopolis, a pile of Roman ruins between the Dead Sea and the Red Sea. One should not over-estimate this promotion. In the world Roncalli had entered, his new dignity was scarcely more significant than the title of monsignor in a large American archdiocese today.

Exile in Bulgaria

Roncalli was frankly distressed about the appointment. He tried to get out of it, as he had tried to avoid the mission job four years previously, pleading to Cardinal Gasparri that he lacked diplomatic experience and knew nothing about Bulgaria. Gasparri confessed ignorance himself.

> Listen, Monsignor, I'm told the situation in Bulgaria is very confused. Everyone seems to be fighting with everyone else: the Moslems with the Orthodox, the Greek Catholics with the Latins, and the Latins with each other. Could you go there and find out what is really happening?

Was the appointment a matter of obedience, Roncalli asked. It was, the cardinal assured him. Upon hearing Roncalli's name the Holy Father had exclaimed: "Splendid! This is the man sent by Providence." That clinched the matter — as Cardinal Ferrari's letter about the mission appointment had sealed Roncalli's fate four years before.

Roncalli chose the feast of Saint Joseph, March 19, 1925, for his episcopal ordination. For his bishop's motto he took the words repeated by the sixteenth-century church historian Caesare Baronius, the disciple of Saint Philip Neri, on his daily visits to the statue of Saint Peter in the Vatican basilica: *"Obedientia et pax"* (Obedience and peace). More than a motto, the words furnish a valuable key to Roncalli's whole life.

His relatives were present for this ordination, looking stiff and uncomfortable in their Sunday clothes. The next day Roncalli took them to the Vatican Grottoes for his first episcopal Mass, the site of his first Mass twenty-one years before and of his burial thirty-eight years later.

The situation Roncalli encountered on arrival in Sofia was as confused as Cardinal Gasparri had indicated. The first papal representative to Bulgaria in five centuries, Roncalli found a tiny flock of only 62,000 Catholics in an overwhelmingly Orthodox country. This did not protect him, however, from Orthodox attacks as the agent of Roman "proselytism" and "imperialism."

The Catholics were themselves divided: 48,000 (mostly city folk) belonged to Roncalli's own Latin Rite, 14,000 (scattered in rural areas) were Eastern Rite Catholics. These were the "Greek Catholics" Gasparri had mentioned. They worshiped in the same way as their Orthodox neighbors, had married priests and celibate bishops, but unlike the Orthodox were in communion with the Pope. As such they were regarded as turncoats and traitors in a country in which Orthodoxy (rather like Latin Rite Catholicism in Poland and Ireland) was considered the paramount expression of national culture and patriotism.

Roncalli set about visiting this scattered flock. "I went to seek them out in the most distant villages," he recalled 1954. "I entered their modest homes and became their neighbor." Travel was difficult. A contemporary photograph shows Archbishop Roncalli sitting sideways in an oxcart, better suited for hauling potatoes or manure than people.

A few years previously Achille Ratti, now reigning as Pope Pius XI, had received a chilly reception from Catholic prelates in Poland, resentful at the presence of an uninvited agent of Rome. Archbishop Sapieha of Krakow (during World War II the protector of the seminarian Karol Wojtyla) actually shut in Ratti's face the door of a room where the Polish bishops were meeting. Ratti never forgot this slight. Sapieha had to wait until 1946 to receive from Pius XII the red hat which normally went with his position.

The situation in Bulgaria was quite different. Catholics there welcomed Roncalli with open arms, grateful that someone in Rome was aware of their existence. There was more to Roncalli's success than that, however. He ascribed his warm reception to the fact that he was the Pope's representative. Equally important was his personality. People experienced him as a pastor not as a diplomat. He would never forget the people he came to love in Bulgaria. In 1949, when he was nuncio in France, he wrote a friend:

> I still keep a fine collection of photographs of these beautiful country places, and when I am tired I look through them again. Believe me, when I remember those dear people, my heart is moved and my eyes are full of tears.

Roncalli's friendliness and pastoral concern overcame prejudice and resentment even among some of the Orthodox. A special friend was the aged Armenian patriarch in Bulgaria, Archbishop Hovagnimian. With about 50,000 of his flock, he had escaped the Turkish massacres of 1896, and the even worse pogrom of 1915 (denied to this day by the Turkish government). To Roncalli, who met him in 1927, the eighty-year-old patriarch poured out the griefs of a lifetime.

The Ecumenical Patriarch in Constantinople (honorary head of the autonomous Orthodox churches) had refused to recognize him. In 1893, he told Roncalli, he had received the Pope's representative in his cathedral with the honors due a patriarch. Roncalli gave the old man a medal of Pius XI.

On October 13, 1962, two days after the start of the Second Vatican Council, Roncalli told the non-Catholic observers about this gift and the man who had received it. "When a short time later he was dying, he asked that the medal should be placed upon his heart. I saw it there myself, and the memory moves me still."

In a pre-ecumenical age, Roncalli was learning about ecumenism in the school of experience. He also learned its pitfalls. One of the most painful was the flap over the marriage of the Bulgarian King Boris to the Italian Princess Giovanna. German by birth, like his royal cousins in neighboring Greece, Boris had been baptized as a Latin Rite Catholic, but had converted to Orthodoxy out of political necessity. Before their Catholic marriage in Assisi on October 25, 1930, Boris and his bride gave the customary promise to have their children baptized and reared as Catholics. Upon returning to Sofia from Italy, the couple underwent a second, equally grand, Orthodox marriage ceremony. When Pius

XI heard about it, he hit the ceiling. Part of the blame for this treachery, as it was considered in Rome, was assigned to Roncalli.

Papal indignation erupted afresh when the couple's first child received Orthodox baptism in January 1933. Roncalli wrote a letter of protest, and received a reply from Boris reminding him that he was "by family and baptism a Catholic." He had acted "solely out of concern for the interest of my country." The Orthodox, egged on by communists at home and next door in the Soviet Union, were beginning to question their King's loyalty to the state church. Roncalli understood all this much better than his superiors in Rome. As a kindness he invited the young Italian Queen to attend Mass in his domestic chapel (rather than in a public church), and gave her a handsome missal.

The promised posting to Argentina never materialized. There is no evidence that this was due to malice. Roncalli was the victim of nothing worse than bureaucratic amnesia. Banished from Rome to a temporary post in a distant country with few Catholics, his superiors at headquarters soon forgot about him as they turned their attention to more pressing matters closer to home.

In February 1929 there was a flurry of rumors that Roncalli was being considered for the vacant See of Milan. He had excellent qualifications. He was from the Milan church province. He was editing the Acts of Milan's great archbishop, Saint Charles Borromeo. He had been a friend of Cardinal Ferrari. At forty-eight, he was the right age. Roncalli wrote home telling his relatives "not to waste time imagining things. On the reverse side of greater honors lie also great and incredible sufferings." He would live to see those words verified. But the time was not yet. The appointment went to the Benedictine Abbot Ildefonso Schuster. Some time later the Italian press reported that Roncalli was to become nuncio in Bucharest. It would have been a promotion. Rumania had far more Catholics than Bulgaria. The previous nuncio was returning to Rome as a cardinal. Once again, however, Roncalli was passed over.

At Easter 1930 Roncalli wrote his family:

> I continue to be well and to live peacefully and happily, without any thought other than to do the will of the Lord. In part I owe this tranquil disposition and ability to let myself go in the arms of Providence and obedience to being born in the country, into a family that is poor in material goods but rich in faith and the fear of the Lord, and that is used to the simple realities of nature coming round day by day and year by year. So a sound organism, without any desire for extraordinary things, since what the Lord

has given us every day according to nature is already so beautiful and wonderful.

The journal of the retreat he made shortly after this letter was written, tells a somewhat different story:

The trials, with which in recent months the Lord has tested my patience, have been many: anxieties concerning the arrangements for founding the Bulgarian seminary [*it never got off the ground*]; the uncertainty which has now lasted for more than five years about the exact scope of my mission in this country; my frustrations and disappointments at not being able to do more, and my enforced restriction to my life of a complete hermit, in opposition to my longing for work directly ministering to souls; my interior discontent with what is left of my natural human inclinations, even if until now I have succeeded in holding all this under control. . . . I must do my best to preserve this cheerfulness in my soul and in my outward behavior. One must learn how to bear suffering without letting anyone know it is there. Was this not one of the last lessons I learned from Msgr. Radini of revered memory?

Journal entries from his annual retreats in the years following are similar.

My prolonged mission as papal representative in this country often causes me acute and intimate suffering, but I try not to show this (*September 1933*).

Do not be concerned about your future but think that perhaps you are drawing near the gateway of eternal life. [*He was approaching fifty-three.*] At the same time be ever more content to live like this, hidden from the world, perhaps forgotten by your superiors, and do not grieve at being little appreciated but try to find an even greater joy in "being esteemed of little worth" [*Imitation of Christ* I, ii, 25]. . . . What has Msgr. Roncalli been doing during these monotonous years at the Apostolic Delegation? Trying to make himself holy and with simplicity, kindness and joy opening a source of blessings and graces for all Bulgaria, whether he lives to see it or not (*August 1934*).

Relief was at hand — of a sort. Shortly after writing these lines Roncalli was asked if he would be willing to become apostolic delegate in Istanbul (still called Constantinople by Roncalli and his superiors). He replied (as he reported in a letter to a friend)

that I was always ready to go where obedience demanded, even if that meant doing a provisional stint in hell; but as to whether I liked the idea or not, I had no illusions about the place. I believe Constantinople is a good post for someone content to hold together what remains of the beleaguered Catholic flock, while waiting patiently for the doors to be opened for an apostolate among the Turks.

This somber evaluation reflects the severe restrictions placed on all Christian activities by Turkey's militantly secular government.

Announcement of the new appointment came on November 17, 1934. The Secretary of State, Cardinal Pacelli, never mentioned it, however, when he received Roncalli on that day. Ten years in Sofia had made him something of an expert on the Balkans. At the home office, however, he was still an outsider.

Roncalli's 1934 Christmas sermon was his farewell to Bulgaria:

I think I have been well understood by them [*the Orthodox — possibly a response to criticisms that he had been too friendly*]. The respect I've always tried to have for everyone, both in public and in private; my unbroken and non-judgmental silence; the fact that I never stooped to pick up the stones that were cast at me from this or that side of the street — all this leaves me with the clear certainty that I have shown everyone that I love them in the Lord with that fraternal, heartfelt and sincere charity that is taught in the gospels.

Roncalli said the Holy See had granted his request to change his See from Areopolis to Mesembria, Bulgaria. He would remain its titular archbishop until he became Patriarch of Venice in 1953. The concluding passage, recalling the Irish custom of placing a candle in the window at Christmas to welcome the Holy Family, is well known, but merits quotation here:

Dear brothers, nobody knows the paths of the future. Wherever I may go if a Bulgarian passes by my door, whether it's night-time or whether he's poor, he will find that candle lighted at my window. Knock, knock. You won't be asked whether you're a Catholic or not; the title of Bulgarian brother is enough. Come in. Two fraternal arms will welcome you, and the heart of a friend will make it a feast-day. Such is the charity of the Lord whose graces have made life sweet during my ten-year stay in Bulgaria. *Pax hominibus bonae voluntatae* [Peace to all of good will].

Roncalli's arrival in Sofia ten years before had passed unnoticed, apart from the attacks in the Orthodox press noted above. When he boarded the Orient

Express for Istanbul on January 4, 1935, representatives of the King and the Orthodox archbishop were on hand to give him a grand send-off.

"Ant's work, bee's work"

Roncalli would spend exactly ten years in Istanbul. He arrived at the beginning of January 1935 by train. He departed two days after Christmas 1944 by air. The contrasting means of transport symbolize the dramatic events of this decade, half of it a time of increasingly fragile peace, the other dominated by the agony of war.

Roncalli was still marveling at his new situation at the end of his first year in Istanbul. "Since the end of August 1934," he wrote during his retreat in December 1935, "what unexpected alterations in my affairs! I am in Turkey." He also recorded a friendly message passed to him by a cardinal in Rome: "By sending me here the Holy Father has wished to point out the impression made on him by my silence, maintained for ten years, about being kept in Bulgaria, without ever complaining or expressing the wish to be moved elsewhere. This was in order to honor a resolution I had made, and I am glad I was always faithful to it." The resolution was a fruit of his bishop's motto: *Obedientiae et pax.*

There were fewer Catholics in Turkey than in Bulgaria. But whereas Catholics there had their own bishops, Roncalli now had pastoral responsibility for the 35,000 Catholics who lived in and around Istanbul. This made the work more congenial to him. He was responsible as well for the little Catholic flock in neighboring Greece, most of them belonging to his own Latin Rite. In both Greece and Turkey there were also small numbers of Eastern Rite Catholics with their own bishops. Building on his previous experience in Bulgaria, Roncalli tried from the start to show friendship toward the 100,000 Orthodox Christians gathered round the Ecumenical Patriarch in the Phanar (his official residence) in Istanbul. Such contacts were especially difficult in Greece, to this day the most virulently anti-Catholic of all Orthodox lands.

Cultivating good relations with the Turkish authorities was difficult for different reasons. The regime regarded all religions as obstacles to the country's modernization. Shortly after Roncalli's arrival in Istanbul, a law forbade the wearing of any kind of religious garb in public. Roncalli invited his clergy to join him in a demonstration of obedience. On June 15, 1935, the day the law came into effect, he marched with a group of them out of the church of St.

Anthony in a dark suit and necktie. For the rest of his time in Turkey he would wear the cassock in church buildings only. Where fundamental principles were not involved, he would obey even militantly secular civil authority.

As a further gesture of goodwill Roncalli, while struggling to learn Turkish himself, had some of the prayers at extraliturgical devotions recited in Turkish. When people walked out of church in protest and denounced him to Rome, he refused to budge. "The Apostolic Vicar is a bishop for everyone," he explained in his journal, "and intends honoring the gospel, which does not admit national monopolies, does not become a fossil, looks to the future."

Most of Roncalli's work, especially prior to the outbreak of war in September 1939, was on this modest scale: "ant's work, bee's work," he called it in the imagery of his youth. He became a good friend of the Reverend Austin Oakley, chaplain at the British Embassy and the Archbishop of Canterbury's personal representative to the Ecumenical Patriarch. Such a friendship was unusual in those years. Even more unusual were Roncalli's visits to Oakley's chapel, where the two men prayed together. He knew the walls between separated Christians could not be demolished quickly. "I try to pull out a brick here and there," he told his Anglican friend.

Such an approach met with little understanding in Rome. Notes from a brief retreat back home in Bergamo in October 1936 show that Roncalli suffered from his superiors' disapproval.

> I feel quite detached from everything, from all thoughts of advancement or anything else. I know I deserve nothing and I do not feel any impatience. It is true, however, that the difference between my way of seeing situations on the spot and certain ways of judging the same things in Rome hurts me considerably: it is my only real cross. I want to bear it humbly, with great willingness to please my principal superiors, because this and nothing else is what I desire. I shall always speak the truth, but with mildness, keeping silence about what might seem a wrong or injury done to myself, ready to sacrifice myself or be sacrificed. The Lord sees everything and will deal justly with me. Above all, I wish to continue always to render good for evil, and in all things to endeavor to prefer the gospel truth to the wiles of human politics.

This preference would continue to bring Roncalli criticism to his life's end — and beyond.

Evidence of the success of Roncalli's low-key diplomacy was the attendance at the requiem Mass he celebrated in Istanbul on February 19, 1939 for

Pius XI. Present, in addition to the usual members of the diplomatic corps, were representatives of the Turkish government, the Grand Rabbi, and the Armenian and Ecumenical Patriarchs. The latter was also represented at the *Te Deum* for the election of Pius XII. When Roncalli visited the patriarch on May 27, 1939 to thank him and exchange the kiss of peace, his host greeted him in faultless Latin (significant in view of the negative historical associations of that language for the hypersensitive Orthodox): *"Haec est dies quam fecit Dominus"* ("This is the day the Lord has made" — from the Latin liturgy for Easter Day).

Roncalli's journal entries from his Istanbul years show little of the frustration of the decade in Bulgaria. "I am pleased with my new ministry in Turkey, in spite of so many difficulties," he wrote during this same retreat in October 1936, adding: "I am fond of the Turks, to whom the Lord has sent me." Further acquaintance deepened this sentiment: "I love the Turks," he wrote in November 1939, "I appreciate the natural qualities of these people who have their own place reserved in the march of civilization." By the time Roncalli wrote those words, however, civilization's march had been disrupted by the coming of war.

"This murderous war"

The pre-war years brought recurrent rumors that Roncalli was marked for promotion. In 1936 there were efforts to make him nuncio to Poland. In the summer of 1939 he received (as he wrote in the November retreat notes cited above) "an extremely benevolent and encouraging welcome in Rome" from his superiors, including the new Pope Pius XII.

> There is no lack of rumor around me, murmurs that "greater things are in store." I am not so foolish as to listen to this flattery, which is, yes, I admit it, for me too a temptation. I try very hard to ignore these rumors which speak of deceit and spite. I treat them as a joke: I smile and pass on.

With the outbreak of war in September 1939 the rumors ceased. Istanbul, though still an ecclesiastical backwater, became an important political listening post and one of the few places from which attempts might be launched to alleviate Europe's sufferings and to rescue Jews from Hitler's Holocaust.

Roncalli realized that a prerequisite for such efforts was strict neutrality between the combatants. Roncalli's retreat notes from November 1940 are significant in this regard:

> This murderous war which is being waged on the ground, on the seas and in the air is truly a vindication of divine justice because the sacred laws governing human society have been transgressed and violated. It has been asserted, and is still being asserted, that God is bound to preserve this or that country, or grant it invulnerability and final victory. . . . But he has not given any guarantee of special and privileged assistance, except to the race of believers, that is to holy Church as such. And even his assistance to his Church, although it preserves her from final defeat, does not guarantee her immunity from trials and persecutions. . . .

> Patriotism, which is right and may be holy, but may also degenerate into nationalism, which in my case would be most detrimental to the dignity of my episcopal ministry, must be kept above all nationalistic disputes. The world is poisoned with morbid nationalism, built up on the basis of race and blood, in contradiction to the gospel.

Roncalli's wartime efforts to help Jews have been the subject of numerous reports, some of them exaggerated. He was on good terms with the German ambassador to Turkey, Franz von Papen, a reactionary Catholic who, in 1933, had joined Hitler's first cabinet as Vice Chancellor in the naive belief that he could "control" the Fuehrer. Von Papen told the postulator of Pope John's beatification cause on oath that during the war Roncalli had "helped 24,000 Jews with clothes, money, and documents." There is no way to verify this figure. It is clear, however, that Roncalli did what he could.

The thousands of false "baptismal certificates" which Roncalli is said to have issued to Hungarian and Bulgarian Jews were actually "Immigration Certificates" issued by the Palestine Jewish Agency and forwarded by Roncalli to Vatican diplomats in the Balkans. The most moving of many testimonies to Roncalli's rescue efforts came from Isaac Herzog, Grand Rabbi of Jerusalem, who wrote Roncalli on February 28, 1944:

> I want to express my deepest gratitude for the energetic steps that you have undertaken and will undertake to save our unfortunate people. . . . You follow in the tradition, so profoundly humanitarian, of the Holy See, and you follow the feelings of your own heart. The people of Israel will never forget the help brought to its unfortunate brothers and sisters by the Holy See and its highest representatives at this saddest moment of our history.

Chaim Barlas, the representative in Turkey of the Jewish Agency, who met often with Roncalli, reported after the war that "the Nuncio Roncalli worked and toiled indefatigably on behalf" of Jews in the Balkans. The Jewish writer Saul Friedlander wrote in his book *Pius XII and the Third Reich* (which is severely critical of that Pope):

> The Zionist archives contain numerous documents concerning the unceasing activities of Nuncio Roncalli in favor of Jews. Let us underline that Monsignor Roncalli has declared that all he did in this field was upon papal urging.

Roncalli also tried to alleviate wartime hunger in Greece, which was under German and Italian occupation. This required the utmost tact, since as an Italian and a Catholic he was doubly suspect to the Greeks. In the autumn of 1941 he had a two-hour secret meeting with the Metropolitan of Athens, Archbishop Damaskinos, who as regent for the Greek government-in-exile in London had made the relief of his countrymen's needs his highest priority. The amount of material aid Roncalli was able to supply was modest. But the meeting was a great success ecumenically. "We began with a handshake," he reported to Rome, "but said farewell with a heart-felt embrace and with sincere joy in our hearts."

Preaching on Pentecost 1944, when the war was drawing to a close, Roncalli said that the Holy Spirit alone could demolish the barriers between nations and races which were causing such terrible suffering.

> Jesus came to break down all these barriers; he died to proclaim universal brotherhood; the central point of his teaching is charity, that is the love which binds all men to him as the elder brother, and binds us all with him to the Father.

On December 6, 1944 a coded telegram arrived in the Apostolic Delegation in Istanbul from Monsignor Tardini, Roncalli's superior in Rome. The secretary who usually decoded such messages was absent. Roncalli laboriously deciphered the cable himself. When he was finished, he could hardly believe the words in front of him. They said he had been appointed nuncio to France. He wrote in his journal the next day:

> Late at night Tardini's coded telegram arrived, like a thunderbolt. I was astonished and dismayed. I went to the chapel to ask Jesus whether I should elude the burden and the cross, or just accept it according to the principle *non recuso laborem* (I do not refuse work). That was how I spent the night between the feasts of St. Nicholas and St. Ambrose, two men who were called to the episcopacy and became great saints and sanctifiers.

Nuncio in France

Roncalli had good reason to be astonished at what Saint Nicholas, the legendary distributor of gifts to children, had brought him. To be plucked from twenty years' oblivion in the Orient and given one of the most prestigious positions in the papal diplomatic service was a reversal of fortune which fully justified his designation of thunderbolt. Roncalli mentioned Saint Ambrose, not only because he is commemorated on December 7, but, more importantly, because his choice as bishop of Milan in 374 was an even greater thunderbolt. Ambrose was prefect of the city and an unbaptized catechumen when he was named bishop by popular acclamation.

Roncalli was not Rome's first choice for the Paris nunciature. Three days before Tardini's telegram to Roncalli, the job had been offered to Archbishop Joseph Fietta, since 1936 the nuncio to Argentina. He declined for reasons of health. Did Fietta know what he would be facing? We cannot say. For months General de Gaulle, the *de facto* head of the French republic and already the personification of French *grandeur* (years later, as President, he would invite journalists at his magnificently staged press conferences to "supply some questions for my answers") had been demanding the removal of the nuncio Valerio Valeri and twenty-five of the French bishops, three cardinals among them, because of their alleged support for the collaborationist regime of Marshall Pétain. Anyone who took over Valeri's post would be walking into a hornets' nest. There were people at Rome who felt that for such a position Roncalli was just right. A French journalist seeking information about the new nuncio was told by a curial prelate: "He's an old fogey."

The official letter of appointment did not reach Roncalli until December 22. It was signed by his old friend Montini, like Tardini one of the two "Substitutes" for the Secretary of State whom Pius XII declined to appoint, preferring to exercise that office himself. Roncalli was told that he must be in Paris in time to present New Year's greetings to General de Gaulle on behalf of the diplomatic corps, of which the papal nuncio (according to a rule established at the Congress of Vienna in 1815 to prevent national rivalries) was dean. Otherwise the greetings would be presented by the ambassador of the Soviet Union, as senior diplomat in Paris — a prospect which Pius XII found insupportable.

Visiting the Secretariat of State in Rome three days after Christmas, Roncalli asked who was responsible for his promotion. Tardini replied with his customary gruff bluntness that it had come from "the man upstairs," and hinted that he did not approve. Pius XII himself told Roncalli on December 29: "I want to make it clear that I was the one who acted in this nomination, thought of it and arranged it all. " With the self-assurance which was a hallmark of his pontificate the Pope added: "For that reason you may be sure that the will of God could not be more manifest or encouraging." Roncalli was grateful, but not carried away. To friends who congratulated him on his promotion, he quoted an old Lombard proverb: "Where horses break down, an ass gets through."

Before leaving Rome Roncalli met also with his ousted predecessor Valerio Valeri, who handed him the text of the speech he had prepared for his successor to deliver in Paris three days later. Roncalli knew that Valeri had been sacrificed on the altar of political expediency. Thirteen years later he would show his sympathy by voting for Valeri in the 1958 conclave.

On New Year's day, with the Soviet ambassador standing beside him, Roncalli told de Gaulle, on behalf of the assembled diplomatic corps, that France had recovered her liberty and faith in her own destiny "thanks to your political sagacity." The deeper significance of this tribute was not lost on its recipient. It signaled the Holy See's recognition of de Gaulle's still provisional government and its admission that the Vichy regime had been a temporary aberration.

Roncalli's position in Paris was very different from his two previous postings. In Bulgaria, Turkey, and Greece Catholics were tiny minorities, grateful for the presence of the Pope's representative. Catholics in France, still glorying in the title of the Church's "eldest daughter," were wary of Roman interference. Though he was accredited to the government, as he had not been in Sofia, Istanbul, and Athens, Roncalli could travel to Church functions in France only by episcopal invitation.

The French bishops were aware of de Gaulle's demand for a purge of their ranks. They had not forgotten (how could they?) Pius VII's removal of the entire French hierarchy in 1801. The Holy See had already replaced the nuncio. Had his successor come to find further victims? Roncalli moved swiftly to reassure the bishops. On the feast of the Epiphany, January 6, 1945, he wrote them "a humble and simple letter" in which he treated the bishops with respect, praised Valeri, and made it clear that he had no mandate to effect sweeping changes. The bishops were grateful: about a hundred wrote personal replies.

The sequel showed that the bishops' fears were exaggerated. The demand for a wholesale cleansing of the episcopate had come in the summer of 1944 from Catholics in the resistance movement. By the time Roncalli reached Paris, passions had begun to cool. In July 1945 seven prelates were quietly replaced, three of them in French overseas dioceses. Roncalli asked one of the ousted bishops, an auxiliary of Paris, to be his confessor — a typical gesture of kindness.

Roncalli's French was reasonably fluent but sounded (as this writer clearly recalls from a public audience in 1959) exactly like Italian. An anecdote, better authenticated than many of those which clustered round him, illustrates both his command of the language and the informality which came naturally to him. Preaching from a Parisian pulpit during a solemn ceremony, the nuncio's attempts to be heard were defeated by feedback from a defective microphone. Roncalli abandoned his prepared text and the pulpit to tell the congregation from the center aisle of the church: "Dear children, you have heard nothing of what I was saying. That doesn't matter. It wasn't very interesting. I don't speak French very well. My saintly old mother, who was a peasant, didn't make me learn it early enough." In the triumphalist Church of Pius XII a prelate who spoke like that was rare — and irresistible. The Pope himself, however, disapproved of such conduct. Hearing that his representative in Paris went for daily walks in the streets of the capital, Pius said that this was undignified. Obedient as always, Roncalli desisted.

A barbed wire seminary

The two major questions which troubled Church life during Roncalli's French years were the controversy over "worker priests" and the "new theology." Before recounting those episodes, however, we must record a project dear to Roncalli's heart which his biographers have mostly overlooked: his support for a "barbed wire seminary" in the camp for German prisoners of war near Chartres. Its rector was a remarkable German priest named Franz Stock.

Ordained in 1932 for the archdiocese of Paderborn, Stock (who had done some of his theological studies in Paris and spoke beautiful French) was sent to Paris two years later as chaplain to German-speaking Catholics in the French capital. He remained there throughout the war and the German occupation. This brought him the grim task of ministering to captured French resistance fighters and innocent hostages, condemned to death in reprisal for attacks on the

German occupation troops. The Abbé Stock, as he was known in France, is estimated to have accompanied over two thousand prisoners to their execution by his own countrymen.

In March 1945, two months before the German surrender, Stock was asked to become rector of a seminary for German prisoners of war who wished to study for the priesthood. The initiative for this undertaking came from another remarkable priest, the French Abbé Le Meur. He had been imprisoned in 1944 for aiding the resistance, escaped, and was condemned to death *in absentia*. Despite these harrowing experiences, Le Meur devoted himself, as soon as France was liberated, to the relief of German prisoners of war. At his urging the French military authorities gave permission for German priests in the prisoner of war camps to minister freely to their fellow prisoners, and granted Le Meur's further request that aspirants to the priesthood be assembled in the camp near Chartres.

Franz Stock, then officially an American prisoner of war, visited Roncalli in Paris in April 1945 to tell him of the planned seminary. The nuncio was delighted and promised to give all possible help, including official approval from the responsible Roman congregation. Further visits followed, both in Paris and Chartres, culminating in the ordination of two priests by Roncalli in the prison chapel at Easter 1947. The "barbed wire seminary" went out of existence shortly thereafter, due to the repatriation of German prisoners in France. At the peak of its activity it had enrolled an astonishing 949 seminarians, of whom more than 600 were ultimately ordained.

Roncalli was deeply impressed with the seminary and with the man who headed it. He said he would use his influence at Rome to have the Abbé Stock made a bishop, predicting that he would be "the bishop of Franco-German reconciliation." It was not to be. Franz Stock died suddenly on February 24, 1948 at the early age of forty-three, his will to live broken by the terrible scenes he had witnessed during his wartime ministry to the victims of Nazi terror. His cause of beatification was introduced by the French bishops in 1981.

Breaking out of the ghetto

In early July 1945, Roncalli attended an open-air evening Mass near the Eiffel Tower in Paris to give thanks for the return of French concentration camp inmates and prisoners of war. He wrote a friend:

Many thousands were present, including all those who have returned from the German camps of suffering and death: a great crowd of women in mourning; and a hundred priests, still dressed as prisoners, distributed holy communion.

The letter contains no hint of realization that these priests, having suffered side by side with men who visited parish churches in France (if they entered them at all) only for baptisms, weddings, and funerals, might not be willing to return to the closed clerical world they had left. It was the experience of these priests, combined with sociological research which showed that only one percent of French working-class males practiced the faith into which most of them were still baptized, which produced the experiment of worker-priests. They worked full-time in industry, wore secular dress (in a day when French priests still wore cassocks everywhere), and said Mass on kitchen tables rather than in parish churches.

There were never more than a hundred worker-priests. But they deeply shocked traditional Catholics in France, who inundated Roncalli with horror stories about these radical clerics who, their critics charged, were communists in all but name. Not all the complaints were frivolous. In their zeal to identify with French workers, some worker-priests became officers in communist-dominated unions. Realizing that the silent Latin Mass was meaningless to dechristianized workers, many of these priests indulged in liturgical experiments then considered shocking. There were also problems with celibacy.

Roncalli passed on the complaints to Rome, as he was bound to do. He also listened to the bishops who defended the worker-priests, notably Cardinal Suhard of Paris. Suhard had become aware of the problem of dechristianization a decade before the war, as bishop of Bayeux. Translated to Rheims in 1935 and to Paris in 1940, Suhard founded the *Mission de France* and later the *Mission de Paris* to train carefully selected seminarians to work as missionaries to the alienated rather than as chaplains for the devout. Suhard vigorously defended the worker-priests until his death in 1949.

It is unclear where Roncalli stood on this question. An early letter to his family showed that he was aware of the problem addressed by the worker-priests: "Paris is a city of five million inhabitants, and many of them lead a life that is completely cut off from the church." His deeply conservative piety made it difficult for him to sympathize with the worker-priests. Yet his strong pastoral sense made him open to the argument of his friend Montini in Rome: "When so much is at stake, risks must be taken, lest one should be guilty of failing to do all that is possible for the salvation of the world."

In October 1949 Roncalli wrote a characteristically mild letter about the worker-priests to Suhard's successor, Maurice Feltin (in whose appointment as Archbishop of Paris Roncalli had played a leading role). The letter offered "suggestions made in the Lord," and expressed "the desire to preserve in all circumstances the fervor, piety, and sacred character of the priesthood" while "coming close to the workers and bringing them the breath of light and grace." Feltin, like his predecessor, continued to defend the worker-priests against their critics. Only in 1953, after Roncalli's departure from Paris, did Rome issue restrictions which effectively crippled the experiment (e.g., limitation of manual labor to three hours a day).

While the worker-priests tried to reach the post-Christian masses with new pastoral methods, academic theologians in France were trying to break out of the ghetto of neo-scholasticism to restate the Church's unchanging faith in terms that would be meaningful to people more familiar with modern philosophers than with Aquinas and the other great thinkers of the Middle Ages. These "new theologians" — men like the Jesuits Henri de Lubac, Jean Daniélou, and Teilhard de Chardin, and the Dominicans Yves-Marie Congar and Marie-Dominique Chenu — helped shape the Vatican II documents. Daniélou and de Lubac became cardinals.

In the pontificate of Pius XII, however, their *nouvelle théologie*, with its return to patristic sources and use of modern philosophy, was suspect. Condemnation came in the encyclical *Humanae generis*, issued in August 1950. This decried the attempts of unnamed theologians "to weaken the significance of the dogmas . . . by seeking to free them from concepts and formulations long held by the church and to return instead to the language of the Bible and the Fathers." All those named above, and others as well, were subject to disciplinary measures such as loss of teaching positions, prohibition to publish, and (in Congar's case) exile to England.

Roncalli, who was uninvolved in this purge, furnished few clues to his views about the new theology. He seems to have gained most of his knowledge of theological developments in France from conversation. The time he could find for serious reading after dealing with official correspondence and attending public functions was devoted to his first love: history. He became an expert on the history of the Paris nunciature. Visiting the Palais des Papes at Avignon, he astonished the archivists with his knowledge of the Pontiffs who had lived there, in particular John XXII (1316-1334), the last legitimate Pope of that name.

On November 14, 1952 Roncalli received a "Private and confidential" letter from Montini in Rome asking in the name of the Pope whether he would be willing to succeed the Patriarch of Venice who was gravely ill. Roncalli wrote in his journal:

> I prayed, thought about it, and answered *Obedientia et pax*. A totally unexpected new direction to my life. I remember St. Joseph and follow his example. So I push my donkey off in a new direction and bless the Lord.

Two weeks later, on November 29, Montini again communicated with Roncalli, this time by telegram, to tell him that Pius was going to make him a cardinal at the coming consistory on January 12, 1953. According to custom, this meant that he must leave Paris. If the Patriarch of Venice survived, Roncalli would go to a curial position in Rome, a prospect he did not relish. When Archbishop Feltin, who was also to get a red hat in January, visited Roncalli to congratulate him, he found the nuncio "sad, gloomy, and troubled."

> I can't really see myself in Rome [*Roncalli explained*], going along day after day to meeting after meeting and concerned with administration. That's not what I'm good at. I'm really a pastor.

Roncalli had been forbidden to tell anyone about the death watch in Venice. It continued until December 29, when Roncalli read in the press of the Venetian Patriarch's death. He had narrowly escaped the Roman curia.

Roncalli's leave-taking was prolonged and affectionate, a tribute to his wide-ranging friendships. On January 15, 1953, President Vincent Auriol, exercising an ancient privilege of the head of the French State, presented the red cardinal's biretta to Roncalli. Auriol recorded later how moved he had been as Roncalli knelt before him, a professed unbeliever, to receive the emblem of his new dignity. On February 5 Roncalli hosted a dinner at the nunciature for Edouard Herriot, the anti-clerical president of the National Assembly and, like Auriol, a warm admirer, and the eight prime ministers of France since 1945. Only under the nuncio's roof, people remarked, could politicians of such diverse views gather in such a friendly fashion.

The diplomatic corps, fifty-nine strong, bade Roncalli farewell on February 19. On February 23 he boarded an early train for Italy: "A silent emotional farewell at 7:30, with a few tears here and there. I bless the Lord and thank him *pro universis beneficiis suis*, for all his kindness to me." He was going home, to be what in his heart he had always longed to be: a pastor. At age seventy-one, it was obviously his last assignment.

Pastor et Pater

Pius XII, who personally chose Roncalli for both Paris and Venice, had been, in his day, a great Pope. Elected on March 2, 1939 at the third ballot of a one-day conclave with forty-eight out of fifty-three votes, his pontificate was shadowed from the start by the clouds of war. During the conflict he agonized daily over how to limit hostilities and aid the victims of wartime atrocities. The judgment of D'Arcy Osborne, British Minister to the Holy See and a non-Catholic, as required by British diplomatic practice, is worth recording.

> So far from being a cool (which, I suppose implies cold-blooded and inhumane) diplomatist, Pius XII was the most warmly humane, kind, generous, sympathetic (and incidentally saintly) character that it has been my privilege to meet in the course of a long life. I know that his sensitive nature was acutely and incessantly alive to the tragic volume of human suffering caused by the war and, without the slightest doubt, he would have been ready and glad to give his life to redeem humanity from its consequences. And this quite irrespective of nationality or faith. But what effectively could he do?

Adding to the Pontiff's anguish was the realization that, although sheltered from suffering himself, the slightest misstep could put millions of Catholics in the Axis-controlled territories at risk, and accelerate the engine of destruction. (This was the result, for instance, of the Dutch bishops' public protest against the persecution of Jews on July 26, 1942. In retaliation the Nazis immediately arrested and sent to Auschwitz all Catholic Jews in the Netherlands, including the Carmelite nun Edith Stein, beatified by Pope John Paul II on May 1, 1987 as a "martyr for her people and her faith.")

In this agonizing situation, Pius XII opted for a policy of deeds before words. The widespread belief that he remained silent is a myth. His protests (notably at Christmas 1942), though infrequent and too elliptical to satisfy the Allies, were well understood by the Nazis, who were furious. On the basis of research in the Vad Yashem archive in Jerusalem, the Jewish writer Pinchas E.

Lapide estimates the total number of Jews saved from the Holocaust by the Pope's much maligned "silence" at 800,000. Included in this figure are the five-sixths of Italy's Jews who survived the war.

Concurrent with this rescue work went an exercise of the papal teaching office which surpassed even that of Leo XIII. Especially notable were the encyclicals *Mystici corporis* on the Church and *Divino afflante Spiritu*, encouraging the use of modern critical methods in the exposition of Scripture — both published in 1943; and in 1947 *Mediator Dei*, which encouraged the active participation of the laity in the Mass. All three encyclicals were, for their day, revolutionary. The scope of Pius XII's achievement is apparent in the documents of Vatican II, which cite him far more often than any other Pope.

The pontificate reached its zenith in the Holy Year 1950, which drew millions of pilgrims to Rome. This was also the year, however, of the harsh condemnations in *Humani generis* and the definition of Mary's bodily assumption into heaven, which was criticized at the time as unnecessary (since the doctrine was undisputed by Catholics) and a barrier to ecumenism. By the time Roncalli reached Venice, the Pope's health was failing. A year later, in March 1954, he was thought to be dying. He recovered, but power passed increasingly to a narrow and not always scrupulous circle whose reactionary views cast dark shadows over Pius XII's declining years.

Roncalli's star, on the other hand, was clearly in the ascendant as he rode, beaming with delight, in the patriarch's barge up the Grand Canal on March 15, 1953 and, in St. Mark's Cathedral, presented himself to the Venetian people and clergy in an address which went straight to their hearts.

> Like every other man on earth, I come from a particular family and place. I have been blessed with good physical health and enough common sense to grasp things quickly and clearly; I also have an inclination to love people, which keeps me faithful to the law of the gospel and respectful of my own rights and those of others. It stops me doing harm to anyone; it encourages me to do good to all.
>
> I come from a modest family and was brought up in contented and blessed poverty — a poverty that has few needs, builds up the highest virtues and prepares one for the great adventure of life.
>
> Providence took me away from my native village and led me along the roads of East and West. It allowed me to come close to people

> of different religions and ideologies, and to study grave and menacing social problems. Yet Providence also allowed me to maintain a balanced and calm judgment. I have always been more concerned with what unites than with what separates and causes differences. . . .

> No doubt the great position entrusted to me exceeds all my capacities. But above all I commend to your kindness someone who simply wants to be your brother, kind, approachable, and understanding. . . .

To remind himself of the spirit in which he undertook his new charge Roncalli placed over the door of his study the words *Pastor et Pater* ("Shepherd and Father").

The "contented and blessed poverty" of which he spoke accompanied him even as patriarch. Notes from his first Venetian retreat in May 1953 record

> two painful problems here, amidst all the splendor of ecclesiastical state, and the veneration shown to me as Cardinal and Patriarch: the scantiness of my revenue and the throng of poor folk with their requests for employment and financial help. . . . I prefer to bless the Lord for this poverty, which is rather humiliating and often embarrassing. It draws me closer to Jesus, who was poor, and to St. Francis and, after all, I am sure I shall not die of hunger!

The humility which he had worked a lifetime to achieve did not diminish his childlike delight in what these notes call "the splendor of ecclesiastical state." The same journal entry mentions "my triumphal entry into Venice." Triumphalism in the pejorative sense would be discovered only at the council. Until then Roncalli rejoiced in the ecclesiastical pomp which was as natural to him as uniforms and salutes are to members of the military.

In this same retreat Roncalli resolved to strive for "humility, simplicity, fidelity to the gospel in word and works, with unfaltering gentleness, inexhaustible patience and fatherly and insatiable enthusiasm for the welfare of souls." That Roncalli had no expectation in 1953 of "higher things" is evident from his final resolution:

> to add to my will the request that I should have a resting place reserved for me in the crypt of the basilica, near the tomb of the Evangelist who has now become so familiar to my soul and to my prayers: Mark, son to St. Peter, and his disciple and interpreter.

Preferring the gospel to politics

Roncalli's choice of "gospel truth" over "the wiles of human politics," and the consequent disapproval of his Roman superiors, remained in Venice, as it had been years before in Istanbul, his "only real cross." The difference was less over principles than in what his critics judged expedient. People of equal good will often differ in their choice of tactics. In most cases only time discloses which side has judged rightly.

Roncalli's Venetian years witnessed a climax of papal anti-communism. During the Second World War, Pius XII, faithful to his policy of strict neutrality, had steadfastly refused to translate the Church's condemnation of communism into approval of Hitler's attack on the Soviet Union. Faced after the war in Italy, however, with the most powerful communist party in the Western world, the Pope in 1949 approved the decree of the Holy Office which excommunicated those who voted for communist candidates in Italian elections. Thereafter Cardinal Ottaviani, the author of this decree, liked to boast that "you can say what you like about the divinity of Christ but if, in the remotest village in Sicily, you vote communist, your excommunication will arrive the next day."

Roncalli had no taste for such hard-line measures. In his first address as patriarch, he had stated his preference for "what unites" over "what separates." Separation was the essence of party politics. Roncalli wanted to be pastor of the whole flock entrusted to him, including those whose political judgments were mistaken. He made this clear in his first meeting with the Venetian city council, which included socialists and communists.

> I am happy to be here, even though there may be some present who do not call themselves Christians, but who can be acknowledged as such because of their good deeds. To all I give my paternal blessing.

His pre-election pastoral on May 30, 1953 contained the advice, then obligatory for an Italian bishop, "not to campaign for those who profess anti-Christian doctrines which the Catholic Church has condemned." The tone, however, was mild. Especially noteworthy was the statement that fifty years of "trying to create social justice without Christ's gospel" had proved a failure. Few Italian bishops of that era were willing to credit communists with the attempt to create social justice.

Roncalli tried to be loyal to the party line. But he disapproved of some of its leading spokesmen, notably Father Ricardo Lombardi, S.J. Known as "God's microphone" and regarded by his brethren (in the words of the erstwhile Jesuit Peter Hebblethwaite) "as a gifted if slightly crazed prima donna," Lombardi was the founder of the "Movement for a Better World" and believed to have the ear of Pius XII. Sitting under Father Lombardi during his retreat in May 1955, Roncalli confessed himself troubled by the Jesuit's "historical judgments and his one-sided view of the state of the modern world . . . and his aggressive, pessimistic, trouble-shooting tone."

Roncalli's reservations were shared by Montini, increasingly his most-trusted confidant. In December 1954, however, Montini's curial opponents told the aging Pius XII that his right-hand man had become too "dangerous" to retain at headquarters and should be made Archbishop of Milan. Thereafter Montini's foes concentrated their efforts on eliminating him from the next conclave by seeing that he was not made a cardinal. Roncalli was distressed at all this. But he refused to change his ways.

> I would not mind being thought a fool [*he wrote during his retreat in June 1956*] if this could help people to understand what I firmly believe and shall assert as long as I live, that the gospel teaching is unalterable, and that in the gospel Jesus teaches us to be *gentle and humble*; naturally this is not the same thing as being weak and easy-going.

The reference to "being thought a fool" betrays Roncalli's awareness of how he was regarded by his numerous critics. A year later his retreat notes focused on old age and death.

> "Give me more light as evening falls." O Lord, we are now in the evening of our life. . . . Three-quarters of my contemporaries have passed over to the far shore. So I must always be ready for the great moment. The thought of death does not alarm me. . . .
>
> My poor life, now such a long one, has unwound itself as easily as a ball of string, under the sign of simplicity and purity. It costs me nothing to acknowledge that *I am nothing* and *worth precisely nothing*. . . .
>
> I think the Lord has in store for me, before I die, for my complete mortification and purification and in order to admit me to his everlasting joy, some great suffering and affliction of body and spirit. Well, I accept everything with all my heart, if it is for his glory

and the good of my soul and for the souls of my dear spiritual children. . . .

There are two gates to paradise: innocence and penance. Which of us, poor frail creatures, can expect to find the first of these wide open? But we may be sure of the other: Jesus passed through it, bearing the cross in atonement for our sins, and he invites us to follow him. But following him means doing penance, letting oneself be scourged, and scourging oneself a little too.

My Jesus, amidst the many joys of my episcopal ministry there are also continual opportunities for mortification. I welcome them. Sometimes they hurt my pride a little, but I rejoice at this suffering and repeat before God: "It is good for me to be humiliated." St. Augustine's great saying is always in my mind and comforts me.

An open conclave

Pius XII died at Castel Gandolfo in the early hours of Thursday, October 9, 1958. A series of disedifying incidents ensued which cast harsh light onto the decay into which a once great pontificate had fallen. (The underlying problem remains unresolved to this day: how to conclude the reign of a dysfunctional Pope with dignity and pastoral efficiency as long as resignation remains excluded by tradition and the fear of creating a precedent that could bind successors.)

The papal physician, a jumped-up optometrist and self-styled professor named Dr. Galeazzi Lisi, immediately sold to the world press the candid photographs he had taken of the Pontiff in his last agony. The British minister to the Holy See, paying an official visit of condolence on Thursday morning, found the papal summer residence deserted and the Pope's body unattended. Thereafter Dr. Lisi prepared the remains for display and burial in the manner (he blandly explained at a press conference) used for Jesus Christ after his crucifixion. The result was a mortician's nightmare.

Meanwhile, back in Rome, the French curial Cardinal Tisserant, now in command as dean of the sacred college (Pius XII having declined, characteristically, to fill the vacant post of *camerlengo* or chamberlain), gave the papal housekeeper Mother Pasqualina twenty-four hours to clear out. In the Pontiff's later years this Bavarian nun's strict control of access to her employer had earned her the Vatican sobriquet (taken from the Litany of Loreto) of *Virgo potens* — "Powerful virgin." Before the Pope's funeral, newspapers round the world published pictures of her climbing into a taxi in St. Peter's Square clutching a brace of bird cages containing the late Pontiff's canaries. (The resourceful Sister landed on her feet, however. Through the good offices of Cardinal Spellman, who owed her more favors than we may ever know, she found a berth in the kitchen of Rome's North American College.)

Roncalli, who traveled to Rome by train from Venice on Sunday, October 12, devoted must of his diary entry on Monday to disapproving comments on details of the Pope's funeral, which he had just attended. (It had had to be moved up to October 13 because of Galeazzi Lisi's bungling.) The patriarch also wrote his priest-nephew Don Battista Roncalli, whose attempts to cash in on his uncle's fame had already earned him more than one avuncular rebuke, strictly forbidding him to come to Rome. To make sure his instructions were obeyed, Roncalli repeated them to the nephew's bishop, explaining: "The atmosphere here is so foul with verbal malice and the press that the tired old saw is bound to be heard: 'Here's the nephew, here come the relatives.'"

For reasons best known to himself, Pius XII held only two consistories for the creation of cardinals in his reign of almost two decades: in 1946 and most recently in 1953. As a result the papal electors had been reduced at the Pope's death to fifty-three (from the full complement, at that time, of seventy). Of these two would be harvested by the Grim Reaper before the conclave began on Saturday, October 25.

The fifty-one cardinals who went into seclusion on that day to elect the new Pope were also an immensely aged body. Twenty-four were older than Roncalli, who was only weeks from his seventy-seventh birthday. Following one of the daily meetings of cardinals a few days previously, Cardinal Dalla Costa of Florence had surveyed the ample girth of his Venetian colleague and declared: "You'd make a good Pope."

Roncalli demurred: "But I'm seventy-six."

"That's ten years younger than me," Dalla Costa replied.

Roncalli knew in advance, therefore, that he was a candidate. He also knew there were others. So the outcome was uncertain. He viewed the prospect of his election with dismay. Almost three decades previously he had written, in response to rumors that he was under consideration as Archbishop of Milan, that greater honors brought with them "also great and incredible sufferings."

Evidence from the pre-conclave period shows his awareness that the fulfillment of these words might be at hand. To a Venetian visitor he remarked: "Venice is a bed of roses compared with Rome. Rome will be a bed of thorns." And to the bishop of Bergamo he wrote on October 23 "just a word as I enter the conclave" to request prayers "from the bishop and diocese that as a good Bergamesque I hold most dear."

> My soul finds comfort in the confidence that a new Pentecost can blow through the church, renewing its head, leading to a new ordering of the ecclesiastical body and bringing fresh vigor in progress towards the victory of truth, goodness and peace. It little matters whether the next Pope is from Bergamo or not. Our common prayers will ensure that he will be a prudent and gentle administrator, a saint and a sanctifier. You follow me, your excellency?

The conclave began Saturday afternoon October 25. Voting began on Sunday, with two ballots each morning and afternoon until the necessary majority of thirty-five was reached (two-thirds of the votes plus one). Fortunately for the historian, papal electors do not always interpret strictly the secrecy imposed on their proceedings. By piecing together seemingly innocent remarks and indiscretions, it is usually possible to draw a reasonably accurate picture of what has happened.

One of the most valuable indiscretions following the 1958 conclave came from the new Pope himself. Visiting the Armenian College three months later, Pope John recalled that as the votes of successive conclave ballots were announced, the names of Roncalli and Agagianian "went up and down like two chickpeas in boiling water." So this native Armenian, who like many long-term expatriates in the Eternal City had become more Roman than the Romans, was Roncalli's principal rival. There were others as well.

Eight ballots over two days failed to produce the necessary majority. By evening of Monday October 27, Roncalli had over thirty votes. He celebrated Mass privately at six o'clock on Tuesday morning the 28th, served by his Venetian secretary Loris Capovilla — and immediately afterwards served Capovilla's Mass. (This was then standard liturgical practice: the ancient rite of concelebration was not revived until 1965.)

The ninth and tenth ballots later that morning still produced no result. Capovilla tells us that immediately afterwards, the patriarch returned to his cell from the Sistine Chapel (accessible only to cardinals) and asked to be left alone.

When Capovilla returned to take him to lunch, Roncalli said they would eat together in his cell. Following a sparse and largely silent meal, Roncalli took a brief siesta.

Then he sat down at his desk to draft the statement he realized would soon be required of him. At the top of the paper he wrote the words with which, within hours, he would astonish first the cardinals, then the entire world —

"Vocabor Joannes"

At four-fifty in the afternoon, the result of the eleventh ballot was announced: thirty-eight votes for Roncalli. The bearded Cardinal Tisserant, dean of the sacred college, approached Roncalli to ask the ritual question, "Do you accept the election?" Roncalli replied:

> Listening to your voice, I tremble and am seized with fear. What I know of my poverty and smallness is enough to cover me with confusion. But seeing the sign of God's will in the votes of my brother cardinals of the Holy Roman Church, I accept their decision; I bow my head before the cup of bitterness and my shoulders before the yoke of the cross. . . .

With the utterance of these words he became Pope. Before responding to Tisserant's next question, "By what name do you wish to be known?" the new Pontiff first knelt and prayed in silence. Rising, he drew from his pocket the paper he had written in his cell and read:

> *Vocabor Joannes* — I will be called John. This name is especially dear to me because it was my father's name, and because John is the patron of the humble parish where we were baptized. It is the noble name of countless cathedrals the world over, above all of the Lateran basilica, our cathedral.
>
> In the long list of Roman bishops it is the name which occurs most often. Indeed there have been twenty-two legitimate popes named John. Almost all had brief pontificates.

After recalling that Mark, patron of the cathedral and local church of Venice and beloved spiritual son of Saint Peter, was also called John, Roncalli continued:

> But we also love the name John, so dear to the whole church, especially because of the men who were so close to our Lord

Jesus Christ: the Lord's forerunner, "who was not the light, but a witness to the light" [*Jn 1:8*] . . . ; and the other John, the apostle and evangelist, especially loved by our Lord and his mother, who at the last supper leaned on the Lord's breast and thus derived a love which endured into old age. May these two Johns speak to the church today through our humble pastoral ministry.

Pope John closed by recalling the exhortation of John's first epistle:

My children, love one another. Love one another because this is the greatest commandment of the Lord. Venerable brethren, may God in his mercy grant that we, bearing the name John, may with the help of divine grace have his holiness of life and strength of soul, even unto the shedding of blood, if God so wills.

The choice of a name not used for over six centuries has been widely interpreted as a break with tradition. This is mistaken. Roncalli was deeply traditional. But his lifelong study of history had made him aware that church tradition was far richer than commonly supposed. By choosing a name from the distant past, he was declaring his independence of recent tradition, his determination to be his own man.

His first papal act revived another tradition that had fallen into desuetude. When the conclave secretary, Monsignor di Jorio, approached to present the white papal *zuchetto* (skull cap), John placed his cardinal's *zuchetto* on di Jorio's head — signifying that he would be made a cardinal in the next consistory. Noting the secretary's confusion (di Jorio had been out of favor under Pius XII), John reassured him: "No, I mean it. You have my skull cap now."

Another breach with the recent past was John's second papal act: his request that the cardinals remain in conclave until the next morning. What many took to be an innovation reflected John's knowledge of ancient Church order. The cardinals in their three orders of bishops, priests, and deacons, are, historically and juridically, the clergy of the diocese of Rome. Rome's bishop was signaling his desire to confer privately with his clergy before withdrawing into the isolation of "supreme pontiff." Four years before the debates over collegiality at Vatican II, John XXIII was already practicing it.

This prolongation of the conclave was unknown, however, to the small army of aides waiting impatiently outside the Sistine Chapel. Seeing the chapel door open, and the canopies over all the cardinals' thrones save that of the Patriarch of Venice lowered, these *conclavisti* (as they are called) swarmed in to share the general rejoicing and receive the new Pope's first blessing. Whereupon the dean, Cardinal Tisserant, a former French army officer and a stickler for discipline, thundered: "You're violating the conclave — you're excommunicated!" Told of this incident later, Pope John responded in characteristic fashion: "We'll have to use our influence to get the excommunication lifted."

John meanwhile was in the sacristy, exchanging his cardinal's gear for that of a Pope. None of the white cassocks prepared in advance would encompass his ample girth. The embarrassed papal tailor Annibale Gammarelli did the best he could with safety pins, concealing his handiwork with a surplice.

At six-twenty in the evening, just an hour and a half after his election, Pope John appeared on the *loggia* of St. Peter's for his first papal blessing *Urbi et Orbi*. He recorded his feelings later:

> I remembered Jesus' warning: "Learn of me, for I am meek and humble of heart." Dazzled by television lights, I could see nothing but an amorphous, swaying mass. I blessed Rome and the world as though I were a blind man. As I came away I thought of all the cameras and lights that from now on, at every moment, would be directed at me. And I said to myself: if you don't remain a disciple of the gentle and humble Master, you'll understand nothing even of temporal realities. Then you'll be really blind.

Opening windows

The windows of the Vatican Palace, shuttered and sealed for the conclave, remained closed overnight. John spent his first night as Pope not in the papal apartment, but in that of the Secretary of State, uninhabited since the death of its last occupant, Cardinal Luigi Maglione, in 1944. It was there that he had his first audience with his erstwhile superior, Monsignor Domenico Tardini. John asked him to be his Secretary of State.

Though Tardini had long discharged the duties of this office, without the title, his appointment was a surprise. Tardini had no great opinion of the new Pope's abilities. During the war he had written on a dispatch from Roncalli reporting (too naively, Tardini thought) a long conversation with the German ambassador to Turkey, von Papen: "This fellow hasn't a clue." John was well aware of Tardini's mistrust. In John's eyes Tardini represented the world of the Roman curia which, because it utilized (as he had written way back in 1936) "the wiles of human politics," had long been his "only real cross." John had every reason therefore to bring in his own man as his principal assistant. He declined to do so. Why?

The answer is another instance of John's preference for what he called "gospel truth" over politics. John knew that the curia could make or break any pontificate. Should he start by demonstrating his independence, and risk changing mistrust into determined opposition? Or should he reach out to his critics, at the risk of being thought weak? John never doubted which course was right.

In his first address in Venice he had spoken of his "inclination to love people," his "respect for my own rights and those of others," his concern with "what unites [rather] than with what separates and causes differences." That was the path he had followed all his life. He was too old to change now. And if that were not decisive, the gospel call to follow "the gentle and humble Master" was. His critics were human beings too, with feelings like his. They too thought they were serving the best interests of the Church. Reconciliation was always preferable to confrontation. John would pursue this policy to the end. Long before his death, knowledgeable people in Rome were already saying: "He's made all his enemies cardinals."

Tardini told John that he was too old to be Secretary of State, and too worn out — and produced a medical certificate to prove it. He reminded him of their past disagreements. John listened to it all, said he understood, but that Tardini was still the man he wanted: "We're both priests, and have to submit to the will of God." In the end Tardini yielded: "Finally I knelt down," he told his protégé (later a cardinal) Sebastiano Baggio, "and offered him my obedience. Such is life."

In the days following, John worked with Tardini on the appointment of new cardinals. With Tardini's agreement, he placed Montini at the head of the list, followed by Tardini himself. When they reached the full complement of seventy set by Sixtus V in 1586, John asked: "Why stop now?" The Church's growth justified a larger sacred college. The final list of twenty-three names (bringing the total to seventy-four) gave cardinals, for the first time ever, to the Philippines, Japan, Mexico, and Africa.

In the meantime John had delivered, on the day after his election, his first papal address, broadcast on Vatican radio. Strongly anti-communist, in the tradition of Pius XII, it sounded a gentler and more conciliatory tone. The Pope prayed for the end of "inhuman persecutions, not only because they threaten the peace and tranquillity of these peoples, but also because they are in open contrast with modern civilization and the rights of man." He deplored the vast sums squandered for armaments which could be used "for all classes of society, especially the least favored." Quoting Jesus' prayer "that they may be one" (Jn 17:11), John also sent greetings to "all those who are separated from this Apostolic See."

The old warrior, Don Luigi Sturzo, back from exile in the United States and since 1952 a life member of the Italian Senate, commented on this speech in a newspaper article: "Peace, justice, liberty, mutual understanding of rights and duties — all in the accents of love."

John's sermon at his coronation on November 4, the feast of his beloved Saint Charles Borromeo, was in the same vein. He made it clear he would not try to replicate Pius XII. He wanted to be above all a pastor.

> There are those who expect the pontiff to be a statesman, a diplomat, a scholar, the organizer of the collective life of society, or someone whose mind is attuned to every form of modern knowledge. . . . The new Pope, through the events and circumstances of his life, is like the son of Jacob who, meeting with his brothers, burst into tears and said: "I am Joseph, your brother."
>
> Other human qualities — learning, diplomatic cleverness and skill, organizing ability — may embellish and fill out a pontificate, but they cannot be a substitute for being a shepherd of the whole flock.

The curia had been aghast at the prospect of holding the coronation only six days after the Pope's election. John was told that the elaborate ceremony could not possibly be mounted in so brief a time. John treated these objections as he did those of Tardini to his appointment as Secretary of State: he listened patiently, said he understood perfectly, but that his mind was made up. The coronation would go ahead as scheduled. And it would include a homily — though this was not part of the customary rite. In the end the ceremony took five hours.

Chatting with his secretary, Loris Capovilla, that evening, John said that being carried shoulder-high in the *sedia gestatoria* (a custom he put up with as the best way for the Pope to be seen by vast crowds) reminded him of riding on his father's shoulders in Sotto il Monto more than seventy years before.

Two days later Pope John met the world press. Though journalists are not notably sentimental, some of them admitted afterwards that they were in tears. "His face is constantly illumined by a confident and humorous smile," one of them wrote. "The listener feels that he is gradually caught up in a family atmosphere and that he is taking part in a conversation." The contrast with the magisterial speeches of John's austere predecessor could not have been more striking.

On Sunday, November 23 John "took possession" of his cathedral as Bishop of Rome: St. John Lateran. Though the ceremony was almost as long as the coronation, he described it as

> one of the most wonderful days of my life. . . . The return from the Lateran to the Vatican: simply triumphal. The homage of the Roman people, all along the route, to their new bishop of Rome, was moving and unexpected, and therefore all the more precious.
>
> On the way there and back arranged to be accompanied by cardinals Tisserant, the dean, and Pizzardo. They wept with emotion. All I could do was remain in a state of humiliation, a sacrificial offering for my people; in abandonment but with great and confident simplicity.

On November 25 he turned seventy-seven. Two days later he visited his old seminary, now the Lateran Atheneum, and reminisced about his own student days. He told the students he was still having difficulty remembering, when people spoke of "the Pope," that "the person they are talking about is me" and not "our holy father Pope Pius XII, whom I venerated and loved so much." They must pray for him, "that I may be granted the grace of the holiness that is attributed to me. . . . Nothing counts, nothing has value for history and human life, nothing has any value for the church and for souls, unless the pontiff is holy in deed as well as in title."

At Christmas he revived two customs that had lapsed: a visit to the Babin' Gesù hospital on Christmas day, and to Rome's Regina Coeli prison the day following. "Generally edifying emotion," John noted in his journal. The understatement was typical. The children, the prisoners, and their guards were ecstatic — as were the journalists, who trumpeted to the world the transparent goodness of a Pope so different from the prevailing stereotype. John himself found the notice taken, of his prison visit especially, surprising. "For me it was such a simple and natural thing," he wrote in his journal.

The image of John opening the windows of the Vatican to let in fresh air has been repeated so often that people assume it was his own. His secretary, Capovilla, says he never heard John use this language; and that he disliked drafts. The metaphor is apt nonetheless. By year-end he had been Pope for just three months. There was a new atmosphere in Rome. People all over the world found the papacy interesting, in a way they could not previously remember.

John knew, however, that this initial euphoria could not last. On November 28 he had told Capovilla that it would cost him nothing to retire if a commission of cardinals should ask him to do so. Only the new year would disclose the significance of these cryptic words — and of those which followed:

> I'm not afraid of opposition and do not refuse suffering. I think of myself as the last of all, but I have in mind a program of work and I'm not fussing about it any more. In fact, I am pretty well decided.

A sudden inspiration?

On September 15, 1962 on the sixth day of the private retreat John made to prepare for the council, which would begin three weeks later, Pope John wrote

> a summary of great graces bestowed on a man who has a low esteem of himself but receives good inspirations and humbly and trustfully proceeds to put them into practice.
>
> **First grace.** To have accepted with simplicity the honor and burden of the pontificate, with the joy of being able to say that I did nothing to obtain it, absolutely nothing; indeed I was most careful and conscientious to avoid anything that might direct attention to myself. As the voting in conclave wavered to and fro, I rejoiced when I saw the chances of my being elected diminishing and the likelihood of others, in my opinion truly most worthy and venerable persons, being chosen.
>
> **Second grace.** To have been able to accept as simple and capable of being immediately put into effect certain ideas which were not in the least complex in themselves, indeed perfectly simple, but far-reaching in their effects and full of responsibilities for the future. I was immediately successful in this, which goes to show that one must accept the good inspirations that come from the Lord, simply and confidently.

266

> Without any forethought, I put forward, in one of my first talks with my Secretary of State, on 20 January 1959, the idea of an ecumenical council, a diocesan synod and the revision of the code of canon law, all this being quite contrary to any previous supposition or idea of my own on this subject.
>
> I was the first to be surprised at my proposal, which was entirely my own idea.

That was how John remembered it almost four years later. But, as Shakespeare has reminded us, "Old men forget. . . ." On January 20, 1959 John did tell Tardini that he intended to call an ecumenical council. Both men made notes of their conversation the same evening. Tardini's memo also mentioned the Roman synod and revision of canon law. John's omission of these two matters shows only that they were less important in his mind. While Tardini was the first member of the curia to whom John disclosed his intentions (which explains his diary note, "I was rather hesitant and nervous"), he had been thinking about a council almost from the day of his election. And he had already discussed it with others.

Capovilla says that John mentioned a council only two days after he became Pope. John himself recorded that he discussed the subject with Cardinal Ruffini of Palermo on November 2, 1958. This audience was one of many he had in the first fortnight of his pontificate with the non-curial cardinals, before they returned to their dioceses. They complained that too often the curia did not understand the problems of their local churches. John never supposed that he could resolve these tensions. Why not get all the bishops together to discuss things?

John continued to talk about this idea with others in the weeks following. In December 1958 he called for archival studies of the preparations for the First Vatican Council. They had lasted six years. At age seventy-seven John felt he did not have that much time. The Church had grown enormously since then. But communication and travel were much swifter. The preparation this time would have to be shorter.

The archives also disclosed that John's two predecessors had both considered a council. Pius XI dropped the idea in order to settle "the Roman question" (through the Lateran Treaties of 1929). Pius XII had set up five preparatory commissions, but lost interest when he realized the complexities involved, and the expense.

On January 9, 1959 John told Don Giovanni Rossi, who had been secretary to John's old friend and mentor, Cardinal Ferrari, four decades before: "I want to tell you something marvelous. But you must promise to keep it secret. Last night I had the great idea of holding a council." Given his previous conversations on the subject and the archival research, this could only mean: 'Last night I finally made up my mind.' The remarks which followed show the spirit in which John approached the council: "You know, it's not true to say that the Spirit assists the Pope. The Holy Spirit doesn't help the Pope. I'm simply his helper. He did everything. The council is his idea."

John decided to announce the council at an "extraordinary consistory" of cardinals to be held at the Benedictine Basilica of St. Paul's Outside the Walls following a liturgical ceremony for the conclusion of the octave of prayer for Christian Unity on Sunday, January 25. At the end of a long and uncharacteristically pessimistic discourse on the declension of morals and the rise of error in the modern world (best explained as an attempt to place himself on his hearers' wave length), John came to the point:

> Venerable brothers and beloved sons! Trembling with emotion, and yet with a humble resolution, we put before you the proposal of a double celebration: a diocesan synod for Rome and an ecumenical council for the universal church.

John concluded by requesting prayers for

> a good beginning, a successful implementation, and a happy outcome for those projects that will involve hard work for the enlightenment, the edification, and the joy of the christian people, and a friendly and renewed invitation to our brothers of the separated christian Churches to share with us in this banquet of grace and brotherhood, to which so many souls in every corner of the world aspire.

If the cardinals shared John's emotion, they concealed it successfully. They seemed not to react at all. John was deeply hurt. "Humanly speaking," he confided later, "we would have expected that the cardinals, after listening to our address, might have crowded round to express their approval and good wishes." Instead they departed in silence.

Next day the front page story in *Osservatore Romano* was about the Pope's indictment of modern immorality and error. Readers had to turn to page three to find the announcement of the council. When the official text of John's allocution to the cardinals was published, his words had been altered (not for the first time — or the last). The "brothers of the separated Christian Churches" were brethren no longer but simply "faithful." The bodies to which they belonged had been downgraded from "churches" to "communities." And the sharing in the banquet of grace and brotherhood for which John had prayed had become an invitation to "search, in good will, for unity and grace."

Reading John's discourse, Cardinal Lercaro, who had not been present at the consistory, found the Pope boring no longer. In private remarks disclosed only years later, Lercaro wondered whether John had not taken leave of his senses:

> How dare he summon a council after one hundred years, and only three months after his election? Pope John has been rash and impulsive. His inexperience and lack of culture brought him to this pass, to this paradox. An event like this will ruin his already shaky health, and make the whole of his supposed moral and theological virtues come tumbling down.

Even John's old friend, Montini, was skeptical. On the evening of the announcement Montini telephoned an old friend to share his dismay: "This holy old boy doesn't seem to realize what a hornet's nest he's stirring up." This was the general opinion of Roman insiders. A gathering of all the world's bishops meant chaos, loss of control.

Montini's confidant reassured him. "Don't worry, Don Battista. Relax. The Holy Spirit is still awake in the church." John would have been delighted with this response, had he known about it. It was the message he had already given to Don Giovanni Rossi on January 9.

The bed of thorns

In August 1961, during a retreat at the papal summer residence of Castel Gandolfo in preparation for his eightieth birthday in November, Pope John wrote in his Journal:

> When on October 28, 1958, the cardinals of the Holy Roman Church chose me to assume the supreme responsibility of ruling the universal flock of Jesus Christ, at seventy-seven years of age, everyone was convinced that I would be a provisional and transitional Pope. Yet here I am, already on the eve of the fourth year of my pontificate, with an immense program of work in front of me

to be carried out before the eyes of the whole world, which is watching and waiting. As for myself, I feel like St. Martin, who "neither feared to die, nor refused to live."

During the three years since his election, John had had ample opportunity to recall his pre-conclave prediction that Rome would be a bed of thorns compared to the roses he had experienced in Venice. We have already noted the cardinals' chilly reception to his proclamation of the council. Efforts to delay the gathering, and in any case to control it, began at once.

John countered pleas for more time by advancing the date. He first envisaged the autumn of 1963 for the start of the council. Each time he was told that an undertaking so vast would require lengthier preparations, John shortened them until, on February 2, 1962, he announced that the first session would begin on October 11 the same year. The advocates of postponement (some of whom hoped that the Pontiff's advanced age might yet spare them the ordeal of a council altogether) were themselves to blame for the fact that Vatican II began a year earlier than originally planned.

The curia's efforts to determine the agenda (inspired by knowledge that he who controls the agenda controls the meeting) were more successful. They accomplished this through a well-oiled machinery of interlocking membership in the curial congregations whose key officials easily dominated the preparatory commissions which evaluated the responses of more than 2,000 bishops, the heads of all male religious orders, and the world's thirty-seven catholic universities to the request for suggestions of topics for conciliar action. By entrusting the drafting of the proposed conciliar documents (*schemata*) exclusively to "reliable" theologians in Rome and elsewhere, this group did all in their power to limit the damage from the harebrained scheme of an out-of-control Pontiff whose prudence (in their eyes) was clearly no match for his piety.

Never a curial man himself, and mistrusting "the wiles of human politics," John found it difficult to counter opposition from those who were supposed to be his closest collaborators. He first attempted to loosen their grip by the creation of new cardinals. In just over four years John would create fifty-four cardinals, only two less that Pius XII had created in almost twenty years. Roughly half of John's creations were from the curia. The reason he was creating so many, he explained at his first consistory on December 15, 1958, was so that the work might be shared more equitably. When nobody took this hint, John showed that he could be tough when forced to it. In 1959 he wrote (and had published in *Osservatore Romano*) letters to two of the most notorious pluralists, the cardinals Tisserant and Pizzardo, thanking them publicly for offering to resign some of their offices. Not disclosed, on the other hand, was the flat refusal of certain other cardinals to make way for others. Accustomed to obey all his life, John was incredulous. "They refused the Pope," he told intimates. "They refused the Pope."

In establishing the Central Preparatory Commission for the council at Pentecost 1960, John also tried to loosen the curia's tight grip by explaining that the council curia were quite separate.

> The Ecumenical Council has its own structure and organization which cannot be confused with the ordinary functions of the Roman Curia. . . . The preparation for the Council will not be the task of the Roman Curia but, together with the illustrious prelates and consultors of the Roman Curia, bishops and scholars from all over the world will offer their contribution.

John also took this occasion to clarify the council's aims by saying that it would be a demonstration to the world of the Church's vigor of life and truth. Its discipline and practice should also be brought up to date (the Pope's much discussed *aggiornamento*). Church teaching should be brought to bear on the problems of the modern world. "If after this is accomplished," John declared, "our separated brethren wish to realize a common desire for unity, they will find the way open to a meeting and a return to the church."

The Jesuit Cardinal Bea, whom John had just put in charge of his newly established Secretariat for Christian Unity, managed to eliminate references to the separated brethren's "return" in future papal utterances. The expression implied that Catholics were in no way to blame for Christian disunity and could simply wait — and pray — until the separated brethren re-entered the family home they should never have left in the first place.

Few members of the curia shared Bea's outlook, however. Most continued to view the coming council with feelings ranging from resigned acceptance to outright alarm. They feared that the Pontiff did not really understand the theological complexities involved in the reunion question. His warm-hearted declarations on this subject were giving encouragement to dangerous theological upstarts — men like the youthful Hans Küng in Tübingen, the brothers Hugo and Karl Rahner in Innsbruck, and Yves Congar (a survivor of *Humanae generis* now back in France) — whom the curia accused of offering the treasures of Catholic faith to outsiders at fire-sale prices.

No less alarming to John's numerous critics was the prospect that the world's bishops, once assembled in Rome, would be emboldened by numbers to air their grievances against the whole system of central control by Vatican diplomats and the Roman curia — which, to be fair, derived much of its power from the readiness of bishops throughout the world to submit to Roman bureaucrats endless petty questions and scruples that could easily have been decided locally.

John's guide for dealing with this opposition was a maxim attributed to Saint Bernard: "See everything, turn a blind eye to much, correct a little." In his retreat notes from August 1961, he called his opponents *saccenti*, an Italian word inadequately translated as "know-it-alls" or "wiseacres."

> It is commonly believed and considered fitting that even the everyday language of the Pope should be full of mystery and awe [*clearly a reference to unfavorable comparisons with Pius XII*]. But the example of Jesus is more closely followed in the most appealing simplicity. . . . Wiseacres may show disrespect, if not scorn, for the simple man. But those wiseacres are of no account; even if their opinions and conduct inflict some humiliations, no notice should be taken of them at all: in the end everything ends in their defeat and confusion. The "simple, upright, God-fearing man" is always the worthiest and the strongest. Naturally he must always be sustained by a wise and gracious prudence. He is a simple man who is not ashamed to profess the gospel, even in the face of men who consider it to be nothing but weakness and childish nonsense, and to profess it entirely, on all occasions, and in the presence of all; he does not let himself be deceived or prejudiced by his fellows, nor does he lose his peace of mind, however they may treat him.

The Roman synod

A marked contrast to these defensive remarks was John's reference, in these same retreat notes, to "the unexpectedly successful outcome of the Diocesan Synod" over which he had presided in the last week of January 1960. John regarded the synod as a kind of trial run for the council. Few people shared his optimistic assessment of its achievement.

John had experienced synods as episcopal secretary in Bergamo, and in Venice, where he presided himself. The Roman synod was part of John's effort to take seriously his position as Bishop of Rome — something of which his curial critics disapproved. During the first year of his pontificate, John had steadily pushed the pastors and theologians responsible for preparing the synod to draft what ultimately became 755 articles. These proposed synodal acts were read out over four days in John's cathedral, the Basilica of St. John Lateran. The clergy and religious of the diocese were invited to submit written proposals for changes. Many were incorporated into the final version promulgated on June 28, 1960, the vigil of the feast of the apostles Peter and Paul.

A number of the synod's regulations brought greater joy to John's critics than to those who hoped that the council would enable Catholics to break out of their self-imposed ghetto into the mainstream of modern life. Clerics were reminded of their obligation to wear the cassock at all times, to shave their tonsures (the bald spot on the crown of the head which, since the Middle Ages, had been the cleric's distinguishing mark), to avoid "public spectacles" (operas, plays, movies: in Rome with its thousands of clerical students a means of curbing popular resentment against a highly visible group capable of cornering the market in tickets).

There were also directions about how to pursue holiness amid the distractions of modern life. When canonists complained that these provisions were "not law," John responded that they were not meant to be. If the synod had had a purely legal purpose, it would have been enough to reprint sections of the Church's universal code of canon law.

John himself wrote the provision about priests who had left active ministry:

> Priests laboring under censure or other penalties, or who have perhaps unhappily left the church, should never cease to trust in the Lord's mercy or the humanity or decency of ecclesiastical superiors. Other priests, especially their friends, moved by heavenly charity, should strive to build up this trust. No one is to be denied the friendship of his fellow priests or consolation in his difficulties or even material help should it be needed.

This was new. Some of these men had been John's fellow students at the Roman Seminary. Church law labeled them *vitandi* ("to be shunned"). The Italian Concordat barred their employment in the civil service. This excluded them from teaching positions, for which many were well qualified, and from the postal service — in Italy the employer of last resort for thousands who could not find jobs elsewhere. John's concern for these men was a triumph of charity over legalism.

"On the slopes of the sacred mountain"

"After three years of preparation, certainly laborious but also joyful and serene, we are now on the slopes of the sacred mountain. May the Lord give us strength to bring everything to a successful conclusion!" Thus did John conclude his retreat notes (already cited above) on September 15, 1962.

Few of those entrusted with preparing the council would have described their labors as "serene." As with every council in church history, there had been struggle, intrigue, compromise, and (for some) bitter disappointment. Closely linked with the contest over control of the council was the fundamental question of its purpose. Was it to be a defensive, apologetic gathering, concerned above all with condemning errors? Or was it to be a positive proclamation of the gospel and a manifestation, to the separated brethren first and then to the world, of the Church's unity and vigor?

The clearest evidence of John's wishes was his address to the Central Preparatory Commission on June 15, 1961. "The Council is not a speculative assembly," John said on that occasion, "but a living and vibrant organism which embraces everyone in the light and love of Christ." It should aim at "the recomposition of the whole mystical flock of Christ." This would require "a change in mentalities, ways of thinking and prejudices, all of which have a long history." Above all, John said, "the language we use in the Council should be serene and tranquil; it should throw light on and remove misunderstandings; and it should dissipate errors by the force of truth."

Those to whom John entrusted the council's preparation, however, were bent on condemnations. Leading them was John's Secretary of State, Cardinal Tardini. His sudden death on July 30, 1961 removed a major obstacle to the realization of the Pope's plans. On the evening of Tardini's funeral, John chose as his new Secretary of State a fellow village boy from north Italy, whom he had made cardinal in his first consistory, Amleto Cicognani.

A skilled canonist, Cicognani had served an unprecedented quarter century (1933-1958) as apostolic delegate in the United States. Known to a whole generation of American prelates as "Chick," his affection for their country never extended to mastery of its language. Only the most gauche identified this as a handicap, however, in a day in which the liturgy and official Church documents were in Latin, and most of those with whom the delegate had official dealings had picked up a rudimentary knowledge of Italian during their student days in Rome.

Though two years younger than John, Cicognani was well past his prime at the time of his appointment. He was useful nonetheless. As a relative newcomer to the curia, he was untainted by ancient quarrels, belonged to no particular faction, and had few fixed ideas of what kind of gathering the coming council should be.

The real work of shaping the council in accordance with John's wishes fell to others: the Jesuit Augustin Bea, Suenens of Belgium, and John's old friend Montini in Milan. Bea, who enjoyed the great advantage with "the men of Pius XII" of having been that Pope's confessor, educated John — and Catholics generally — ecumenically, while skillfully negotiating to bring non-Catholic observers to the council and enable them to have a role in its proceedings. Suenens helped reduce the mountain of material (amounting at one point to seventy-two draft schemata) to manageable proportions, dividing it between proposals touching the inner life of the Church and others affecting relations with the world.

Montini, who soon overcame his initial skepticism, was especially helpful, given his decades of service in the Roman curia. In his 1962 Lenten Pastoral, a lecture at the Catholic University of Milan on March 25 of that year, and in meetings of the Central Preparatory Commission, Montini pleaded for a "pastoral" council of renewal and *aggiornamento*, "of positive rather than punitive reforms, and of exhortations rather than anathemas."

The central theme of the council, Montini said, would be the mystery of the Church. It would have to speak about the relationship between the bishops and the Pope, left unresolved by Vatican I, which adjourned after emphasizing papal authority, leaving the Church with a lopsided ecclesiology. Montini also anticipated the council's liturgical reforms by advocating liturgy in the vernacular, concelebration at the Chrism Mass of Holy Thursday morning, with the evening Mass of that day a celebration of the priesthood, and the elimination of the "cursing psalms" from the Breviary.

On September 11, 1962, exactly a month before the council was to begin, John spoke about it on Vatican radio. "Has there ever been an ecumenical council," he asked rhetorically, "which was not a way of self-renewal through an encounter with the risen Jesus, the glorious and immortal king, whose light illumines the whole church for the salvation, the joy, and the glory of all peoples?" The council, he added, would present the Church "in the under-developed countries as the church of all, and especially of the poor." The draft texts did not mention this theme. When "the church of the poor" came to prominence toward the end of the first council session, its champions eagerly quoted these words from the Pope's address of September 11.

In the week following John underwent medical tests to determine the cause of the intestinal pains which had troubled him for some time. On September 23 the doctors told him he had stomach cancer. That afternoon (it was a Sunday) he descended to the crypt of St. Peter's, the site of his first Masses as priest and bishop, to pray at the tombs of his predecessors and inspect the niche he had designated in December 1960 as his own last resting place. He decided to carry on as if nothing were wrong. Any announcement about his health would start wild rumors and jeopardize the success of the council. On May 14, 1963 John would tell the last bishop he received in private audience, the Belgian Emile de Smedt: "There are so many people here who have the Pope's name constantly on their lips, and use it whenever it suits them; but they take no notice of him when they don't feel like it." John did not want to give them any encouragement.

On October 4 John went by train to Loreto and Assisi to pray for the success of the council. Apart from visits to Castel Gandolfo, it was the first official trip of a Pope outside Rome since 1870. The council was only a week away. John had done all he could to prepare. In August he had told Cardinal Suenens, who visited him at Castel Gandolfo where the Pope was laboring over drafts of the council documents: "I know what my own part will be in this Council: it will be suffering."

John underestimated his role. He had been writing a council document of his own: his opening discourse. It would be the speech of his life.

The prophets of doom

Mother church rejoices because, by a singular gift of divine providence, the desired day has finally dawned.

Thus did John begin his homily at the end of the council's opening Mass. He spoke in a clear, sonorous voice that could be heard throughout St. Peter's Basilica. Nothing in his opening paragraphs suggested a departure from the rotund pontifical oratory expected on such an occasion. He had called the council, John said, "to assert once again the church's unfailing and imperishable magisterium . . . to consider the errors, requirements, and opportunities of our time. . . ." His critics were reassured. Errors were precisely what worried them. There were so many about.

Then without warning, almost disingenuously, in the guise of giving "our assessment of the happy circumstances under which the Ecumenical Council begins," John ignited his first bombshell:

> In the daily exercise of our pastoral office, sometimes (much to our regret), we have to listen to people who, even though very zealous, do not have too much discretion or judgment. These people can see nothing but calamities and ruin in these modern times. Comparing our era to previous centuries, they say we are becoming worse. By their actions they show that they have learned nothing from history, which is the teacher of life. These people seem to think that in times of previous councils everything was just right for Christian thinking and living and true religious liberty.

Those council fathers still able, after several hours of mind-numbing ceremonial, to follow the Pope's Latin did not have to search far for the causes of his regret. One of them, the large-hearted cardinal deacon and prefect of the Holy Office, Alredo Ottaviani, was at John's right elbow as he spoke. Others were in the cardinals' tribune nearby. Ottaviani at least, a man of keen intelligence, would have had no difficulty understanding John as he continued:

> We feel that we must disagree with these prophets of doom who are always forecasting disaster, as if the end of the world were imminent.

Divine providence, the Pope went on, "is leading us to a new order of human relations." The Church must bring herself up to date, never departing from "the sacred patrimony of truth received from the Fathers," but "looking to the present, to new conditions and new forms of life introduced into the modern world, which have opened new avenues to the catholic apostolate."

He had not called the council, John said, "to discuss one article or another of the fundamental doctrines of the church . . . which is presumed well known and familiar to all; for this a Council was not necessary." The world expected "a leap forward in doctrinal insight and the formation of consciences. This must of course be "in conformity with authentic doctrine." But this doctrine should be "studied and expounded according to the methods of research and literary forms of modern thought." John's second bombshell followed:

> The substance of the ancient teaching of the deposit of faith is one thing; the manner in which it is presented is another. . . . Everything must be measured in the form and proportion of a magisterium which is predominantly pastoral in character.

In the past, John said, the church had condemned errors with the greatest severity.

> Today, however, the bride of Christ prefers to make use of the medicine of mercy rather than that of severity. She considers that she meets the needs of the present day by demonstrating the validity of her teaching rather than by condemnation.

John concluded his address by saying that the Catholic Church considered it her duty to work actively for "the mystery of unity" — not only of all Christians, but of "those who follow non-christian religions." The key to this unity was "the fullness of christian charity." The Pope thus mandated what would soon be called "catholic ecumenism."

This address was a frontal attack on the immobilist, ahistorical, and defensive mentality of those who had dominated the council's preparation. They at once set about editing the Pope's words to render them innocuous. The Latin text of his speech printed the next day in *Osservatore Romano*, and later in the official *Acta Apostolicae Sedis*, omitted John's "leap forward in doctrinal insight," substituting for it the duty of "faithful obedience to certain and immutable doctrine," which must be "investigated in the way our age demands." (His reference to "the methods of research and literary forms of modern thought" disappeared altogether.)

John's distinction between the substance of the deposit of faith and the way it was presented also vanished. The edited version had him saying: "The deposit of faith itself, or the truths which are contained in our venerable doctrine, is one thing, and the way in which they are expressed is another, retaining however the same sense and meaning" — language taken from the anti-Modernist oath of 1910.

Aware of these falsifications, John told his secretary, Capovilla: "I would like the first Italian draft of this speech to be published, not because I want to be praised for it but because I want to take responsibility for it; it should be known that it belongs to me from the first to the last." In the months following John several times quoted crucial portions of this address, always in his original Italian version, not in the sanitized Latin text produced by his anonymous editors. Yet attempts to claim that the bowdlerized version is authentic continue.

Surprising Saint Joseph

Having spoken his piece, John withdrew. He wanted the council fathers to deliberate freely, without the papal domination which had been so prominent at Vatican I. John followed the proceedings on closed circuit television in his study, turning up the sound only when he saw an interesting speaker, or one he knew. "The Council is like a big ship," John told the French Cardinal Garonne. "I got it out to sea, but someone else will have to maneuver it into port."

Garonne, Archbishop of Toulouse since 1956, played a crucial role at the start of the council. Studying the rules of procedure the previous summer, Garonne realized the critical importance of the permanent commissions. They would have to make changes in *schemata* found defective by the council. If the permanent commissions were largely identical with the preparatory commissions which had drafted the documents, the result would be deadlock. When he got to Rome, Garonne was alarmed to find that the curia's list of candidates for the permanent commissions consisted almost entirely of the original drafters. It was essential that the council elect its own men.

After trying unsuccessfully in Rome to get others to grasp this vital point, Garonne got through to Cardinal Liénart of Lille, one of the eight council presidents. On Saturday, October 13, the council's first working day, Liénart — brushing aside the efforts of his fellow President Cardinal Tisserant, who was presiding, to prevent him from speaking — seized the microphone and moved that the scheduled election of commissioners be postponed until the fathers had had time to confer over the weekend. The motion was immediately seconded by Cardinal Frings of Cologne, another council president, in the name of his fellow cardinals Döpfner of Munich and König of Vienna. It passed by acclamation and the council's first congregation was over in fifteen minutes.

To the end of his life Frings, who played a major role in the council debates, maintained that this had been his most important conciliar intervention. The commissioners elected, from new lists prepared by thirty-four bishops' conferences, included many not on the slate proposed in advance by the curia. John's role in the affair came on October 20, when he suspended the requirement of a two-thirds majority (which would have unduly lengthened the elections) in favor of a simple majority.

In the meantime the Pope was active outside the council hall. On the afternoon of October 13, he received in the Sistine Chapel more than two hundred journalists accredited to the council. He spoke of the importance of the press in the modern world, and of their responsibility to report truthfully — a task rendered unnecessarily difficult by the official secrecy imposed on the proceedings.

From the Sistine Chapel, John went to the Hall of the Consistory, where he received the forty-six non-Catholic observers (including two Russian Orthodox who had arrived only the day before as the result of top-secret negotiations with Moscow). John sat with his guests, drawn up in a square, in a chair rather than on the raised throne used for the Pope's meetings with the cardinals.

Speaking in French on the Lord's high priestly prayer "that they may be one" (Jn 17:11), John reminisced about his ecumenical contacts in the East, including the story of the Armenian patriarch recounted above, in the section on John's Bulgarian exile. "Though we did not debate," John said, "we loved each other." Controversy was useless, he told the observers. What was needed was mutual understanding and "the christian virtue of patience — which must not be allowed to harm the virtue of prudence, which is equally fundamental."

The Pope's words, and even more his manner, went straight to his hearers' hearts, creating an atmosphere without precedent in Roman and conciliar annals. Thanks to Cardinal Bea and his Secretariat of Unity, the observers received full conciliar documentation, the best seats at the general congregations (along with simultaneous translations envied by many of the bishops, who followed the locally accented Latin of their peers with difficulty), and opportunity to comment on the proceedings to the appropriate commissions.

Despite these hopeful initial developments, the council soon bogged down in procedural difficulties and tedious debates, first over the liturgy, then over the *schema* on *The Sources of Revelation* (drafted by Cardinal Ottaviani's team at the Holy Office). This treated revelation as a set of logical propositions drawn from two independent sources: Scripture and tradition. Though most of the fathers knew this theology from the dogmatic manuals they had used in seminary decades before, the debate showed that it had become a minority view.

On November 20 a motion to send the *schema* back to the commission for redrafting passed by 1,378 to 822. Since this was 105 votes short of the necessary two-thirds majority, however, the rules required that the debate continue — on a document rejected by a substantial majority. The next day Pope John ended the impasse by referring the draft to a new commission chaired jointly by the two principal contenders in the debate: the cardinals Ottaviani and Bea. The fathers received this news with relief — and eagerly repeated the French name for the new body: *la Commission des deux sources.*

Debate over the document on revelation enlisted the interest of the theologically sophisticated. On liturgy everyone was an expert — as any parish priest knows who has tried to rearrange the furnishings in his church. Discussion centered on the use of the vernacular in the liturgy. Underlying the arguments was disagreement about the Church itself. Had it received from its divine founder a fixed constitution, valid for all ages? Or did the gift of the Spirit, promised by Christ "to teach you everything, and remind you of all that I have said to you" (Jn 14:26), empower the Church to reshape afresh in accordance with the changing conditions of each age its life, its worship, and even the articulation of its unchanging faith?

On November 10 Pope John saw on his television screen a man he knew from his years in the Balkans: the aged Bishop of Mostar, Petar Cule. Visibly nervous, he stumbled over his Latin text as he pleaded, with many repetitions, that the name of Saint Joseph be included in the canon of the Mass. Amid murmurs of impatience, Cardinal Ruffini of Palermo, who was presiding, admonished the speaker: "Complete your holy and eloquent speech. We all love St. Joseph and we hope there are many saints in Yugoslavia." The mortified bishop concluded as best he could and the meeting ended shortly thereafter with the customary Angelus and Gloria Patri. Ruffini then brought down the house by trumpeting into the microphone: *"Sancte Joseph"* — to which the bishops responded amid general hilarity: *"Ora pro nobis!"*

Three days later the bishops were astonished to learn that Pope John had ordered the insertion of Saint Joseph's name in the hitherto sacrosanct Roman canon. Only a handful were aware of the background. John knew that Bishop Cule's nervous manner was the result of his ordeal as the victim of a communist show trial which had sentenced him to four years in a concentration camp. The train which took him there had been deliberately wrecked in an attempt to kill as many of the prisoners on board as possible. The crash broke both the bishop's hips, but he survived. Despite poor health, he had come to the council to make his plea for his beloved Saint Joseph. John could not stand to see a good man hurt. He was determined to grant this modern confessor his wish.

A year later, speaking at the council's tribute to Pope John on October 28, 1963, Cardinal Suenens told the fathers:

> He lived completely in the world of the supernatural, in the familiar company of the angels and saints. He loved to share his preferences with others, and here also he showed the courage that characterized his friendships. He surprised St. Joseph by introducing him into the canon of the Mass. . . .

Roses — and more thorns

The closing weeks of the council's first session brought recurrent rumors about the Pope's health. On November 29 *Osservatore Romano* published the first medical bulletin. It spoke of a worsening "gastric disturbance" and "rather severe anemia." This was true, but not the whole truth. John himself had divined from the words of his doctors that his cancer was inoperable and his life-span limited. He appeared at the window of his apartment for the noon Angelus on Sunday, December 2 and spoke about his returning health. He did the same the Wednesday following, when a vast crowd of bishops was present in St. Peter's Square, the council having been adjourned early for this tribute to the Holy Father.

The bishops were shocked, however, at John's appearance at the close of the council's first session on December 8, the feast of the Immaculate Conception. Many felt they were seeing him for the last time. Apart from concern over the Pope's health, there was gloom over the lack of any visible result. Not a single document had been approved. John did not share this pessimism. The first session, he said, had been "like the slow and majestic prelude to a great masterpiece." Bishops from all over the world "had first to become acquainted." There had been

> in all charity, a sharp divergence of views. Such difference of opinion can be disturbing at times, but it is no cause for surprise. In fact, it was providential, for it served to clarify issues, and to demonstrate to the world the existence in the church of the holy freedom of the sons of God.

John urged the bishops to work diligently on the revised drafts that would be sent out during the nine-month recess, in the hope that the council could conclude at Christmas 1963, the 400th anniversary (John reminded the bishops) of the conclusion of the Council of Trent.

Remarking that they were parting on the anniversary of the opening of the First Vatican Council in 1869, John quoted the words of Pius IX on that occasion about the peace which Christ gave to his apostles, which "casts out fear [and] shuts its ears to uninformed talk." Anniversaries like these appealed to John's historical sense. Mentioning them was his way of reassuring those distressed at what seemed to them the abandonment of tradition that the latest council was a continuation of the two which had preceded it.

John repeated his exhortation to complete the council in a personal letter sent at Epiphany 1963 to all the bishops, addressed "Venerable and dearest brother." Every bishop was to regard conciliar business as "the apple of his eye" and give it priority over everything else. They were to fire the people of their local churches to pray for the success of the council

> *instanter, instantius, instantissime* . . . a prayer full of confident assurance, looking forward with joy to the wealth of God's grace. . . . Information comes to us from all quarters concerning the confidence with which, since the Council's inception, public opinion has veered toward a peaceful and christian settlement of the major issues of the day.

In the five months of life which remained to him, the conclusion of the council, and work for unity and peace, not only among separated Christians (mentioned prominently in his Epiphany letter to the bishops) but also among nations, would dominate the Pope's thinking and actions.

The Cuban missile crisis, which brought the world to the brink of atomic war, had coincided with the opening of the council in October. Pope John had played an important behind-the-scenes role in defusing the crisis — and received private messages of thanks from both President Kennedy and Nikita Khruschev. When the Soviet leader sent Christmas greetings to John in December, the Pope rejected the stiff, formal response drafted for him by the Secretariat of State and replied in warm, personal terms with "joyful good wishes for the prosperity of the Russian people and all the peoples of the world." Thereafter things moved rapidly.

Since October John had been thinking about an encyclical on peace. He wanted it to embody his lifelong preference for "what unites over what separates and causes differences." In December he asked Monsignor Pietro Pavan, professor of social doctrine at the Lateran University, to draft it for him. It must contain no condemnations, John told Pavan. "I can't attribute ill will to one side or the other. If I do, there will be no dialogue, and all doors will be closed." Pavan gave the Pope a first draft the day after Epiphany.

At the beginning of February, Archbishop Josef Slipyi, Metropolitan of the Ukrainian Catholic Church which had been forcibly united with the Russian Orthodox Church by Josef Stalin, was released from the Siberian prison camp where he had languished since 1948. To obtain Slipyi's liberation, John had promised that it would not be exploited for anti-Soviet propaganda — a concession for which he was bitterly criticized as soon as it became known. On February 10, the anniversary of the death of Pius XI who had made him a bishop, John had a double joy. He was able to open the process of beatification for his old friend, Cardinal Ferrari of Milan. And he announced Slipyi's release, calling it

> an event which in the secret designs of God can help the church and all honest people grow in sincere faith and the apostolate of peace. Let us not wreck the mysterious plan with which God invites everyone to collaborate, bringing into unity the threads of a cloth woven by his grace and the readiness of innocent, humble, and generous souls to serve him.

John and Slipyi met the same evening for a deeply moving conversation of an hour and twenty minutes. Slipyi showed the Pope his prison uniform, told him of other bishops and priests still in captivity, and gave John a map of the Soviet Union with all the prison camps marked on it. John kept it with him till he died, having written on it: "The heart is closer to those who are further away; prayer hastens to seek out those who have the greatest need to feel understood and loved." In his long life, John had always been loved. He had often been misunderstood. The closing months of his life would deepen this misunderstanding.

On February 28 Nikita Khrushchev's son-in-law, the journalist Alexis Adzhubei, arrived in Rome with his wife, Rada, and requested an audience with the Pope, to whom he wished to present a gift from his father-in-law. John's advisers told him to refuse. Receiving the representative of a man whose hands were still covered with the blood of martyrs and countless prisoners who, unlike Slipyi, had not been released, would be a betrayal of these victims of religious persecution. When John decided to grant the audience, his critics started a press campaign portraying him as a man betrayed by his own goodness, too naive to realize that he was walking into a carefully prepared trap.

The meeting took place on March 7. Because of continuing opposition within the Vatican, the Russian couple had to be smuggled into the Pope's private library at the end of an audience for a group of journalists. Adzhubei conveyed Khruschev's desire for some means of dealing with problems as they arose, possibly even establishing diplomatic relations. John's response was the model of prudence and discretion. He spoke of the biblical story of creation. God first created light. The remaining stages of creation lasted six days — each of them long epochs.

> Today is the first day of creation, the day of light. . . . It all takes time. . . . The light is in my eyes and in your eyes. If the Lord so wills it, he will show us the way to go. We must go gently, gradually in these matters, preparing minds.

The rest of the conversation was more personal. John spoke of his time in Bulgaria, his love for Slav music, and the peasant origin he shared with Khruschev. He asked Nada to tell him the names of her three sons, "because when a mother speaks the names of her children, something very special happens." When she named the youngest, Ivan, John said that was his name too. When she got home, she must give the boys hugs from the Pope, but "a special one for Ivan: the others won't mind."

The only witness to the meeting was the Pope's Jesuit interpreter. John had him write a full account and wanted it published. The editor of *Osservatore Romano* refused — on orders from the Secretariat of State. John was incredulous, and deeply hurt. In his own account of the meeting, written "for history" and not disclosed until after his death, John wrote: "I deplore and pity those who in these last few days have lent themselves to unspeakable maneuvers. *Ignosco et dimitto.*" These Latin words ("I forgive and forget") were from the vesting prayers of a bishop before Mass.

The first day of March, just six days before this meeting, it was announced that John had been awarded the Balzan Peace Prize, "for his activity in favor of brotherhood between all men and all people, and his appeals for peace and good will in the recent diplomatic intervention" (a reference to his mediation in the Cuban missile crisis the previous October).

Some of John's advisers in the Secretariat of State objected strongly to his accepting the prize, which they considered undignified for a Pope. John rejected this advice. But he refused to receive the award in St. Peter's, explaining: "It isn't right to honor a pope on the tomb of the crucified St. Peter." The ceremony was held on May 10, in the Vatican Throne Room. In his acceptance speech, John said that the award was as much for his predecessors as for himself: the five Popes of his lifetime had all "worked untiringly to maintain, develop, and consolidate peace among men."

Before that, however, John had issued the encyclical which he intended as a kind of last will and testament, summing up the message of his life.

Pacem in terris

John's previous encyclical on social justice, *Mater et magistra*, had been announced six months before its appearance on May 15, 1961, the seventieth anniversary of *Rerum novarum*. Stung by negative reactions to that document, John kept *Pacem in terris* under wraps until he announced it on March 31, 1963. He signed the first five copies in his private library before television cameras on April 9, Tuesday in Holy Week, wearing a stole to emphasize the event's religious nature. It was dated two days later, Holy Thursday, when the Church commemorates Jesus' new commandment of love.

In *Rerum novarum* Leo XIII had condemned class warfare but not the class system as such. The role of the state was to promote justice between classes, a patriarchal system reflected in the English verses:

> The worker in his cottage,
> The master in the hall,
> The scholar in his study,
> The Lord God made them all.

In *Mater et magistra* John XXIII went farther and accepted the welfare state as a legitimate means of promoting the common good. In 1961 right-wing Catholics found this uncomfortably close to socialism, even to communism. The American William F. Buckley, Jr., spoke for many when he commented: "Mater si, magistra no." But the United States was far away. More important for the Pope was the hostile reaction of critics in Italy to his "opening to the left" (as it was quickly dubbed). Opposition to *Mater et magistra* carried over into the first session of the council and reached a climax of indignation with John's audience for Khruschev's son-in-law and *Pacem in terris*.

Though addressed, unlike previous encyclicals, not only to the Church's hierarchy but to "all people of good will" (No. 172), *Pacem in terris* differed from other papal documents not so much in content (the encyclical quoted liberally from previous popes, especially from Pius XII) as in tone. Its list of "three things which characterize our modern age," for instance, was not the negative catalogue people had come to expect from Popes. Having so recently criticized the "prophets of doom" in opening the council, John chose to see the good in the modern world. As examples he cited "a progressive improvement in the economic and social condition of working people"; greater awareness of "the natural dignity of women," with a corresponding growth in their political activity; and the decline of colonialism, class warfare, and racism (Nos. 39-44).

Most disturbing to those who looked to the Pope for leadership in the struggle against communism was John's plea for cooperation not only with "those christians who are separated from the Apostolic See," but even with people "who may not be christians but who nevertheless are reasonable men, and men of natural moral integrity" (No. 157).

> It is perfectly legitimate to make a clear distinction between a false philosophy . . . and economic, social, cultural, and political undertakings, even when such undertakings draw their origin and inspiration from that philosophy. . . . Besides, who can deny the possible existence of good and commendable elements in these undertakings. . . ? (*No.* 159)

Coupled with this was a passage, written by John himself, which attacked the philosophical tenet, championed (among others) by the prefect of the Holy Office, Cardinal Ottaviani, that "error has no rights."

> It is always perfectly justifiable to distinguish between error as such and the person who falls into error. . . . A man who has fallen into error does not cease to be a man.

He retains the capacity "to break through the barriers of error and seek the road to truth."

> Catholics who, in order to achieve some external good, collaborate with unbelievers . . . may possibly provide the occasion or even the incentive for their conversion to the truth (*No.* 158).

Coming from a Pope who had just exchanged gifts with the emissary of the world's leading communist ruler, this could only mean that it was legitimate for Catholics to cooperate with communists — and even to vote for them in defiance of the excommunication imposed in Italy on anyone who did so. With a crucial national election impending on April 28, John's critics were understandably alarmed.

When the communists gained over a million votes more than they had received five years previously, people were quick to blame John — and not only in Italy. A German newspaper published an open letter from a Catholic in that country who told the Pope bluntly: "You have misused the Chair of Peter." And on the first of May, John McCone, director of the American CIA and a Knight of Malta, delivered much the same message in a private audience and warned that Khruschev was not to be trusted. John's diary entry shows that he remained unrepentant: "I'm not going to be put off by the unseemly fuss that some people try to impress churchmen with. I bless all people, and withhold my confidence from none."

In truth the fuss did come only from "some people." The worldwide reaction to *Pacem in terris* was overwhelmingly positive — even in the Soviet Union (which John's critics seized on, of course, as grist for their mill). The attacks hurt John deeply, nonetheless, coming as they did from some of his closest associates.

By this time, however, John had more pressing concerns. His illness was becoming grave. On this same first of May he became confused and lost his place at Mass. He had less than five weeks to live.

"The church is no one's enemy"

The day following, May 2, John worked on the revised schemata for the next session of the council. When Cardinal Cicognani sent them to the bishops shortly thereafter, he included John's hand-written comment: "All these *schemata* have been *personally* gone through with great attention by the Holy Father, who reserves the right to see them again before they are definitively approved." He still hoped he would be able to see the council through to its conclusion.

Five days later, sensing the Pope's distress at press attacks blaming him for the communist gains in the April 28 election, Capovilla asked whether it might have been better to have delayed publication of *Pacem in terris* until after the election. John would have none of it.

> The doctrine expounded in the encyclical is in accord with the Lord's gospel and in harmony with papal teaching over the last sixty years. The meeting with Adzhubei fitted in with the overall line of my ministry. I've said it clearly enough several times

already, that one could publish the text of our conversation in perfect tranquillity.

Two days later John again defended the audience, this time to Archbishop Marty of Rheims:

> I have to welcome everyone who knocks on my door. I saw them, and we talked about the children . . . I saw that Madame Adzhubei had tears in her eyes. I gave her a rosary, explaining that she probably didn't know how to use it and that, obviously, I wasn't asking her to. I told her that looking at it would remind her that there once existed a perfect mother.

The day following, Friday, May 10, came the award of the Balzan Peace Prize, recounted above. After the private ceremony in the Vatican there was a public celebration in St. Peter's with a vigorous speech by the Pope defending his work for peace. At the end he was carried from the basilica in the *sedia gestatoria* with his head in his hands, too exhausted to respond to the applause.

The next day John made an official visit to President Segni of Italy in the Quirinal — until the end of the papal state in 1870 a papal residence. Conclaves had been held there. From its windows on July 10, 1809 Pius VII and his Secretary of State Cardinal Pacca had watched Napoleon's troops haul down the papal flag over the Castel Sant' Angelo and replace it with the French tricolor. (See p. 176 above.) John's visit, the first by a Pope since 1870, was the final act of reconciliation between the papacy and the Italian republic begun by Pius XI with the Lateran Treaties of 1929. John prepared by two hours of prayer, on his knees.

In the car John was in great pain. Passing the monument to Italy's Unknown Soldier in the Piazza Venezia, he managed, however, to raise his hand in salute to the men he had ministered to as a chaplain in the First World War. "I'm making this visit as an act of deference towards my country," he told Capovilla who was riding with him, "because I owe so much not only to Bergamo but to Italy."

At the Quirinal John's simple speech thanking Segni for his welcome moved the President so deeply that he sank to his knees. Raising him to his feet, the Pope embraced him, with the words: "For you, and for Italy." Only an Italian can fully appreciate the significance of this exchange.

On May 13 Cardinal Suenens presented *Pacem in terris* to the United Nations in New York and spoke in the crowded assembly chamber for over an hour. Asked in the question period afterwards, "Does the Pope bless communism?" Suenens replied:

> The encyclical makes a distinction between the doctrine of a movement, the movement itself, and the people involved in it. The communist doctrine is incompatible with our faith. A movement can be more or less imbued with a particular doctrine. As for the people themselves, they are often worth much more than the doctrines they espouse. We christians are always worth less than our doctrine.

In his memoirs Suenens reports "a delighted response from my listeners." Had John known about Suenens' words, he would surely have shared this delight.

Vesting for Mass the next day, May 14, John winced in pain. Asked by Capovilla how he felt, John replied: "Like St. Lawrence on the gridiron." (According to legend, this early Roman martyr had been roasted to death.) The same evening John had a two-hour conversation with Bishop de Smedt of Bruges, whose council speech on December 1 criticizing "triumphalism, clericalism, and juridicism" in the *schema* on the Church had been a turning point in the first session.

The evening of May 16, John received his Under-Secretary of State Agostino Casaroli, just back from Prague and Budapest. Eight years later Casaroli would describe his experiences on this trip in terms reminiscent of Consalvi's report about the Congress of Vienna in 1815 (see p. 182 above):

> It was quite evident that these communist leaders were convinced that the Pope was sincere, trustworthy, and loved them as well. These feelings of warmth and affection melted the ice-floes that had kept us apart for so long. Their judgment on Pope John was always positive.

The same article reported John's response to Casaroli's account of this trip: "Monsignor, the church may have many enemies, but she is no one's enemy." John needed the encouragement that Casaroli brought him. Two days later the press briefing sent to him daily from the Secretariat of State was full of fresh attacks on him as a naive dupe of communist trickery. John responded as before: "*Ignosco et dimitto.*"

"This bed is an altar"

On Friday, May 17 John celebrated what he realized would be his last Mass. He started saying his goodbyes the same day. The first was to the Irish priest who had been his secretary in Istanbul in 1943-1944, Father Thomas Ryan. "I never managed to speak English as I wanted to in those distant days when you gave me my first lessons," John told him. "But you enabled me to read and understand the language. I hope that my efforts will be remembered as an act of reverence towards all the English-speaking peoples."

John remained in his bedroom over the weekend. On Sunday he was able to appear at his window for the midday Angelus. On Monday Cardinal Wyszynski and four Polish bishops were coming to see him. Capovilla said he should receive them in his bedroom: His guests would be honored. (There was precedent for this. On January 17, 1937 Pius XI had received five German bishops in his sickroom to discuss his planned encyclical *Mit brennender Sorge*, a searing indictment of Nazi treachery.) Pope John insisted on going downstairs to meet his guests in the library.

At the end of the audience Wyszynski said, "Goodbye until September." John told him he might greet a different Pope then. "It takes only a month, you know: the funeral of one and the elevation of another." And then a characteristic remark: "If it weren't for this blessed protocol, I'd come down to the bronze door with you."

John returned to his bed the same afternoon, plagued by severe pains and hemorrhages. He had not lost his sense of humor, however. Seeing the anxiety on the face of his doctor, Professor Gambarrini, he said: "Don't look so worried. My bags are packed, and I'm ready to go."

Thursday, May 23, the feast of the Ascension, John was able to appear again at his window and intone the *Regina coeli* in a voice that was still strong and musical. That evening he had a visit from a man he regarded as his spiritual son, Gustavo Testa. John had known him since he was a nineteen-year-old seminarian. He had been John's secretary in Istanbul. When John made him a cardinal he took the motto *Sola gratia tua* ("By your grace alone"), explaining that without John's favor (*gratia*), he would never have reached the ranks of the *porporati*. Now Testa broke down weeping. John comforted him:

> Dear Don Gustavo, we have to take things as they are. I've had
> a long life and served the church and left some sort of mark on

history. By God's grace I haven't behaved badly: so, not a day more. If the Lord wants me to remain a little longer, well and good, otherwise — we're off.

When Testa had gone, John remarked to the Passionist laybrother who was nursing him that he wished he could say Mass. Knowing that this was impossible, the brother replied: "But this bed is your altar."

"You're right," John responded. "This bed is an altar, an altar needs a victim, and I'm ready. I wouldn't mind going tonight on the feast of the Ascension." But he stayed. He had appealed for prayers for the council during the nine days between Ascension and Pentecost, the Church's original novena. John would make it on his sickbed.

From various witnesses it is possible to piece together things John said during these nine days, as he declined and then rallied. Readers may notice parallels with recurrent themes in the speeches of Pope John Paul II.

Today more than ever, certainly more than in previous centuries, we are called to serve man as such, and not merely catholics; to defend above all and everywhere the rights of the human person, and not merely those of the Catholic Church. Today's world, the needs made plain in the last fifty years, and a deeper understanding of doctrine have brought us to a new situation, as I said in my opening speech to the Council. It is not that the gospel has changed: it is that we have begun to understand it better. Those who have lived as long as I have were faced with new tasks in the social order at the start of the century; those who, like me, were twenty years in the East and eight in France, were enabled to compare different cultures and traditions, and know that the moment has come to discern the signs of the times, to seize the opportunity and to look far ahead.

Shown some of the messages which were pouring in from all over the world, not only from Catholics, John asked:

Aren't all these demonstrations of affection around a dying old man perhaps a *sign of the times?* At the beginning of the century official Rome ignored the death agony of Leo XIII. As a young seminarian on my way to the Vatican to get news of the Pope, I can remember hearing disrespectful and insulting remarks on the streets. Times have changed for the better.

Long before, John had asked Loris Capovilla to tell him when death was approaching, so that he could die "as a bishop and a pope should." On Friday,

May 31 the doctors told Capovilla they could do no more. Fighting back tears, Capovilla knelt beside the bed and said: "Holy Father, I'm keeping my promise. I have to do for you what you did for Monsignor Radini at the end of his life. The time has come. The Lord calls you."

As he was about to receive the final anointing, John interrupted the rite to tell those gathered round his bed:

> The secret of my ministry is in that crucifix you see opposite my bed. It's there so I can see it in my first waking moment and before going to sleep. It's there also so that I can talk to it during the long night hours. Look at it, see it as I see it. Those open arms have been the program of my pontificate: they say that Christ died for all, for all. No one is excluded from his love, from his forgiveness.
>
> What did Christ leave to his church? He left us "*ut omnes unum sint*" ("that all may be one": Jn 10:16).
>
> I had the great grace to be born into a christian family, modest and poor but with the fear of the Lord. I had the grace to be called by God as a child: I never thought of anything else, I never had any other ambition. Along the way I've met holy priests and good superiors. Oh! Don Francesco Rebuzzini [*the priest who baptized him and nurtured his vocation*], Monsignor Radini, Cardinal Ferrari . . . all helped me and loved me. I had lots of encouragement.
>
> For my part, I'm not aware of having offended anyone, but if I have, I beg their forgiveness; and if you know anyone who has not been edified by my attitudes or actions, ask them to have compassion on me and to forgive me. In this last hour I feel calm and sure that my Lord, in his mercy, will not reject me. Unworthy though I am, I wanted to serve him, and I've done my best to pay homage to truth, justice, charity, and the meek and humble heart of the gospel.
>
> My time on earth is drawing to a close. But Christ lives on and the church continues his work. Souls, souls. *Ut unum sint! Ut unum sint!*

That was Friday morning. In the evening he spoke to Capovilla the words placed at the head of this chapter: "We've worked together and served the church without stopping to pick up and throw back the stones that have sometimes blocked our path. You've put up with my defects, and I've put up with yours. We'll always be friends. . . . I'll protect you from heaven. . . . When all this is over, get some rest and go see your mother."

Later Montini arrived from Milan, bringing members of the Roncalli family with him. They watched through the night and all the next day, the Vigil of Pentecost. John drifted in and out of consciousness, imagining himself first in France, then in Sotto il Monte.

At noon on Pentecost John awoke and asked the time. Upon being told, he looked at the window where he had stood so often at that hour to pray the Angelus with the crowd below, now swollen to a vast throng. Seeing his nephew, Zaverio, standing at the foot of the bed, he said to him gently: "Out of the way. You're hiding the crucifix from me."

At three o'clock on Monday morning, June 3, John awoke and repeated twice, with emphasis, Peter's words from John 21:15: "You know that I love you."

Towards evening Cardinal Luigi Traglia, Pro-Vicar for the diocese of Rome, began the Mass "For the sick" in St. Peter's Square below. At seven-forty-five p.m. those in the Pope's bedroom heard from the loudspeakers the concluding words, *"Ite, missa est."* As if on cue, the sound of labored breathing from the bed ceased.

A few final prayers, and the Angelus window was thrown open and the floodlights illuminating it turned on. Immediately the thousands in the square below — and within minutes the whole world — knew.

The village boy from Sotto il Monte had gone home.

"A death in the family"

These words appeared in a Washington newspaper on June 4, 1963 over a drawing of the earth shrouded in mourning. Cardinal Suenens used the identical words in his tribute to Pope John on October 28, 1963 cited above. "Never has the whole world taken part at such close quarters in the poignant stages of a mortal sickness," Suenens said on that occasion. "Never has it shown such unanimity of feeling."

It was true. In Paris news of the Pope's death covered the front page of the communist paper *L'humanité*. In London and Belfast, still the undisputed bastion of Northern Ireland's Protestant ascendency, the Union Jack flew at half-mast over government buildings.

A few weeks before, John had said in the course of an audience: "Every day is a good day to be born, and every day is a good day to die. I know in whom I have believed." Cardinal Suenens comments: "He went to meet his end with the serenity of a child going home, knowing that its father is waiting there with open arms."

Speaking of the self-forgetfulness which was one of this Pope's most endearing qualities, Suenens said: "He put himself beyond all earthly vanity. . . . This fundamental humility allowed him to speak of himself with detachment and with humor, as if he were speaking of somebody else."

Turning to the event for which John will always be chiefly known, Suenens recalled the Pope saying once: "When it comes to the Council, we are all novices. The Holy Spirit will be present when the bishops assemble; we'll see." To which Suenens added his own comment:

> Indeed, for him, the Council was not first of all a meeting of the bishops with the Pope, a horizontal coming together. It was first and above all a collective gathering of the whole episcopal college with the Holy Spirit, a vertical coming together, an entire openness to an immense outpouring of the Holy Spirit, a kind of new Pentecost.

The American Redemptorist Francis X. Murphy, whose "Letters from Vatican City" (under the pen name of Xavier Rynne) set a new standard for religious journalism during the council, wrote of John's pontificate:

> History will record that what he did for the church in the twentieth century was similar to what Leo the Great did for it in the fifth, Gregory the Great in the seventh, and Gregory VII in the eleventh centuries. Above all he desired to return the church to the spirit which animated the earliest christian communities.

The last word goes to Cardinal Suenens — the final sentence of the tribute which he says in his memoirs was the most intense emotional experience, and one of the greatest moments, of his whole life:

"At his departure, he left us closer to God, and the world a better place in which to live."

Sources

Introduction

Quotations taken from Gustave Thils, *L'infallibilité pontificale* (Gembloux, 1969), p. 81 and Ives Congar, "Dominicans and worker-priests," in *Doctrine and Life* 40 (March 1990), p. 127.

Chapter I: Simon the Rock

The *Quo vadis* story is in W. Norman Pittenger, *The Life of Saint Peter* (Franklin Watts: New York, 1971), a short popular work without scholarly pretensions. The Protestant Oscar Cullmann, *Peter: Disciple, Apostle, Martyr* (SCM Press: London, 2nd edition 1962) presents the evidence for Peter's Roman martyrdom and argues that he had a personal primacy that died with him. A team of Protestant and Catholic scholars headed by Raymond E. Brown reviews the evidence in a scholarly consensus work, *Peter in the New Testament* (Paulist/Augsburg: New York and Minneapolis, 1973). A masterly but dense work typical of the best German scholarship is Rudolf Pesch, *Simon Petrus* (A. Hiersemann: Stuttgart, 1980). Pesch shares the view of many modern exegetes that Jesus' commission to Peter in Matthew 16:18 was a post-resurrection appearance. He contends that the full implications of this commission became clear only after the dispute between Peter and Paul at Antioch. He also argues that Luke has combined two separate apostolic meetings in Acts 15, only one of which preceded the Antioch dispute.

Chapter II: Leo the Great

The only modern biography of Leo in English is by the Anglican Trevor Jalland, *The Life and Times of St. Leo the Great* (SPCK: London, 1941). R. V. Sellers, *The Council of Chalcedon: A Historical and Doctrinal Survey* (SPCK: London, 1953) is useful for those who do not read German. Both books need to be corrected, however, by Stephan Otto Horn, *PETROU KATHEDRA. Der*

Bischof von Rom und die Synoden von Ephesus (449) und Chalcedon (Bonifatius: Paderborn, 1982). Leo's development of the idea that the Pope is Peter's heir is discussed by Walter Ullmann, "Leo I and the theme of Papal Primacy," in: *Jour. of Theological Studies* 11 (1960) 25-51. There are English translations of Leo's more important letters (from which the excerpts reprinted here are taken) by Edmund Hunt in *The Fathers of the Church* vol. 34 (New York, 1957). Eastern support for Leo's claims to universal primacy is discussed in two books by Francis Dvornik, *The Idea of Apostolicity in Byzantium* (Harvard: Cambridge, Mass., 1958), and *Byzantium and the Roman Primacy* (Fordham: New York, 1966), translated from the French. Leo's "moderation" is the theme of an essay by Hugo Rahner, "Leo der Grosse, der Papst des Konzils," in: A. Grillmeier and H. Bacht, *Das Konzil von Chalkedon* vol. 1 (Echter: Würzburg, 1951) pp. 323-39.

Chapter III: Gregory the Great

The chapter is heavily dependent on, and several excerpts are taken from, Jeffrey Richards, *Consul of God: The Life and Times of Gregory the Great* (Routledge & Kegan Paul: London and Boston, 1980). For background I have used and quoted briefly from Jeffrey Richards, *The Popes and the Papacy in the Early Middle Ages 476-752* (same publisher, 1979); also Walter Ullmann, *The Growth of Papal Government in the Middle Ages* (Bradford & Dickens: London, 2nd edition 1962), and Walter Ullmann, *A Short History of the Papacy in the Middle Ages* (Methuen: London, 1972). I have followed Jeffries in presenting Gregory's missionary activity as the response to pastoral needs, and not the result of the "grand design" claimed by Ullmann. A useful presentation of Gregory's thought, despite biographical inaccuracies, is Robert E. McNally, "Gregory the Great and his declining world," in: *Archivum Historiae Pontificiae* 16 (1978) 7-26.

Chapter IV: Gregory VII

A. J. Macdonald, *Hildebrand: A Life of Gregory VII* (Methuen: London, 1932) is strongly biased against Gregory and in favor of Henry IV. H. X. Arquillière, *Saint Grégoire VII. Essaie sur sa conception du pouvoir pontifical* (J. Vrin: Paris, 1934) manifests the opposite bias. Gregory's oath to Henry III is discussed by Tilmann Schmidt, "Zu Hildebrands Eid vor Kaiser Heinrich

III." in: *Archivum Historiae Pontificiae* 11 (1973) 372-86. The confrontation with Henry at Canossa is discussed in Harald Zimmermann, *Der Canosagang vom 1077, Wirkungen und Wirklichkeit* (F. Steiner: Mainz-Wiesbaden, 1975). I have followed the well-documented study of Gregory's mentality and motivation by August Nitschke, "Die Wirksamkeit Gottes in der Welt Gregors VII.", in *Studi Gregoriani* 5 (1956) 115-219. For the narrative of his pontificate, I am indebted to F. X. Seppelt and Georg Schwaiger, *Geschichte der Päpste* vol. 3 (Kösel: Munich, 1956). Useful selections from Gregory's letters are in Ephraim Emerton, *The Correspondence of Pope Gregory VII: Selected Letters from the Registrum* (Octagon: New York, 1966 reprint of 1932 edition) and H. E. J. Cowdrey, *The* Epistolae Vagantes *of Pope Gregory VII* (Clarendon: Oxford, 1972). The original *Register* is edited by Erich Caspar in *Monumenta Germaniae Historica. Epistolae selectae*, 2 vols. (Berlin, 1920-23) and commented on in his article, "Gregor VII. in seinen Briefen", in: *Historische Zeitschrift* 130 (1924) 1-30. Gregory's last words are analyzed with the thoroughness characteristic of German scholarship by Paul Egon Hübinger, *Die letzten Worte Gregors VII.* (Westdeutscher Verlag, Opladen: 1973).

Chapter V: Innocent III

The chapter's primary source is Helena Tillmann, *Pope Innocent III* (North Holland Publishing Co.: Amsterdam/NY & Oxford, 1980), well translated from the (1954) German original. Reference was made also to Seppelt-Schwaiger, *Geschichte der Päpste* and Walter Ullmann, *Short History of the Papacy in the Middle Ages* (already cited); Christopher R. Cheney, *Pope Innocent III and England* (A. Hiersemann: Stuttgart, 1976); *ibid.*, "The Letters of Pope Innocent III", in: *Bulletin of John Rylands Library* 35 (1952) 23-43; W. Imkam, *Das Kirchenbild Innocenz' III.*, (A. Hiersemann: Stuttgart, 1983, Kenneth Pennington, *Pope and Bishops: the Papal Monarchy in the 12th and 13th Centuries* (Fortress: Philadelphia, 1984); *ibid.* "Pope Innocent's views on Church and State: a gloss to *Per Venerabilem*," in: K. Pennington & Robt. Sommerville, *"Law, Church, and Society"* (Univ. of Pennsylvania: Philadelphia, 1977); Friedrich Kempf, *Papsttum u. Kaisertum bei Innocenz III* (Univ. Gregoriana: Rome, 1954); David Knowles and Dimitri Obolensky, *The Middle Ages (The Christian Centuries* vol. 2) (Darton, Longman and Todd: London, 1969).

Chapter VI: Boniface VIII

For Celestine I have used the definitive account by Peter Herde, *Cölestin V* (1294) (A. Hiersemann: Stuttgart, 1981); for Boniface the excellent biography by T. S. R. Boase, *Boniface the Eighth* (Constable: London, 1933); and Seppelt-Schwaiger, *Geschichte der Päpste* vol. iv pp. 9-55.

Chapter VII: Leo X

I have followed the accounts in F. X. Seppelt and George Schwaiger, *Geschichte der Päpste* vol. iv: and in Ludwig Pastor, *History of the Popes* vol. vii & viii (B. Herder: St. Louis, 1923). For Luther's early career and theology, I have used the account by Erwin Iserloh in Hubert Jedin *et al., Handbuch der Kirchengeschichte* vol. iv., (Herder: Freiburg, 1967); also Jared Wicks, *Man Yearning for Grace: Luther's Early Spiritual Teaching* (Corpus: Washington, D.C., 1968). Several excerpts within this chapter are taken from Colman J. Barry (ed.), *Readings in Church History* (Christian Classics: Westminster, Md., 1985). I have made my own translations of Luther's words from the original Latin and German in the standard Weimar edition of his works.

Chapter VIII: Pius V

I have followed the accounts in F. X. Seppelt, *op. cit.,* vol. v., and Ludwig Pastor, *op. cit.,* vols. xvii and xviii. For the excommunication of Elizabeth, I consulted also John Bossy, *The English Catholic Community 1570-1850* (Darton, Longman and Todd: London, 1975); Patrick McGrath, *Papists and Puritans under Elizabeth I* (Walker: New York, 1967); Adrian Morey, *The Catholic Subjects of Elizabeth I* (Rowman & Littlefield: Totowa, N.J., 1978); Arnold Pritchard, *Catholic Loyalism in Elizabethan England* (Univ. of North Carolina: Chapel Hill, N.C., 1979; and A. O. Meyer, *England the Catholic Church under Queen Elizabeth* (Barnes & Noble: New York, 1967; revised edition: original 1915). Interesting and now largely forgotten is G. K. Chesterton's long romantic poem *Lepanto.* Excerpts from the documents of the Second Vatican Council are taken from *Vatican Council II: Conciliar and Post Conciliar Documents*, Austin Flannery, O.P., gen. ed. (Costello: New York, 1975).

Chapter IX: Pius VII

I have relied heavily on the two fine books by E. E. Y. Hales: *Revolution and Papacy 1769-1846* (Notre Dame Press: Notre Dame, Ind., 1966), and *The Emperor and the Pope: The Story of Napoleon and Pius VII* (Doubleday: New York, 1961); also on Margaret M. O'Dwyer, *The Papacy in the Age of Napoleon and the Restoration: Pius VII, 1800-1823* (Univ. of America Press: Lanham, Md., 1985). For the French Revolution, I have used John McManners, *The French Revolution and the Church* (Harper: New York, 1970). I have also used the chapters by Roger Aubert in R. Aubert *et al., Die Kirche in der Gegenwart: die Kirche zwischen Revolution und Restauration (= Handbuch der Kirchengeschichte*, Band VI/1) (Herder: Freiburg, 1971). John Martin Robinson, *Cardinal Consalvi, 1757-1824* (St. Martin's Press: New York, 1987) has very little about ecclesiastical or religious matters.

Chapter X: Leo XIII

There is no satisfactory biography of Leo XIII. I have used Joseph Schmidlin, *Papstgeschichte der neuesten Zeit*, vol. 2 (Kösel: Munich, 1934); also Roger Aubert *et al., Die Kirche in der Gegenwart: die Kirche zwischen Revolution und Restauration [Handbuch der Kirchengeschichte* Bd. vi/2] (Herder: Freiburg, 1971). For the nineteenth-century background, I have used Derek Holmes, *The Triumph of the Holy See: a Short History of the Papacy in the Nineteenth Century* (Burns, Oates: London, 1978); Karl Otmar von Aretin, *Papstum und moderne Welt* (Kindler: Munich, 1970; English translation, McGraw Hill: New York, 1970); Alec R. Vidler, *The Church in an Age of Revolution: 1789 to the Present Day* (Penguin: London and Baltimore, 1961); and H. J. Pottmeyer, "Ultramontanismus und Ekklesiologie" in *Stimmen der Zeit* 210/7 (July 1992), 449-464. The section on Leo's early life contains material from Willy Lorenz, "Die Jugend des Joachim Pecci" in *Stimmen der Zeit* 165 (1959-60), 419-423; and from James Ward, "In Quest of Leo XIII" in *Dublin Review* 242 (1968), 3-15. The section on France draws on John McManners, *Church and State in France, 1870-1914* (Harper & Row: New York, 1972). The section on the opening of the Vatican archives is based on Owen Chadwick, *Catholicism and History: The Opening of the Vatican Archives* (Cambridge Univ. Press, 1978). The section on *Rerum novarum* draws on William Murphy, "*Rerum novarum*," in: George Weigel and Robert Royal (eds.), *A Century of Catholic Social Thought* (Univ. Press of America: Lanham,

Md., 1991), 1-26; and on Paul Misner, *Social Catholicism in Europe: from the Onset of Industrialization to the First World War* (Crossroad: New York, 1991). The section on ecumenism draws on *Handbuch der Kirchengeschichte* Bd. vi/2 and on J. J. Hughes, *Absolutely Null and Utterly Void: The Papal Condemnation of Anglican Orders 1896* (Sheed & Ward; London, and Corpus: Washington, D.C., 1968). The account of Americanism is based on material in Gerald P. Fogarty, *The Vatican and the American Hierarchy from 1870 to 1965* (Glazier: Wilmington, Del., 1985) and Marvin R. O'Connell, *John Ireland and the American Catholic Church* (Minnesota Historical Society: St. Paul, 1988). Excerpts are taken from Barry, Aretin, and Holmes.

Chapter XI: John XXIII

Cardinal Lercaro's remark about "that bore Roncalli" is reported by Andrea Tornielli, "The Friends of His Eminence," in: *30 Days* No. 3, 1993, 38-43, at p. 41; Cardinal Spellman's characterization is in John Cooney, *The American Pope* (Times Books: New York, 1984), 261. The primary source for the chapter, including numerous excerpts, is Peter Hebblethwaite, *Pope John XXIII, Shepherd of the Modern World* (Doubleday: Garden City, N.Y., 1987). I have also used Meriol Trevor, *Pope John* (Macmillan/St. Martin's Press: London/New York, 1967); Giancarlo Zizola, *The Utopia of Pope John* (Orbis: Maryknoll, N.Y., 1978); Ernesto Balducci, *Pope John: The Transitional Pope* (Burns, Oates: London, 1965); Loris Capovilla, *Johannes XXIII.* (Sailer: Nürnberg & Eichstätt, 1963); Pope John XXIII, *Journal of a Soul* (Harper-Collins: London, 1965); Helmuth Nürnberger, *Johannes XXIII.* (Rowohlt: Hamburg, 1985). Information about Roncalli's wartime efforts to save Jews has been drawn in part from Pinchas E. Lapide, *The Last Three Popes and the Jews* (Souvenir Press: London, 1967).

For Franz Stock see Anton Albert, *Das war Abbé Stock. Ein Leben zwischen den Fronten* (Herder: Freiburg, 1960) and Augustine Stock, "Franz Stock, the Prisoners' Priest" in: *The Priest*, Aug. 1989, 37-40. Rome's dealings with the French worker-priests and "new theologians" are recounted in Thomas O'Meara, " 'Raid on the Dominicans': The Repression of 1954" in *America*, Feb. 5, 1994, pp. 8-16, which is based on F. Leprieur, *Quand Rome condamne* (Paris, 1989).

D'Arcy Osborne's judgment of Pius XII is in Owen Chadwick, *Britain and the Vatican during the Second World War* (Cambridge Univ. Press, 1986), 316.

Details of Pius XII's death and funeral are taken from Paul Hofmann, *O Vatican! A Slightly Wicked View of the Holy See* (Congdon & Weed: New York, 1984), a more serious book than its title suggests. The post-mortem visit of the British minister to Castel Gandolfo was related to me by another British diplomat in April 1959.

The bowdlerization of John's opening speech to the council is meticulously documented in: Ludwig Kaufmann & Nikolaus Klein, *Johannes XXIII. Prophetie im Vermächtnis* (Exodus: Fribourg/Brig, 1990).

Important corrections to interpretations of John's life based more on ideology than on fact are supplied by Victor Conzemius, "Mythes et contre-mythes autour de Jean XXIII," in: *Cristianesimo nella Storia* 10 (1989) 553-577.

The closing sections contain material from *The Encyclicals and other Messages of John XXIII* (The Pope Speaks: Washington, D.C., 1964); and from Leon-Joseph Suenens, *Memories and Hopes* (Veritas: Dublin, 1992).

Index

a

Acton, Lord 213
Adrian I, Pope 54
Adrian VI, Pope (Adrian Florensz) 141
Adzhubei, Alexis 284, 285, 288, 289
Aeterni patris 211
Affre, Denis-August 209
Agagianian, Cardinal 259
Agapitus, Pope 49
Aggiornamento 271, 275
Alaric, General 28
Albigensians 99, 100
Albrecht 130, 131, 134, 135
Aleander, Hieronymus 128
Alexander II, Pope (Anselmo da Baggio) 67, 74, 77, 201
Alexander II, Russian Czar 201
Alexander IV, Pope (Rinaldo, Count of Segni) 112
Alexander VI, Pope (Rodrigo Borgia) 122, 123, 125, 127, 139
Alexander VIII, Pope (Pietro Ottoboni) 158
Ambrose, Saint 13, 149, 244, 245
Ananias 19
Ancien régime 161, 162, 166, 169-171, 174, 187, 188, 190, 206, 219
Andrew, Saint 14, 15, 17
Andrew, St. (monastery) 51, 53, 54, 61
Anglican orders 2, 216, 217, 302
Antonelli, Cardinal 191, 197
Apostolicae curae 218
Au milieu des sollicitudes 208
Augustine, Saint 28, 29, 32, 50, 98, 101, 124, 148, 149, 211, 257
Augustine of Canterbury, Saint 61-64
Auriol, Vincent 251

Auschwitz 252
Ausculta fili 116
Avignon Captivity 121

b

Baggio, Sebastiano 263
Balzan Peace Prize 285, 289
Barlas, Chaim 243
Barnabas 22, 23
Bartolini, Cardinal 198
Batiffol, Pierre 32, 65
Bea, Cardinal 271, 275, 280, 281
Bellisomi, Cardinal 164
Belloy, Archbishop 178
Benedict VIII, Pope (Theophylactus) 68
Benedict IX, Pope (Theophylactus, nephew of Benedict VIII) 68, 69, 71
Benedict X (John of Velletri) 73
Benedict XIV, Pope (Prospero Lambertini) 163
Benedict XV, Pope (Giacomo della Chiesa) 231, 232, 234
Berengar 72
Bernard of Clairvaux, Saint 92
Bismarck, Otto von 203-206
Black cardinals 177, 180
Black Death 121
Bokenkotter, Thomas 36
Boleyn, Anne 151
Boniface, Saint 63
Boniface VIII, Pope (Benedict Caetani) 92, 107, 109-121, 152, 300
Bossuet, Bishop J. B. 157
Breviary 51, 123, 149, 275
Brinkmann, Bishop 204
Buckley, William F. 286
Butler, Abbot Cuthbert 192

c

Caesaropapism 44
Caetani, Cardinal Benedict (see Boniface VIII, Pope)
Cajetan, Cardinal 135-137
Cano, Melchior 11

Capitulation 126, 154, 155, 178

Capovilla, Monsignor Loris 225, 259, 260, 264, 266, 267, 278, 288-293, 302

Caprara, Cardinal 171, 175

Casaroli, Agostino 290

Caspar, Erich 65, 299

Cassian, John 29

Cathari (see also Albigensians) 99

Catherine of Aragon 150

Celestine I, Pope Saint 28, 29, 300

Celestine III, Pope (Giacinto Bobone) 89, 90, 104

Celestine V, Pope Saint (Pietro del Moronne) 107-111, 113, 114

Celidonius, Bishop 34, 35

Center Party 204, 205, 208

Chadwick, Owen 213, 214, 301, 302

Chalcedon 41-45, 297, 298

Charlemagne 54, 69, 173

Charles Borromeo, Saint 12, 144, 146, 216, 229, 237, 264

Charles II, King of Naples 108, 110

Charles V, King, Holy Roman Emperor 128, 136, 137, 142, 154

Cheetham, Nicholas 68

Chenu, Marie-Dominique 250

Chrysaphios 38, 39, 42

Chrysologus, Peter 38

Chrysostom, Saint John 29, 149

Cicognani, Cardinal Amleto 274, 275, 288

Civil Constitution of the Clergy 161

Claudius, Emperor 24

Clement I, Pope Saint 24

Clement II, Pope (Suitger of Bamberg) 69, 71

Clement III (Archbishop Wibert of Ravenna) 84, 85

Clement III, Pope (Paul Scolari) 90

Clement VII, Pope (Giulio de' Medici) 122, 141, 142, 150

Clement X, Pope (Emilio Altieri) 156

Clement XI, Pope (Giovanni Francesco Albani) 156

Clement XIV, Pope (Giovanni Vincenzo Antonio Ganganelli) 158

Clerical celibacy 49, 70, 73

Clericis laicos 107, 111, 112

College of Cardinals 28

Collegiality 56, 261

Colonna, Cardinals James and Peter 109, 113-115

Commendatory abbots 150, 160

Commission des deux sources 281
Communism 255, 286, 287, 290
Communist Manifesto 209
Conciliarism 121, 122
Concordat 8, 167, 171, 172, 176, 178-180, 184, 188, 205-208, 273
Congar, Yves-Marie 12, 250, 271, 297
Consalvi, Cardinal Ercole 166, 167, 169, 170, 172-175, 177, 180-182, 185, 197, 290, 301
Constitutional Church 161-163, 168, 169
Costa, Cardinal Dalla 258
Creeping infallibility 183, 192
Crusades 96, 111, 146
Cuban missile crisis 283, 285
Cum postquam 136
Curia 29, 91, 104, 108, 112, 126, 129, 130, 136, 138, 175, 184, 199, 201, 212-215, 251, 262-264, 267, 270-272, 275, 279
Cyril of Alexandria, Patriarch 29
Cyril, Saint 215

d

Damaskinos, Archbishop 244
Damasus II, Pope (Poppo) 71
Daniélou, Jean 250
Darboy, Archbishop 208
de Chardin, Teilhard 250
de Gaulle, Charles 245, 246
de Lubac, Henri 250
de Montor, Artaud 166
de Sauvigny, Bertier 185
de Smedt, Bishop Emile 276, 290
Democracy 101, 166, 190, 219, 220
Devotio moderna 124
di Jorio, Monsignor 261
Dictatus papae 86
Dioscorus, Patriarch 40-44
Diuturnum 201
Divino afflante Spiritu 253
Döllinger, Ignaz von 212
Don John 154-155
Dominic, Saint 100-102

Donation of Constantine 94
Döpfner, Cardinal 279
Droz, Jacques 184
Duchesne, Louis 229

e

Eastern Rite 215, 235, 240
Ecumenical patriarch 56, 66, 236, 240, 241
Edward VII, King of England 222
Elizabeth I, Queen of England 300
Engels, Friedrich 209
Enlightenment 146, 157, 158, 160, 187, 189, 201, 268
Ephesus 23, 29, 36-39, 41, 42, 298
Episcopal collegiality 56
Erasmus 125
Estates General 159
Eulogius, Patriarch 47, 55
Eutyches, Abbot 36-40, 42
Exurge Domine 137

f

Febronius (J. N. von Hontheim) 158
Felix III, Pope 47, 49
Felton, John 152
Feltin, Cardinal Maurice 250, 251
Ferrari, Cardinal Andrea Carlo 228, 229, 231, 234, 237, 268, 284, 293
Fesch, Cardinal 173
Fietta, Archbishop Joseph 245
Flavian, Patriarch 36-42
Francis I, King 128, 137
Francis II, Roman Emperor 163, 164, 166, 167, 172, 173
Franz Josef, Emperor of Austria 200
Frederick II, Roman Emperor 95, 102
Frémont, Abbé 209
French Revolution 8, 159, 181, 183, 184, 187-189, 191, 219, 301
Freppel, Bishop 206-208
Friedlander, Saul 244
Frings, Cardinal 279
Fuenzalida, Diego José 165
Fuggers 124, 130, 134

g

Gallicanism 157, 161, 171, 183
Gambarrini 291
Gammarelli, Annibale 262
Garonne, Cardinal 279
Gasparri, Cardinal 233-235
Geiseric, King 46
Gibbons, Cardinal James 220
Giovanna, Princess 236
Gnosticism 99
Grammar of Assent 180
Grande munus christiani 215
Gratian, John 68
Great Western Schism 121
Greek Catholics 234, 235
Grégoire, Bishop 169
Gregorian Sacramentary 65
Gregory II, Pope Saint 63, 65
Gregory IV, Pope 65
Gregory the Great, Pope Saint 6, 47-66, 75, 85, 86, 145, 149, 185, 200, 295, 298
Gregory VI, Pope (John Gratian) 68-71, 86
Gregory VII, Pope (Hildebrand) 6, 67, 86, 88, 91, 92, 94-96, 295, 298, 299
Gregory VIII, Pope (Alberto de Morra) 90
Gregory X, Blessed Pope (Teobaldo Visconti) 107
Gregory XI, Pope (Pierre Roger de Beaufort) 121
Gregory XIII, Pope (Ugo Buoncompagni) 156
Gregory XVI, Pope (Bartolomeo Alberto Cappellari)) 189, 190, 196, 222

h

Hales, E. E. Y. 166, 301
Halifax, Lord 216-218
Hecker, Isaac 220
Heenan, Cardinal 227
Henry II, King 90
Henry III, King 69, 71, 72, 74, 75, 79, 298
Henry IV, King 72, 74-76, 83, 91, 298
Henry VI, King 94, 95
Henry VII, King of England 151
Henry VIII, King of England 13, 138, 150-152, 169
Hergenröther, Cardinal Josef 212-214

Herod 14, 20, 21
Herriot, Eduouard 251
Herzog, Isaac 243
Hilary, Bishop 34, 35, 39-41
Hildebrand (See Gregory VII, Pope)
Holocaust 242, 253
Honorius I, Pope 28
Honorius II, Pope 74
Hontheim, J. N. von (Febronius) 158
Hormisdas, Pope Saint 49
Horn, Stephan Otto 43, 297
Hovagnimian, Archbishop 236
Hugh the White 79, 84, 87
Hughes, John Jay 12, 302
Hughes, Philip 141
Humanae generis 250, 271
Humiliati 99
Hundred Years War 121

i

Ignatius, Saint 25, 182
Ignosco et dimitto 285, 290
Imitation of Christ 124
Immortale Dei 201, 202, 219
In excelso throno 114
Inculturation 62
Index of Forbidden Books 142, 147, 229
Indulgences 115, 123, 124, 129, 131, 132, 134-136
Ineffabilis 112
Infallibility 183, 192, 193, 203, 212, 216, 229
Innocent III, Pope (Lothar of Segni) 7, 23, 89, 97, 111, 112, 152, 222, 299
Innocent VIII, Pope (Giovanni Battista Cibò) 124
Inquisition 142-144, 148
Inscrutabili Dei 199
Ireland 61, 78, 153, 189, 235
Ireland, Archbishop John 219-221, 302
Isidore, Saint 52
Istrian Schism 48, 53

j

James, Saint (brother of Saint John; James the Greater) 15, 17, 18, 113, 220, 301
James, Saint, of Jerusalem (James the Less) 14, 19, 20, 21, 22
Jerome, Saint 50, 149
Jesuits 148, 158, 159, 163, 165, 195, 204-206, 250
Jewel, Bishop 152, 153
John, Deacon 54
John, King of England 94
John, Saint (Apostle) 17, 20, 37
John Chrysostom, Saint (See Chrysostom, Saint John)
John Gratian 68
John of Austria 154
John Lateran, St. (Basilica) 53, 64, 67, 68, 71, 89, 105, 126, 222, 260, 273
John Paul I, Pope (Albino Luciani) 142
John Paul II, Pope (Karol Wojtyla) 141, 198, 223, 252, 292
John the Baptist, Saint 15, 125
John the Evangelist, Saint 16
John the Faster 56
John the Monk 118
John VIII, Pope 54, 65
John XXII, Pope (Jacques d'Euse) 121, 251
John XXIII, Pope (Angelo Roncalli) 8, 72, 145, 156, 192, 222, 225-227, 229, 233, 243, 259, 260-295, 302, 303
Joseph II, Roman Emperor 158
Joseph, Saint 125, 225, 235, 251, 281, 282
Josephine, Empress of France 173, 177
Josephinism 158
Julian, Bishop of Eclanum 29
Julian, Bishop of Kos 39
Julius II, Pope (Giuliano della Rovere) 123, 125-129
Julius III, Pope (Giovanni Maria Ciocchi del Monte) 142, 144
Justinian, Emperor 48, 50, 58, 59

k

Kelly, J. N. D. 159
Ketteler, Bishop Wilhelm Emmanuel von 209, 210
Khruschev, Nikita 283, 285, 286, 288
Klein, Abbé Félix 220, 303
König, Cardinal 279
Kulturkampf 204, 205, 223

Küng, Hans 271

l

Lapide, Pinchas E. 253, 302
Lapsis abscissus 114
Lateran Basilica (See John Lateran, St.)
Lateran Council III 110
Lateran Council IV 97, 100-102
Lateran Council V 126, 129
Lateran Treaties 182, 233, 267, 289
Lateran University 232, 265, 283
Lavigerie, Cardinal Charles de 207, 208
Lawrence, St. (Church at Perugia) 105
Lawrence, St. (Basilica) 200
Lawrence Justinian, St. 225, 290
Lay investiture 7, 73, 77-79, 83
Le Meur, Abbé 248
Leander, Bishop of Seville 52, 55
Ledóchowski, Cardinal 205
Lefebvre, Archbishop 184, 209
Leo I, Pope Saint (the Great) 27-46, 48, 49, 295, 297, 298
Leo III, Pope Saint 69
Leo IX, Pope Saint (Bruno) 71, 72, 75, 85
Leo X, Pope (Giovanni de' Medici) 45, 121, 126-130, 132, 135-139, 141, 300
Leo XII, Pope (Annibale della Genga) 189, 195
Leo XIII, Pope (Gioacchino Pecci) 105, 187, 189, 191, 193-223, 225, 227, 228, 253, 286, 292, 301
Lepanto 155, 156, 300
Lercaro, Cardinal 226, 269, 302
"Letters from Vatican City" 295
Lisi, Dr. Galeazzi 257, 258
Lombardi, Father Ricardo, S.J. 256
Lortz, Joseph 133
Louis IX, King 113
Louis XIII, King 152
Louis XVI, King 159, 160
Luc, Abbé 190, 211
Luca, Vice Chancellor 214
Luigi d'Aragona, Cardinal 124
Lukacs, John 157
Luke, Saint 16, 18-20, 297

Luther, Martin 23, 130-139, 141, 142, 147, 148, 203, 300

m

Maglione, Cardinal Luigi 262
Magna Carta 43, 94
Malabranca, Cardinal Latino 107
Manicheans 32, 34
Manning, Cardinal 193
Marcellus II, Pope (Marcello Cervini) 142
Marcian 41, 42
Marengo 167, 168
Marie Louise, Princess 173, 177
Marinus I, Pope 30
Mark, Saint 15-18, 44, 65, 225, 254, 260
Martin IV, Pope (Simon de Brie) 105
Martiniana, Cardinal 168
Marty, Cardinal 289
Marx, Karl 209
Mary Stuart, Queen 151
Mater et magistra 286
Mattei, Cardinal 164
Matthew, Saint 15-18, 86, 297
Maurice (son in law of Emperor Tiberius) 52, 53, 59
McCone, John 288
Mediator Dei 253
Melchers, Cardinal 205
Metternich, Austrian Prime Minister 190, 191
Michael VII, Eastern Emperor 76
Mirari vos 189
Mit brennender Sorge 291
Morals on Job 50, 57, 64
Morton, Nicholas 151
Murphy, Father Francis F. 295, 301
Mystici corporis 253

n

Napoleon Bonaparte 162, 167, 212
National Assembly 117, 160, 251
Nero 13, 14, 23-25

Nestorius 36
Newman, Cardinal John Henry 180, 183, 193, 197, 212
Nicaea 30, 37, 38, 40, 42, 44
Nicholas, Saint 244, 245
Nicholas II, Pope (Gerard) 73
Nicholas IV, Pope (Girolamo Masci) 107
Nicolaism 70
Non expedit 200

O

Oakley, Reverend Austin 241
Odoacer 47
Old Catholic Church 203
Opera dei Congressi 228
Oreglia, Cardinal 221
Organic Articles 170-172, 174
Osborne, D'Arcy 252, 302
Osservatore Romano 234, 268, 271, 278, 282, 285
Ottaviani, Cardinal 255, 277, 280, 281, 287
Otto I, German Emperor 214
Otto of Brunswick 95

P

Pacca, Cardinal 176, 180, 181, 289
Pacem in terris 9, 286, 288, 289
Paisley, Ian 153
Papal states 109, 113, 162-165, 172, 178, 182, 188-190, 194, 195, 199, 201, 214, 233
Papen, Franz von 243, 262
Pascal, Blaise 159
Pasqualina, Mother 257
Pasquier, Duke Étienne 185
Pastor, Ludwig von 125, 126, 139, 150, 215, 300
Pastoral Rule 55, 57, 64
Paul, Saint 15, 17, 19-25, 32, 45, 58, 75, 80, 83, 98, 134, 273, 297
Paul III, Pope (Alessandro Farnese) 142, 144
Paul IV, Pope (Gian Pietro Carafa) 142-144
Paul V, Pope (Camillo Borghese) 87
Paul the Deacon 54, 55

Paul VI, Pope (Giovanni Battista Montini) 26, 233
Paul's Outside the Walls, St. (Church) 71, 165, 268
Pavan, Monsignor Pietro 283, 284
Pelagianism 29, 33
Pelagius 51-53
Pétain, Marshall 245
Peter, Patrimony of St. 58, 176
Peter, Saint 11, 13, 14, 17-26, 30-32, 35, 37, 42-46, 50, 63, 77, 80, 81, 83, 85, 86,
     91, 92, 107, 115, 120, 139, 162, 175, 235, 254, 260, 273, 285, 288, 294, 297, 298
Peter Chrysologus, Saint 38
Peter Damian, Saint 87
Peter in Chains, St. (Church) 74
Peter of Castelnau 100
Peter's, Basilica of St. 46, 53, 65, 69, 123, 130, 132, 185, 198, 199, 200, 222, 225,
     232, 262, 276, 285, 289
Peter the Deacon 64
Peter Waldo 99
Philip II, King (France) 92, 100, 104
Philip II, King (Spain) 148, 151, 154
Philip IV, King (France) 112
Philip of Swabia 95
Pisa, Council of 122
Pitra, Cardinal 214
Pius II, Pope (Enea Silvio Piccolomini) 122
Pius III, Pope (Francesco Todeschini-Piccolomini) 123
Pius IV, Pope (Giovanni Angelo de' Medici) 143, 144
Pius V, Pope Saint (Antonio-Michele Ghislieri) 141, 142, 146-156, 227, 300
Pius VI, Pope (Giovanni Angelo Braschi) 162-165, 167, 169
Pius VII, Pope (Luigi Barnab là Chiaramonti) 157, 159, 164, 166-172, 174-176,
     178, 180-185, 188, 189, 205, 212, 246, 289, 301
Pius VIII, Pope (Francesco Saverio Castiglioni) 195
Pius IX, Pope (Giovanni M. Mastai-Ferretti) 12, 183, 184, 190-194, 197, 198, 200,
     204, 222, 283
Pius X, Pope Saint (Giuseppe Sarto) 38, 141, 198, 221, 223, 225, 227-230
Pius XI, Pope (Achille Ratti) 182, 222, 223, 232-236, 242, 267, 284, 289, 291
Pius XII, Pope (Eugenio Pacelli) 12, 225, 235, 242, 244-247, 250, 252, 253, 255-
     258, 261, 263-265, 267, 270, 275, 287, 302, 303
Pizzardo, Cardinal 265, 271
Pluralism 103, 129, 144, 146, 158
Pole, Cardinal Reginald 13
Portal, Abbé Fernand 216-218

Pragmatic Sanction 48, 59
Prierias, Sylvester 135
Prisoner of the Vatican 182, 192, 193
Privilegium Ottonis 214
Pulcheria, Empress 27, 39, 41

q

Quanta cura 191
Quirinal Palace 167, 175

r

Radini-Tedeschi, Bishop 228, 230, 234, 238, 293
Rahner, Hugo 271, 298
Rahner, Karl 271
Ralliement 208, 209, 218, 219, 223
Rampolla, Cardinal 207, 208, 216, 217, 222, 223, 228
Ranke, Ludwig von 145
Raphael 45, 123
Ratzinger, Cardinal Joseph 142
Reformation 103, 121, 123, 124, 131, 141, 143, 187
Regnans in excelsis 150, 152, 153
Reign of Terror 162
Rerum novarum 8, 209-211, 215, 223, 286, 301
Richard I, King (The Lionheart) 104
Richer, Edmond 158, 160, 261
Robber synod 42
Romulus Augustus, Emperor 47
Rosi-Bernardini, Monsignor 213
Rossi, Count Pellagrino 191, 268, 269
Ruffini, Cardinal 267, 281
Ryan, Father Thomas 291
Rynne, Xavier (Francis Murphy) 295

s

Sacrosanctis salvatoris et redemptoris 130
Saphira 19
Sapieha, Cardinal (Krakow) 235
Sciat maxima fatuitas 117
Sedia gestatoria 200, 264, 289

Segni, President Antonio 89, 90, 289
"Servant of the servants of God" 66, 75
Sickel, Theodore 214
Siege mentality 156
Silvester III, Pope (antipope) 68, 69
Simon the Magician 19, 26, 37, 68
Simony 68, 70, 72, 74, 77, 78, 81, 114, 126
Sixtus III, Pope Saint 28-30
Sixtus V, Pope (Felice Peretti) 156, 263
Slipyi, Archbishop Josef 284
Soderini, Eduardo 221
Spellman, Cardinal 226, 258, 302
Spina, Monsignor Giuseppe 169
Stalin, Josef 284
Staupitz 135
Stein, Blessed Edith 252
Stephen IX, Pope (Frederick of Lorraine) 72
Stock, Franz 85, 247, 248, 302
Sturzo, Don Luigi 233, 264
Suenens, Cardinal 275, 276, 282, 289, 290, 294, 295
Suhard, Cardinal 249, 250
Super Petri solio 119
Syllabus of Errors 184, 191

t
Talleyrand, Bishop 169
Tardini, Cardinal 244, 245, 262-264, 267, 274
Taxil, Leo 199
Tertullian 183
Testa, Cardinal Gustavo 291, 292
Testem benevolentiae 220, 221
Tetzel, Johannes 130-132, 135, 137
Theodosius II, Eastern Emperor 36, 37, 39, 41, 52
Three Chapters 48
Tiberius 52
Tierny, Brian 120
Tisserant, Cardinal 257, 260, 262, 265, 271, 279
Tolentino, Treaty of 164, 165, 174
Tome (of Pope Leo) 38-40, 42
"Tower Experience," (Martin Luther's) 134

Traglia, Cardinal Luigi 294
Transubstantiation 137
Trent, Council of 11, 38, 123, 129, 138, 142, 143, 146, 148, 227, 229, 282
Trevor, Meriol 233, 297, 302
Turibius, Bishop of Austria 33, 34

u

Ultramontanism 158, 183, 188
Unam sanctam 7, 107, 117, 118
United Nations 289
Urban II, Blessed Pope (Otto di Lagery) 96
Urban IV, Pope (Jacques Pantaléon) 105
Urban VI, Pope (Bartolomeo Prignano) 122
Urban VIII, Pope (Maffeo Barberini) 152
Urbi et Orbi 198, 232, 262

V

Valentinian III, Western Emperor 30, 35, 36, 41, 45
Valeri, Cardinal Valerio 245, 246
Vatican Council 45, 47, 56, 64, 72, 104, 144, 147, 148, 171, 183, 185, 192, 212, 223, 236, 267, 283, 300
Vaughan, Cardinal 217, 218
Veuillot, Louis 191
Vicar of Christ 91, 191, 217
Victor II, Pope (Gebhard) 72, 75
Victor III, Blessed Pope (Dauferius) 75
Vienna 166, 167, 172, 173, 181, 188, 190, 200, 205, 245, 279, 290
Vigilius, Pope 48
Voltaire 156, 200

W

Wagram, Battle of 176
Waldensians 23, 99
Waldo, Peter 99
Wibert, Archbishop 67, 75, 84, 85, 87
Wilhelm I, Kaiser 204
Wilhelm II, Kaiser 222
William of Nogaret 118, 119
Windhorst, Ludwig 204, 208

Woodward, Kenneth L. 226

Z
Zozimus, Pope Saint 28, 29, 34